Intelligent Projects Using Python

9 real-world AI projects leveraging machine learning and deep learning with TensorFlow and Keras

Santanu Pattanayak

Packt

BIRMINGHAM - MUMBAI

Intelligent Projects Using Python

Commissioning Editors: Sunith Shetty
Acquisition Editor: Joshua Nadar
Content Development Editors: Karan Thakkar
Technical Editor: Sushmeeta Jena
Copy Editor: Safis Editing
Language Support Editor: Mary McGowan, Storm Mann
Project Coordinator: Namrata Swetta
Proofreader: Safis Editing
Indexers: Pratik Shirodkar
Graphics: Jisha Chirayil
Production Coordinator: Deepika Naik

First published: January 2019

Production reference: 1310119

Published by Packt Publishing Ltd.
Livery Place
35 Livery Street
Birmingham
B3 2PB, UK.

ISBN 978-1-78899-692-1

www.packtpub.com

Contributors

About the author

Santanu Pattanayak works as a Staff Machine Learning Specialist at Qualcomm Corp R&D and is an author of the deep learning book Pro Deep Learning with TensorFlow - A Mathematical Approach to Advanced Artificial Intelligence in Python. He has around 12 years of work experience and has worked at GE, Capgemini, and IBM before joining Qualcomm. He graduated with a degree in electrical engineering from Jadavpur University, Kolkata and is an avid math enthusiast. Santanu is currently pursuing a master's degree in data science from Indian Institute of Technology (IIT), Hyderabad. He also participates in Kaggle competitions in his spare time where he ranks in top 500. Currently, he resides in Bangalore with his wife.

About the reviewer

Manohar Swamynathan is a data science practitioner and an avid programmer, with over 14 years of experience in various data-science-related areas, including data warehousing, BI, analytical tool development, ad hoc analysis, predictive modeling, consulting, formulating strategy, and executing analytics program. He's had a career covering the life cycle of data across different domains, such as US mortgage banking, retail/e-commerce, insurance, and Industrial IoT. He has a bachelor's degree with a specialization in physics, mathematics, and computers, and a master's degree in project management.

He has written *Mastering Machine Learning With Python – In Six Steps*, and has also been a technical review of books on Python and R.

Packt is searching for authors like you

If you're interested in becoming an author for Packt, please visit `authors.packtpub.com` and apply today. We have worked with thousands of developers and tech professionals, just like you, to help them share their insight with the global tech community. You can make a general application, apply for a specific hot topic that we are recruiting an author for, or submit your own idea.

Table of Contents

Preface

Python Artificial Intelligence Projects will help you to build smart and practical AI-based systems leveraging deep learning and reinforcement learning. The projects illustrated in this book cover a wide range of domain problems related to healthcare, e-commerce, expert systems, surveillance fashion industry, mobile-based applications, and self-driving cars using techniques such as convolutional neural networks, deep reinforcement learning, LSTM-based RNNs, restricted Boltzmann machines, generative adversarial networks, machine translation, and transfer learning. The theoretical aspects of building the intelligent applications illustrated in this book will enable the reader to extend the projects in interesting ways and get them up to speed in building impactful AI applications. By the end of this book, you will be skilled enough to build your own smart models to tackle any kind of problem without any hassle.

Who this book is for

This book is intended for data scientists, machine learning professionals, and deep learning practitioners who are ready to extend their knowledge of AI. If you want to build real-life smart systems that play a crucial role in every complex domain, then this book is what you need.

What this book covers

`Chapter 1`, *Foundations of Artificial Intelligence Based Systems*, covers the basics of how to build smart artificial systems using machine learning, deep learning, and reinforcement learning. We will be discussing various artificial neural networks, including CNNs for image processing purposes and RNNs for natural language processing purposes.

`Chapter 2`, *Transfer Learning*, covers how to use transfer learning to detect diabetic retinopathy conditions in the human eye, and to determine the retinopathy's severity. We will explore CNNs and learn how to train a model with CNN that is capable of detecting diabetic retinopathy in fundus images of the human eye.

`Chapter 3`, *Neural Machine Translation*, covers the basics of **recurrent neural network** (**RNN**) architectures. We will also learn about three different machine translation systems: rule-based machine translation, statistical machine translation, and neural machine translation.

`Chapter 4`, *Style Transfer in Fashion Industry using GANs*, explains how to create a smart AI model to generate shoes with a similar style to a given handbag and vice versa. We will be using the Vanilla GAN to implement the project using customized versions of the GAN, such as a DiscoGAN and a CycleGAN.

`Chapter 5`, *Video Captioning Application*, discusses the role of CNNs and LSTMs in video captioning and explains how to build a video captioning system leveraging the sequence to sequence—video to text architecture.

`Chapter 6`, *The Intelligent Recommender System*, discusses recommender systems, which are information filtering systems that deal with the problem of digital data overload to pull out items or information according. We will be using latent factorization for collaborative filtering and use a restricted Boltzmann machine to build recommendation systems.

`Chapter 7`, *Mobile App for Movie Review Sentiment Analysis*, explains how machine learning as a service is used to benefit mobile apps. We will be creating an Android mobile app using TensorFlow that will take reviews of movies as input and provide a rating based on sentiment analysis.

`Chapter 8`, *Conversational AI Chatbots for Customer Service*, explains how chatbots have evolved during and looks at the benefits of having conversational chatbots. We will also be looking into how to create chatbots and what LSTM sequence-to-sequence models are. We will also be building a sequence-to-sequence model for a Twitter support chatbot.

`Chapter 9`, *Autonomous Self-Driving Car Through Reinforcement Learning*, explains reinforcement learning and Q-learning. We will also be crating a self-driving car using deep learning and reinforcement learning.

`Chapter 10`, *CAPTCHA from a Deep-Learning Perspective*, we discusses what CAPTCHAs are and why they are needed. We will also be creating a model to break CAPTCHAs using deep learning and then how to generate them using adversarial learning.

To get the most out of this book

The readers should have previous knowledge of Python and artificial intelligence to go through the projects in the book.

Download the example code files

You can download the example code files for this book from your account at `www.packt.com`. If you purchased this book elsewhere, you can visit `www.packt.com/support` and register to have the files emailed directly to you.

You can download the code files by following these steps:

1. Log in or register at `www.packt.com`.
2. Select the **SUPPORT** tab.
3. Click on **Code Downloads & Errata**.
4. Enter the name of the book in the **Search** box and follow the onscreen instructions.

Once the file is downloaded, please make sure that you unzip or extract the folder using the latest version of:

- WinRAR/7-Zip for Windows
- Zipeg/iZip/UnRarX for Mac
- 7-Zip/PeaZip for Linux

The code bundle for the book is also hosted on GitHub at `https://github.com/PacktPublishing/Intelligent-Projects-using-Python`. In case there's an update to the code, it will be updated on the existing GitHub repository.

We also have other code bundles from our rich catalog of books and videos available at `https://github.com/PacktPublishing/`. Check them out!

Download the color images

We also provide a PDF file that has color images of the screenshots/diagrams used in this book. You can download it here: `https://www.packtpub.com/sites/default/files/downloads/9781788996921_ColorImages.pdf`.

Code in action

Visit the following link to check out videos of the code being run:
`http://bit.ly/2Ru8rlU`

Conventions used

There are a number of text conventions used throughout this book.

`CodeInText`: Indicates code words in text, database table names, folder names, filenames, file extensions, pathnames, dummy URLs, user input, and Twitter handles. Here is an example: "Mount the downloaded `WebStorm-10*.dmg` disk image file as another disk in your system."

A block of code is set as follows:

```
def get_im_cv2(path,dim=224):
    img = cv2.imread(path)
    resized = cv2.resize(img, (dim,dim), cv2.INTER_LINEAR)
    return resized
```

When we wish to draw your attention to a particular part of a code block, the relevant lines or items are set in bold:

```
adam = optimizers.Adam(lr=0.00001, beta_1=0.9, beta_2=0.999, epsilon=1e-08,
decay=0.0)
```

Any command-line input or output is written as follows:

```
Cross Validation Accuracy: 0.6383708345200797
Validation Quadratic Kappa Score: 0.47422998110380984
```

Bold: Indicates a new term, an important word, or words that you see onscreen. For example, words in menus or dialog boxes appear in the text like this. Here is an example: "Select **System info** from the **Administration** panel."

Warnings or important notes appear like this.

Tips and tricks appear like this.

Get in touch

Feedback from our readers is always welcome.

General feedback: If you have questions about any aspect of this book, mention the book title in the subject of your message and email us at `customercare@packtpub.com`.

Errata: Although we have taken every care to ensure the accuracy of our content, mistakes do happen. If you have found a mistake in this book, we would be grateful if you would report this to us. Please visit `www.packt.com/submit-errata`, selecting your book, clicking on the Errata Submission Form link, and entering the details.

Piracy: If you come across any illegal copies of our works in any form on the Internet, we would be grateful if you would provide us with the location address or website name. Please contact us at `copyright@packt.com` with a link to the material.

If you are interested in becoming an author: If there is a topic that you have expertise in and you are interested in either writing or contributing to a book, please visit `authors.packtpub.com`.

Reviews

Please leave a review. Once you have read and used this book, why not leave a review on the site that you purchased it from? Potential readers can then see and use your unbiased opinion to make purchase decisions, we at Packt can understand what you think about our products, and our authors can see your feedback on their book. Thank you!

For more information about Packt, please visit `packt.com`.

1
Foundations of Artificial Intelligence Based Systems

Artificial intelligence (**AI**) has been at the forefront of technology over the last few years, and has made its way into mainstream applications, such as expert systems, personalized applications on mobile devices, machine translation in natural language processing, chatbots, self-driving cars, and so on. The definition of AI, however, has been a subject of dispute for quite a while. This is primarily because of the so-called **AI effect** that categorizes work that has already been solved through AI in the past as non-AI. According to a famous computer scientist:

> *Intelligence is whatever machines haven't done yet.*
>
> *– Larry Tesler*

Building an intelligent system that could play chess was considered AI until the IBM computer Deep Blue defeated Gary Kasparov in 1996. Similarly, problems dealing with vision, speech, and natural language were once considered complex, but due to the AI effect, they would now only be considered computation rather than true AI. Recently, AI has become able to solve complex mathematical problems, compose music, and create abstract paintings, and these capabilities of AI are ever increasing. The point in the future at which AI systems will equal human levels of intelligence has been referred to by scientists as the **AI singularity**. The question of whether machines will ever actually reach human levels of intelligence is very intriguing.

Many would argue that machines will never reach human levels of intelligence, since the AI logic by which they learn or perform intelligent tasks is programmed by humans, and they lack the consciousness and self-awareness that humans possess. However, several researchers have proposed the alternative idea that human consciousness and self-awareness are like infinite loop programs that learn from their surroundings through feedback. Hence, it may be possible to program consciousness and self-awareness into machines, too. For now, however, we will leave this philosophical side of AI for another day, and will simply discuss AI as we know it.

Put simply, AI can be defined as the ability of a machine (generally, a computer or robot) to perform tasks with human-like intelligence, possessing such as attributes the ability to reason, learn from experience, generalize, decipher meanings, and possess visual perception. We will stick to this more practical definition rather than looking at the philosophical connotations raised by the AI effect and the prospect of the AI singularity. While there may be debates about what AI can achieve and what it cannot, recent success stories of AI-based systems have been overwhelming. A few of the more recent mainstream applications of AI are depicted in the following diagram:

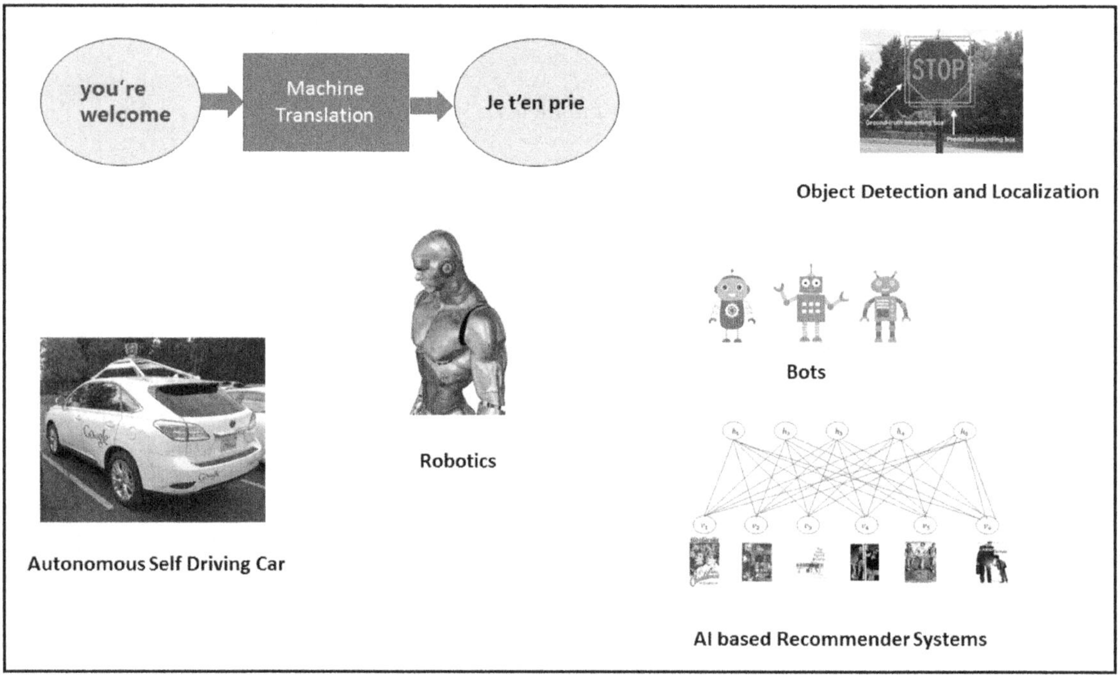

Figure 1.1: Applications of AI

This book will cover the detailed implementation of projects from all of the core disciplines of AI, outlined as follows:

- Transfer learning based AI systems
- Natural language based AI systems
- **Generative adversarial network** (**GAN**) based applications
- Expert systems
- Video-to-text translation applications
- AI-based recommender systems
- AI-based mobile applications
- AI-based chatbots
- Reinforcement learning applications

In this chapter, we will briefly touch upon the concepts involving machine learning and deep learning that will be required to implement the projects that will be covered in the following chapters.

Neural networks

Neural networks are machine learning models that are inspired by the human brain. They consist of neural processing units they are interconnected with one another in a hierarchical fashion. These neural processing units are called **artificial neurons**, and they perform the same function as axons in a human brain. In a human brain, dendrites receive input from neighboring neurons, and attenuate or magnify the input before transmitting it on to the soma of the neuron. In the soma of the neuron, these modified signals are added together and passed on to the axon of the neuron. If the input to the axon is over a specified threshold, then the signal is passed on to the dendrites of the neighboring neurons.

An artificial neuron loosely works perhaps on the same logic as that of a biological neuron. It receives input from neighboring neurons. The input is scaled by the input connections of the neurons and then added together. Finally, the summed input is passed through an activation function whose output is passed on to the neurons in the next layer.

A biological neuron and an artificial neuron are illustrated in the following diagrams for comparison:

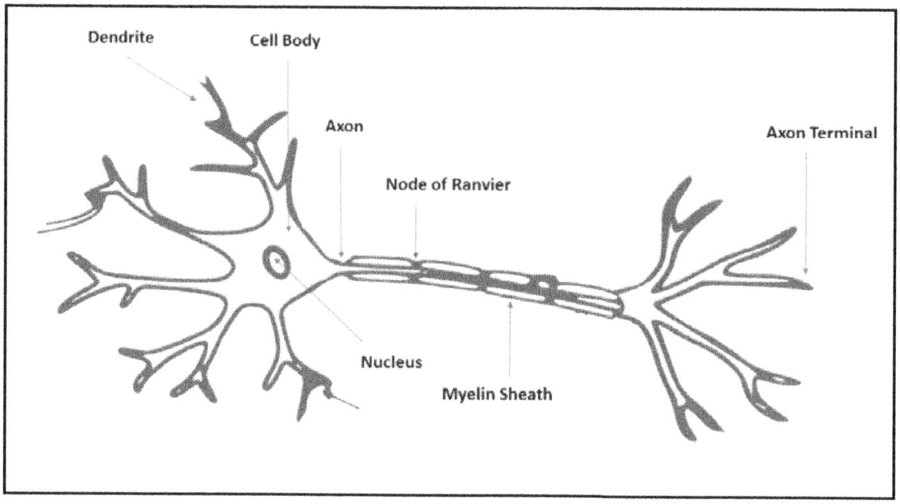

Figure 1.2: Biological neuron

An artificial neuron are illustrated in the following diagram:

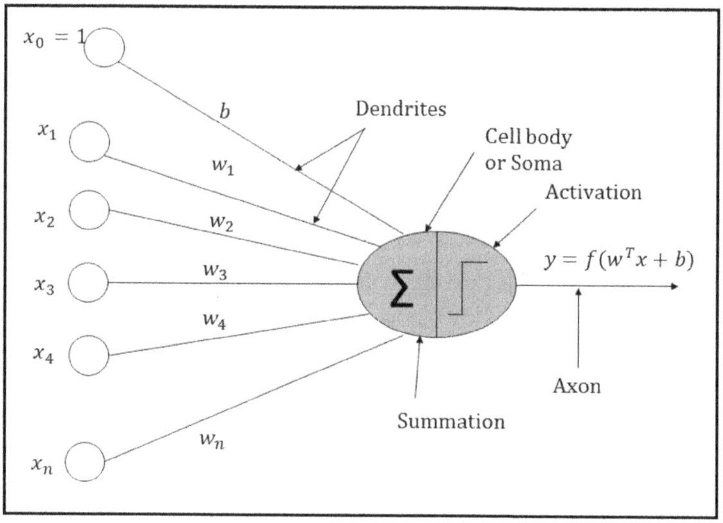

Figure 1.3: Artificial neuron

Now, let's look at the structure of an artificial neural network, as illustrated in the following diagram:

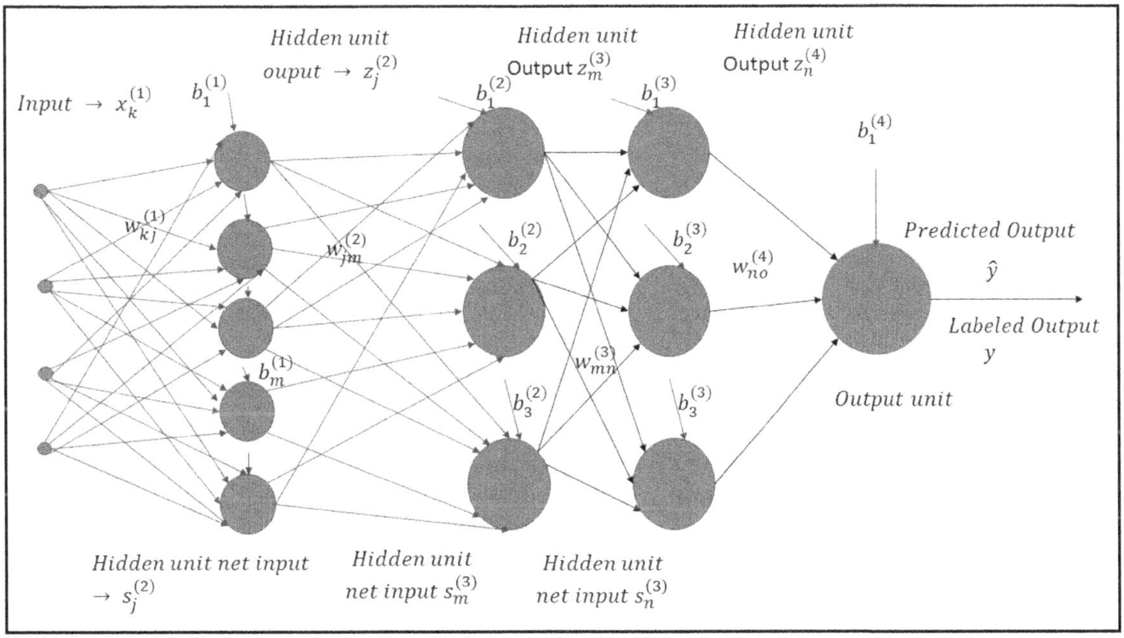

Figure 1.4: Artificial neural network

The input, $x \in R^N$, passes through successive layers of neural units, arranged in a hierarchical fashion. Each neuron in a specific layer receives an input from the neurons of the preceding layers, attenuated or amplified by the weights of the connections between them. The weight, $w_{ij}^{(l)}$, corresponds to the weight connection between the ith neuron in layer l and the jth neuron in layer $(l+1)$. Also, each neuron unit, i, in a specific layer, l, is accompanied by a bias, $b_i^{(l)}$. The neural network predicts the output, $\hat{y}$, for the input vector, $x \in R^N$. If the actual label of the data is y, where y takes continuous values, then the neuron network learns the weights and biases by minimizing the prediction error, $(y - \hat{y})^2$. Of course, the error has to be minimized for all of the labeled data points: $(x_i, y_i) \forall_i \in 1, 2, \ldots m$.

If we denote the set of weights and biases by one common vector, *W*, and the total error in the prediction is represented by *C*, then through the training process, the estimated *W* can be expressed as follows:

$$\hat{W} = \underbrace{argmin}_{W} C = \underbrace{argmin}_{W} \sum_{i} (y_i - \hat{y}_i)^2$$

Also, the predicted output, $\hat{y}$, can be represented by a function of the input, x, parameterized by the weight vector, *W*, as follows:

$$\hat{y} = f_W(x)$$

Such a formula for predicting the continuous values of the output is called a **regression problem**.

For a two-class binary classification, cross-entropy loss is minimized instead of the squared error loss, and the network outputs the probability of the positive class instead of the output. The cross-entropy loss can be represented as follows:

$$C = -\sum_{i} [y_i logp_i + (1 - y_i)log(1 - p_i)]$$

Here, p_i is the predicted probability of the output class, given the input x, and can be represented as a function of the input, x, parameterized by the weight vector, as follows:

$$p = P(y = 1/x; W) = f_W(x)$$

In general, for multi-class classification problems (say, of n classes), the cross-entropy loss is given via the following:

$$C = -\sum_{i} y_i^{(j)} log(p_i^{(j)})$$

Here, $y_i^{(j)}$ is the output label of the jth class, for the ith datapoint.

Neural activation units

Several kinds of neural activation units are used in neural networks, depending on the architecture and the problem at hand. We will discuss the most commonly used activation functions, as these play an important role in determining the network architecture and performance. Linear and sigmoid unit activation functions were primarily used in artificial neural networks until **rectified linear units (ReLUs)**, invented by Hinton et al., revolutionized the performance of neural networks.

Linear activation units

A **linear activation unit** outputs the total input to the neuron that is attenuated, as shown in the following graph:

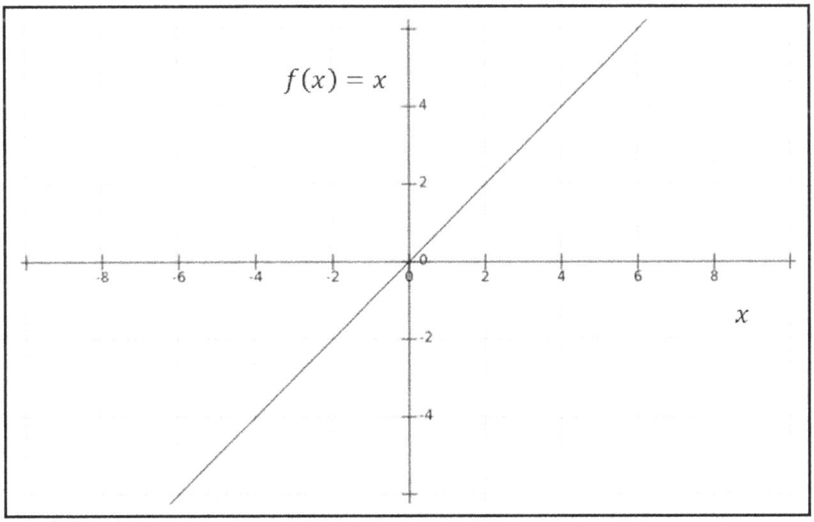

Figure 1.5: Linear neuron

If x is the total input to the linear activation unit, then the output, y, can be represented as follows:

$$y = f(x) = x$$

Sigmoid activation units

The output of the **sigmoid activation unit**, y, as a function of its total input, x, is expressed as follows:

$$y = f(x) = \frac{1}{1 + e^{-x}}$$

Since the sigmoid activation unit response is a nonlinear function, as shown in the following graph, it is used to introduce nonlinearity in the neural network:

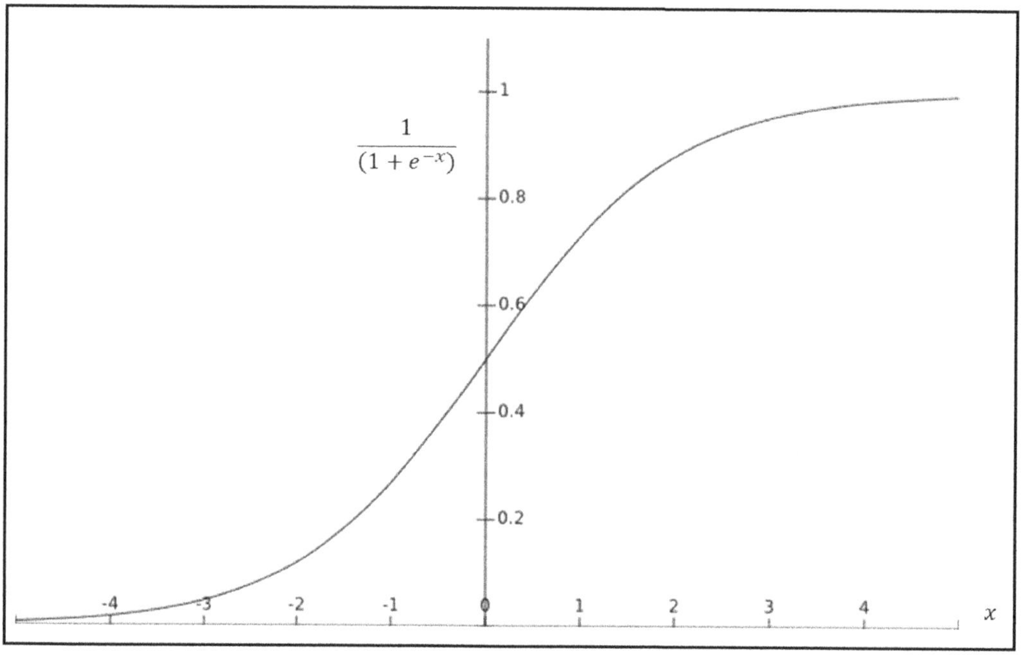

Figure 1.6: Sigmoid activation function

Any complex process in nature is generally nonlinear in its input-output relation, and hence, we need nonlinear activation functions to model them through neural networks. The output probability of a neural network for a two-class classification is generally given by the output of a sigmoid neural unit, since it outputs values from zero to one. The output probability can be represented as follows:

$$\hat{p} = \frac{1}{1 + e^{-x}}$$

Here, x represents the total input to the sigmoid unit in the output layer.

The hyperbolic tangent activation function

The output, y, of a **hyperbolic tangent activation function** (**tanh**) as a function of its total input, x, is given as follows:

$$y = f(x) = \frac{e^{x} - e^{-x}}{e^{x} + e^{-x}}$$

The tanh activation function outputs values in the range **[-1, 1]**, as you can see in the following graph:

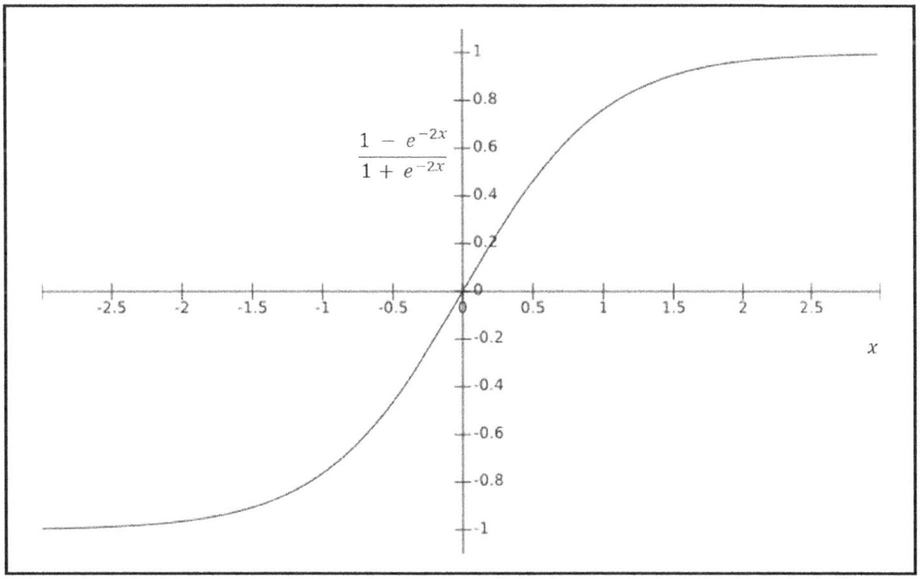

Figure 1.7: Tanh activation function

One thing to note is that both the sigmoid and the tanh activation functions are linear within a small range of the input, beyond which the output saturates. In the saturation zone, the gradients of the activation functions (with respect to the input) are very small or close to zero; this means that they are very prone to the vanishing gradient problem. As you will see later on, neural networks learn from the backpropagation method, where the gradient of a layer is dependent on the gradients of the activation units in the succeeding layers, up to the final output layer. Therefore, if the units in the activation units are working in the saturation region, much less of the error is backpropagated to the early layers of the neural network. Neural networks minimize the prediction error in order to learn the weights and biases (*W*) by utilizing the gradients. This means that, if the gradients are small or vanish to zero, then the neural network will fail to learn these weights properly.

Rectified linear unit (ReLU)

The output of a ReLU is linear when the total input to the neuron is greater than zero, and the output is zero when the total input to the neuron is negative. This simple activation function provides nonlinearity to a neural network, and, at the same time, it provides a constant gradient of one with respect to the total input. This constant gradient helps to keep the neural network from developing saturating or vanishing gradient problems, as seen in activation functions, such as sigmoid and tanh activation units. The ReLU function output (as shown in *Figure 1.8*) can be expressed as follows:

$$f(x) = max(0, x)$$

The ReLU activation function can be plotted as follows:

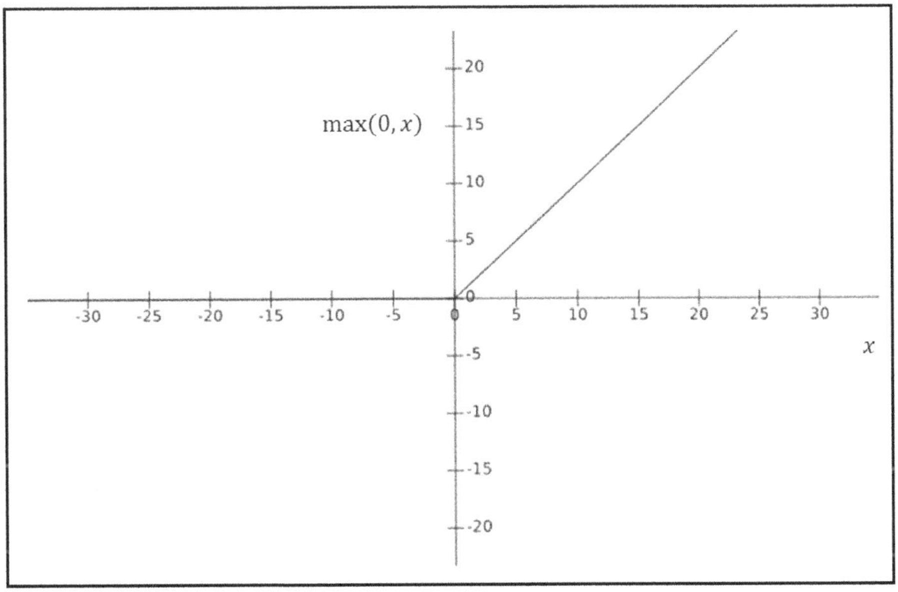

Figure 1.8: ReLU activation function

One of the constraints for ReLU is its zero gradients for negative values of input. This may slow down the training, especially at the initial phase. Leaky ReLU activation functions (as shown in *Figure 1.9*) can be useful in this scenario, where the output and gradients are nonzero, even for negative values of the input. A leaky ReLU output function can be expressed as follows:

$$f(x) = x, x > 0$$

$$= \alpha x, x \leq 0$$

The α parameter is to be provided for leaky ReLU activation functions, whereas for a parametric ReLU, α is a parameter that the neural network will learn through training. The following graph shows the output of the leaky ReLU activation function:

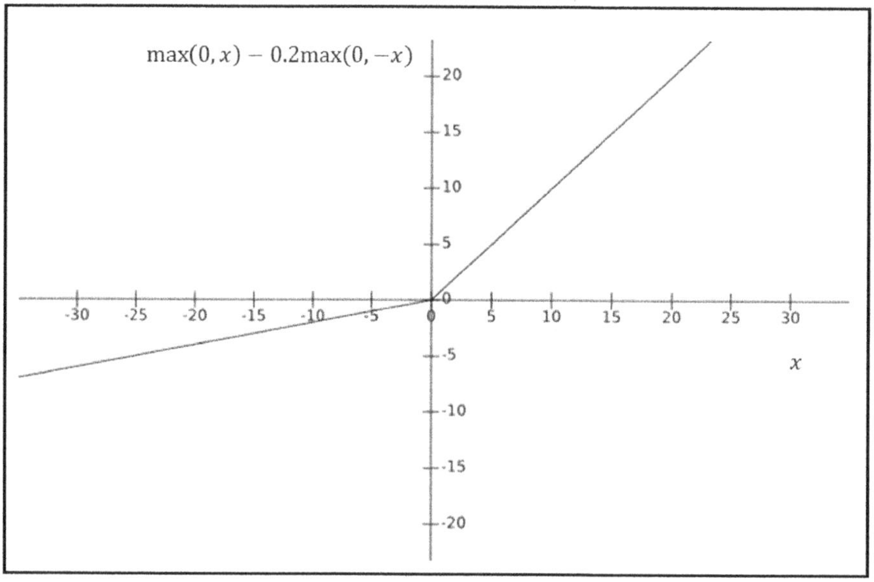

Figure 1.9: Leaky ReLU activation function

The softmax activation unit

The **softmax activation unit** is generally used to output the class probabilities, in the case of a multi-class classification problem. Suppose that we are dealing with an n class classification problem, and the total input corresponding to the classes is given by the following:

$$x = \left[x^{(1)} x^{(2)} \ldots x^{(n)}\right]^T$$

In this case, the output probability of the kth class of the softmax activation unit is given by the following formula:

$$p^{(k)} = \frac{e^{x^{(k)}}}{\sum_{i=1}^{n} e^{x^{(i)}}}$$

There are several other activation functions, mostly variations of these basic versions. We will discuss them as we encounter them in the different projects that we will cover in the following chapters.

The backpropagation method of training neural networks

In the backpropagation method, neural networks are trained through the gradient descent technique, where the combined weights vector, *W*, is updated iteratively, as follows:

$$W^{(t+1)} = W^{(t)} - \eta \nabla C(W^{(t)})$$

Here, η is the learning rate, $W^{(t+1)}$ and $W^{(t)}$ are the weight vectors at iterations *(t+1)* and *(t)*, respectively, and $\nabla C(W^{(t)})$ is the gradient of the cost function or the error function, with respect to the weight vector, *W*, at iteration *(t)*. The previous algorithm for an individual weight or bias generalized by $w \in W$ can be represented as follows:

$$w^{(t+1)} = w^{(t)} - \eta \frac{\partial C(w^{(t)})}{\partial w}$$

As you can gather from the previous expressions, the heart of the gradient descent method of learning relies on computing the gradient of the cost function or the error function, with respect to each weight.

From the chain rule of differentiation, we know that if we have $y = f(x)$, $z = f(y)$, then the following is true:

$$\frac{\partial z}{\partial x} = \frac{\partial z}{\partial y}\frac{\partial y}{\partial x}$$

This expression can be generalized to any number of variables. Now, let's take a look at a very simple neural network, as illustrated in the following diagram, in order to understand the backpropagation algorithm:

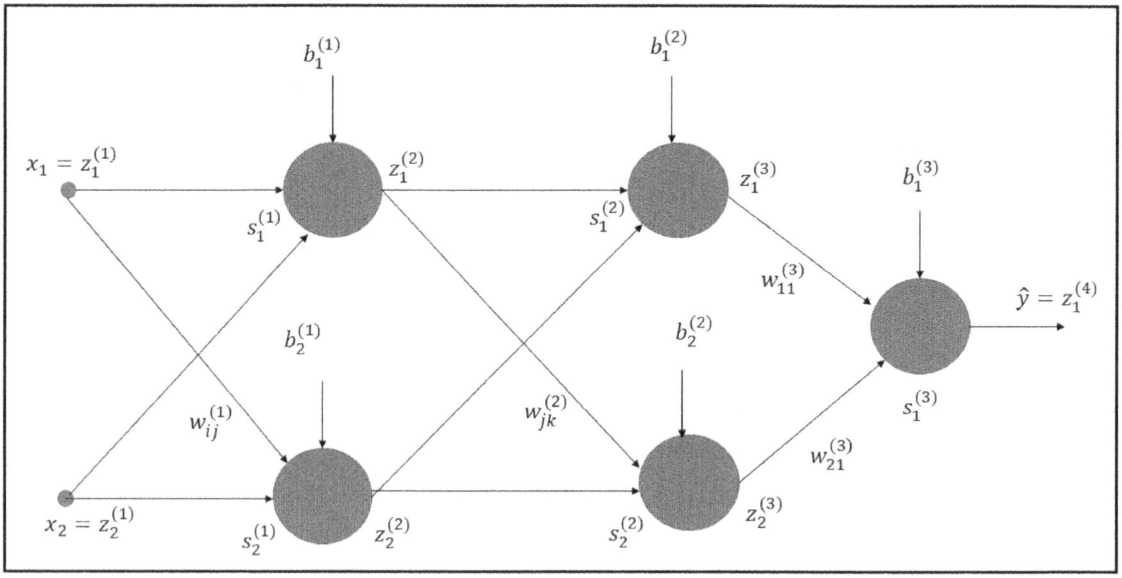

Figure 1.10: A network illustrating backpropagation

Let the input to the network be a two-dimensional vector, $x = [x_1\ x_2]^T$, and the corresponding output label and prediction be y and $\hat{y}$, respectively. Also, let's assume that all of the activation units in the neural network are sigmoids. Let the generalized weight connecting any unit i in layer $(l-1)$ to unit j in layer l be denoted by $w_{ij}^{(l)}$, while the bias in any unit i in layer l should be denoted by $b_i^{(l)}$. Let's derive the gradient for one data point; the total gradient can be computed as the sum of all of the data points used in training (or in a mini-batch). If the output is continuous, then the loss function, C, can be chosen as the square of the error in prediction:

$$C = \frac{1}{2}(y - \hat{y})^2$$

The weights and biases of the network, cumulatively represented by the set *W*, can be determined by minimizing the cost function with respect to the *W* vector, which is as follows:

$$\hat{W} = \underbrace{argmin}_{W} C(W)$$

To perform the minimization of the cost function iteratively through gradient descent, we need to compute the gradient of the cost function with respect to each weight, $w \in W$, as follows:

$$w^{(t+1)} = w^{(t)} - \eta \frac{\partial C(W)}{\partial w} | W = W^{(t)}$$

Now that we have everything that we need, let's compute the gradient of the cost function, *C*, with respect to the weight, $w_{21}^{(3)}$. Using the chain rule of differentiation, we get the following:

$$\frac{\partial C}{\partial w_{21}^{(3)}} = \frac{\partial C}{\partial \hat{y}} \frac{\partial \hat{y}}{\partial s_1^{(3)}} \frac{\partial s_1^{(3)}}{\partial w_{21}^{(3)}}$$

Now let's look at the following formula:

$$\frac{\partial C}{\partial \hat{y}} = -(y - \hat{y}) = (\hat{y} - y)$$

As you can see in the previous expression, the derivative is nothing but the error in prediction. Generally, the output unit activation function is linear in the case of regression problems, and hence the following expression applies:

$$\frac{\partial \hat{y}}{\partial s_1^{(3)}} = 1$$

So, if we were to compute the gradient of the cost function with respect to the total input at the output unit, it would be $\frac{\partial C}{\partial s_1^{(3)}}$. This is still equal to the error in prediction of the output.

The total input at the output unit, as a function of the incoming weights and activations, can be expressed as follows:

$$s_1^{(3)} = w_{11}^{(3)} z_1^{(3)} + w_{21}^{(3)} z_2^{(3)} + b_1^{(3)}$$

This means that, $\frac{\partial s_1^{(3)}}{\partial w_{21}^{(3)}} = z_2^{(3)}$ and the derivative of the cost function with respect to the weight, $w_{21}^{(3)}$, contributing to the input of the output layer is given via the following:

$$\frac{\partial C}{\partial w_{21}^{(3)}} = (\hat{y} - y) z_2^{(3)}$$

As you can see, the error is backpropagated in computing the gradient of the cost function, with respect to the weights in the layers preceding the final output layer. This becomes more obvious when we compute the gradient of the cost function with respect to the generalized weight, $w_{jk}^{(2)}$. Let's take the weight corresponding to *j=1* and *k=2*; that is, $w_{jk}^{(2)}$. The gradient of the cost function, *C*, with respect to this weight can be expressed as follows:

$$\frac{\partial C}{\partial w_{12}^{(2)}} = \frac{\partial C}{\partial s_2^{(2)}} \frac{\partial s_2^{(2)}}{\partial w_{12}^{(2)}}$$

Now, $\frac{\partial s_2^{(2)}}{\partial w_{12}^{(2)}} = z_1^{(2)}$, which means that, $\frac{\partial C}{\partial w_{12}^{(2)}} = \frac{\partial C}{\partial s_2^{(2)}} z_1^{(2)}$.

So, once we have figured out the gradient of the cost function with respect to the total input to a neuron as $\frac{\partial C}{\partial s}$, the gradient of any weight, *w*, contributing to the total input, *s*, can be obtained by simply multiplying the activation, *z*, associated with the weight.

Now, the gradient of the cost function with respect to the total input, $s_2^{(2)}$, can be derived by chain rule again, as follows:

$$\frac{\partial C}{\partial s_2^{(2)}} = \frac{\partial C}{\partial s_1^{(3)}} \frac{\partial s_1^{(3)}}{\partial z_2^{(3)}} \frac{\partial z_2^{(3)}}{\partial s_2^{(2)}} \qquad (1)$$

Since all of the units of the neural network (except for the output unit) are sigmoid activation functions, the following is the case:

$$\frac{\partial z_2^{(3)}}{\partial s_2^{(2)}} = z_2^{(3)}(1 - z_2^{(3)}) \qquad (2)$$

$$\frac{\partial s_1^{(3)}}{\partial z_2^{(3)}} = w_{21}^{(3)} \qquad (3)$$

Combining *(1)*, *(2)*, and *(3)*, we get the following:

$$\frac{\partial C}{\partial s_2^{(2)}} = \frac{\partial C}{\partial s_1^{(3)}} \frac{\partial s_1^{(3)}}{\partial z_2^{(3)}} \frac{\partial z_2^{(3)}}{\partial s_2^{(2)}} = (\hat{y} - y)w_{21}^{(3)} z_2^{(3)}(1 - z_2^{(3)})$$

In the preceding derived gradient expressions, you can see that the error in prediction, $(\hat{y} - y)$, is backpropagated by combining it with the relevant activations and weights (as per the chain rule of differentiation) for computing the gradients of the weights at each layer, hence, the name backpropagation in AI nomenclature.

Convolutional neural networks

Convolutional neural networks (**CNNs**) utilize convolutional operations to extract useful information from data that has a topology associated with it. This works best for image and audio data. The input image, when passed through a convolution layer, produces several output images, known as **output feature maps**. The output feature maps detect features. The output feature maps in the initial convolutional layer may learn to detect basic features, such as edges and color composition variation.

The second convolutional layer may detect slightly more complicated features, such as squares, circles, and other geometrical structures. As we progress through the neural network, the convolutional layers learn to detect more and more complicated features. For instance, if we have a CNN that classifies whether an image is of a cat or a dog, the convolutional layers at the bottom of the neural network might learn to detect features such as the head, the legs, and so on.

Figure 1.11 shows an architectural diagram of a CNN that processes images of cats and dogs in order to classify them. The images are passed through a convolutional layer that helps to detect relevant features, such as edges and color composition. The ReLU activations add nonlinearity. The pooling layer that follows the activation layer summarizes local neighborhood information in order to provide an amount of **translational invariance**. In an ideal CNN, this convolution-activation-pooling operation is performed several times before the network makes its way to the dense connections:

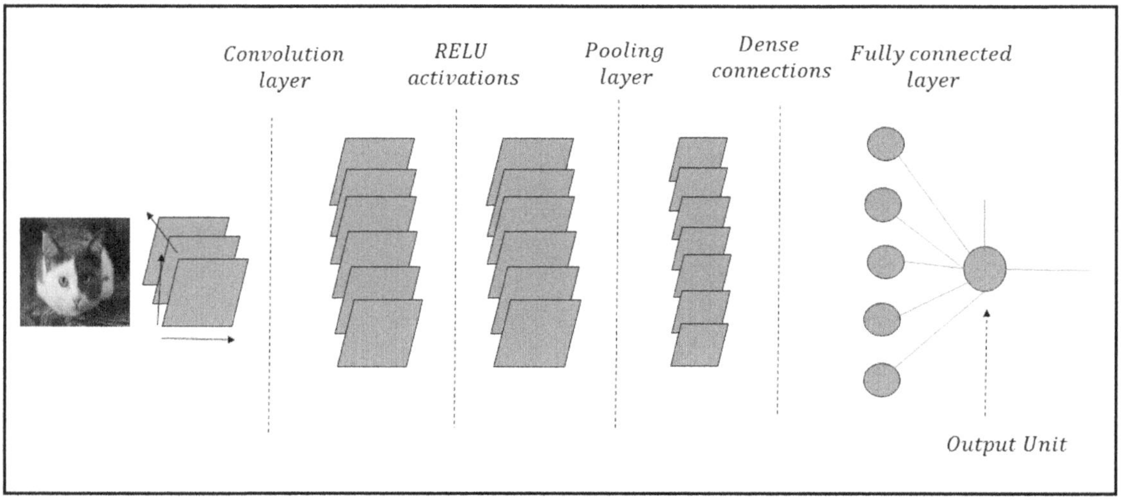

Figure 1.11: CNN architecture

As we go through such a network with several convolution-activation-pooling operations, the spatial resolution of the image is reduced, while the number of output feature maps is increased in every layer. Each output feature map in a convolutional layer is associated with a filter kernel, the weights of which are learned through the CNN training process.

In a convolutional operation, a flipped version of a filter kernel is laid over the entire image or feature map, and the dot product of the filter-kernel input values with the corresponding image pixel or the feature map values are computed for each location on the input image or feature map. Readers that are already accustomed to ordinary image processing may have used different filter kernels, such as a Gaussian filter, a Sobel edge detection filter, and many more, where the weights of the filters are predefined. The advantage of convolutional neural networks is that the different filter weights are determined through the training process; This means that, the filters are better customized for the problem that the convolutional neural network is dealing with.

When a convolutional operation involves overlaying the filter kernel on every location of the input, the convolution is said to have a stride of one. If we choose to skip one location while overlaying the filter kernel, then convolution is performed with a stride of two. In general, if *n* locations are skipped while overlaying the filter kernel over the input, the convolution is said to have been performed with a stride of *(n+1)*. Strides of greater than one reduce the spatial dimensions of the output of the convolution.

Generally, a convolutional layer is followed by a pooling layer, which basically summarizes the output feature map activations in a neighborhood, determined by the receptive field of the pooling. For instance, a 2 x 2 receptive field will gather the local information of four neighboring output feature map activations. For max-pooling operations, the maximum value of the four activations is selected as the output, while for average pooling, the average of the four activations is selected. Pooling reduces the spatial resolution of the feature maps. For instance, for a 224 x 224 sized feature map pooling operation with a 2 x 2 receptive field, the spatial dimension of the feature map will be reduced to 112 x 112.

One thing to note is that a convolutional operation reduces the number of weights to be learned in each layer. For instance, if we have an input image of a spatial dimension of 224 x 224 and the desired output of the next layer is of the dimensions 224 x 224, then for a traditional neural network with full connections, the number of weights to be learned is 224 x 224 x 224 x 224. For a convolutional layer with the same input and output dimensions, all that we need to learn are the weights of the filter kernel. So, if we use a 3 x 3 filter kernel, we just need to learn nine weights as opposed to 224 x 224 x 224 x 224 weights. This simplification works, since structures like images and audio in a local spatial neighborhood have high correlation among them.

The input images pass through several layers of convolutional and pooling operations. As the network progresses, the number of feature maps increases, while the spatial resolution of the images decreases. At the end of the convolutional-pooling layers, the output of the feature maps is fed to the fully connected layers, followed by the output layer.

The output units are dependent on the task at hand. If we are performing regression, the output activation unit is linear, while if it is a binary classification problem, the output unit is a sigmoid. For multi-class classification, the output layer is a softmax unit.

In all of the image processing projects in this book, we will use convolutional neural networks, in one form or another.

Recurrent neural networks (RNNs)

Recurrent neural networks (**RNNs**) are useful in processing sequential or temporal data, where the data at a given instance or position is highly correlated with the data in the previous time steps or positions. RNNs have already been very successful at processing text data, since a word at a given instance is highly correlated with the words preceding it. In an RNN, at each time step, the network performs the same function, hence, the term **recurrent** in its name. The architecture of an RNN is illustrated in the following diagram:

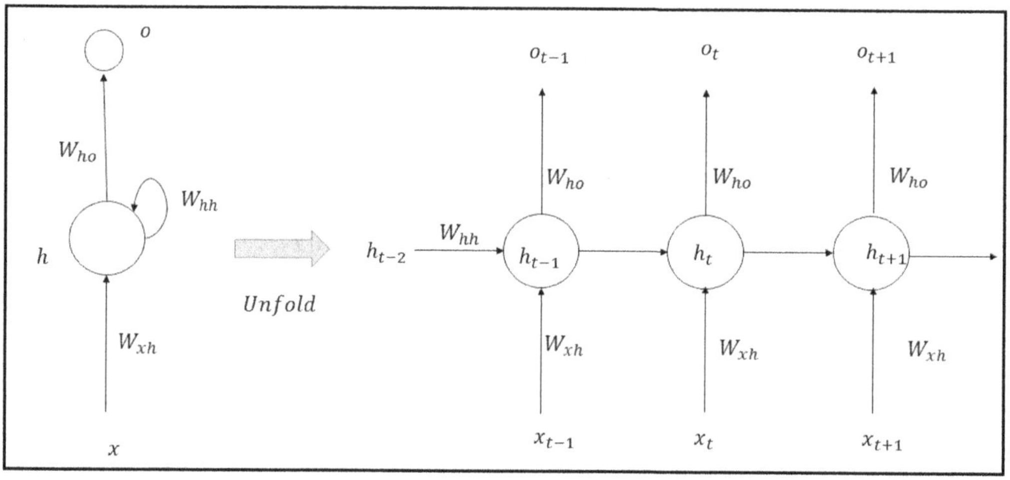

Figure 1.12: RNN architecture

At each given time step, t, a memory state, h_t, is computed, based on the previous state, h_{t-1}, at step *(t-1)* and the input, x_t, at time step t. The new state, h_t, is used to predict the output, o_t, at step t. The equations governing RNNs are as follows:

$$h_t = f_1(W_{hh}h_{t-1} + W_{xh}x_t + b^{(1)}) \quad (1)$$

$$o_t = f_2(W_{ho}h_t + b^{(2)}) \quad (2)$$

If we are predicting the next word in a sentence, then the function f_2 is generally a softmax function over the words in the vocabulary. The function f_1 can be any activation function based on the problem at hand.

In an RNN, an output error in step t tries to correct the prediction in the previous time steps, generalized by $k \in 1, 2, \ldots t-1$, by propagating the error in the previous time steps. This helps the RNN to learn about long dependencies between words that are far apart from each other. In practice, it isn't always possible to learn such long dependencies through RNN because of the vanishing and exploding gradient problems.

As you know, neural networks learn through gradient descent, and the relationship of a word in time step t with a word at a prior sequence step k can be learned through the gradient of the memory state $h_t^{(i)}$ with respect to the gradient of the memory state $h_i^{(t)} \forall i$. This is expressed in the following formula:

$$\frac{\partial h_t^{(i)}}{\partial h_k^{(i)}} = \prod_{g=k+1}^{t} \frac{\partial h_g^{(i)}}{\partial h_{g-1}^{(i)}} = \frac{\partial h_{k+1}^{(i)}}{\partial h_k^{(i)}} \frac{\partial h_{k+2}^{(i)}}{\partial h_{k+1}^{(i)}} \cdots \frac{\partial h_t^{(i)}}{\partial h_{t-1}^{(i)}} \quad (3)$$

If the weight connection from the memory state $h_k^{(i)}$ at the sequence step k to the memory state $h_{k+1}^{(i)}$ at the sequence step *(k+1)* is given by $u_{ii} \in W_{hh}$, then the following is true:

$$\frac{\partial h_{k+1}^{(i)}}{\partial h_k^{(i)}} = u_{ii} \frac{\partial f_2(s_{k+1}^{(i)})}{\partial s_{k+1}^{(i)}} \quad (4)$$

In the preceding equation, $s_{k+1}^{(i)}$ is the total input to the memory state *i* at the time step *(k+1)*, such that the following is the case:

$$s_{k+1}^{(i)} = W_{hh}[i,:]h_k + W_{xh}[i,:]x_{t+1} = u_{ii}h_k^{(i)} + \sum_{j \neq i} u_{ij}h_k^{(j)} + W_{xh}[i,:]x_{t+1}$$

$$f_2(s_{k+1}^{(i)}) = h_{k+1}^{(i)}$$

Now that we have everything in place, it's easy to see why the vanishing gradient problem may occur in an RNN. From the preceding equations, *(3)* and *(4)*, we get the following:

$$\frac{\partial h_t^{(i)}}{\partial h_k^{(i)}} = (u_{ii})^{t-k} \prod_{k=k}^{t-1} \frac{\partial f_2(s_{k+1}^{(i)})}{\partial s_{k+1}^{(i)}}$$

For RNNs, the function f_2 is generally sigmoid or tanh, which suffers from the saturation problem of having low gradients beyond a specified range of values for the input. Now, since the f_2 derivatives are multiplied with each other, the gradient $\frac{\partial h_t^{(i)}}{\partial h_k^{(i)}}$ can become zero if the input to the activation functions is operating at the saturation zone, even for relatively moderate values of *(t-k)*. Even if the f_2 functions are not operating in the saturation zone, the gradients of the f_2 function for sigmoids are always less than *1*, and so it is very difficult to learn distant dependencies between words in a sequence. Similarly, there might be exploding gradient problems stemming from the factor $u_{ii}^{(t-k)}$. Suppose that the distance between steps *t* and *k* is around *10*, while the weight, u_{ii}, is around two. In such cases, the gradient would be magnified by a factor of two, $2^{10} = 1024$, leading to the exploding gradient problem.

Long short-term memory (LSTM) cells

The vanishing gradient problem is taken care of, to a great extent, by a modified version of RNNs, called **long short-term memory** (**LSTM**) cells. The architectural diagram of a long short-term memory cell is as follows:

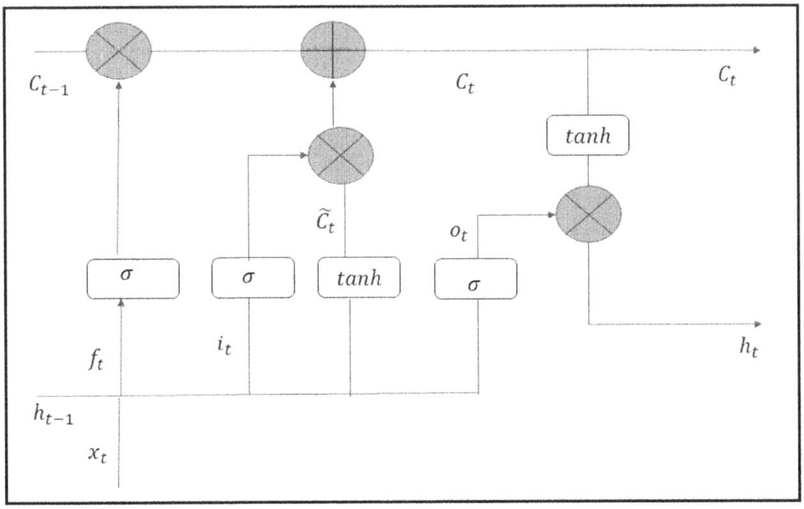

Figure 1.13: LSTM architecture

LSTM introduces the cell state, C_t, in addition to the memory state, h_t, that you already saw when learning about RNNs. The cell state is regulated by three gates: the forget gate, the update gate, and the output gate. The forget gate determines how much information to retain from the previous cell states, C_{t-1}, and its output is expressed as follows:

$$f_t = \sigma(U_f h_{t-1} + W_f x_t) \qquad (1)$$

The output of the update gate is expressed as follows:

$$i_t = \sigma(U_i h_{t-1} + W_i x_t) \qquad (2)$$

The potential new candidate cell state, $\tilde{C}_t$, is expressed as follows:

$$\tilde{C}_t = tanh(U_c h_{t-1} + W_c x_t) \qquad (3)$$

Based on the previous cell state and the current potential cell state, the updated cell state output is given via the following:

$$C_t = f_t * C_{t-1} + i_t * \widetilde{C_t} \qquad (4)$$

Not all of the information of the cell state is passed on to the next step, and how much of the cell state should be released to the next step is determined by the **output gate**. The output of the output gate is given via the following:

$$o_t = \sigma(U_o h_{t-1} + W_o x_t) \qquad (5)$$

Based on the current cell state and the output gate, the updated memory state passed on to the next step is given via the following:

$$h_t = o_t * tanh(C_t) \qquad (6)$$

Now comes the big question: How does LSTM avoid the vanishing gradient problem? The equivalent of $\frac{\partial h_t^{(i)}}{\partial h_k^{(i)}}$ in LSTM is given by $\frac{\partial C_t^{(i)}}{\partial C_k^{(i)}}$, which can be expressed in a product form as follows:

$$\frac{\partial C_t^{(i)}}{\partial C_k^{(i)}} = \prod_{g=k+1}^{t} \frac{\partial C_g^{(i)}}{\partial C_{g-1}^{(i)}} = \frac{\partial C_{k+1}^{(i)}}{\partial C_k^{(i)}} \frac{\partial C_{k+2}^{(i)}}{\partial C_{k+1}^{(i)}} \cdots \frac{\partial C_t^{(i)}}{\partial C_{t-1}^{(i)}} \qquad (7)$$

Now, the recurrence in the cell state units is given by the following:

$$C_t^{(i)} = f_t^{(i)} C_{t-1}^{(i)} + i_t^{(i)} \widetilde{C_t^{(i)}} \qquad (8)$$

From this, we get the following:

$$\frac{\partial C_t^{(i)}}{\partial C_{t-1}^{(i)}} = f_t^{(i)}$$

As a result, the gradient expression, $\frac{\partial C_t^{(i)}}{\partial C_k^{(i)}}$, becomes the following:

$$\frac{\partial C_t^{(i)}}{\partial C_k^{(i)}} = \prod_{g=k+1}^{t} \frac{\partial C_g^{(i)}}{\partial C_{g-1}^{(i)}} = \prod_{g=k+1}^{t} f_g^{(i)} \qquad (9)$$

As you can see, if we can keep the forget cell state near one, the gradient will flow almost unattenuated, and the LSTM will not suffer from the vanishing gradient problem.

Most of the text-processing applications that we will look at in this book will use the LSTM version of RNNs.

Generative adversarial networks

Generative adversarial networks, popularly known as **GANs**, are generative models that learn a specific probability distribution through a generator, *G*. The generator *G* plays a zero sum minimax game with a discriminator *D* and both evolve over time, before the Nash equilibrium is reached. The generator tries to produce samples similar to the ones generated by a given probability distribution, *P(x)*, while the discriminator *D* tries to distinguish those fake data samples generated by the generator *G* from the data sample from the original distribution. The generator *G* tries to generate samples similar to the ones from *P(x)*, by converting samples, *z*, drawn from a noise distribution, *P(z)*. The discriminator, *D*, learns to tag samples generated by the generator *G* as *G(z)* when fake; *x* belongs to *P(x)* when they are original. At the equilibrium of the minimax game, the generator will learn to produce samples similar to the ones generated by the original distribution, *P(x)*, so that the following is true:

$$P(G(z)) \sim P(x)$$

The following diagram illustrates a GAN network learning the probability distribution of the MNIST digits:

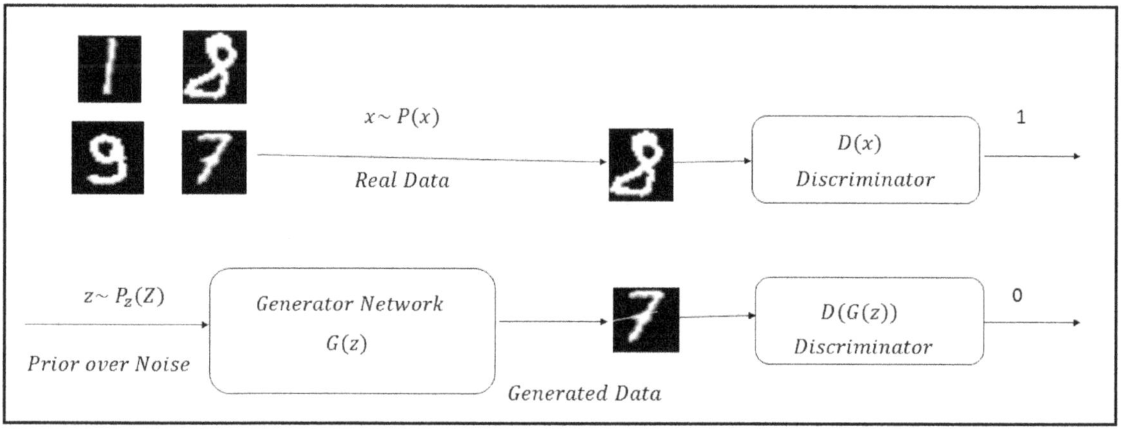

Figure 1.14: GAN architecture

The cost function minimized by the discriminator is the binary cross-entropy for distinguishing the real data points belonging to the probability distribution *P(x)* from the fake ones generated by the generator (that is, *G(z)*):

$$U(G, D) = -\mathbb{E}_{x \sim P(x)}[\log D(x)] - \mathbb{E}_{G(z) \sim P(G(z))}[\log(1 - D(G(z))] \qquad (1)$$

The generator will try to maximize the same cost function given by **(1)**. This means that, the optimization problem can be formulated as a minimax player with the utility function *U(G,D)*, as illustrated here:

$$\underbrace{min}_{D}\,\underbrace{max}_{G}\,U(G, D) = \underbrace{min}_{D}\,\underbrace{max}_{G} - \mathbb{E}_{x \sim P(x)}[\log D(x)] - \mathbb{E}_{G(z) \sim P(G(z))}[\log(1 - D(G(z))] \qquad (2)$$

Generally, to measure how far a given probability distribution matches that of a given distribution, *f*-divergence measures are used, such as the **Kullback–Leibler (KL)** divergence, the Jensen Shannon divergence, and the Bhattacharyya distance. For example, the KL divergence between two probability distributions, *P* and *Q*, is given by the following, where the expectation is with respect to the distribution, *P*:

$$KL(P||Q) = \mathbb{E}_P \log \frac{P}{Q}$$

Similarly, the Jensen Shannon divergence between P and Q is given as follows:

$$JSD(P||Q) = \mathbb{E}_P \log \frac{P}{\frac{P+Q}{2}} + \mathbb{E}_Q \log \frac{Q}{\frac{P+Q}{2}}$$

Now, coming back to *(2)*, the expression can be written as follows:

$$-\mathbb{E}_{x\sim P(x)}[\log D(x)] - \mathbb{E}_{x\sim G(x)}[\log(1 - D(x)] \qquad (3)$$

Here, $G(x)$ is the probability distribution for the generator. Expanding the expectation into its integral form, we get the following:

$$U(G,D) = -\int_{x\sim P(x)} P(x)[\log D(x)] - \int_{x\sim G(x)} [\log(1 - D(x)] \qquad (4)$$

For a fixed generator distribution, $G(x)$, the utility function will be at a minimum with respect to the discriminator if the following is true:

$$D(x) = \hat{D}(x) = \frac{P(x)}{P(x) + G(x)} \qquad (5)$$

Substituting $D(x)$ from *(5)* in *(3)*, we get the following:

$$V(G,\hat{D}) = -\mathbb{E}_{x\sim P(x)} \log \frac{P(x)}{P(x) + G(x)} - \mathbb{E}_{x\sim G(x)} \log \frac{G(x)}{P(x) + G(x)} \qquad (7)$$

Now, the task of the generator is to maximize the utility, $V(G,\hat{D})$, or minimize the utility, $-V(G,\hat{D})$. The expression for $-V(G,\hat{D})$ can be rearranged as follows:

$$-V(G,\hat{D}) = \mathbb{E}_{x\sim P(x)} \log \frac{P(x)}{P(x) + G(x)} + \mathbb{E}_{x\sim G(x)} \log \frac{G(x)}{P(x) + G(x)}$$

$$= -\log 4 + \mathbb{E}_{x\sim P(x)} \log \frac{P(x)}{\frac{P(x)+G(x)}{2}} + \mathbb{E}_{x\sim G(x)} \log \frac{G(x)}{\frac{P(x)+G(x)}{2}}$$

$$-\log 4 + JSD(P||G)$$

Hence, we can see that the generator minimizing $-V(G, \hat{D})$ is equivalent to minimizing the Jensen Shannon divergence between the real distribution, *P(x)*, and the distribution of the samples generated by the generator, *G* (that is, *G(x)*).

Training a GAN is not a straightforward process, and there are several technical considerations that we need to take into account while training such a network. We will be using an advanced GAN network to build a cross-domain style transfer application in `Chapter 4`, *Style Transfer in Fashion Industry using GANs*.

Reinforcement learning

Reinforcement learning is a branch of machine learning that enables machines and/or agents to maximize some form of reward within a specific context by taking specific actions. Reinforcement learning is different from supervised and unsupervised learning. Reinforcement learning is used extensively in game theory, control systems, robotics, and other emerging areas of artificial intelligence. The following diagram illustrates the interaction between an agent and an environment in a reinforcement learning problem:

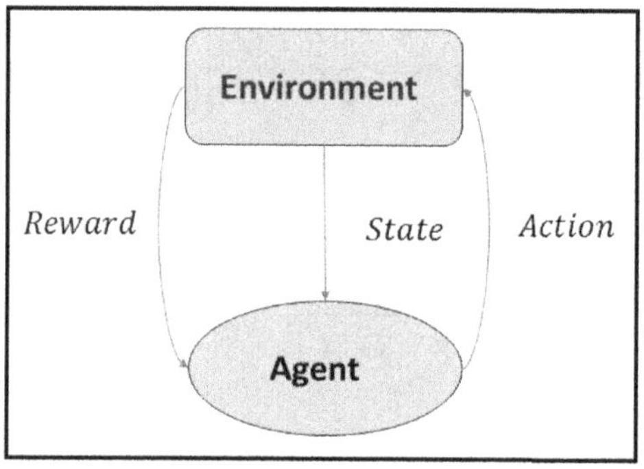

Figure 1.15: Agent-environment interaction in a reinforcement learning model

Q-learning

We will now look at a popular reinforcement learning algorithm, called **Q-learning**. Q-learning is used to determine an optimal action selection policy for a given finite Markov decision process. A **Markov decision process** is defined by a state space, *S*; an action space, *A*; an immediate rewards set, *R*; a probability of the next state, $S^{(t+1)}$, given the current state, $S^{(t)}$; a current action, $a^{(t)}$; $P(S^{(t+1)}/S^{(t)};r^{(t)})$; and a discount factor, γ. The following diagram illustrates a Markov decision process, where the next state is dependent on the current state and any actions taken in the current state:

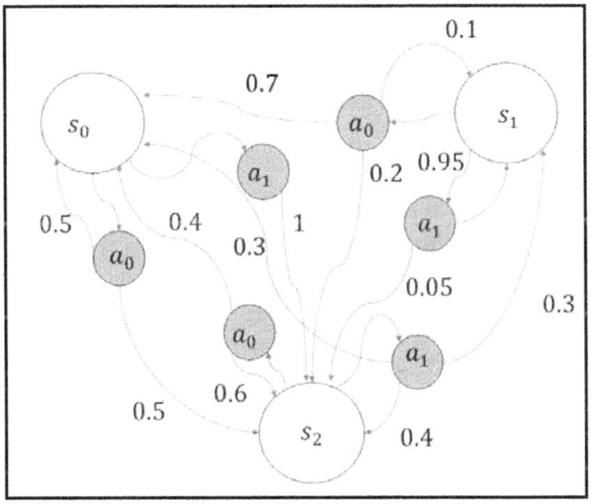

Figure 1.16: A Markov decision process

Let's suppose that we have a sequence of states, actions, and corresponding rewards, as follows:

$$s^{(1)}, a^{(1)}, r^{(1)}, s^{(2)}, a^{(2)}, r^{(2)}, \ldots\ldots\ s^{(t)}, a^{(t)}, r^{(t)}, s^{(t+1)} \ldots s^{(T)}, a^{(T)}, r^{(T)}$$

If we consider the long term reward, R_t, at step *t*, it is equal to the sum of the immediate rewards at each step, from *t* until the end, as follows:

$$R_t = r_t + r_{t+1} + \ldots. + r_T$$

Now, a Markov decision process is a random process, and it is not possible to get the same next step, $S^{(t+1)}$, based on $S^{(t)}$ and $a^{(t)}$ every time; so, we apply a discount factor, γ, to future rewards. This means that, the long-term reward can be better represented as follows:

$$R_t = r_t + \gamma r_{t+1} + \gamma^2 r_{t+2} \ldots . + \gamma^{(T-t)} r_T = r_t + \gamma (r_{t+1} + \gamma r_{t+2} \ldots . + \gamma^{(T-t-1)} r_T) = r_t + \gamma R_{t+1}$$

Since at the time step, *t*, the immediate reward is already realized, to maximize the long-term reward, we need to maximize the long-term reward at the time step *t+1* (that is, R_{t+1}), by choosing an optimal action. The maximum long-term reward expected at a state $S^{(t)}$ by taking an action $a^{(t)}$ is represented by the following Q-function:

$$Q(s^{(t)}, a^{(t)}) = max\ R_t = r_t + \gamma\ max\ R_{t+1} = r_t + \gamma \underbrace{max}_{a} Q(s^{(t+1)}, a) \qquad (1)$$

At each state, $s \in S$, the agent in Q-learning tries to take an action, $a \in A$, that maximizes its long-term reward. The Q-learning algorithm is an iterative process, the update rule of which is as follows:

$$Q(s^{(t)}, a^{(t)}) = (1 - \alpha) Q(s^{(t)}, a^{(t)}) + \alpha (r^{(t)} + \gamma \underbrace{max}_{a} Q(s^{(t+1)}, a)) \qquad (2)$$

As you can see, the algorithm is inspired by the notion of a long-term reward, as expressed in *(1)*.

The overall cumulative reward, $Q(s^{(t)}, a^{(t)})$, of taking action $a^{(t)}$ in state $s^{(t)}$ is dependent on the immediate reward, $r^{(t)}$, and the maximum long-term reward that we can hope for at the new step, $s^{(t+1)}$. In a Markov decision process, the new state $s^{(t+1)}$ is stochastically dependent on the current state, $s^{(t)}$, and the action taken $a^{(t)}$ through a probability density/mass function of the form $P(S^{(t+1)}/S^{(t)};r^{(t)})$.

The algorithm keeps on updating the expected long-term cumulative reward by taking a weighted average of the old expectation and the new long-term reward, based on the value of α.

Once we have built the $Q(s,a)$ function through the iterative algorithm, while playing the game based on a given state s we can take the best action, $\hat{a}$, as the policy that maximizes the Q-function:

$$\pi(s) = \hat{a} = \underbrace{argmax}_{a} Q(s, a) \quad (2)$$

Deep Q-learning

In Q-learning, we generally work with a finite set of states and actions; this means that, tables suffice to hold the Q-values and rewards. However, in practical applications, the number of states and applicable actions are mostly infinite, and better Q-function approximators are needed to represent and learn the Q-functions. This is where deep neural networks come to the rescue, since they are universal function approximators. We can represent the Q-function with a neural network that takes the states and actions as input and provides the corresponding Q-values as output. Alternatively, we can train a neural network using only the states, and have the output as Q-values corresponding to all of the actions. Both of these scenarios are illustrated in the following diagram. Since the Q-values are rewards, we are dealing with regression in these networks:

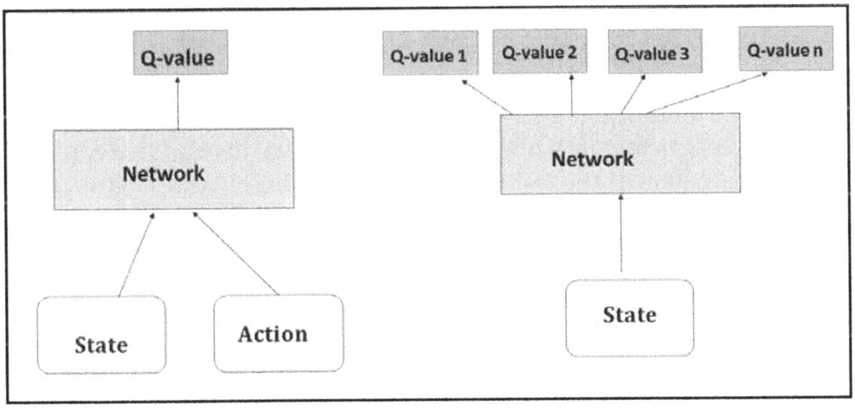

Figure 1.17: Deep Q-learning function approximator network

In this book, we will use reinforcement learning to train a race car to drive by itself through deep Q-learning.

Transfer learning

In general, **transfer learning** refers to the notion of using knowledge gained in one domain to solve a related problem in another domain. In deep learning, however, it specifically refers to the process of reusing a neural network trained for a specific task for a similar task in a different domain. The new task uses the feature detectors learned from a previous task, and so we do not have to train the model to learn them.

Deep-learning models tend to have a huge number of parameters, due to the nature of connectivity patterns among units of different layers. To train such a large model, a considerable amount of data is required; otherwise, the model may suffer from overfitting. For many problems requiring a deep learning solution, a large amount of data will not be available. For instance, in image processing for object recognition, deep-learning models provide state-of-the-art solutions. In such cases, transfer learning can be used to create features, based on the feature detectors learned from an existing trained deep-learning model. Then, those features can be used to build a simple model with the available data in order to solve the new problem at hand. So the only parameters that the new model needs to learn are the ones related to building the simple model, thus reducing the chances of overfitting. The pretrained models are generally trained on a huge corpus of data, and thus, they have reliable parameters as the feature detectors.

When we process images in CNNs, the initial layers learn to detect very generic features, such as curls, edges, color composition, and so on. As the network grows deeper, the convolutional layers in the deeper layers learn to detect more complex features that are relevant to the specific kind of dataset. We can use a pretrained network and choose to not train the first few layers, as they learn very generic features. Instead, we can concentrate on only training the parameters of the last few layers, since these would learn complex features that are specific to the problem at hand. This would ensure that we have fewer parameters to train for, and that we use the data judiciously, only training for the required complex parameters and not for the generic features.

Transfer learning is widely used in image processing through CNNs, where the filters act as feature detectors. The most common pretrained CNNs that are used for transfer learning are `AlexNet`, `VGG16`, `VGG19`, `Inception V3`, and `ResNet`, among others. The following diagram illustrates a pretrained `VGG16` network that is used for transfer learning:

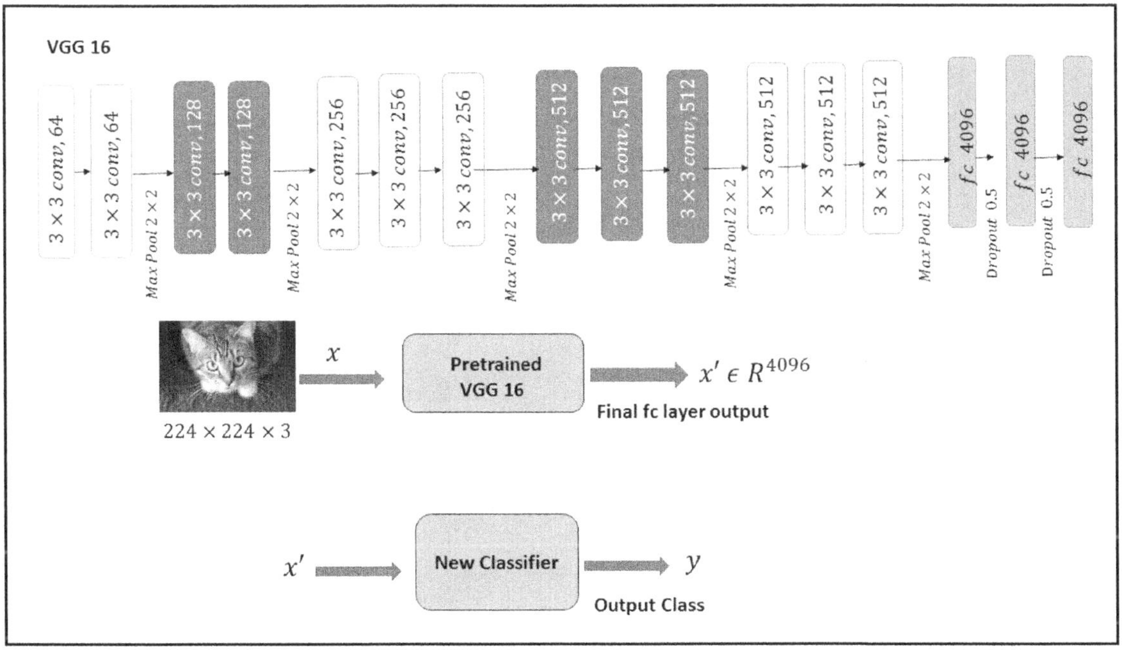

Figure 1.18: Transfer learning with a pretrained VGG 16 network

The input images represented by **x** are fed to the **Pretrained VGG 16** network, and the **4096** dimensional output feature vector, **x'**, is extracted from the last fully connected layer. The extracted features, **x'**, along with the corresponding class label, **y**, are used to train a simple classification network, reducing the data required to solve the problem.

We will solve an image classification problem in the healthcare domain by using transfer learning in `Chapter 2`, *Transfer Learning*.

Restricted Boltzmann machines

Restricted Boltzmann machines (**RBMs**) are an unsupervised class of machine learning algorithms that learn the internal representation of data. An RBM has a visible layer, $v \in R^m$, and a hidden layer, $h \in R^n$. RBMs learn to present the input in the visible layer as a low-dimensional representation in the hidden layer. All of the hidden layer units are conditionally independent, given the visible layer input. Similarly, all of the visible layers are conditionally independent, given the hidden layer input. This allows the RBM to sample the output of the visible units independently, given the hidden layer input, and vice versa.

The following diagram illustrates the architecture of an RBM:

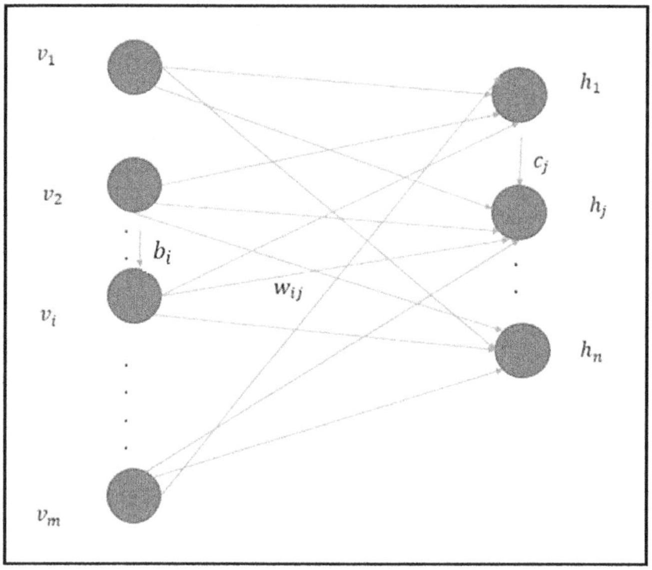

Figure 1.19: Restricted Boltzmann machines

The weight, $w_{ij} \in W$, connects the visible unit, i, to the hidden unit, j, where $W \in R^{m \times n}$ is the set of all such weights, from visible units to hidden units. The biases in the visible units are represented by $b_i \in b$, whereas the biases in the hidden units are represented by $c_j \in c$.

Inspired by ideas from the Boltzmann distribution in statistical physics, the joint distribution of a visible layer vector, v, and a hidden layer vector, h, is made proportional to the exponential of the negative energy of the configuration:

$$P(v,h) \propto e^{-E(v,h)} \quad (1)$$

The energy of a configuration is given by the following:

$$E(v,h) = v^T W h + b^T v + c^T h \quad (2)$$

The probability of the hidden unit, *j*, given the visible input vector, v, can be represented as follows:

$$P(h_j/v) = \sigma(\sum_i v_i w_{ij} + b_j = \sigma(v^T W[:, j] + c_j) \quad (2)$$

Similarly, the probability of the visible unit, *i*, given the hidden input vector, h, is given by the following:

$$P(v_i/h) = \sigma(\sum_j h_j w_{ij} + c_i = \sigma(h^T W^T[:, i] + c_j) \quad (3)$$

So, once we have learned the weights and biases of the RBM through training, the visible representation can be sampled, given the hidden state, while the hidden state can be sampled, given the visible state.

Similar to **principal component analysis** (**PCA**), RBMs are a way to represent data in one dimension, provided by the visible layer, v, into a different dimension, provided by the hidden layer, h. When the dimensionality of the hidden layer is less than that of the visible layer, the RBMs perform the task of dimensionality reduction. RBMs are generally trained on binary data.

RBMs are trained by maximizing the likelihood of the training data. In each iteration of gradient descent of the cost function with respect to the weights and biases, sampling comes into the picture, which makes the training process expensive and somewhat computationally intractable. A smart method of sampling, called **contrastive divergence**—which uses Gibbs sampling—is used to train the RBMs.

We will be using RBMs to build recommender systems in `Chapter 6`, *The Intelligent Recommender System*.

Autoencoders

Much like RBMs, **autoencoders** are a class of unsupervised learning algorithms that aim to uncover the hidden structures within data. In **principal component analysis** (**PCA**), we try to capture the linear relationships among input variables, and try to represent the data in a reduced dimension space by taking linear combinations (of the input variables) that account for most of the variance in data. However, PCA would not be able to capture the nonlinear relationships between the input variables.

Autoencoders are neural networks that can capture the nonlinear interactions between input variables while representing the input in different dimensions in a hidden layer. Most of the time, the dimensions of the hidden layer are smaller to those of the input. This we skipped, with the assumption that there is an inherent low-dimensional structure to the high-dimensional data. For instance, high-dimensional images can be represented by a low-dimensional manifold, and autoencoders are often used to discover that structure. The following diagram illustrates the neural architecture of an autoencoder:

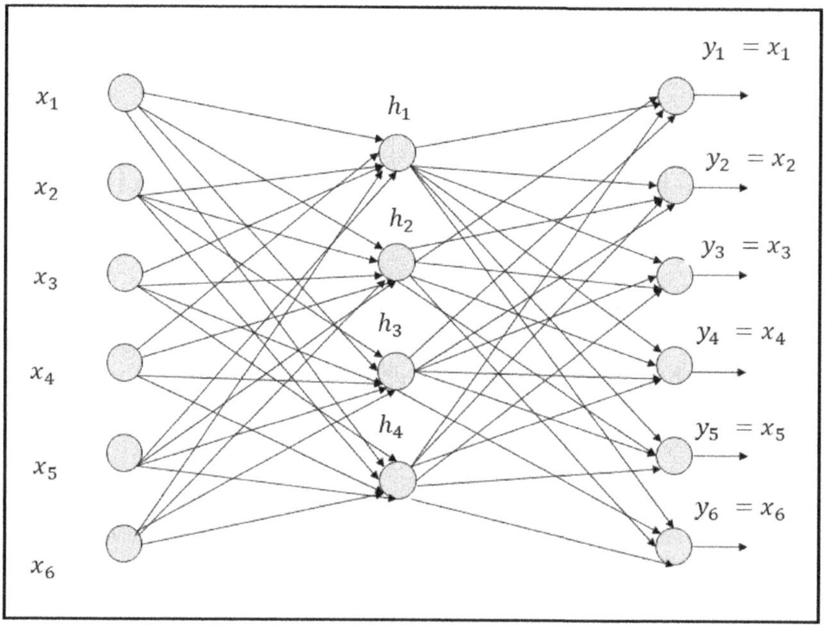

Figure 1.20: Autoencoder architecture

An autoencoder has two parts: an encoder and a decoder. The encoder tries to project the input data, x, into a hidden layer, h. The decoder tries to reconstruct the input from the hidden layer h. The weights accompanying such a network are trained by minimizing the reconstruction error that is, the error between the reconstructed input, $\tilde{x}$, from the decoder and the original input. If the input is continuous, then the sum of squares of the reconstruction error is minimized, in order to learn the weights of the autoencoder.

If we represent the encoder by a function, $f_W(x)$, and the decoder by $f_U(x)$, where W and U are the weight matrices associated with the encoder and the decoder, then the following is the case:

$$h = f_W(x) \qquad (1)$$

$$\tilde{x} = f_U(h) \qquad (2)$$

The reconstruction error, C, over the training set, x_i, $i = 1, 2, 3, ...m$, can be expressed as follows:

$$C(W, U) = \frac{1}{m}\sum_{i=1}^{m} ||x_i - \widetilde{x_i}||_2^2 \qquad (3)$$

The autoencoder optimal weights, $\hat{W}, \hat{U}$, can be learned by minimizing the cost function from *(3)*, as follows:

$$\hat{W}, \hat{U} = \underbrace{argmin}_{W,U}\, C(W, U) \qquad (4)$$

Autoencoders are used for a variety of purposes, such as learning the latent representation of data, noise reduction, and feature detection. Noise reduction autoencoders take the noisy version of the actual input as their input. They try to construct the actual input that acts as a label for the reconstruction. Similarly, autoencoders can be used as generative models. One such class of autoencoders that can work as generative models is called **variational autoencoders**. Currently, variational autoencoders and GANs are very popular as generative models for image processing.

Summary

We have now come to the end of this chapter. We have looked at several variants of artificial neural networks, including CNNs for image processing purposes and RNNs for natural language processing purposes. Additionally, we looked at RBMs and GANs as generative models and autoencoders as unsupervised methods that cater to a lot of problems, such as noise reduction or deciphering the internal structure of the data. Also, we touched upon reinforcement learning, which has made a big impact on robotics and AI.

You should now be familiar with the core techniques that we are going to use when building smart AI applications throughout the rest of the chapters in this book. While building the applications, we will take small technical digressions when required. Readers that are new to deep learning are advised to explore more about the core technologies touched upon in this chapter for a more thorough understanding.

In subsequent chapters, we will discuss practical AI projects, and we will implement them using the technologies discussed in this chapter. In `Chapter 2`, *Transfer Learning*, we will start by implementing a healthcare application for medical image analysis using transfer learning. We hope that you look forward to your participation.

2
Transfer Learning

Transfer learning is the process of transferring the knowledge gained in one task in a specific domain to a related task in a similar domain. In the deep learning paradigm, transfer learning generally refers to the reuse of a pre-trained model as the starting point for another problem. The problems in computer vision and natural language processing require a lot of data and computational resources, to train meaningful deep learning models. Transfer learning has gained a lot of importance in the domains of vision and text, since it alleviates the need for a large amount of training data and training time. In this chapter, we will use transfer learning to solve a healthcare problem.

Some key topics related to transfer learning that we will touch upon in this chapter are as follows:

- Using transfer learning to detect diabetic retinopathy conditions in the human eye, and to determine the retinopathy's severity
- Exploring the advanced pre-trained convolutional neural architectures that can be used to train a **convolutional neural network** (**CNN**) that is capable of detecting diabetic retinopathy in fundus images of the human eye
- Looking at the different image preprocessing steps required for the practical implementation of a CNN
- Learning to formulate a cost function that is appropriate for the problem at hand
- Defining the appropriate metrics for measuring the performance of a trained model
- Generating additional data using affine transformations
- Training intricacies related to the appropriate learning rate, the selection of the optimizer, and so on
- Going over an end-to-end Python implementation

Technical requirements

You will require to have basic knowledge of Python 3, TensorFlow, Keras and OpenCV.

The code files of this chapter can be found on GitHub:
`https://github.com/PacktPublishing/Intelligent-Projects-using-Python/tree/master/Chapter02`

Check out the following video to see the code in action:
`http://bit.ly/2t6LLyB`

Introduction to transfer learning

In a traditional machine learning paradigm (see *Figure 2.1*), every use case or task is modeled independently, based on the data at hand. In transfer learning, we use the knowledge gained from a particular task (in the form of architecture and model parameters) to solve a different (but related) task, as illustrated in the following diagram:

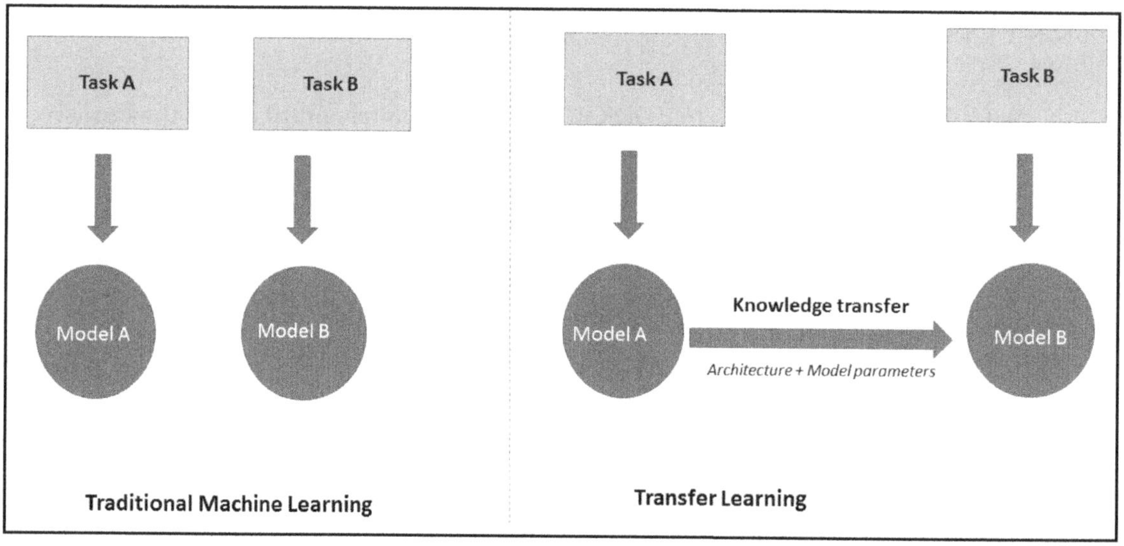

Figure 2.1: Traditional machine learning versus transfer learning

Andrew Ng, in his 2016 NIPS tutorial, stated that transfer learning would be the next big driver of machine learning's commercial success (after supervised learning); this statement grows truer with each passing day. Transfer learning is now used extensively in problems that need to be solved with artificial neural networks. The big question, therefore, is why this is the case.

Training an artificial neural network from scratch is a difficult task, primarily due to the following two reasons:

- The cost surface of an artificial neural network is non-convex; hence, it requires a good set of initial weights for a reasonable convergence.
- Artificial neural networks have a lot of parameters, and thus, they require a lot of data to train. Unfortunately, for a lot of projects, the specific data available for training a neural network is insufficient, whereas the problem that the project aims to solve is complex enough to require a neural network solution.

In both cases, transfer learning comes to the rescue. If we use pre-trained models that are trained on a huge corpora of labeled data, such as ImageNet or CIFAR, problems involving transfer learning will have a good set of initial weights to start the training; those weights can then be fine-tuned, based on the data at hand. Similarly, to avoid training a complex model on a smaller amount of data, we may want to extract the complex features from a pre-trained neural network, and then use those features to train a relatively simple model, such as an SVM or a logistic regression model. To provide an example, if we are working on an image classification problem and we already have a pre-trained model—say, a `VGG16` network on 1,000 classes of ImageNet—we can pass the training data through the weights of `VGG16` and extract the features from the last pooling layer. If we have *m* training data points, we can use the equation $(x^{(i)}, y^{(i)})_{i=1}^{m}$, where *x* is the feature vector and *y* is the output class. We can then derive complex features, such as vector *h*, from the pre-trained `VGG16` network, as follows:

$$h = f_W(x) \qquad (1)$$

Here, *W* is the set of weights of the pre-trained `VGG16` network, up to the last pooling layer.

We can then use the transformed set of training data points, $(h^{(i)}, y^{(i)})_{i=1}^{m}$, to build a relatively simple model.

Transfer learning and detecting diabetic retinopathy

In this chapter, using transfer learning, we are going to build a model to detect diabetic retinopathy in the human eye. Diabetic retinopathy is generally found in diabetic patients, where high blood sugar levels cause damage to the blood vessels in the retina. The following image shows a normal retina on the left, and one with diabetic retinopathy on the right:

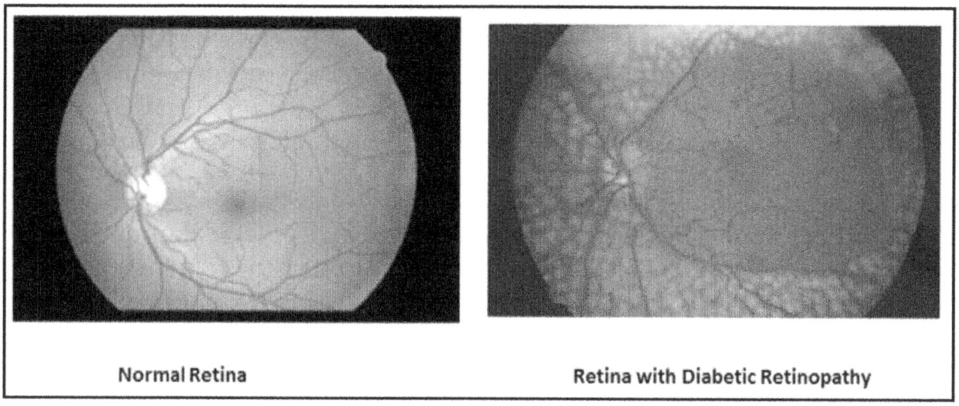

Figure 2.2: A normal human retina versus a retina with diabetic retinopathy

In healthcare, diabetic retinopathy detection is generally a manual process that involves a trained physician examining color fundus retina images. This introduces a delay in the process of diagnosis, often leading to delayed treatment. As a part of our project, we are going to build a robust artificial intelligence system that can take the color fundus images of the retina and classify the severity of the condition of the retina, with respect to diabetic retinopathy. The different conditions into which we are going to classify the retina images are as follows:

- **0**: No diabetic retinopathy
- **1**: Mild diabetic retinopathy
- **2**: Moderate diabetic retinopathy
- **3**: Severe diabetic retinopathy
- **4**: Proliferative diabetic retinopathy

The diabetic retinopathy dataset

The dataset for the building the Diabetic Retinopathy detection application is obtained from Kaggle and can be downloaded from following the link: `https://www.kaggle.com/c/classroom-diabetic-retinopathy-detection-competition/data`.

Both the training and the holdout test datasets are present within the `train_dataset.zip` file, which is available at the preceding link.

We will use the labeled training data to build the model through cross-validation. We will evaluate the model on the holdout dataset.

Since we are dealing with class prediction, accuracy will be a useful validation metric. Accuracy is defined as follows:

$$a_c = \frac{c}{N}$$

Here, c is the number of correctly classified samples, and N is the total number of evaluated samples.

We will also use the **quadratic weighted kappa** statistics to determine the quality of the model, and to have a benchmark as to how good the model is, compared to Kaggle standards. The quadratic weighted kappa is defined as follows:

$$\kappa = 1 - \frac{\sum_{i,j} w_{i,j} O_{i,j}}{\sum_{i,j} w_{i,j} E_{i,j}}$$

The weight $(w_{i,j})$ in the expression for quadratic weighted kappa is as follows:

$$w_{i,j} = \frac{(i-j)^2}{N-1}$$

In the preceding formula, the following applies:

- N represents the number of classes
- O_{ij} represents the number of images that have been predicted to have class i, and where the actual class of the image is j
- E_{ij} represents the expected number of observations for the predicted class which is i, and the actual class being j, assuming independence between the predicted class and the actual class

To better understand kappa metrics components, let's look at a binary classification of apples and oranges. Let's assume that the confusion matrix of the predicted and actual classes is as shown in the following diagram:

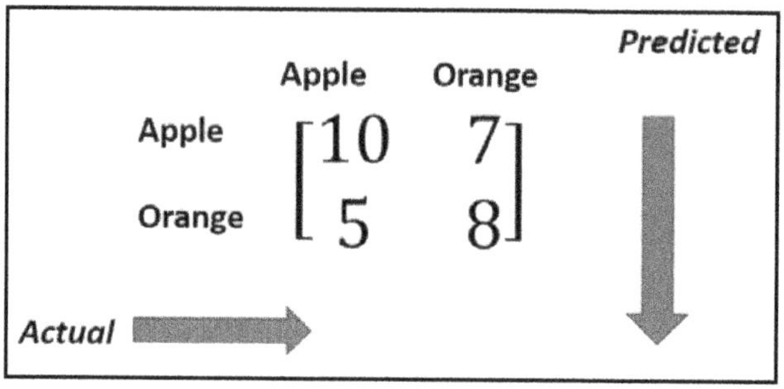

Figure 2.3: Kappa metric terms

The expected count of predicting *Apple* when the true label is *Orange,* assuming independence between the labels, is given by the following formula:

$$E[i =\text{" Apple "}, j =\text{" Orange "}] = P(i =\text{" Apple "})P(j =\text{" Orange "}) * (Total\ of\ \text{" Apples " and " Oranges "})$$
$$= \frac{(10+7)}{30}\frac{(5+8)}{30}30 = \frac{(17*13)}{30} = 11.05$$

This expected count is the worst error that you can make, given that there is no model.

If you're familiar with the chi-square test for independence between two categorical variables, the expected count in each cell of the contingency table is computed based on the same formula, assuming independence between the categorical variables.

The observed count of the model predicting *Apple* when the true label is *Orange* can be directly traced from the confusion matrix, and is equal to 5, as follows:

$$O[i =\text{" Apple "}, j =\text{" Orange "}] = 5$$

Hence, we can see that the error the model makes in predicting *Orange* as *Apple* is less than the error we would obtain if we were to use no model. Kappa generally measures how well we are doing in comparison to predictions made without a model.

If we observe the expression for the quadratic weights, ($w_{i,j}$), we can see that the value of the weights is higher when the difference between the actual and the predicted label is greater. This makes sense, due to the ordinal nature of classes. For example, let's denote an eye in perfect condition with the class label zero; a mild diabetic retinopathy condition with one; a moderate diabetic retinopathy condition with two; and a severe condition of diabetic retinopathy with three. This quadratic term weight, ($w_{i,j}$), is going to be higher when a mild diabetic retinopathy condition is wrongly classified as severe diabetic retinopathy, rather than as moderate diabetic retinopathy. This makes sense, since we want to predict a condition as close to the actual condition as possible, even if we don't manage to predict the actual class.

We will be using `sklearn.metrics.cohen_kappa_score` with `weights="quadratic"` to compute the kappa score. The higher the weights, the lower the kappa score will be.

Formulating the loss function

The data for this use case has five classes, pertaining to no diabetic retinopathy, mild diabetic retinopathy, moderate diabetic retinopathy, severe diabetic retinopathy, and proliferative diabetic retinopathy. Hence, we can treat this as a categorical classification problem. For our categorical classification problem, the output labels need to be one-hot encoded, as shown here:

- **No diabetic retinopathy**: $[1\ 0\ 0\ 0\ 0]^T$
- **Mild diabetic retinopathy**: $[0\ 1\ 0\ 0\ 0]^T$
- **Moderate diabetic retinopathy**: $[0\ 0\ 1\ 0\ 0]^T$
- **Severe diabetic retinopathy**: $[0\ 0\ 0\ 1\ 0]^T$
- **Proliferative diabetic retinopathy**: $[0\ 0\ 0\ 0\ 1]^T$

Softmax would be the best activation function for presenting the probability of the different classes in the output layer, while the sum of the categorical cross-entropy loss of each of the data points would be the best loss to optimize. For a single data point with the output label vector y and the predicted probability of p, the cross-entropy loss is given by the following equation:

$$L = -\sum_{j=1}^{5} y_j \log p_j \quad (1)$$

Here, $y = [y_1 ... y_j .. y_5]^T$ and $p = [p_1 ... p_j .. p_5]^T$.

Similarly, the average loss over M training data points can be represented as follows:

$$L = -\frac{1}{M}\sum_{i=1}^{M}\sum_{j=1}^{5}[y_j^{(i)} \log p_j^{(i)}] \qquad (2)$$

During the training process, the gradients of a mini batch are based on the average log loss given by *(2)*, where *M* is the chosen batch size. For the validation log loss that we will monitor in conjunction with the validation accuracy, *M* is the number of validation set data points. Since we will be doing **K-fold cross-validation** in each fold, we will have a different validation dataset in each fold.

Now that we have defined the training methodology, the loss function, and the validation metric, let's proceed to the data exploration and modeling.

Note that the classifications in the output classes are of an ordinal nature, since the severity increases from class to class. For this reason, regression might come in handy. We will try our luck with regression in place of categorical classification, as well, to see how it fares. One of the challenges with regression is to convert the raw scores to classes. We would use a simple scheme and hash the scores to its nearest integer severity class.

Taking class imbalances into account

Class imbalance is a major problem when it comes to classification. The following diagram depicts the class densities of the five severity classes:

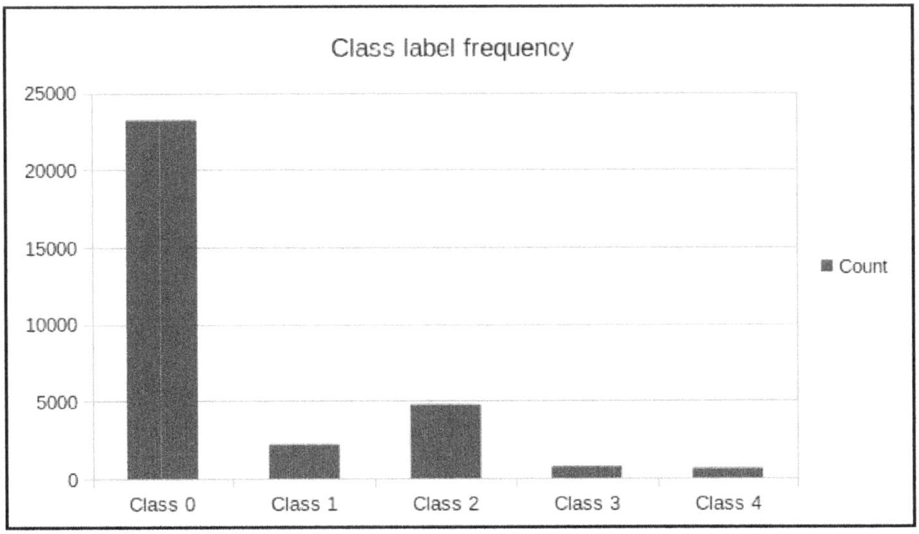

Figure 2.4: Class densities of the five severity classes

As we can see from the preceding chart, nearly 73% of the training data belongs to **Class 0**, which stands for no diabetic retinopathy condition. So if we happen to label all data points as **Class 0**, then we would have 73% percent accuracy. This is not desirable in patient heath conditions. We would rather have a test say a patient has a certain heath condition when it doesn't (false positive) than have a test that misses detecting a certain heath condition when it does (false negative). A 73% accuracy may mean nothing if the model learns to classify all points as belonging to **Class 0**.

Detecting the higher severity classes are more important than doing well on the *no severity class*. The problem with classification models using the log loss or the cross entropy cost function is that it favors the majority class. This is because the cross entropy error is derived from the maximum likelihood principles which tends to assign higher probability to majority classes. We can do two things:

- Discard data from the classes with more samples or up sample the low frequency classes to keep the distribution of samples among classes uniform.
- In the loss function assigns a weight to the classes in inverse proportion to their densities. This will ensure that the low frequency classes impose a higher penalty on the cost function when the model fails to classify them.

We will work with scheme two since it doesn't involve having to generate more data or throw away existing data. If we take the class weights to be proportional to the inverse of the class frequencies, we get the following class weights:

Severity classes	**Class weights**
`Class 0`	`0.0120353863`
`Class 1`	`0.1271350558`
`Class 2`	`0.0586961973`
`Class 3`	`0.3640234214`
`Class 4`	`0.4381974727`

We will use these weights while training the classification network.

Preprocessing the images

The images for the different classes will be stored in different folders, so it will be easy to label their classes. We will read the images using `Opencv` functions, and will resize them to different dimensions, such as 224 x 224 x 3. We'll subtract the mean pixel intensity channel-wise from each of the images, based on the ImageNet dataset. This means subtraction will bring the diabetic retinopathy images to the same intensity range as that of the processed ImageNet images, on which the pre-trained models are trained. Once each image has been prepossessed, they will be stored in a `numpy` array. The image preprocessing functions can be defined as follows:

```
def get_im_cv2(path,dim=224):
    img = cv2.imread(path)
    resized = cv2.resize(img, (dim,dim), cv2.INTER_LINEAR)
    return resized

def pre_process(img):
    img[:,:,0] =    img[:,:,0] - 103.939
    img[:,:,1] =    img[:,:,0] - 116.779
    img[:,:,2] =    img[:,:,0] - 123.68
    return img
```

The images are read through the `opencv` function `imread`, and then resized to `(224,224,3)` or any given dimension using an interlinear interpolation method. The mean pixel intensity in the red, green, and blue channels for the ImageNet images are `103.939`, `116.779`, and `123.68`, respectively; the pre-trained models are trained after subtracting these mean values from the images. This activity of mean subtraction is used to center the data. Centering the data around zero helps fight vanishing and exploding gradient problem, which in turn helps the models converge faster. Also, normalizing per channel helps to keep the gradient flow into each channel uniformly. Since we are going to use pre-trained models for this project, it makes sense to mean correct our images based on the channel wise mean pixel values before feeding them into the pre-trained networks. However, its not mandatory to mean correct the images based on the mean values of ImageNet on which the pre-trained network is based on. You can very well normalize by the mean pixel intensities of the training corpus for the project.

Similarly, instead of performing channel wise mean normalization, you can choose to do a mean normalization over the entire image. This entails subtracting the mean value of each image from itself. Imagine a scenario where the object to be recognized by the CNN is exposed under different lighting conditions such as in the day and night. We would like to classify the object correctly irrespective of the light conditions, however different pixel intensities would activate the neurons of the neural network differently, leading to a possibility of wrong classification of the object. However, if we subtract the mean of each image from itself, the object would no longer be affected by the different lighting conditions. So depending on the nature of the images that we work with, we can choose for ourselves the best image normalizing scheme. However any of the default ways of normalization tend to give reasonable performance.

Additional data generation using affine transformation

We will use the `keras ImageDataGenerator` to generate additional data, using **affine transformation** on the image pixel coordinates. The transformations that we will primarily use are rotation, translation, and scaling. If the pixel spatial coordinate is defined by $x = [x_1 x_2]^T \in R^2$, then the new coordinate of the pixel can be given by the following:

$$x' = Mx + b$$

Here, $M = R^{2x2}$ is the affine transformation matrix, and $b = [b_1\ b_2]^T \in R^2$ is a translation vector.

The term b_1 specifies the translation along one of the spatial directions, while b_2 provides the translation along the other spatial dimension.

These transformations are required, because neural networks are not, in general, translational invariant, rotational invariant, or scale invariant. Pooling operations do provide some translational invariance, but it is generally not enough. The neural network doesn't treat one object in a specific location in an image and the same object at a translated location in another image as the same thing. That is why we require several instances of an image at different translated positions for the neural network to learn better. The same explanation applies to rotation and scaling.

Rotation

The following is the affine transformation matrix for rotation, where θ represents the angle of rotation:

$$M = \begin{bmatrix} cos\theta & -sin\theta \\ sin\theta & cos\theta \end{bmatrix}$$

The translation vector, b, is zero, in this case. We can get rotation followed by translation by selecting a non-zero b.

As an example, the following image shows a photo of a retina, and then the same photo, rotated 90 degrees:

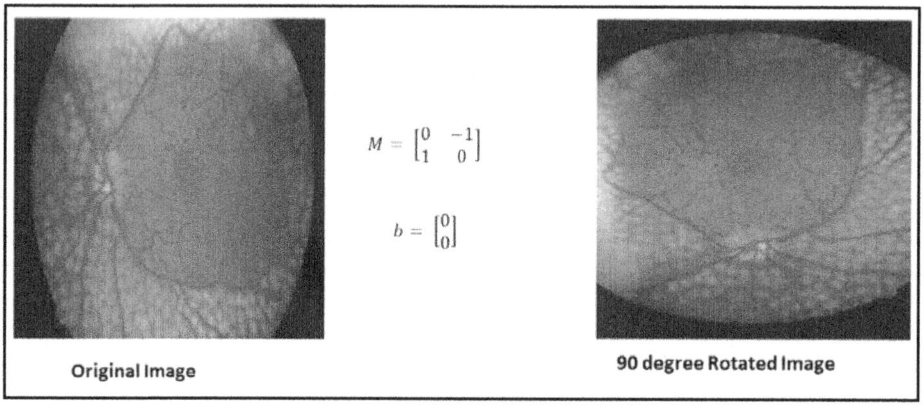

Figure 2.5: Rotated photo of the retina

Translation

For translation, the affine transformation matrix is the identity matrix, and the translation vector, *b*, has a nonzero value:

$$M = I = \begin{bmatrix} 1 & 0 \\ 0 & 1 \end{bmatrix}$$

$$b \neq 0$$

For instance, for a translation of five pixel positions along the vertical direction and three pixel positions along the horizontal direction, we can use $b = [5\ 3]^T$, with *M* as the identity matrix.

The following is an image translation of a retina by 24 pixel locations, along both the width and height of the image:

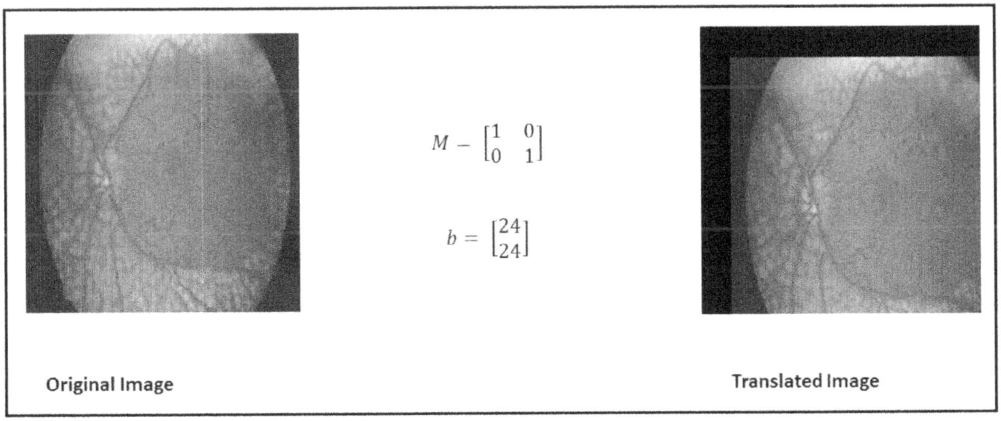

Figure 2.5: Image translation of the retina

Scaling

Scaling can be performed by a diagonal matrix, $M \in R^{2x2}$, as shown here:

$$M = \begin{bmatrix} s_v & 0 \\ 0 & s_h \end{bmatrix}$$

Here, S_v denotes the scale factor along the vertical direction, and S_h denotes the scale factor along the horizontal direction (see *Figure 2.6* for an illustration). We can also choose to follow up the scaling with a translation, by having a nonzero translation vector, b:

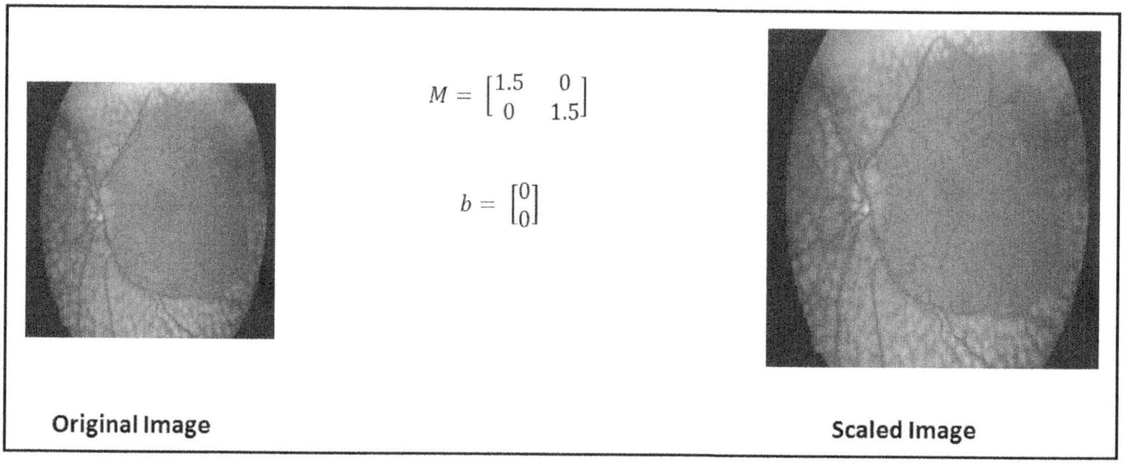

Figure 2.6 Image scaling of the retina

Reflection

The reflection about a line, L, making an angle of θ with the horizontal, can be obtained by the transformation matrix $T \in R^{2x2}$, as follows:

$$T = \begin{bmatrix} \cos 2\theta & \sin 2\theta \\ \sin 2\theta & -\cos 2\theta \end{bmatrix}$$

The following image shows a horizontal flip of a retina photo:

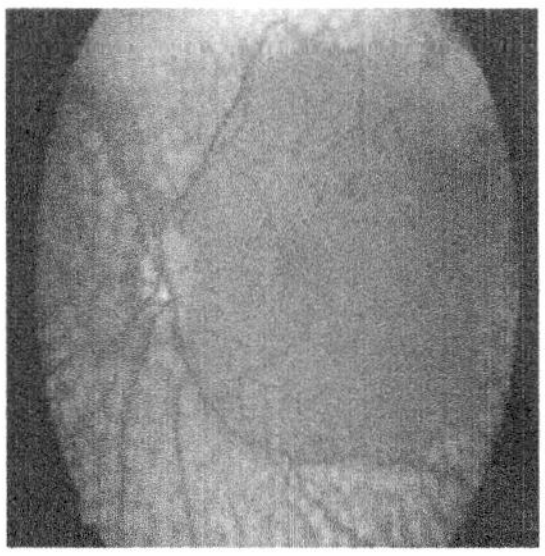

$$M = \begin{bmatrix} 1 & 0 \\ 0 & -1 \end{bmatrix}$$

$$b = \begin{bmatrix} 0 \\ 0 \end{bmatrix}$$

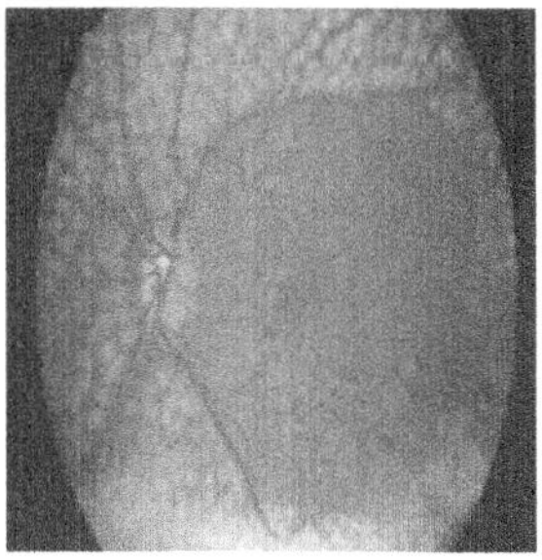

Original Image

Horizontally Flipped Image

Figure 2.7: Horizontal flip of a retina photo

Additional image generation through affine transformation

The `keras` image generator would work for our task using the following class:

```
datagen = ImageDataGenerator(
              horizontal_flip = True,
                              vertical_flip = True,
                              width_shift_range = 0.1,
                              height_shift_range = 0.1,
                              channel_shift_range=0,
                              zoom_range = 0.2,
                              rotation_range = 20)
```

As you can see from the defined generator, we have enabled horizontal and vertical flipping, which is nothing but a reflection of the images along the horizontal and vertical axes, respectively. Similarly, we have defined the image translations along the width and the height to be within 10% of the pixel locations along those directions. The range of rotation is confined to an angle of `20` degrees, whereas the scale factor is defined to be within `0.8` to `1.2` of the original image.

Network architecture

We will now experiment with the pre-trained `ResNet50`, `InceptionV3`, and `VGG16` networks, and find out which one gives the best results. Each of the pre-trained models' weights are based on ImageNet. I have provided the links to the original papers for the ResNet, `InceptionV3`, and `VGG16` architectures, for reference. Readers are advised to go over these papers, to get an in-depth understanding of these architectures and the subtle differences between them.

The VGG paper link is as follows:

- **Title**: *Very Deep Convolutional Networks for Large-Scale Image Recognition*
- **Link**: `https://arxiv.org/abs/1409.1556`

The ResNet paper link is as follows:

- **Title**: *Deep Residual Learning for Image Recognition*
- **Link**: `https://arxiv.org/abs/1512.03385`

The InceptionV3 paper link is as follows:

- **Title**: *Rethinking the Inception Architecture for Computer Vision*
- **Link**: `https://arxiv.org/abs/1512.00567`

To explain in brief, `VGG16` is a 16-layered CNN that uses 3 x 3 filters and 2 x 2 receptive fields for convolution. The activation functions used throughout the network are all ReLUs. The VGG architecture, developed by Simonyan and Zisserman, was the runner up in the ILSVRC 2014 competition. The `VGG16` network gained a lot of popularity due to its simplicity, and it is the most popular network for extracting features from images.

`ResNet50` is a deep CNN that implements the idea of residual block, quite different from that of the `VGG16` network. After a series of convolution-activation-pooling operations, the input of the block is again fed back to the output. The ResNet architecture was developed by Kaiming He, et al., and although it has 152 layers, it is less complex than the VGG network. This architecture won the ILSVRC 2015 competition by achieving a top five error rate of 3.57%, which is better than the human-level performance on this competition dataset. The top five error rate is computed by checking whether the target is in the five class predictions with the highest probability. In principle, the ResNet network tries to learn the residual mapping, as opposed to directly mapping from the output to the input, as you can see in the following residual block diagram:

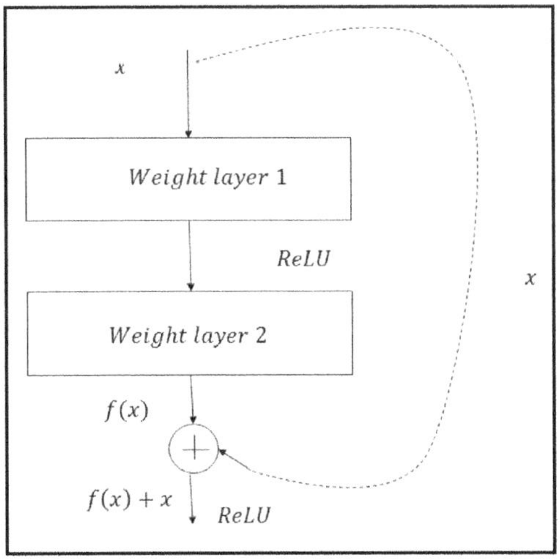

Figure 2.8: Residual block of ResNet models

InceptionV3 is the state-of-the-art CNN from Google. Instead of using fixed-sized convolutional filters at each layer, the InceptionV3 architecture uses filters of different sizes to extract features at different levels of granularity. The convolution block of an InceptionV3 layer is illustrated in the following diagram:

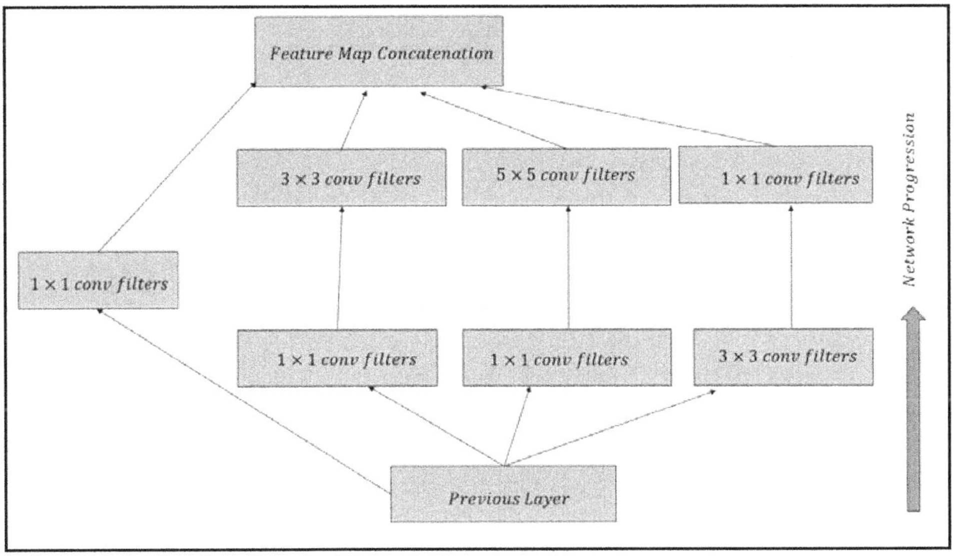

Figure 2.9: InceptionV3 convolution block

Inception V1 (GoogleNet) was the winner of the ILSVRC 2014 competition. Its top 5% error rate was very close to human-level performance, at 6.67%.

The VGG16 transfer learning network

We will take the output from the last pooling layer in the pre-trained `VGG16` network and add a couple of fully connected layers of 512 units each, followed by the output layer. The output of the final pooling layer is passed from a global average pooling operation before the fully connected layer. We can just flatten the output of the pooling layer, instead of performing global average pooling—the idea is to ensure that the output of the pooling is not in a two-dimensional lattice format, but rather, in a one-dimensional array format, much like a fully connected layer. The following diagram illustrates the architecture of the new `VGG16`, based on the pre-trained `VGG16`:

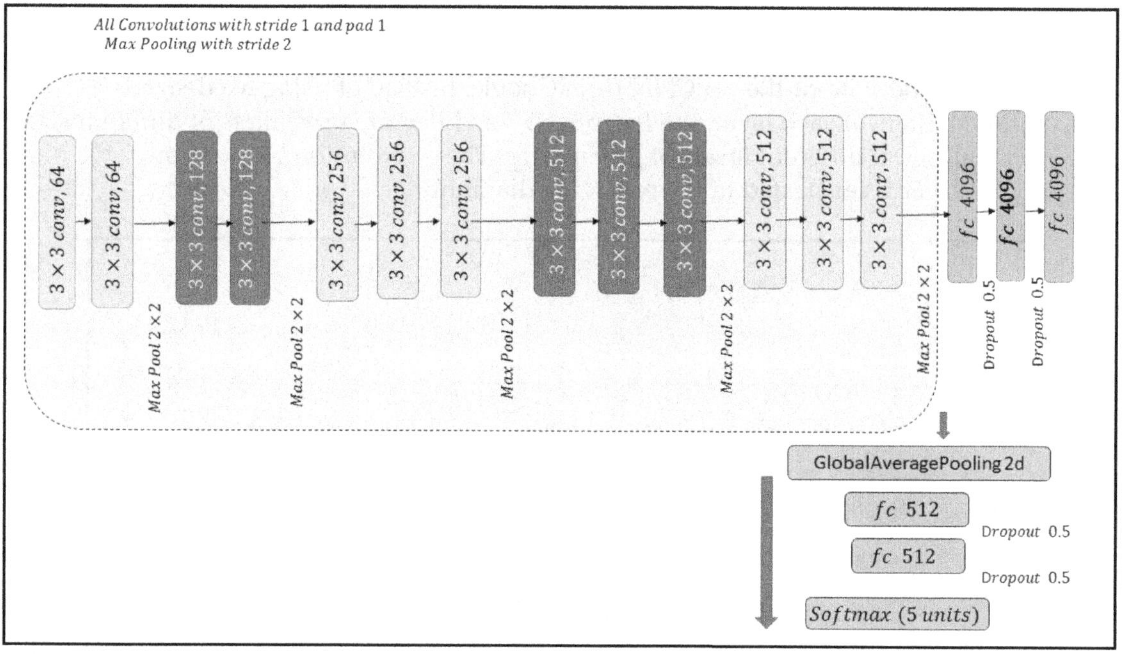

Figure 2.10: The VGG16 transfer learning network

As shown in the preceding diagram, we will extract the output from the last max-pooling layer in the pre-trained network and attach two fully connected layers before the final output layer. Based on the preceding architecture, the VGG definition function can be defined as shown the following code block, using `keras`:

```
def VGG16_pseudo(dim=224,freeze_layers=10,full_freeze='N'):
   # model_save_dest = {}
    model = VGG16(weights='imagenet',include_top=False)
    x = model.output
    x = GlobalAveragePooling2D()(x)
    x = Dense(512, activation='relu')(x)
    x = Dropout(0.5)(x)
    x = Dense(512, activation='relu')(x)
    x = Dropout(0.5)(x)
    out = Dense(5,activation='softmax')(x)
    model_final = Model(input = model.input,outputs=out)
    if full_freeze != 'N':
        for layer in model.layers[0:freeze_layers]:
         layer.trainable = False
    return model_final
```

We are going to use the weights from the pre-trained `VGG16` trained on ImageNet as the initial weights of the model, and then fine-tune the model. We are also freezing the weights of the first few layers (`10` is the default) since, in a CNN, the first few layers learn to detect generic features, such as edges, color composition, and so on. Hence, the features will not vary much across domains. Freezing a layer refers to not training the weights that are specific to that layer. We can experiment with the number of layers to freeze, and take the one that provides the best validation score. Since we are performing multi-class classification, the softmax activation function has been chosen for the output layer.

The InceptionV3 transfer learning network

The `InceptionV3` network for our task is defined in the following code block. One thing to note is that since `InceptionV3` is a much deeper network, we can have a greater number of initial layers. The idea of not training all of the layers in each of the models has another advantage, with respect to data availability. If we use less data training, the weights of the entire network might lead to overfitting. Freezing the layers reduces the number of weights to train, and hence, provides a form of regularization.

Since the initial layers learn generic features irrespective of the domain of the problem, they are the best layers to freeze. We have also used dropout in the fully connected layer, to prevent overfitting:

```
def inception_pseudo(dim=224,freeze_layers=30,full_freeze='N'):
    model = InceptionV3(weights='imagenet',include_top=False)
    x = model.output
    x = GlobalAveragePooling2D()(x)
    x = Dense(512, activation='relu')(x)
    x = Dropout(0.5)(x)
    x = Dense(512, activation='relu')(x)
    x = Dropout(0.5)(x)
    out = Dense(5,activation='softmax')(x)
    model_final = Model(input = model.input,outputs=out)
    if full_freeze != 'N':
        for layer in model.layers[0:freeze_layers]:
         layer.trainable = False
    return model_final
```

The ResNet50 transfer learning network

The `ResNet50` model for transfer learning can be defined similarly to the `VGG16` and `InceptionV3` networks, as follows:

```
def resnet_pseudo(dim=224,freeze_layers=10,full_freeze='N'):
   # model_save_dest = {}
    model = ResNet50(weights='imagenet',include_top=False)
    x = model.output
    x = GlobalAveragePooling2D()(x)
    x = Dense(512, activation='relu')(x)
    x = Dropout(0.5)(x)
    x = Dense(512, activation='relu')(x)
    x = Dropout(0.5)(x)
    out = Dense(5,activation='softmax')(x)
    model_final = Model(input = model.input,outputs=out)
    if full_freeze != 'N':
        for layer in model.layers[0:freeze_layers]:
       layer.trainable = False
    return model_final
```

The optimizer and initial learning rate

The **Adam** optimizer (**adaptive moment estimator**) is used in training that implements an advanced version of stochastic gradient descent. The Adam optimizer takes care of the curvature in the cost function, and at the same time, it uses momentum to ensure steady progress toward a good local minima. For the problem at hand, since we are using transfer learning and want to use as many of the previously learned features from the pre-trained network as possible, we will use a small initial learning rate of `0.00001`. This will ensure that the network doesn't lose the useful features learned by the pre-trained networks, and fine-tunes to an optimal point less aggressively, based on the new data for the problem at hand. The Adam optimizer can be defined as follows:

```
adam = optimizers.Adam(lr=0.00001, beta_1=0.9, beta_2=0.999, epsilon=1e-08,
decay=0.0)
```

The `beta_1` parameter controls the contribution of the current gradient in the momentum computation, whereas the `beta_2` parameter controls the contribution of the square of the gradient in the gradient normalization, which helps to tackle the curvature in the cost function.

Cross-validation

Since the training dataset is small, we will perform five-fold cross-validation, to get a better sense of the model's ability to generalize to new data. We will also use all five of the models built in the different folds of cross-validation in training, for inference. The probability of a test data point belonging to a class label would be the average probability prediction of all five models, which is represented as follows:

$$\hat{p} = \frac{1}{5}\sum_{i=1}^{5} p_i$$

Since the aim is to predict the actual classes and not the probability, we would select the class that has the maximum probability. This methodology works when we are working with a classification-based network and cost function. If we are treating the problem as a regression problem, then there are a few alterations to the process, which we will discuss later on.

Model checkpoints based on validation log loss

It is always a good practice to save the model when the validation score chosen for evaluation improves. For our project, we will be tracking the validation log loss, and will save the model as the validation score improves over the different epochs. This way, after the training, we will save the model weights that provided the best validation score, and not the final model weights from when we stopped the training. The training will continue until the maximum number of epochs defined for the training is reached, or until the validation log loss hasn't reduced for `10` epochs in a row. We will also reduce the learning rate when the validation log loss doesn't improve for `3` epochs. The following code block can be used to perform the learning rate reduction and checkpoint operation:

```
reduce_lr = keras.callbacks.ReduceLROnPlateau(monitor='val_loss',
factor=0.50,
 patience=3, min_lr=0.000001)

 callbacks = [
 EarlyStopping(monitor='val_loss', patience=10, mode='min', verbose=1),
 CSVLogger('keras-5fold-run-01-v1-epochs_ib.log', separator=',',
append=False),reduce_lr,
 ModelCheckpoint(
 'keral-5fold-run-01-v1-fold-' + str('%02d' % (k + 1)) + '-run-' +
str('%02d' % (1 + 1)) + '.check',
 monitor='val_loss', mode='min', # mode must be set to max or keras will be
confused
 save_best_only=True,
 verbose=1)
 ]
```

As you can see in the preceding code block, the learning rate reduces to half (`0.50`) if the validation loss hasn't improved in `3` (`patience=3`) epochs. Similarly, we stop the training (by performing `EarlyStopping`) if the validation loss is not reduced in `10` (`patience = 10`) epochs. The model is saved whenever the validation log loss reduces, as shown in the following code snippet:

```
'keral-5fold-run-01-v1-fold-' + str('%02d' % (k + 1)) + '-run-' +
str('%02d' % (1 + 1)) + '.check'
```

The validation log loss in each epoch of the training process is tracked in the `keras-5fold-run-01-v1-epochs_ib.log` log file, and is referred to in order to save the model if the validation log loss improves, or to decide when to reduce the learning rate or stop the training.

The models in each fold are saved by using the `keras save` function in user-defined paths, while during inference, the models are loaded into memory by using the `keras.load_model` function.

Python implementation of the training process

The following Python code block shows an end-to-end implementation of the training process. It consists of all of the functional blocks that were discussed in the preceding sections. Let's start by calling all of the Python packages that are required, as follows:

```
import numpy as np
np.random.seed(1000)

import os
import glob
import cv2
import datetime
import pandas as pd
import time
import warnings
warnings.filterwarnings("ignore")
from sklearn.model_selection import KFold
from sklearn.metrics import cohen_kappa_score
from keras.models import Sequential,Model
from keras.layers.core import Dense, Dropout, Flatten
from keras.layers.convolutional import Convolution2D, MaxPooling2D,
ZeroPadding2D
from keras.layers import GlobalMaxPooling2D,GlobalAveragePooling2D
from keras.optimizers import SGD
from keras.callbacks import EarlyStopping
from keras.utils import np_utils
from sklearn.metrics import log_loss
import keras
from keras import __version__ as keras_version
from keras.applications.inception_v3 import InceptionV3
from keras.applications.resnet50 import ResNet50
from keras.applications.vgg16 import VGG16
from keras.preprocessing.image import ImageDataGenerator
from keras import optimizers
from keras.callbacks import EarlyStopping, ModelCheckpoint, CSVLogger,
Callback
from keras.applications.resnet50 import preprocess_input
```

```
import h5py
import argparse
from sklearn.externals import joblib
import json
```

Once we have imported the required library, we can define the `TransferLearning` class:

```
class TransferLearning:
  def __init__(self):
    parser = argparse.ArgumentParser(description='Process the inputs')
    parser.add_argument('--path',help='image directory')
    parser.add_argument('--class_folders',help='class images folder
                        names')
    parser.add_argument('--dim',type=int,help='Image dimensions to
                        process')
    parser.add_argument('--lr',type=float,help='learning
                        rate',default=1e-4)
    parser.add_argument('--batch_size',type=int,help='batch size')
    parser.add_argument('--epochs',type=int,help='no of epochs to
                        train')
    parser.add_argument('--initial_layers_to_freeze',type=int,help='the
                        initial layers to freeze')
    parser.add_argument('--model',help='Standard Model to
                        load',default='InceptionV3')
    parser.add_argument('--folds',type=int,help='num of cross
                        validation folds',default=5)
    parser.add_argument('--outdir',help='output directory')
    args = parser.parse_args()
    self.path = args.path
    self.class_folders = json.loads(args.class_folders)
    self.dim = int(args.dim)
    self.lr = float(args.lr)
    self.batch_size = int(args.batch_size)
    self.epochs = int(args.epochs)
    self.initial_layers_to_freeze = int(args.initial_layers_to_freeze)
    self.model = args.model
    self.folds = int(args.folds)
    self.outdir = args.outdir
```

Next, let's define a function that can read the images and resize them to a suitable dimension, as follows:

```
  def get_im_cv2(self,path,dim=224):
    img = cv2.imread(path)
    resized = cv2.resize(img, (dim,dim), cv2.INTER_LINEAR)
    return resized

  # Pre Process the Images based on the ImageNet pre-trained model
```

```
    Image transformation
  def pre_process(self,img):
    img[:,:,0] = img[:,:,0] - 103.939
    img[:,:,1] = img[:,:,0] - 116.779
    img[:,:,2] = img[:,:,0] - 123.68
    return img
  # Function to build X, y in numpy format based on the
    train/validation datasets
  def read_data(self,class_folders,path,num_class,dim,train_val='train'):
    print(train_val)
    train_X,train_y = [],[]
    for c in class_folders:
      path_class = path + str(train_val) + '/' + str(c)
      file_list = os.listdir(path_class)
      for f in file_list:
        img = self.get_im_cv2(path_class + '/' + f)
        img = self.pre_process(img)
        train_X.append(img)
        train_y.append(int(c.split('class')[1]))
    train_y =
keras.utils.np_utils.to_categorical(np.array(train_y),num_class)
    return np.array(train_X),train_y
```

Following that, we will now define the three models for transfer learning, starting with `InceptionV3`:

```
def inception_pseudo(self,dim=224,freeze_layers=30,full_freeze='N'):
    model = InceptionV3(weights='imagenet',include_top=False)
    x = model.output
    x = GlobalAveragePooling2D()(x)
    x = Dense(512, activation='relu')(x)
    x = Dropout(0.5)(x)
    x = Dense(512, activation='relu')(x)
    x = Dropout(0.5)(x)
    out = Dense(5,activation='softmax')(x)
    model_final = Model(input = model.input,outputs=out)
    if full_freeze != 'N':
      for layer in model.layers[0:freeze_layers]:
        layer.trainable = False
    return model_final
```

Then, we will define the `ResNet50` Model for transfer learning:

```
def resnet_pseudo(self,dim=224,freeze_layers=10,full_freeze='N'):
  model = ResNet50(weights='imagenet',include_top=False)
  x = model.output
  x = GlobalAveragePooling2D()(x)
  x = Dense(512, activation='relu')(x)
```

```
    x = Dropout(0.5)(x)
    x = Dense(512, activation='relu')(x)
    x = Dropout(0.5)(x)
    out = Dense(5,activation='softmax')(x)
    model_final = Model(input = model.input,outputs=out)
    if full_freeze != 'N':
      for layer in model.layers[0:freeze_layers]:
        layer.trainable = False
    return model_final
```

Lastly, we will define the `VGG16` model:

```
  def VGG16_pseudo(self,dim=224,freeze_layers=10,full_freeze='N'):
    model = VGG16(weights='imagenet',include_top=False)
    x = model.output
    x = GlobalAveragePooling2D()(x)
    x = Dense(512, activation='relu')(x)
    x = Dropout(0.5)(x)
    x = Dense(512, activation='relu')(x)
    x = Dropout(0.5)(x)
    out = Dense(5,activation='softmax')(x)
    model_final = Model(input = model.input,outputs=out)
    if full_freeze != 'N':
      for layer in model.layers[0:freeze_layers]:
        layer.trainable = False
    return model_final
```

Now, let's define the training function, as follows:

```
def train_model(self,train_X,train_y,n_fold=5,batch_size=16,epochs=40,
dim=224,lr=1e-5,model='ResNet50'):
    model_save_dest = {}
    k = 0
    kf = KFold(n_splits=n_fold, random_state=0, shuffle=True)

    for train_index, test_index in kf.split(train_X):
      k += 1
      X_train,X_test = train_X[train_index],train_X[test_index]
      y_train, y_test = train_y[train_index],train_y[test_index]
      if model == 'Resnet50':
        model_final =
        self.resnet_pseudo(dim=224,freeze_layers=10,full_freeze='N')
      if model == 'VGG16':
        model_final =
        self.VGG16_pseudo(dim=224,freeze_layers=10,full_freeze='N')
      if model == 'InceptionV3':
        model_final =
self.inception_pseudo(dim=224,freeze_layers=10,full_freeze='N')
```

```
    datagen = ImageDataGenerator(
        horizontal_flip = True,
        vertical_flip = True,
        width_shift_range = 0.1,
        height_shift_range = 0.1,
        channel_shift_range=0,
        zoom_range = 0.2,
        rotation_range = 20)
    adam = optimizers.Adam(lr=lr, beta_1=0.9, beta_2=0.999,
      epsilon=1e-08, decay=0.0)
    model_final.compile(optimizer=adam,
     loss= ["categorical_crossentropy"],metrics=['accuracy'])
    reduce_lr = keras.callbacks.ReduceLROnPlateau(monitor='val_loss',
      factor=0.50, patience=3, min_lr=0.000001)
    callbacks = [
          EarlyStopping(monitor='val_loss', patience=10, mode='min',
           verbose=1),
      CSVLogger('keras-5fold-run-01-v1-epochs_ib.log',
      separator=',', append=False),reduce_lr,
          ModelCheckpoint(
              'keral-5fold-run-01-v1-fold-' + str('%02d' % (k + 1)) +
              '-run-' + str('%02d' % (1 + 1)) + '.check',
              monitor='val_loss', mode='min',
              save_best_only=True,
              verbose=1)
        ]
    model_final.fit_generator(datagen.flow(X_train,y_train,
                              batch_size=batch_size),
    steps_per_epoch=X_train.shape[0]/batch_size, epochs=epochs,
       verbose=1, validation_data= (X_test,y_test),
       callbacks=callbacks, class_weight=
       {0:0.012,1:0.12,2:0.058,3:0.36,4:0.43})

    model_name = 'keral-5fold-run-01-v1-fold-' + str('%02d' % (k +
                 1)) + '-run-' + str('%02d' % (1 + 1)) + '.check'
    del model_final
    f = h5py.File(model_name, 'r+')
    del f['optimizer_weights']
    f.close()
    model_final = keras.models.load_model(model_name)
    model_name1 = self.outdir + str(model) + '___' + str(k)
    model_final.save(model_name1)
    model_save_dest[k] = model_name1
  return model_save_dest
```

We will also define an `inference` function for the holdout dataset, as follows:

```
def inference_validation(self,test_X,test_y,model_save_dest,
  n_class=5,folds=5):
  pred = np.zeros((len(test_X),n_class))

  for k in range(1,folds + 1):
    model = keras.models.load_model(model_save_dest[k])
    pred = pred + model.predict(test_X)
  pred = pred/(1.0*folds)
  pred_class = np.argmax(pred,axis=1)
  act_class = np.argmax(test_y,axis=1)
  accuracy = np.sum([pred_class == act_class])*1.0/len(test_X)
  kappa = cohen_kappa_score(pred_class,act_class,weights='quadratic')
  return pred_class,accuracy,kappa
```

Now, let's call the `main` function, to trigger the training process, as follows:

```
def main(self):
    start_time = time.time()
    self.num_class = len(self.class_folders)
  if self.mode == 'train':
        print("Data Processing..")
        file_list,labels=
        self.read_data(self.class_folders,self.path,self.num_class,
                      self.dim,train_val='train')
        print(len(file_list),len(labels))
        print(labels[0],labels[-1])
        self.model_save_dest =
        self.train_model(file_list,labels,n_fold=self.folds,
                         batch_size=self.batch_size,
                         epochs=self.epochs,dim=self.dim,
                         lr=self.lr,model=self.model)
        joblib.dump(self.model_save_dest,f'{self.outdir}/model_dict.pkl')
        print("Model saved to dest:",self.model_save_dest)
  else:
        model_save_dest = joblib.load(self.model_save_dest)
        print('Models loaded from:',model_save_dest)
            # Do inference/validation
        test_files,test_y =
        self.read_data(self.class_folders,self.path,self.num_class,
                      self.dim,train_val='validation')
      test_X = []
      for f in test_files:
        img = self.get_im_cv2(f)
        img = self.pre_process(img)
        test_X.append(img)
      test_X = np.array(test_X)
```

```
test_y = np.array(test_y)
print(test_X.shape)
print(len(test_y))
pred_class,accuracy,kappa =
self.inference_validation(test_X,test_y,model_save_dest,
                        n_class=self.num_class,folds=self.folds)
results_df = pd.DataFrame()
results_df['file_name'] = test_files
results_df['target'] = test_y
results_df['prediction'] = pred_class
results_df.to_csv(f'{self.outdir}/val_resuts_reg.csv',index=False)
print("-----------------------------------------------------")
print("Kappa score:", kappa)
print("accuracy:", accuracy)
print("End of training")
print("-----------------------------------------------------")
print("Processing Time",time.time() - start_time,' secs')
```

We can change several parameters, such as learning rate, batch size, image size, and so on, and we can experiment, to come up with a decent model. During the training phase, the model locations are saved in the `model_save_dest` dictionary that is written to the `dict_model` file.

During the inference phase, the model just makes predictions on the new test data, based on the trained models.

The script for transfer learning named `TransferLearning.py` can be invoked as follows:

```
python TransferLearning.py --path '/media/santanu/9eb9b6dc-b380-486e-b4fd-c424a325b976/book AI/Diabetic Retinopathy/Extra/assignment2_train_dataset/' --class_folders '["class0","class1","class2","class3","class4"]' --dim 224 --lr 1e-4 --batch_size 16 --epochs 20 --initial_layers_to_freeze 10 --model InceptionV3 --folds 5 --outdir '/home/santanu/ML_DS_Catalog-/Transfer_Learning_DR/'
```

The output log of the script is as follows:

```
Model saved to dest: {1: '/home/santanu/ML_DS_Catalog-
/Transfer_Learning_DR/categorical/InceptionV3___1', 2:
'/home/santanu/ML_DS_Catalog-
/Transfer_Learning_DR/categorical/InceptionV3___2', 3:
'/home/santanu/ML_DS_Catalog-
/Transfer_Learning_DR/categorical/InceptionV3___3', 4:
'/home/santanu/ML_DS_Catalog-
/Transfer_Learning_DR/categorical/InceptionV3___4', 5:
'/home/santanu/ML_DS_Catalog-
/Transfer_Learning_DR/categorical/InceptionV3___5'}
validation
```

```
--------------------------------------------------------
Kappa score: 0.42969781637876836
accuracy: 0.5553973227000855
End of training
--------------------------------------------------------
Processing Time 26009.3344039917 secs
```

As we can see from the results in the log, we achieve a decent cross validation accuracy of around `56%` and a quadratic Kappa of around `0.43`.

In this script, we have loaded all the data into memory and then fed the augmented images from the `ImageDataGenerator` to the model for training. If the set of training images are few and/or of moderate dimension, then loading the data into memory might not be of great concern. However, if the image corpus is huge and/or we have limited resources, loading all the data into memory won't be a viable option. Since the machine on which these experiments have been run has 64 GB RAM, we were able to train these models without issues. Even a 16 GB RAM machine might not be sufficient to run these experiments by loading all the data in memory and you might run into a memory error.

The question is, do we need to load all the data into memory at once?

Since neural networks work with mini-batches, we would only require the data corresponding to one mini-batch to train the model through back-propagation at one time. Similarly for the next back-propagation, we can discard the data corresponding to the current batch and process the next batch instead. So in a way the memory requirement at each mini-batch is only the data corresponding to that batch. So we can get around training deep learning models in machines with less memory by creating dynamic batches at training time. Keras has a good function to create dynamic batches at training time which we will discuss in the next section.

Dynamic mini batch creation during training

One of the ways to only load the data corresponding to a mini-batch is to dynamically create mini-batches by processing images randomly from their location. The number of images to be processed in a mini-batch would be equal to the mini-batch size we specify. Of course there would be some bottleneck in the training process because of the dynamic mini-batch creation during training time but that bottleneck is negligible. Specially packages such as `keras` have efficient dynamic batch creation mechanism. We would be leveraging `flow_from_directory` functionality in keras to dynamically create mini-batches during training to reduce the memory requirements of the training process. We will still continue to use `ImageDataGenerator` for image augmentation. The train generator and the validation generator can be defined as follows.

The image preprocessing step of subtracting the mean images pixel intensities from the three channels is done by feeding the `pre_process` function as input to the `preprocessing_function` of the `ImageDataGenerator`:

```
def pre_process(img):
    img[:,:,0] = img[:,:,0] - 103.939
    img[:,:,1] = img[:,:,0] - 116.779
    img[:,:,2] = img[:,:,0] - 123.68
    return img


train_file_names = glob.glob(f'{train_dir}/*/*')
val_file_names = glob.glob(f'{val_dir}/*/*')
train_steps_per_epoch = len(train_file_names)/float(batch_size)
val_steps_per_epoch = len(val_file_names)/float(batch_size)
train_datagen =
ImageDataGenerator(horizontal_flip =
                   True,vertical_flip =
                   True,width_shift_range =
                   0.1,height_shift_range = 0.1,
                   channel_shift_range=0,zoom_range = 0.2,
                   rotation_range = 20,
                   preprocessing_function=pre_process)
val_datagen =
ImageDataGenerator(preprocessing_function=pre_process)
train_generator =
train_datagen.flow_from_directory(train_dir,
                                  target_size=(dim,dim),
                                  batch_size=batch_size,
                                  class_mode='categorical')
val_generator =
val_datagen.flow_from_directory(val_dir,
                                target_size=(dim,dim),
                                 batch_size=batch_size,
                                 class_mode='categorical')
print(train_generator.class_indices)
joblib.dump(train_generator.class_indices,
f'{self.outdir}/class_indices.pkl')
```

The `flow_from_directory` function takes in an image directory as and input and expects a folder pertaining to a class within the image directory. It then infers the class labels from the folder names. If an image directory has the following structure for the image directory then the classes are inferred as `0`, `1`, `2`, `3`, `4`, pertaining to the class folders `'class0'`,`'class1'`,`'class2'`,`'class3'`, and `'class4'`.

The other important inputs to the `flow_from_directory` function is the `batch_size`, `target_size` and `class_mode`. The `target_size` is to specify the dimension of the image to be fed to the neural network while `class_mode` is to specify the nature of the problem. For binary classification `class_mode` is set to binary while for multi class classification the same is set to `categorical`.

We will next train the same model by creating dynamic batches instead of loading all the data to memory at once. We just need to create a generator using `flow_from_directory` option and tie it to the data augmentation object. The data generator object can be generated as follows:

```
# Pre processing for channel wise mean pixel subtraction
def pre_process(img):
    img[:,:,0] = img[:,:,0] - 103.939
    img[:,:,1] = img[:,:,0] - 116.779
    img[:,:,2] = img[:,:,0] - 123.68
    return img


# Add the pre_process function at the end of the ImageDataGenerator,
#rest all of the data augmentation options
# remain the same.

train_datagen =
ImageDataGenerator(horizontal_flip = True,vertical_flip = True,
                   width_shift_range = 0.1,height_shift_range = 0.1,
                   channel_shift_range=0,zoom_range =
                   0.2,rotation_range = 20,
                   preprocessing_function=pre_process)

 # For validation no data augmentation on image mean subtraction
preprocessing
val_datagen = ImageDataGenerator(preprocessing_function=pre_process)


# We build the train generator using flow_from_directory
train_generator = train_datagen.flow_from_directory(train_dir,
        target_size=(dim,dim),
        batch_size=batch_size,
        class_mode='categorical')

# We build the validation generator using flow_from_directory
val_generator = val_datagen.flow_from_directory(val_dir,
        target_size=(dim,dim),
        batch_size=batch_size,
        class_mode='categorical')
```

In the preceding code we pass the ImageDataGenerator an additional task of performing the mean pixel subtraction since we don't have any control of loading the image data in memory and passing it through the pre_process function. In the preprocessing_function option, we can pass any desired custom function for any specific preprocessing task.

Through train_dir, and val_dir we pass the training and validation directories to the train and validation generator that we created with flow_with_directory option. The generators identifies the number of classes by looking at the number of class folders within the training data directory (here train_dir)passed. During training time based on the target_size the images are read into memory based on the specified batch_size

The class_mode helps the generator identify whether its a binary classification or a multi class('categotical') one.

The detailed implementation is laid down in the TransferLearning_ffd.py folder on GitHub at https://github.com/PacktPublishing/Python-Artificial-Intelligence-Projects/tree/master/Chapter02.

The Python script TransferLearning_ffd.py can be invoked as follows:

```
python TransferLearning_ffd.py  --path '/media/santanu/9eb9b6dc-b380-486e-b4fd-c424a325b976/book AI/Diabetic Retinopathy/Extra/assignment2_train_dataset/' --class_folders '["class0","class1","class2","class3","class4"]' --dim 224  --lr 1e-4 --batch_size 32 --epochs 50 --initial_layers_to_freeze 10 --model InceptionV3 --outdir '/home/santanu/ML_DS_Catalog-/Transfer_Learning_DR/'
```

The end of the output log from the job run is as follows:

```
Validation results saved at : /home/santanu/ML_DS_Catalog-/Transfer_Learning_DR/val_results.csv
[0 0 0 ... 4 2 2]
[0 0 0 ... 4 4 4]
Validation Accuracy: 0.5183708345200797
Validation Quadratic Kappa Score: 0.44422008110380984
```

As we can see by reusing an existing network and performing transfer learning on the same we are able to achieve a decent Quadratic Kappa of 0.44.

Results from the categorical classification

The categorical classification is performed by using all three of the neural network architectures: `VGG16`, `ResNet50`, and `InceptionV3`. The best results were obtained using the `InceptionV3` version of the transfer learning network for this diabetic retinopathy use case. In case of categorical classification we are just converting the class with the maximum predicted class probability as the predicted severity label. However since the classes in the problem has an ordinal sense one of the ways in which we can utilize the softmax probabilities is to take the expectation of the class severity with respect to the softmax probabilities and come up with an expected score $\hat{y}$ as follows:

$$\hat{y} = 0p_0 + 1p_1 + 2p_2 + 3p_3 = p_1 + 2p_2 + 3p_3$$

We can rank order the scores and determine three thresholds to determine which class the image belongs to. These thresholds can be chosen by training a secondary model on these expected scores as features. The reader is advised to experiment along these lines and see if it reaps any benefit.

As part of this project we are using transfer learning to get reasonable results on a difficult problem. The model performances could have very well been better by training a network from scratch on the given dataset.

Inference at testing time

The following code can be used to carry out inference on the unlabeled test data:

```
import keras
import numpy as np
import pandas as pd
import cv2
import os
import time
from sklearn.externals import joblib
import argparse

# Read the Image and resize to the suitable dimension size
def get_im_cv2(path,dim=224):
    img = cv2.imread(path)
    resized = cv2.resize(img, (dim,dim), cv2.INTER_LINEAR)
    return resized
```

```
# Pre Process the Images based on the ImageNet pre-trained model Image
transformation
def pre_process(img):
    img[:,:,0] = img[:,:,0] - 103.939
    img[:,:,1] = img[:,:,0] - 116.779
    img[:,:,2] = img[:,:,0] - 123.68
    return img

# Function to build test input data
def read_data_test(path,dim):
    test_X = []
    test_files = []
    file_list = os.listdir(path)
    for f in file_list:
        img = get_im_cv2(path + '/' + f)
        img = pre_process(img)
        test_X.append(img)
        f_name = f.split('_')[0]
        test_files.append(f_name)
    return np.array(test_X),test_files
```

Let us define the inference:

```
def inference_test(test_X,model_save_dest,n_class):
    folds = len(list(model_save_dest.keys()))
    pred = np.zeros((len(test_X),n_class))
    for k in range(1,folds + 1):
        model = keras.models.load_model(model_save_dest[k])
        pred = pred + model.predict(test_X)
    pred = pred/(1.0*folds)
    pred_class = np.argmax(pred,axis=1)
    return pred_class

def main(path,dim,model_save_dest,outdir,n_class):
    test_X,test_files = read_data_test(path,dim)
    pred_class = inference_test(test_X,model_save_dest,n_class)
    out = pd.DataFrame()
    out['id'] = test_files
    out['class'] = pred_class
    out['class'] = out['class'].apply(lambda x:'class' + str(x))
    out.to_csv(outdir + "results.csv",index=False)

if __name__ == '__main__':
    parser = argparse.ArgumentParser(description='arguments')
    parser.add_argument('--path',help='path of images to run inference on')
    parser.add_argument('--dim',type=int,help='Image dimension size to
                        process',default=224)
    parser.add_argument('--model_save_dest',
```

```
                    help='location of the trained models')
parser.add_argument('--n_class',type=int,help='No of classes')
parser.add_argument('--outdir',help='Output DIrectory')
args = parser.parse_args()
path = args.path
dim = args.dim
model_save_dest = joblib.load(args.model_save_dest)
n_class = args.n_class
outdir = args.outdir
main(path,dim,model_save_dest,outdir,n_class)
```

Performing regression instead of categorical classification

One of the things that we discussed in the *Formulating the loss function* section, was the fact that the class labels are not independent categorical classes, but do have an ordinal sense with the increasing severity of the diabetic retinopathy condition. Hence, it would be worthwhile to perform regression through the defined transfer learning networks, instead of classification, and see how the results turned out. The only thing that we would need to change would be the output unit, from a softmax to a linear unit. We will, in fact, change it to be a ReLU, since we want to avoid negative scores. The following code block shows the `InceptionV3` version of the regression network:

```
def inception_pseudo(dim=224,freeze_layers=30,full_freeze='N'):
    model = InceptionV3(weights='imagenet',include_top=False)
    x = model.output
    x = GlobalAveragePooling2D()(x)
    x = Dense(512, activation='relu')(x)
    x = Dropout(0.5)(x)
    x = Dense(512, activation='relu')(x)
    x = Dropout(0.5)(x)
    out = Dense(1,activation='relu')(x)
    model_final = Model(input = model.input,outputs=out)
    if full_freeze != 'N':
        for layer in model.layers[0:freeze_layers]:
         layer.trainable = False
    return model_final
```

Instead of minimizing the categorical cross-entropy (log loss), as in the classification network, we are going to minimize the mean square error for the regression network. The cost function, minimized for the regression problem, is as follows, where $\hat{y}$ is the predicted label:

$$L = \frac{1}{M}\sum_{i=1}^{M}(y^i - \hat{y}^{(i)})^2$$

Once we predict the regression scores, we would round up the scores to their nearest severity condition rank (zero to four).

Using the keras sequential utils as generator

Keras has a good batch generator named `keras.utils.sequence()` that helps you customize batch creation with great flexibility. In fact, with `keras.utils.sequence()` one can design the whole epoch pipeline. We are going to use this utility in this regression problem to get accustomed to this utility. For the transfer learning problem we can design a generator class using `keras.utils.sequence()` as follows:

```
class DataGenerator(keras.utils.Sequence):
    'Generates data for Keras'
    def
__init__(self,files,labels,batch_size=32,n_classes=5,dim=(224,224,3),shuffl
e=True):
        'Initialization'
        self.labels = labels
        self.files = files
        self.batch_size = batch_size
        self.n_classes = n_classes
        self.dim = dim
        self.shuffle = shuffle
        self.on_epoch_end()

    def __len__(self):
        'Denotes the number of batches per epoch'
        return int(np.floor(len(self.files) / self.batch_size))

    def __getitem__(self, index):
        'Generate one batch of data'
        # Generate indexes of the batch
```

```
        indexes = self.indexes[index*self.batch_size:
                               (index+1)*self.batch_size]

        # Find list of files to be processed in the batch
        list_files = [self.files[k] for k in indexes]
        labels = [self.labels[k] for k in indexes]

        # Generate data
        X, y = self.__data_generation(list_files,labels)

        return X, y

    def on_epoch_end(self):
        'Updates indexes after each epoch'
        self.indexes = np.arange(len(self.files))
        if self.shuffle == True:
            np.random.shuffle(self.indexes)

    def __data_generation(self,list_files,labels):
        'Generates data containing batch_size samples' # X : (n_samples,
                                                          *dim, n_channels)
        # Initialization

        X = np.empty((len(list_files),self.dim[0],self.dim[1],self.dim[2]))
        y = np.empty((len(list_files)),dtype=int)
     # print(X.shape,y.shape)

        # Generate data
        k = -1
        for i,f in enumerate(list_files):
            # print(f)
            img = get_im_cv2(f,dim=self.dim[0])
            img = pre_process(img)
            label = labels[i]
            #label =
             keras.utils.np_utils.to_categorical(label,self.n_classes)
            X[i,] = img
            y[i,] = label
       # print(X.shape,y.shape)
        return X,y
```

In the preceding code, we define the `DataGenerator` class using `keras.utils.Sequence`.

We define the data generator to accept the image filename, labels, batch size, the number of classes, and the dimension we want the images to be resized to. Also, we specify whether we want the order in which the images are to be processed in an epoch to be shuffled.

The functions that we've specified are inherited from the `keras.utils.Sequence` and hence the specific activities in each of these functions can't be specified elsewhere. The `len` function is to compute the number of batches in an epoch.

Similarly, within the `on_epoch_end` function, we can specify activities that are to be performed at the end of the epoch such as shuffling the order in which the inputs are to be processed in an epoch. We can create a different set of dataset in each epoch to process. This is generally useful when we have lot of data and we don't want to process all the data in each epoch. The `__getitem__` function helps with batch creation by extracting the data corresponding to all data point indices that are specific to a batch. If the data creation process is more complex, the `__data_generation` function can be utilised to have logic specific to the extraction of each individual data point in the batch. For instance we pass the files names corresponding to the data point indices in the batch to the `__data_generation` function to read each image using `opencv` and also preprocess them using the `preprocess` function that we have to do the mean pixel subtraction.

The train functions for the regression based transfer learning can be coded as follows:

```
def train_model(self,file_list,labels,n_fold=5,batch_size=16,
epochs=40,dim=224,lr=1e-5,model='ResNet50'):
        model_save_dest = {}
        k = 0
        kf = KFold(n_splits=n_fold, random_state=0, shuffle=True)

        for train_index,test_index in kf.split(file_list):

            k += 1
            file_list = np.array(file_list)
            labels = np.array(labels)
            train_files,train_labels =
            file_list[train_index],labels[train_index]
            val_files,val_labels =
            file_list[test_index],labels[test_index]

            if model == 'Resnet50':
                model_final =
self.resnet_pseudo(dim=224,freeze_layers=10,full_freeze='N')

            if model == 'VGG16':
                model_final =
                self.VGG16_pseudo(dim=224,freeze_layers=10,full_freeze='N')

            if model == 'InceptionV3':
                model_final =
self.inception_pseudo(dim=224,freeze_layers=10,full_freeze='N')
```

```
            adam =
            optimizers.Adam(lr=lr, beta_1=0.9, beta_2=0.999, epsilon=1e-08,
                            decay=0.0)
            model_final.compile(optimizer=adam,
loss=["mse"],metrics=['mse'])
            reduce_lr =
            keras.callbacks.ReduceLROnPlateau(monitor='val_loss',
                                              factor=0.50,patience=3,
                                              min_lr=0.000001)
            early =
            EarlyStopping(monitor='val_loss', patience=10, mode='min',
                          verbose=1)
            logger =
            CSVLogger('keras-5fold-run-01-v1-epochs_ib.log', separator=',',
                      append=False)
            checkpoint =
            ModelCheckpoint('kera1-5fold-run-01-v1-fold-'
                            + str('%02d' % (k + 1))
                            + '-run-' + str('%02d' % (1 + 1)) + '.check',
                            monitor='val_loss', mode='min',
                            save_best_only=True,
                            verbose=1)
            callbacks = [reduce_lr,early,checkpoint,logger]
            train_gen =
            DataGenerator(train_files,train_labels,batch_size=32,
            n_classes=
            len(self.class_folders),dim=(self.dim,self.dim,3),shuffle=True)
            val_gen =
            DataGenerator(val_files,val_labels,batch_size=32,
                          n_classes=len(self.class_folders),
                          dim=(self.dim,self.dim,3),shuffle=True)
            model_final.fit_generator(train_gen,epochs=epochs,verbose=1,
            validation_data=(val_gen),callbacks=callbacks)
            model_name =
            'kera1-5fold-run-01-v1-fold-' + str('%02d' % (k + 1)) + '-run-
                                              ' + str('%02d' % (1 + 1)) +
'.check'
            del model_final
            f = h5py.File(model_name, 'r+')
            del f['optimizer_weights']
            f.close()
            model_final = keras.models.load_model(model_name)
            model_name1 = self.outdir + str(model) + '___' + str(k)
            model_final.save(model_name1)
            model_save_dest[k] = model_name1

        return model_save_dest
```

As we can see from the preceding code, the train generator and the validation generator have been created using the `DataGenerator`, which inherits the `keras.utils.sequence` class. The function for inference can be coded as follows:

```
def inference validation(self,test_X,test_y,model_save_dest,n_class=5,
folds=5):
        print(test_X.shape,test_y.shape)
        pred = np.zeros(test_X.shape[0])
        for k in range(1,folds + 1):
            print(f'running inference on fold: {k}')
            model = keras.models.load_model(model_save_dest[k])
            pred = pred + model.predict(test_X)[:,0]
            pred = pred
            print(pred.shape)
            print(pred)
        pred = pred/float(folds)
        pred_class = np.round(pred)
        pred_class = np.array(pred_class,dtype=int)
        pred_class = list(map(lambda x:4 if x > 4 else x,pred_class))
        pred_class = list(map(lambda x:0 if x < 0 else x,pred_class))
        act_class = test_y
        accuracy = np.sum([pred_class == act_class])*1.0/len(test_X)
        kappa = cohen_kappa_score(pred_class,act_class,weights='quadratic')
        return pred_class,accuracy,kappa
```

As we can see from the preceding code, the mean of the prediction from each fold is computed and it is converted to the nearest severity class by rounding off the prediction score. The Python script for regression is in the GitHub link `https://github.com/PacktPublishing/Python-Artificial-Intelligence-Projects/tree/master/Chapter02.` with the name `TransferLearning_reg.py`. The same can be invoked by running the following command:

```
python TransferLearning_reg.py --path '/media/santanu/9eb9b6dc-b380-486e-
b4fd-c424a325b976/book AI/Diabetic
Retinopathy/Extra/assignment2_train_dataset/' --class_folders
'["class0","class1","class2","class3","class4"]' --dim 224 --lr 1e-4 --
batch_size 32 --epochs 5 --initial_layers_to_freeze 10 --model InceptionV3
--folds 5 --outdir '/home/santanu/ML_DS_Catalog-
/Transfer_Learning_DR/Regression/'
```

The output log for training is as follows:

```
Model saved to dest: {1: '/home/santanu/ML_DS_Catalog-
/Transfer_Learning_DR/Regression/InceptionV3___1', 2:
'/home/santanu/ML_DS_Catalog-
/Transfer_Learning_DR/Regression/InceptionV3___2', 3:
'/home/santanu/ML_DS_Catalog-
```

```
/Transfer_Learning_DR/Regression/InceptionV3___3', 4:
'/home/santanu/ML_DS_Catalog-
/Transfer_Learning_DR/Regression/InceptionV3___4', 5:
'/home/santanu/ML_DS_Catalog-
/Transfer_Learning_DR/Regression/InceptionV3___5'}
```

As we can see the `5` models corresponding to the `5` folds have been saved under the Regression folder that we have specified. Next, we can run inference on the validation dataset and see how the regression model fares. The same Python script can be invoked as follows:

```
 python TransferLearning_reg.py  --path '/media/santanu/9eb9b6dc-b380-486e-
b4fd-c424a325b976/book AI/Diabetic
Retinopathy/Extra/assignment2_train_dataset/' --class_folders
'["class0","class1","class2","class3","class4"]' --dim 224  --lr 1e-4 --
batch_size 32 --model InceptionV3  --outdir '/home/santanu/ML_DS_Catalog-
/Transfer_Learning_DR/Regression/' --mode validation  --model_save_dest --
'/home/santanu/ML_DS_Catalog-
/Transfer_Learning_DR/Regression/model_dict.pkl' --folds 5
```

The results of inference are as follows:

```
Models loaded from: {1: '/home/santanu/ML_DS_Catalog-
/Transfer_Learning_DR/Regression/InceptionV3___1', 2:
'/home/santanu/ML_DS_Catalog-
/Transfer_Learning_DR/Regression/InceptionV3___2', 3:
'/home/santanu/ML_DS_Catalog-
/Transfer_Learning_DR/Regression/InceptionV3___3', 4:
'/home/santanu/ML_DS_Catalog-
/Transfer_Learning_DR/Regression/InceptionV3___4', 5:
'/home/santanu/ML_DS_Catalog-
/Transfer_Learning_DR/Regression/InceptionV3___5'}


-----------------------------------------------------
Kappa score: 0.4662660860310418
accuracy: 0.661350042722871
End of training
-----------------------------------------------------
Processing Time 138.52878069877625 secs
```

As we can see from the preceding log, the model achieves a decent validation accuracy of around 66% and a quadratic Kappa score of `0.466` given we have just used the regression scores to map it to the nearest severity condition. The reader is advised to experiment and see whether a secondary model based on the prediction scores the and whether the eye is a left eye or a right eye gives better results than this naive score mapping to the nearest severity class.

Summary

In this chapter, we went over the practical aspects of transfer learning, to solve a real-world problem in the healthcare sector. The readers are expected to further build upon these concepts by trying to customize these examples wherever possible.

The accuracy and the kappa score that we achieved through both the classification and the regression-based neural networks are good enough for production implementation. In `Chapter 3`, *Neural Machine Translation*, we will work on implementing intelligent machine translation systems, which is a much more advanced topic than what was presented in this chapter. I look forward to your participation.

3
Neural Machine Translation

Machine translation, in simple terms, refers to the translation of text from one language to another using a computer. It is a branch of computer linguistics that has now been around for several years. Currently, in the US, translation is a USD 40 billion industry, and it is also growing at a fast pace in Europe and Asia. There is a great social, governmental, economic, and commercial need for translation, and it is used extensively by companies such as Google, Facebook, eBay, and others, in their applications. Google's neural translation system in particular is one of the most advanced translation systems out there, capable of performing translation of multiple languages with just one model.

Early machine translation systems started with the translation of mere words and phrases in a text into a pertinent substitute in the desired target language. However, there were limitations on the quality of translation achieved through these simple techniques for the following reasons:

- Word-to-word mapping from the source language to the target language is not always available.
- Even if exact word-to-word mappings do exist between the source and target languages, the syntactic structures of the languages commonly do not correspond to one another. This problem in machine translation is commonly referred to as *misalignment*.

However, with the recent advances in **recurrent neural network** (**RNN**) architectures, such as LSTMs, GRU, and so on, machine translation not only provides an improved quality of translation, but also the complexity of such systems is far less than those of traditional systems.

Machine translation systems can be broadly classified into three classes: rule-based machine translation, statistical machine translation, and neural machine translation.

In this chapter, we will cover the following topics:

- Rule-based machine translation
- Statistical machine-learning systems
- Neural machine translation
- Sequence-to-sequence neural translation
- Loss function for neural translation

Technical requirements

You will require to have basic knowledge of Python 3, TensorFlow and Keras.

The code files of this chapter can be found on GitHub:
`https://github.com/PacktPublishing/Intelligent-Projects-using-Python/tree/master/Chapter03`

Check out the following video to see the code in action:
`http://bit.ly/2sXYX8A`

Rule-based machine translation

Classic rule-based machine translation systems heavily rely on rules for converting text from the source language to the target language. These rules, often created by linguists, generally work at the syntactic, semantic, and lexical levels. A classical rule-based machine translation system typically has three phases:

- The analysis phase
- The lexical transfer phase
- The generation phase

Illustrated in *Figure 3.1* is a flow diagram of a typical rule-based machine translation system:

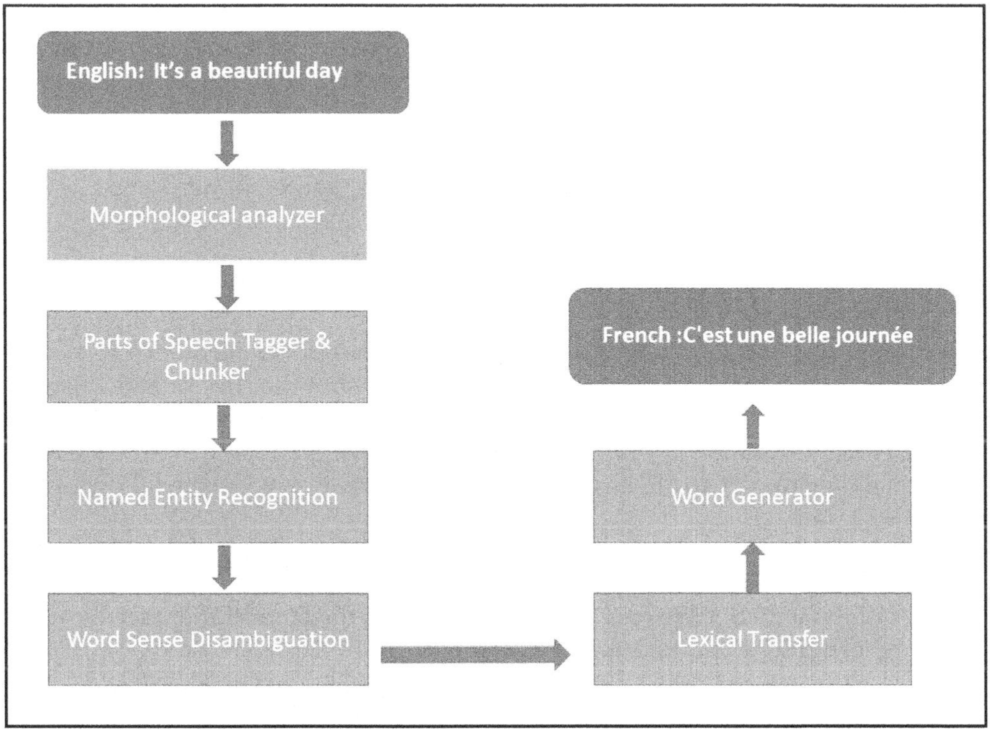

Figure 3.1: A flow diagram of a rule-based machine translation system

The analysis phase

The first phase in rule-based machine translation is the analysis phase, in which the source language text is analyzed to extract information related to morphology, parts of speech, named entity recognition, as well as word sense disambiguation. Morphological information concerns the structure of words, how their stems are derived, the detection of root words, and so on. A part-of-speech tagger tags each word in the text with a possible speech tag, such as noun, verb, adverb, adjective, and so on. This is followed by a **named entity recognition** (**NER**) task that tries to classify named entities into predefined buckets such as the name of a person, location, the name of an organization, and so on. NER is followed by word-sense disambiguation, which tries to identify how a particular word has been used in a sentence.

Lexical transfer phase

The lexical transfer phase follows the analysis phase and has two stages:

- **Word translation**: In word translation, the source root words derived in the analysis phase are translated to the corresponding target root words using a bilingual translation dictionary.
- **Grammar translation**: In the grammar translation phase, syntactic modification is performed, including translating the suffixes, among other things.

Generation phase

In the generation phase, the translated text is validated and corrected so that it is correct with regard to the parts of speech, genders, and agreement of the subject and object, with respect to the verb, before the final translated text is provided as an output. In each of the steps, the machine translation system makes use of predefined dictionaries. For a bare minimal implementation of a rule-based machine translation system, the following dictionaries are required:

- A dictionary for source language morphological analysis
- A bilingual dictionary containing mappings of the source language word to its target language counterpart
- A dictionary containing target-language morphological information for target word generation

Statistical machine-learning systems

Statistical machine translation systems select a target text by maximizing its conditional probability, given the source text. For example, let's say we have a source text *s* and we want to derive the best equivalent text *t* in the target language. This can be derived as follows:

$$\hat{t} = \underbrace{argmax}_{t} P(t/s) \qquad (1)$$

The formulation of *P(t/s)* in *(1)* can be expanded using Bayes' theorem as follows:

$$\hat{t} = \underbrace{argmax}_{t} \frac{P(s/t)P(t)}{P(s)} \qquad (2)$$

For a given source sentence, *P(s)* would be fixed, and, hence, finding the optimal target translation turns out to be as follows:

$$\hat{t} = \underbrace{arg\max}_{t} P(s/t)P(t) \qquad (3)$$

You may wonder why maximizing *P(s/t)P(t)* in place of *P(t/s)* directly would give an advantage. Generally, ill-formed sentences that are highly likely under *P(t/s)* are avoided by breaking the problem into two components, that is, *P(s/t)* and *P(t)*, as shown in the previous formula:

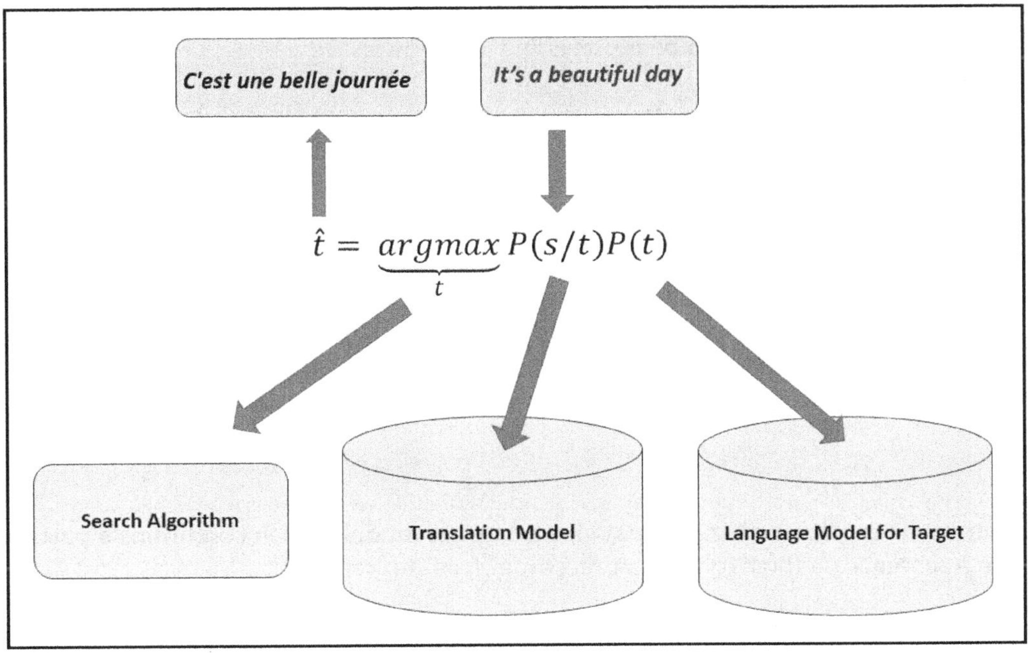

Figure 3.2: Statistical machine translation architecture

As we can see from the preceding diagram, the statistical machine translation problem has been broken down into three distinct sub-problems, as mentioned:

- Building a **Language Model for Target** that allows us to estimate *P(t)*
- Building a **Translation Model** from the target to the source language that allows us to estimate *P(s/t)*
- Carrying out a search across the possible target translations and choosing the one that maximizes *P(s/t)P(t)*

We will discuss each of these three topics, since these functions are inherent to any machine translation problem.

Language model

In a language model, the probability of a sentence is represented as a product of the conditional probabilities of the individual words or phrases as appropriate. Let's say the sentence *t* consists of the words $t_1, t_2, t_3, \ldots t_n$. According to the chain rule of probability, the probability of the sentence *t* can be represented as follows:

$$P(t) = P(t_1 t_2 \ldots . t_n) = P(t_1)P(t_2/t_1)P(t_3/t_1 t_2)\ldots P(t_n/t_1 t_2 \ldots t_{n-1}) = \prod_{i=1}^{n} P(t_i/t_1 \ldots . t_{n-1}) \quad (1)$$

Building a language model based on the preceding formula would require us to estimate conditional probabilities of several orders, which is not practically possible. To make the problem computationally feasible, one simple assumption is to condition a word based on just the previous word, and not on all the words prior to it. This assumption is also known as the **Markov assumption**, and the model is known as a **bigram model**. The conditional probability of a word as per the bigram model can be expressed as follows:

$$P(t_n/t_1 t_2 \ldots t_{n-1}) = P(t_n/t_{n-1}) \quad (2)$$

To improve the results further, we may use a **trigram model**, which conditions a particular word in a sentence on the two words preceding it, as shown here:

$$P(t_n/t_1 t_2 \ldots t_{n-1}) = P(t_n/t_{n-1} t_{n-2}) \quad (3)$$

For bigram models, the conditional probability of the next word being t_2, given the current word t_1, can be estimated by counting the total number of a pairs of (t_1, t_2) in a training corpus and normalizing that by the total occurrences of the word t_1 in the corpus:

$$P(t_2/t_1) = \frac{P(t_1, t_2)}{P(t_1)} = \frac{count(t_1, t_2)}{count(t_1)} \quad (4)$$

For a trigram model, the conditional probability of a current word t_3 given the two words t_1, t_2 preceding it can be estimated as follows:

$$P(t_3/t_1 t_2) = \frac{count(t_1, t_2, t_3)}{count(t_1, t_2)} \quad (5)$$

Going beyond trigram models generally leads to sparsity. Even for a bigram model, we might have conditional probability missing for several bigrams, since they don't appear in the training corpus. However, those missing bigrams might be very relevant, and estimating their conditional probability is very important. Needless to say, the n-gram model tends to estimate high conditional probabilities for the pair of words that appear in the training data, and neglects the ones that don't.

Perplexity for language models

The perplexity metrics are used to evaluate the usefulness of a language model. Let's assume that we have trained a language model on a training corpus and let the learned probability model over sentences or text be *P(.)*. The perplexity of the model *P(.)* is evaluated on a test set corpus drawn from the same population as that of the training corpus. If we represent the test set corpus by the *M* words, say $(w_1, w_2, w_3, \ldots\ldots, w_M)$, then the perplexity of the model over the test set sequence is represented by the following:

$$PP = 2^H = 2^{-\frac{1}{M}\log_2 P(w_1, w_2, \ldots, w_M)} \quad (1)$$

The expression for *H* as shown measures the per-word uncertainty:

$$H = -\frac{1}{M}\log_2 P(w_1, w_2, \ldots . w_M) \quad (2)$$

As per the language model, we can break up the probability expression for the test corpus as follows:

$$P(w_1, w_2, \ldots . w_M) = P(w_1)P(w_2/w_1)P(w_3/w_1w_2)\ldots\ldots P(w_M/w_1w_2\ldots w_{M-1}) \quad (3)$$

If we represent the probability of the ith word in the test set conditioned on the previous words as $p(s_i)$, then the probability of the test corpus is given as follows:

$$P(w_1, w_2, \ldots . w_M) = \prod_{i=1}^{M} \log_2 P(s_i) \quad (4)$$

Here, $p(s_i) = P(w_i/w_1 w_2 \ldots w_{i-1})$. Combining *(1)* and *(4)*, the perplexity can be written as follows:

$$PP = 2^H = 2^{-\frac{1}{M} \prod_{i=1}^{M} P(s_i)} \quad (5)$$

Suppose we have a language model *P(.)* and a test set *I love Machine Learning* to evaluate. According to the language model, the probability of the test set would be as follows:

$$P(\text{" I love Machine Learning "}) = P(\text{" I "})P(\text{" love " / " I "})P(\text{" Machine " / " I love "})P(\text{" Learning " / " I love Machine "})$$

If the training corpus of the language model is also *I love Machine Learning,* the probability of the test set would be one, leading to a log probability of *zero,* and a perplexity of *one*. This means the model can generate the next word with full certainty.

If, on the other hand, we have a more real-world training corpus of a vocabulary of a size *N* = 20,000 and the perplexity of the trained model on the test dataset is 100, then, on average, to predict the next word in the sequence, we have narrowed our search space from 20,000 words to 100 words.

Let's look at the worst-case scenario, in which we manage to build a model in which every word is independent of the previous words in the sequence:

$$P(w_i/w_1w_2w_3\ldots\ldots w_{i-1}) = P(w_i) = \frac{1}{N}$$

For a test set of M words, the perplexity using *(5)* is as follows:

$$PP = 2^{H} = 2^{-\frac{1}{M}\prod_{i=1}^{M}\log_2 P(s_i)} = 2^{-\frac{1}{M}\prod_{i=1}^{M}\log_2 \frac{1}{N}} = 2^{\frac{1}{M}\log_2 N^{M}} = N$$

If we have $N = 20{,}000$ as before, then to predict any word in the sequence, all the N words of the vocabulary need to be considered, since they are equally probable. In this case, we haven't been able to reduce the average search space over words to predict a word in a sequence.

Translation model

The **translation model** can be considered the heart of the machine translation model. In the translation model, we are required to estimate the probability *P(s/t)*, where *s* is the source language sentence and *t* is the target language sentence. Here, the source sentence is given, while the target is the one that we seek to find out. Hence, this probability can termed as the likelihood of the source sentence given the target sentence. For example, let's imagine that we are translating a source text from French to English. So, in the context of *P(s/t)*, our target language is French and our source language is English, while in the context of the actual translation, that is, *P(s/t)P(t)*, our source language is French and our target language is English.

The translation primarily consists of three components:

- **Fertility**: Not all words in the source language have a corresponding word in the target language. For example, the English sentence *Santanu loves math* is translated in French as *Santanu aim les maths*. As we can see, the word *math* in English has been translated to two words in French, as *les maths*. Formally, *fertility* is defined as the probability distribution over the number of words generated by a source-language word in the target language, and can be represented as $P(n/w_s)$, where w_s stands for the source word. Instead of having a hardcoded number n, a probability distribution is used, since the same word might generate translations of different length based on the context.

- **Distortion**: A word-to-word correspondence between the source and the target sentence is important for any machine translation system. However, the position of words in a source-language sentence might not always be in total sync with its corresponding counterpart in the target language sentence. Distortion covers this notion of alignment through a probability function, $P(p_t/p_s, l)$, where p_t and P_s represents the position of the target and source word respectively, while l represents the length of the target sentence. If the source language is English and the target language is French, then $P(p_t/p_s, l)$ represents the probability that an English word at position p_s corresponds to a French word at position p_s in a given French sentence of length l.
- **Word-to-word translation**: Finally, we come to the word-to-word translation, which is generally represented by a probability distribution of the target language word given the source-language word. For a given source-language word, w_s, the probability can be represented as $P(w_t/w_s)$, where w_t stands for the target-language word.

For a language model, the fertility probabilities, the distortion probabilities, and the word-to-word translation probabilities need to be estimated during the training process.

Now, let's come back to the original problem of estimating the probability $P(s/t)$. If we represent the English sentence by E and the French sentences by F, we need to compute the probability of $P(F/E)$. To take the alignment of the words into account, we modify the probability as $P(F, a/E)$, where a stands for the alignment of the target sentence in French. This alignment would help us inject the information related to distortion and fertility.

Let's work through an example to compute the probability $P(F, a/E)$. Let a specific English sentence be represented by a five-word sentence, $e = (e_1, e_2, e_3, e_4, e_5)$, which is in fact the correct translation of the actual French sentence $f = (f_1, f_2, f_3, f_4, f_5, f_6)$. Also, let the corresponding alignments of the words be as follows:

- $e_1 \rightarrow f_6$
- $e_2 \rightarrow$ *doesn't correspond to any word in French*
- $e_3 \rightarrow f_3, f_4$
- $e_4 \rightarrow f_1$
- $e_5 \rightarrow f_2$
- $f_5 \rightarrow$ *doesn't correspond to any word in English*

Since this is a probabilistic model, the algorithm will try different English sentences with different alignments, out of which the correct English sentence with the correct alignment should have the highest probability, given the French sentence.

Let's take the first English word into consideration as e_1—it is aligned to the French word f_6 and also emits one French word, as follows:

$$P(f_6, a/e_1) = P(f_6/e_1)P(a/e_1, f_6) \quad (1)$$

Now, let's take the alignment as a combination of two components: the distortion, a_d, and the fertility, f_d. The expression in *(1)* can be re-written as follows:

$$\begin{aligned} P(f_6, a/e_1) &= P(f_6/e_1)P(a/e_1, f_5) = P(f_6/e_1)P(a_d, a_f/e_1, f_6) \\ &= P(f_5/e_1)P(a_f/e_1)P(a_d/e_1, f_5) \quad (2) \end{aligned}$$

If we observe carefully, $P(f_5/e_1)$ is the translation probability, $P(a_f/e_1)$ is the fertility, whereas $P(a_d/e_1, f_5)$ is the distortion probability. We need to do this activity for all the given English words in an English sentence for all alignments with the given French sentence to compute *P(F, a/E)*. Finally, we need to take the best English sentence, $\hat{E}$, and alignment, $\hat{a}$, that maximizes the probability *P(F, a/E)P(E)*. This looks as follows:

$$\hat{E}, \hat{a} = \underbrace{argmax}_{E,a} P(F, a/E)P(E)$$

One thing to note here is that trying different alignments and different possible word translations in pursuit of finding the best translation might become computationally intractable, and, thus, clever algorithms need to be deployed to find the best translations in minimal time.

Neural machine translation

Neural machine translation (**NMT**) uses deep neural networks to perform machine translation from the source language to the target language. The neural translation machine takes in text in the source language as a sequence of inputs and encodes these to a hidden representation, which is then decoded back to produce the translated text sequence in the target language. One of the key advantages of this NMT system is that the whole machine translation system can be trained from end-to-end together, unlike the rule-based and statistical machine translation systems. Generally, RNN architectures such as **LSTMs** (**long short term memory**) and/or **gated recurrent units** (**GRUs**) are used in the neural translation machine architecture.

A few of the advantages of NMTs over other traditional methods are as follows:

- All of the parameters of an NMT model are trained end to end, based on a loss function, thus reducing the complexity of the model
- These NMT models use a much larger context than traditional methods and thus produce a more accurate translation
- The NMT models exploit word and phrase similarity better
- RNNs allow for better quality text generation, and so the translation is more accurate with respect to the syntax of the translated text

The encoder–decoder model

Illustrated in following diagram is the architecture of a neural translation machine that uses one LSTM as the encoder to encode the input source language sequence into final hidden states h_f and final memory cell states c_f. The final hidden states and cell states $[h_f, c_f]$ will capture the context of the whole input sequence. Thus, $[h_f, c_f]$ becomes a good candidate on which the decoder network can be conditioned.

This hidden and cell state information, $[h_f, c_f]$, is fed to the decoder network as the initial hidden and cell states and then the decoder is trained on the target sequence, with the input target sequence being at a lag of one with respect to the output target sequence. As per the decoder, the first word of the input sequence is the dummy word `[START]`, while the output label is the word *c'est*. The decoder network is just trained as a generative language model, where at any time step *t*, the output label, is just the next word with respect to the input, that is, $y_t = x_{t+1}$. The only new thing is that the final hidden and cell states of the encoder (that is, $[h_f, c_f]$) is fed to the initial hidden and cell states of the decoder to provide content for the translation.

This means the training process can be thought of as building a language model for the target language (represented by the decoder) conditioned on the hidden states of the encoder that represent the source language:

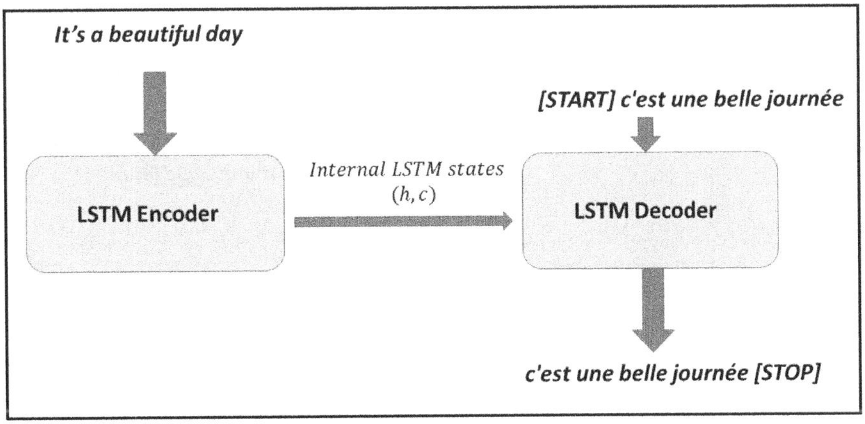

Figure 3.3: High level encoder-decoder architecture of a neural machine translation system

If T is the target language text corresponding to the source language text S, then for training we are just trying to maximize the log probability of $P_w(T_{t+1}/S,T)$ with respect to W, where T_{s+1} represents the target language text shifted by one time step, and W represents the encoder–decoder architecture model parameters.

Now that we have discussed the training procedure for encoder–decoder NMTs, we will now look at how to use the trained model during inference.

Inference using the encoder–decoder model

The architectural flow for running inference on the **NMT** (**neural translation machine**) is a little different than that of training the NMT. The following is the architectural flow for performing inference using the NMT:

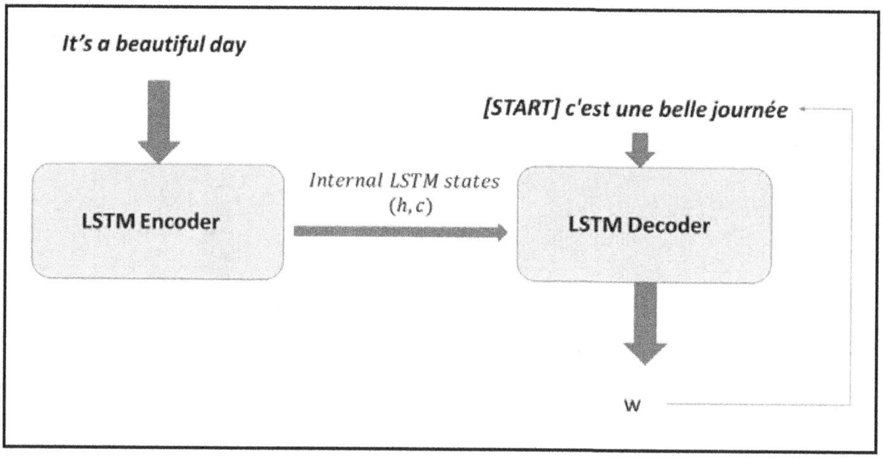

Figure 3.4: Inference from an encoder/decoder-based neural machine translation

During inference, the source language input sequence is fed to the encoder network and the final hidden and cell state produced, $[h_f, c_f]$, is fed to the decoder hidden and cell states. The decoder is converted into a single time step, and the first input fed to the decoder is the dummy `[START]` word. So, based on $[h_f, c_f]$ and the initial dummy word `[START]`, the decoder will output a word, w, and also new hidden and cell states, $[h_d, c_d]$. This word w is fed to the decoder again with the new hidden and cell states, $[h_d, c_d]$, to generate the next word. This process is repeated until we encounter an end-of-sequence character.

Implementing a sequence-to-sequence neural translation machine

We are going to build a neural machine translation system that will learn to translate short English sentences into French. To do this, we are going to use the English-to-French text corpus (`fra-eng/fra.txt`) located at `http://www.manythings.org/anki/`.

Processing the input data

Text data cannot be fed directly into any neural network, since neural networks can understand only numbers. We will treat each word as a one-hot encoded vector of a length that is equal to the number of words present in each corpus. If the English corpus contains 1,000 words, the one-hot encoded vectors v_e would be of a dimension of 1,000, that is, $v_e \in R^{1000 \times 1}$.

We will read through the English and the French corpus and determine the number of unique words in each of them. We will also represent the words by index, and for a one-hot encoded vector for the word, the index corresponding to the word would be set to one, while the rest of the indices would be set to zero. For example, let's assume that in the English corpus, we have four words: *Global warming is real.* We can define the indices of each of the words as follows:

Word	**Index**
Global	0
warming	1
is	2
real	3

In this case, we can define the one-hot encoded vector of the word *Global* as $[1,0,0,0]^T$. Similarly, the one-hot encoded vector of *real* can be represented as $[1,0,0,0]^T$.

Now, turning to the source language input for each sentence or record, we will have a sequence of words represented as a sequence of one-hot encoded vectors. The next obvious question is how to manage the sequence length, since this might vary. The most accepted approach is to have a fixed sequence length either equal to the maximum sequence length of the sentence in the corpus, or a predetermined reasonable length. We will be using the target sentences twice: once as the output sequence of translation from the decoder, and once as the input to the decoder, with the only difference being that the output sequence will be ahead of the input sequence by one time step. So, the first word in the input target sequence would be the dummy word `[START]`, while the last word in the output target sequence would be the dummy word `[END]`, marking the end of the sentence sequence.

If the target French sentence is `Je m'appelle Santanu`, the input target and the output target sequence in the decoder would be as follows:

```
[START],[Je],[m'appelle] [Santanu]
[Je],[m'appelle] [Santanu][END]
```

We have chosen to represent `[START]` by the tab character and the `[END]` by the next line character.

We divide the data creation activity into three parts:

- Reading the input files for the source (English) and target (French) texts
- Building the vocabulary from the source and target language text
- Processing the input English and French corpuses to their numeric representation so that they can be used in the neural machine translation network

The `read_input_file` function illustrated here can be used for reading the source and target language texts:

```
def read_input_file(self,path,num_samples=10e13):
    input_texts = []
    target_texts = []
    input_words = set()
    target_words = set()

    with codecs.open(path, 'r', encoding='utf-8') as f:
        lines = f.read().split('\n')

    for line in lines[: min(num_samples, len(lines) - 1)]:
        input_text, target_text = line.split('\t')
          # \t as the start of sequence
        target_text = '\t ' + target_text + ' \n'
          # \n as the end of sequence
        input_texts.append(input_text)
        target_texts.append(target_text)
        for word in input_text.split(" "):
            if word not in input_words:
                input_words.add(word)
        for word in target_text.split(" "):
            if word not in target_words:
                target_words.add(word)

    return input_texts,target_texts,input_words,target_words
```

The `vocab_generation` function can be used for building the vocabulary set of words for both the source and target languages:

```
def vocab_generation(self,path,num_samples,verbose=True):

    input_texts,target_texts,input_words,target_words =
    self.read_input_file(path,num_samples)
    input_words = sorted(list(input_words))
    target_words = sorted(list(target_words))
    self.num_encoder_words = len(input_words)
    self.num_decoder_words = len(target_words)
    self.max_encoder_seq_length =
```

```
max([len(txt.split(" ")) for txt in input_texts])
self.max_decoder_seq_length =
max([len(txt.split(" ")) for txt in target_texts])

if verbose == True:

    print('Number of samples:', len(input_texts))
    print('Number of unique input tokens:',
          self.num_encoder_words)
    print('Number of unique output tokens:',
           self.num_decoder_words)
    print('Max sequence length for inputs:',
           self.max_encoder_seq_length)
    print('Max sequence length for outputs:',
           self.max_decoder_seq_length)

self.input_word_index =
dict([(word, i) for i, word in enumerate(input_words)])
self.target_word_index =
dict([(word, i) for i, word in enumerate(target_words)])
self.reverse_input_word_dict =
dict((i, word) for word, i in self.input_word_index.items())
self.reverse_target_word_dict =
dict((i, word) for word, i in self.target word_index.items())
```

The input and target texts and the vocabularies built in the previous functions are leveraged by the `process_input` function to convert the text data into numeric form that can be used by the neural translation machine architecture. The code for the `process_input` function is as follows:

```
def process_input(self,input_texts,target_texts=None,verbose=True):

encoder_input_data =
np.zeros((len(input_texts), self.max_encoder_seq_length,
         self.num_encoder_words), dtype='float32')
decoder_input_data =
 np.zeros((len(input_texts), self.max_decoder_seq_length,
          self.num_decoder_words), dtype='float32')

decoder_target_data =
np.zeros((len(input_texts), self.max_decoder_seq_length,
         self.num_decoder_words), dtype='float32')
if self.mode == 'train':
    for i, (input_text, target_text) in
    enumerate(zip(input_texts,target_texts)):
        for t, word in enumerate(input_text.split(" ")):
            try:
                encoder_input_data[i, t,
```

```
                                            self.input_word_index[word]] = 1.
                except:
                    print(f'word {word}
                          encoutered for the 1st time, skipped')
            for t, word in enumerate(target_text.split(" ")):
            # decoder_target_data is ahead of decoder_input_data
              by one timestep
                decoder_input_data[i, t,
                self.target_word_index[word]] = 1.
                if t > 0:
                # decoder_target_data will be ahead by one timestep
                #and will not include the start character.
                    try:
                        decoder_target_data[i, t - 1,
                        self.target_word_index[word]] = 1.
                    except:
                        print(f'word {word}
                               encoutered for the 1st time,skipped')

        return
        encoder_input_data,decoder_input_data,decoder_target_data,
        np.array(input_texts),np.array(target_texts)

    else:
        for i, input_text in enumerate(input_texts):
            for t, word in enumerate(input_text.split(" ")):
                try:
                    encoder_input_data[i, t,
                                            self.input_word_index[word]] = 1.
                except:
                    print(f'word {word}
                    encoutered for the 1st time, skipped')


        return encoder_input_data,None,None,np.array(input_texts),None
```

The `encoder_input_data` variable would contain the input source data and would be a three-dimensional array of the number of records, the number of time steps, and the dimensions of each one-hot encoded vector. Similarly, `decoder_input_data` would contain the input target data, while `decoder_target_data` would contain the target labels. Upon execution of the preceding functions, all the relevant input and output required to train the machine translation system would be generated. The following code block contains the display statistics related to the execution of the `vocab_generation` function with `40000` samples:

```
('Number of samples:', 40000)
('Number of unique input tokens:', 8658)
('Number of unique output tokens:', 16297)
('Max sequence length for inputs:', 7)
('Max sequence length for outputs:', 16)
```

As we can see from the preceding statistics, the number of input English words in the corpus of `40000`, and the number of text sentences is `8658`, while the number of corresponding French words is `16297`. This is an indication of the fact that each of the English words emits around two French words on average. Similarly, we see the maximum number of words in the English sentences is `7`, while in the French sentences, the maximum is `14` if you exclude the `[START]` and `[END]` characters we have added to the French sentences for training purposes. This also confirms the fact that, on average, each English sentence being translated is going to generate double the number of words.

Let's take a look at the shape of the inputs and targets to the neural translation machine:

```
('Shape of Source Input Tensor:',(40000, 7, 8658))
('Shape of Target Input Tensor:',(40000, 16, 16297))
(Shape of Target Output Tensor:',(40000, 16, 16297))
```

The encoder data is of the shape `(40000, 7, 8658)`, where the first dimension is for the number of source-language sentences, the second dimension for the number of time steps and the final dimension is the size of the one-hot encoded vectors, which is `8658`, corresponding to the `8658` source language words in the English vocabulary. Similarly, we see for the target input and output tensor, the one-hot encoded vectors are of a size of `16297`, corresponding to the `16297` words in French vocabulary. The number of time steps for the French sentences is `16`.

Defining a model for neural machine translation

As stated earlier, the encoder will process the source input sequence through an LSTM and encode the source text into a meaningful summary. The meaningful summary would be stored in the final sequence step hidden and cell states h_f and c_f. These vectors together (that is, $[h_f; c_f]$) provide a meaningful context about the source text, and the decoder is trained to produce its own target sequence conditioned on the hidden and cell state vectors $[h_f; c_f]$.

Illustrated in the following diagram, *Figure 3.5,* is a detailed diagram of the training process of an English-to-French translation. The English sentence *It's a beautiful day* is converted to a meaning summary through an LSTM, which is then stored in the hidden and cell state vectors $[h_f; c_f]$. The decoder is then made to generate its own target sequence, conditioned on the input source sentence through the information embedded in $[h_f; c_f]$. The decoder at time step t is made to predict the next target word, that is, the word at time step $t + 1$, given the source sentence. This is why there is a lag of one time step between target input words and target output words. For the first time step, the decoder doesn't have any prior words in the target text sequence, and so the only information available for it to use to predict a target word is the information encoded in $[h_f; c_f]$ that is fed as the initial hidden and cell-state vectors. Like the encoder, the decoder also uses an LSTM, and, as discussed, the output target sequence is ahead of the input target sequence by one time step:

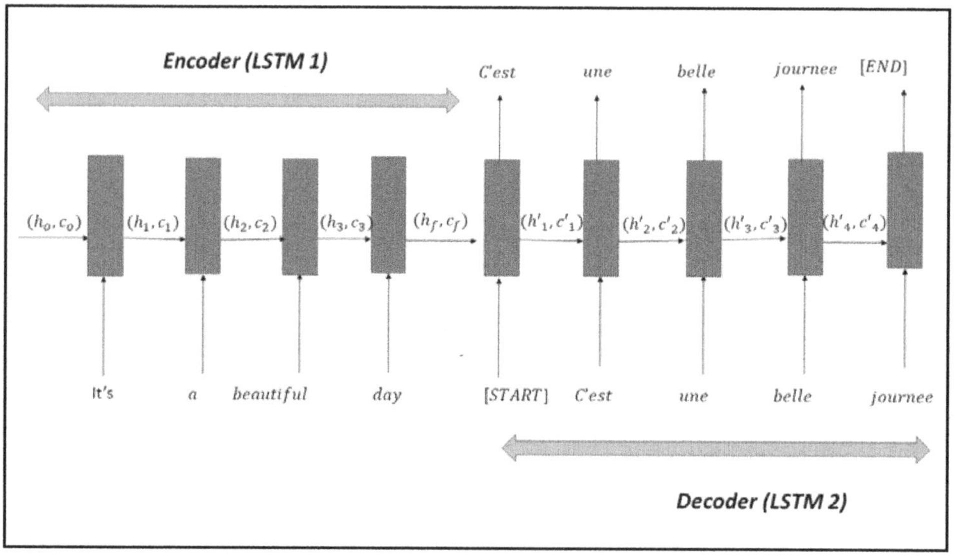

Figure 3.5: Illustration of the machine translation network flow while training

We define the encoder decoder end-to-end model for training in the function `model_enc_dec` based on the architecture illustrated in *Figure 3.5*. Here, the **Encoder (LSTM 1)** takes in the source-language text words sequentially and captures the whole context of the source language sentence or text in the final sequence step of the **Encoder (LSTM 1)**. This context from the encoder is fed as initial state for the **Decoder (LSTM 2)**, which learns to predict the next word based on the current word, since during training we have the sentence/text for the target language, and hence the decoder can just have the inputs to it shifted by just one time step to form the targets:

```
def model_enc_dec(self):
    #Encoder Model
    encoder_inp =
    Input(shape=(None,self.num_encoder_words),name='encoder_inp')
    encoder = LSTM(self.latent_dim, return_state=True,name='encoder')
    encoder_out,state_h, state_c = encoder(encoder_inp)
    encoder_states = [state_h, state_c]

    #Decoder Model
    decoder_inp =
    Input(shape=(None,self.num_decoder_words),name='decoder_inp')
    decoder_lstm =
    LSTM(self.latent_dim, return_sequences=True,
    return_state=True,name='decoder_lstm')
    decoder_out, _, _ =
    decoder_lstm(decoder_inp, initial_state=encoder_states)
    decoder_dense =
    Dense(self.num_decoder_words,
    activation='softmax',name='decoder_dense')
    decoder_out = decoder_dense(decoder_out)
    print(np.shape(decoder_out))
    #Combined Encoder Decoder Model
    model = Model([encoder_inp, decoder_inp], decoder_out)
    #Encoder Model
    encoder_model = Model(encoder_inp,encoder_states)
    #Decoder Model
    decoder_inp_h = Input(shape=(self.latent_dim,))
    decoder_inp_c = Input(shape=(self.latent_dim,))
    decoder_input = Input(shape=(None,self.num_decoder_words,))
    decoder_inp_state = [decoder_inp_h,decoder_inp_c]
    decoder_out,decoder_out_h,decoder_out_c =
    decoder_lstm(decoder_input,initial_state=decoder_inp_state)
    decoder_out = decoder_dense(decoder_out)
    decoder_out_state = [decoder_out_h,decoder_out_c]
    decoder_model = Model(inputs =
    [decoder_input] + decoder_inp_state,output=
    [decoder_out]+ decoder_out_state)
    plot_model(model,show_shapes=True, to_file=self.outdir +
```

```
            'encoder_decoder_training_model.png')
    plot_model(encoder_model,show_shapes=True, to_file=self.outdir +
            'encoder_model.png')
    plot_model(decoder_model,show_shapes=True, to_file=self.outdir +
            'decoder_model.png')

    return model,encoder_model,decoder_model
```

While the model for training is a straightforward end-to-end model, the inference models are not so straightforward, since we don't know the inputs for the decoder at each time step apriori. We talk about the inference model in more detail in the, *Building the inference model* section.

Loss function for the neural translation machine

The loss function for the neural translation machine is the average cross-entropy loss for prediction of each target word in the model sequence. The actual target word and the predicted target word can be any of the *16,297* words in the French corpus that we have taken. The target label at time step *t* would be a one-hot encoded vector $y_t \in \{0,1\}^{16297}$, while the predicted output would be in the form of probability for each of the *16,297* words in the French vocabulary. If we represent the predicted output probability vector as $p_t \in (0,1)^{16297}$, then the average categorical loss in each time step of a particular sentence *s* is given by the following:

$$C_{t,s} = -\sum_{i=1}^{16297} y_t^{(i)} \log p_t^{(i)}$$

We get the loss for the entire sentence by summing up the losses over all the sequence time steps, as shown here:

$$C_s = \sum_t C_{t,s} = -\sum_t \sum_{i=1}^{16297} y_t^{(i)} \log p_t^{(i)}$$

Since we work with mini-batch stochastic gradient descent, the average cost for the mini-batch can be obtained by averaging the loss over all the sentences in the mini-batch. If we take mini-batches of size *m*, the average loss per mini-batch is as follows:

$$C = \frac{1}{m}\sum_{s} C_s = -\frac{1}{m}\sum_{s}\sum_{t}\sum_{i=1}^{16297} y_{s,t}^{(i)} \log p_{s,t}^{(i)}$$

The mini-batch cost is used to compute the gradients for the stochastic gradient descent.

Training the model

We first execute the `model_enc_dec` function to define the model for training as well as `encoder_model` and `decoder_model` for inference and then compile it with `categorical_crossentropy` loss and `rmsprop` optimizer. We can experiment with other optimizers, such as Adam, SDG with momentum, and so on, but, for now, we will stick to `rmsprop`. The `train` function can be defined as follows:

```
# Run training

    def train(self,encoder_input_data,decoder_input_data,
              decoder_target_data):
        print("Training...")
        model,encoder_model,decoder_model = self.model_enc_dec()

        model.compile(optimizer='rmsprop', loss='categorical_crossentropy')

        model.fit([encoder_input_data, decoder_input_data],
                  decoder_target_data,
                  batch_size=self.batch_size,
                  epochs=self.epochs,
                  validation_split=0.2)
        # Save model
        model.save(self.outdir + 'eng_2_french_dumm.h5')
        return model,encoder_model,decoder_model
```

We train the model on 80% of the data and use the remaining 20% for validation. The train/test split is performed by the function defined as follows:

```
def train_test_split(self,num_recs,train_frac=0.8):
        rec_indices = np.arange(num_rccs)
        np.random.shuffle(rec_indices)
        train_count = int(num_recs*0.8)
        train_indices = rec_indices[:train_count]
        test_indices = rec_indices[train_count:]
        return train_indices,test_indices
```

Building the inference model

Let's try to recall the working mechanisms of the inference model and see how we can use components of the already-trained model to build it. The encoder part of the model should work by taking text sentences in the source language as an input, and provide the final hidden and cell state vectors, $[h_{f;} c_f]$, as an output. We can't use the decoder network as is, since the target language input words can no longer be fed to the decoder. Instead, we collapse the decoder network to consist of a single step and provide the output of that step as an input to the next step. We start with the dummy word `[START]` as the first input word to the decoder, along with $[h_{f;} c_f]$, serving as its initial hidden and cell states. The target output word w_1 and the hidden and cell state $[h_{1;} c_1]$ generated by the decoder with `[START]` and $[h_{f;} c_f]$ as the input is again fed to the decoder to generate the next word, and the process repeats until the decoder outputs the dummy word `[END]`. The following diagram illustrates the step-wise representation of the inference procedure for easy interpretation:

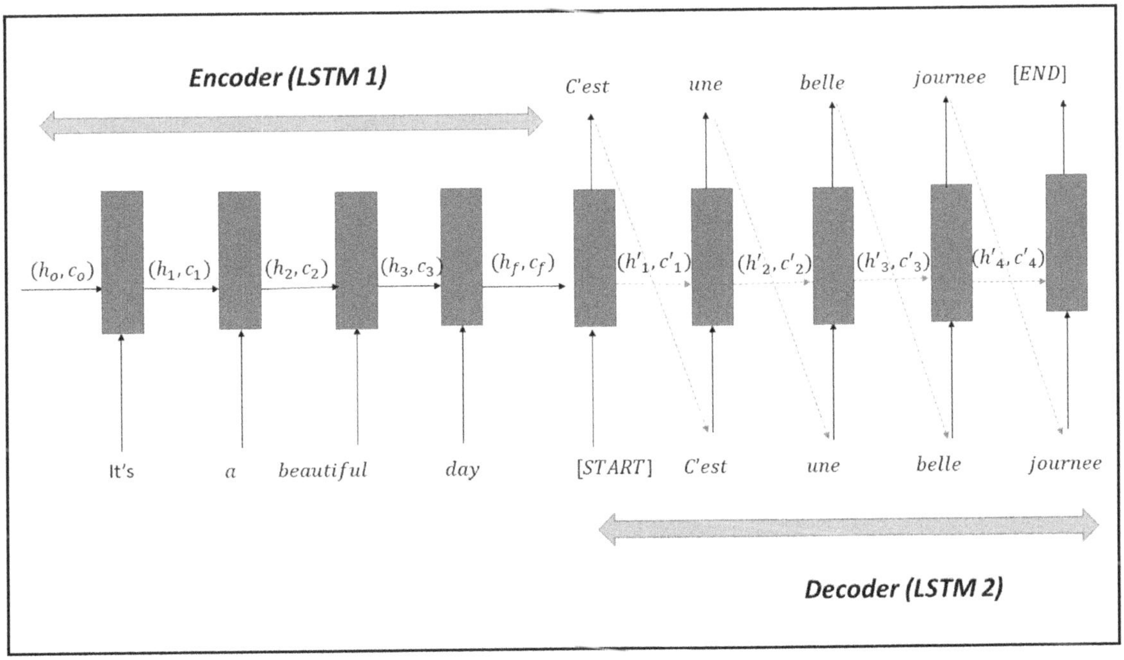

Figure 3.6: Step-wise illustration of the inference process

As we can see from the preceding diagram, the output of the first step of the decoder is `C'est`, while the hidden and cell states are $[h'_1; c'_1]$. This is fed to the decoder again, as shown by the dotted line, to generate the next word, along with the next set of hidden and cell states. The process is repeated, since the decoder outputs the dummy end character `[END]`.

For inference, we could take the encoder part of the network as is, and carry out some modification to collapse the decoder so that it consists of one time step. To recap, no matter whether the RNN consists of one time step or several time steps, the weights associated with the RNN don't change, since all the time steps of an RNN share the same weights.

For inference, we can see that the encoder part of the training model is used as the `encoder_model` in the function `model_enc_dec`. Similarly, a separate `decoder_model` is defined using the same decoder LSTM that takes in input as hidden state, cell state and the input word and outputs the target word and an updated hidden and cell state. The function `model_enc_dec` where we define the inference models, that is `encoder_model` and `decoder_model`, is again repeated for clarity:

```
def model_enc_dec(self):
        #Encoder Model
```

```
encoder_inp =
Input(shape=(None,self.num_encoder_words),name='encoder_inp')
encoder = LSTM(self.latent_dim, return_state=True,name='encoder')
encoder_out,state_h, state_c = encoder(encoder_inp)
encoder_states = [state_h, state_c]

#Decoder Model
decoder_inp =
Input(shape=(None,self.num_decoder_words),name='decoder_inp')
decoder_lstm =
LSTM(self.latent_dim, return_sequences=True,
return_state=True,name='decoder_lstm')
decoder_out, _, _ =
decoder_lstm(decoder_inp, initial_state=encoder_states)
decoder_dense =
Dense(self.num_decoder_words,
activation='softmax',name='decoder_dense')
decoder_out = decoder_dense(decoder_out)
print(np.shape(decoder_out))
#Combined Encoder Decoder Model
model  = Model([encoder_inp, decoder_inp], decoder_out)
#Encoder Model
encoder_model = Model(encoder_inp,encoder_states)
#Decoder Model
decoder_inp_h = Input(shape=(self.latent_dim,))
decoder_inp_c = Input(shape=(self.latent_dim,))
decoder_input = Input(shape=(None,self.num_decoder_words,))
decoder_inp_state = [decoder_inp_h,decoder_inp_c]
decoder_out,decoder_out_h,decoder_out_c =
decoder_lstm(decoder_input,initial_state=decoder_inp_state)
decoder_out = decoder_dense(decoder_out)
decoder_out_state = [decoder_out_h,decoder_out_c]
decoder_model = Model(inputs =
[decoder_input] + decoder_inp_state,output=
[decoder_out]+ decoder_out_state)
plot_model(model,to_file=self.outdir +
           'encoder_decoder_training_model.png')
plot_model(encoder_model,to_file=self.outdir + 'encoder_model.png')
plot_model(decoder_model,to_file=self.outdir + 'decoder_model.png')

return model,encoder_model,decoder_model
```

The decoder will operate one time step at a time. In the first instance, it would take the hidden and cell state from the encoder and guess the first word of the translation based on the dummy word `[START]`. The word predicted in the first step, along with the generated hidden and cell state, is fed to the decoder again to predict the second word, and the process continues till the end of sentence denoted by the dummy word `[END]` is predicted.

Now that we have defined all the functions required for translating a source sentence/text to its target language counterpart, we combine them to build a function that would generate a translated sequence, given a source-language input sequence or sentence:

```
def decode_sequence(self,input_seq,encoder_model,decoder_model):
    # Encode the input as state vectors.
    states_value = encoder_model.predict(input_seq)

    # Generate empty target sequence of length 1.
    target_seq = np.zeros((1, 1, self.num_decoder_words))
    # Populate the first character of target sequence
      with the start character.
    target_seq[0, 0, self.target_word_index['\t']] = 1.

    # Sampling loop for a batch of sequences
    stop_condition = False
    decoded_sentence = ''

    while not stop_condition:
        output_word, h, c = decoder_model.predict(
            [target_seq] + states_value)

        # Sample a token
        sampled_word_index = np.argmax(output_word[0, -1, :])
        sampled_char =
        self.reverse_target_word_dict[sampled_word_index]
        decoded_sentence = decoded_sentence + ' ' + sampled_char

        # Exit condition: either hit max length
        # or find stop character.
        if (sampled_char == '\n' or
        len(decoded_sentence) > self.max_decoder_seq_length):
            stop_condition = True

        # Update the target sequence (of length 1).
        target_seq = np.zeros((1, 1, self.num_decoder_words))
        target_seq[0, 0, sampled_word_index] = 1.

        # Update states
        states_value = [h, c]

    return decoded_sentence
```

Once we train the model, we run inference on the holdout dataset and check the quality of translation. An `inference` function can be coded as follows:

```
def inference(self,model,data,encoder_model,decoder_model,in_text):
    in_list,out_list = [],[]
    for seq_index in range(data.shape[0]):

        input_seq = data[seq_index: seq_index + 1]
        decoded_sentence =
        self.decode_sequence(input_seq,encoder_model,decoder_model)
        print('-')
        print('Input sentence:', in_text[seq_index])
        print('Decoded sentence:',decoded_sentence)
        in_list.append(in_text[seq_index])
        out_list.append(decoded_sentence)
    return in_list,out_list
```

The machine translation model can be trained and validated on the holdout dataset by invoking the Python Script `MachineTranslation.py` as follows:

```
python MachineTranslation.py --path '/home/santanu/ML_DS_Catalog/Machine
Translation/fra-eng/fra.txt' --epochs 20 --batch_size 32 -latent_dim 128 --
num_samples 40000 --outdir '/home/santanu/ML_DS_Catalog/Machine
Translation/' --verbose 1 --mode train
```

The results of the translation of a few English sentences from the holdout dataset where the machine translation model did a good job is illustrated as follows for reference:

```
('Input sentence:', u'Go.')
('Decoded sentence:', u' Va ! \n')
('Input sentence:', u'Wait!')
('Decoded sentence:', u' Attendez ! \n')
('Input sentence:', u'Call me.')
('Decoded sentence:', u' Appelle-moi ! \n')
('Input sentence:', u'Drop it!')
('Decoded sentence:', u' Laisse tomber ! \n')
('Input sentence:', u'Be nice.')
('Decoded sentence:', u' Soyez gentil ! \n')
('Input sentence:', u'Be fair.')
('Decoded sentence:', u' Soyez juste ! \n')
('Input sentence:', u"I'm OK.")
('Decoded sentence:', u' Je vais bien. \n')
('Input sentence:', u'I try.')
('Decoded sentence:', u' Je vais essayer.')
```

There are cases, however, when the machine translation didn't perform so well, as shown here:

```
('Input sentence:', u'Attack!')
('Decoded sentence:', u' ma ! \n')

('Input sentence:', u'Get up.')
('Decoded sentence:', u' un ! \n')
```

In conclusion, the neural machine translation implementation illustrated previously did a decent job of translating the relatively short English sentences to French. One of the things that I want to emphasize is the use of the one-hot encoded vectors to represent input words in each of the languages. As we worked with a relatively small corpus of 40,000 words, the vocabulary was reasonable, and, hence, we were able to work with one-hot encoded vectors of sizes of 8,658 and 16,297 for the English and French vocabularies respectively. With a larger corpus, the size of the one-hot encoded word vectors would increase further. Such sparse high-dimensional vectors don't have any notion of similarity when two words are compared, since their cosine product is going to be *zero*, even if two words have almost the same meaning. In the next section, we are going to see how word vector embeddings that operate in much lower dimensions can be used to solve this problem.

Word vector embeddings

Instead of one-hot encoded vectors, word vector embeddings can be used to represent the words in a dense space of dimensionality much lower than that of the one-hot encoded vectors. The word vector embedding for a word w can be represented by $v_w \in R^m$, where m is the dimensionality of the word vector embeddings. As we can see, while each component of a one-hot encoded vector can take up only binary values of {0,1}, a component of the word vector embedding can take up any real number, and hence has a much denser representation. The notions of similarity and analogy are also related to word vector embeddings.

Word vector embeddings are generally trained through techniques such as the continuous-bag-of-words method, skip-gram, GloVe, and others. We are not going to dwell much on their implementation, but the central idea is to define the word vector embeddings in such a way that similar words are closely placed in the m-dimensional Euclidean space:

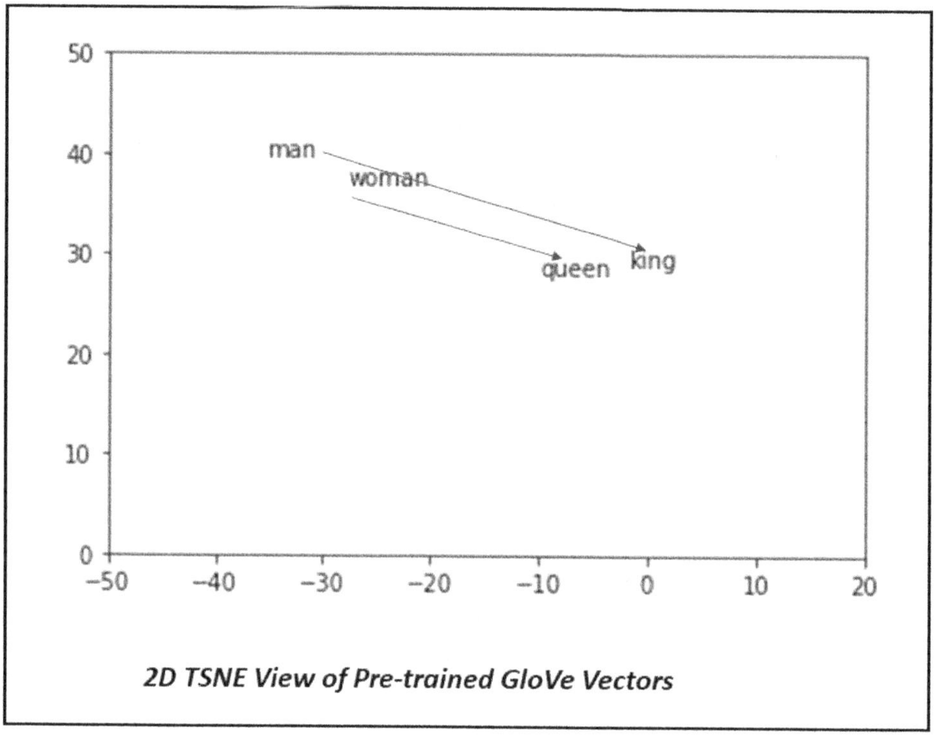

Figure 3.7: Similarity and analogy illustration of GloVe embeddings

In the preceding graph, we plot the 2D TSNE view of the GloVe word vector embeddings for **man**, **woman**, **king**, and **queen**. As we can see, **man** and **woman** have an inherent similarity, as is the case for **king** and **queen**. Also, we see the vector difference between **king** and **man** is almost the same as that of **queen** and **women**, which might stand for some notion of royalty. As we can see, analogies such as *man: king woman: queen* can be expressed by word vector embeddings, in addition to expressing similarity between words. In the next section, we will talk about using the embedding layers in the RNN to express input words as word vector embeddings, instead of one-hot encoded vectors.

Embeddings layer

The embeddings layer takes the index of an input word as an input and provides the word vector embeddings of the word as output. The dimension of the embeddings layer is $R^{d \times V}$, where d is the dimensionality of the word vector embedding and V is the size of the vocabulary. The embeddings layers can learn the embeddings themselves based on the problem, or you can provide a pretrained embeddings layer. In our case, we will let the neural machine translation figure out what the embedding vectors should be for both the source and target language to achieve a good translation. As a result, each of our defined functions should change to accommodate the embeddings layer.

Implementing the embeddings-based NMT

We will need to make a few changes to the existing functions to cater for the embeddings layer. Firstly, `process_input` would process the input to have word indexes in different time steps, instead of the one-hot encoded vectors, as follows:

```
def process_input(self,input_texts,target_texts=None,verbose=True):

  encoder_input data = np.zeros(
      (len(input_texts), self.max_encoder_seq_length),
      dtype='float32')

  decoder_input_data = np.zeros(
      (len(input_texts), self.max_decoder_seq_length),
      dtype='float32')

  decoder_target_data = np.zeros(
      (len(input_texts), self.max_decoder_seq_length,1),
      dtype='float32')

  if self.mode == 'train':
      for i, (input_text, target_text) in
              enumerate(zip(input_texts,target_texts)):
          for t, word in enumerate(input_text.split(" ")):
              try:
                  encoder_input_data[i, t] =
                  self.input_word_index[word]
              except:
                  encoder_input_data[i, t] =
                  self.num_encoder_words

          for t, word in enumerate(target_text.split(" ")):
          # decoder_target_data is ahead of decoder_input_data
```

```
                    by one timestep
                      try:
                          decoder_input_data[i, t] =
                          self.target_word_index[word]
                      except:
                          decoder_input_data[i, t] =
                          self.num_decoder_words
                      if t > 0:
                      # decoder_target_data will be ahead by one timestep
                      #and will not include the start character.
                          try:
                              decoder_target_data[i, t - 1] =
                              self.target_word_index[word]
                          except:
                              decoder_target_data[i, t - 1] =
                              self.num_decoder_words
                print(self.num_encoder_words)
                print(self.num_decoder_words)
                print(self.embedding_dim)
                self.english_emb = np.zeros((self.num_encoder_words + 1,
                                            self.embedding_dim))
                self.french_emb = np.zeros((self.num_decoder_words + 1,
                                            self.embedding_dim))
                return
    encoder_input_data,decoder_input_data,decoder_target_data,np.array(input_te
    xts),
    np.array(target_texts)
            else:
                for i, input_text in enumerate(input_texts):
                    for t, word in enumerate(input_text.split(" ")):
                        try:
                            encoder_input_data[i, t] =
    self.input_word_index[word]
```

The only change from the earlier `process_input` function is that no longer are we representing the words by one-hot encoded vectors but instead by the indices of the words. Also, did you notice we are adding an extra word index for words which are not present in the vocabulary? This shouldn't ideally happen for training data, but during testing a completely new word not in the vocabulary might come up.

The following are the statistics from input processing:

```
Number of samples: 40000
Number of unique input tokens: 8658
Number of unique output tokens: 16297
```

```
Max sequence length for inputs: 7
Max sequence length for outputs: 16
('Shape of Source Input Tensor:', (40000, 7))
('Shape of Target Input Tensor:', (40000, 16))
('Shape of Target Output Tensor:', (40000, 16, 1))
```

As we can see, the source and the target input tensors now have `7` and `16` time steps, but don't have the dimensions for the one-hot encoded vectors. Each of the time steps houses the index for the words.

The next change would be with respect to the encoder and decoder network, to accommodate the embedding layers before the LSTM layers:

```
def model_enc_dec(self):
    #Encoder Model
    encoder_inp = Input(shape=(None,),name='encoder_inp')
    encoder_inp1 =
    Embedding(self.num_encoder_words + 1,
              self.embedding_dim,weights=[self.english_emb])
              (encoder_inp)
    encoder = LSTM(self.latent_dim, return_state=True,name='encoder')
    encoder_out,state_h, state_c = encoder(encoder_inp1)
    encoder_states = [state_h, state_c]

    #Decoder Model
    decoder_inp = Input(shape=(None,),name='decoder_inp')
    decoder_inp1 =
    Embedding(self.num_decoder_words+1,self.embedding_dim,weights=
              [self.french_emb])(decoder_inp)
    decoder_lstm =
    LSTM(self.latent_dim, return_sequences=True,
         return_state=True,name='decoder_lstm')
    decoder_out, _, _ =
    decoder_lstm(decoder_inp1,initial_state=encoder_states)
    decoder_dense = Dense(self.num_decoder_words+1,
                    activation='softmax',name='decoder_dense')
    decoder_out = decoder_dense(decoder_out)
    print(np.shape(decoder_out))
    #Combined Encoder Decoder Model
    model = Model([encoder_inp, decoder_inp], decoder_out)
    #Encoder Model
    encoder_model = Model(encoder_inp,encoder_states)
    #Decoder Model
    decoder_inp_h = Input(shape=(self.latent_dim,))
    decoder_inp_c = Input(shape=(self.latent_dim,))
    decoder_inp_state = [decoder_inp_h,decoder_inp_c]
    decoder_out,decoder_out_h,decoder_out_c =
    decoder_lstm(decoder_inp1,initial_state=decoder_inp_state)
```

```
        decoder_out = decoder_dense(decoder_out)
        decoder_out_state = [decoder_out_h,decoder_out_c]
        decoder_model = Model(inputs =
                        [decoder_inp] + decoder_inp_state,output=
                        [decoder_out]+ decoder_out_state)

        return model,encoder_model,decoder_model
```

The training model needs to be compiled with `sparse_categorical_crossentropy`, since the output target labels are expressed as indices, as opposed to one-hot encoded word vectors:

```
    def train(self,encoder_input_data,decoder_input_data,
              decoder_target_data):
        print("Training...")

        model,encoder_model,decoder_model = self.model_enc_dec()

        model.compile(optimizer='rmsprop',
                      loss='sparse_categorical_crossentropy')
        model.fit([encoder_input_data, decoder_input_data],
                   decoder_target_data,
                  batch_size=self.batch_size,
                  epochs=self.epochs,
                  validation_split=0.2)
        # Save model
        model.save(self.outdir + 'eng_2_french_dumm.h5')
        return model,encoder_model,decoder_model
```

Next, we need to make modifications to the inference-related functions to accommodate the embedding related changes. The `encoder_model` and the `decoder_model` for inference now uses the embeddings layer for English and French vocabulary, respectively.

Finally, we can create the sequence generator function as follows, using `decoder_model` and `encoder_model`:

```
    def decode_sequence(self,input_seq,encoder_model,decoder_model):
        # Encode the input as state vectors.
        states_value = encoder_model.predict(input_seq)

        # Generate empty target sequence of length 1.
        target_seq = np.zeros((1, 1))
        # Populate the first character of target sequence
          with the start character.
        target_seq[0, 0] = self.target_word_index['\t']

        # Sampling loop for a batch of sequences
```

```
        stop_condition = False
        decoded_sentence = ''

        while not stop_condition:
            output_word, h, c = decoder_model.predict(
                [target_seq] + states_value)

            # Sample a token
            sampled_word_index = np.argmax(output_word[0, -1, :])
            try:
                sampled_char =
                self.reverse_target_word_dict[sampled_word_index]
            except:
                sampled_char = '<unknown>'
            decoded_sentence = decoded_sentence + ' ' + sampled_char

            # Exit condition: either hit max length
            # or find stop character.
            if (sampled_char == '\n' or
            len(decoded_sentence) > self.max_decoder_seq_length):
                stop_condition = True

            # Update the target sequence (of length 1).
            target_seq = np.zeros((1, 1))
            target_seq[0, 0] = sampled_word_index

            # Update states
            states_value = [h, c]

        return decoded_sentence
```

The training of the model can be invoked by running the script as follows:

```
python MachineTranslation_word2vec.py --path '/home/santanu/ML_DS_Catalog-
/Machine Translation/fra-eng/fra.txt' --epochs 20 --batch_size 32 --
latent_dim 128 --num_samples 40000 --outdir '/home/santanu/ML_DS_Catalog-
/Machine Translation/' --verbose 1 --mode train --embedding_dim 128
```

The model is trained on GeForce GTX 1070 GPU, and it approximately takes around 9.434 minutes to train on 32,000 records and run inference on 8,000 records. Users are highly recommended to use a GPU, since RNNs are computation heavy and might take hours to train the same model on CPU.

We can run the train the machine translation model and perform validation on the holdout out dataset by running the python script `MachineTranslation.py` as follows:

```
python MachineTranslation.py --path '/home/santanu/ML_DS_Catalog/Machine
Translation/fra-eng/fra.txt' --epochs 20 --batch_size 32 -latent_dim 128 --
num_samples 40000 --outdir '/home/santanu/ML_DS_Catalog/Machine
Translation/' --verbose 1 --mode train
```

The results obtained from the embeddings vector approach are similar to those of the one-hot encoded word vectors. A few translations from the inference of the holdout dataset are provided here:

```
Input sentence: Where is my book?
Decoded sentence:  Où est mon Tom ?
-
Input sentence: He's a southpaw.
Decoded sentence:  Il est en train de
-
Input sentence: He's a very nice boy.
Decoded sentence:  C'est un très bon
-
Input sentence: We'll be working.
Decoded sentence:  Nous pouvons faire
-
Input sentence: May I have a program?
Decoded sentence:  Puis-je une ?

-
Input sentence: Can you make it safe?
Decoded sentence:  Peux-tu le faire
-
Input sentence: We walked to my room.
Decoded sentence:  Nous avons devons
-
Input sentence: Don't stand too close.
Decoded sentence:  Ne vous en prie.
-
Input sentence: Where's the dog?
Decoded sentence:  Où est le chien ?
-
Input sentence: He's a hopeless case.
Decoded sentence:  Il est un fait de
-
Input sentence: Where were we?
Decoded sentence:  Où fut ?
```

Summary

The reader should now have a good understanding of several machine translation approaches and how neural translation machines are different than their traditional counterparts. We should also now have gained an insight into how to build a neural machine translation system from scratch and how to extend that system in interesting ways. With the information and implementation demonstrations provided, the reader is advised to explore other parallel corpus datasets.

In this chapter, we defined embedding layers but didn't load them with pretrained embeddings, such as GloVe, FastText, and so on. The reader is advised to load the embedding layers with pretrained word vector embeddings and see whether this yields better results. In `Chapter 4`, *Style Transfer in Fashion Industry using GANs*, we are going to work through a project related to style transfer in the fashion industry using generative adversarial networks, a modern revolution in the field of artificial intelligence.

4
Style Transfer in Fashion Industry using GANs

The concept of **style transfer** refers to the process of rendering the style of a product into another product. Imagine that your fashion-crazy friend bought a blue-printed bag and wanted to get a pair of shoes of a similar print to go with it. Up until 2016, this might not have been possible, unless they were friends with a fashion designer who would first have to design a shoe before it was approved for production. With the recent progress in generative adversarial networks, however, this kind of design process can be carried out easily.

A generative adversarial network is a network that learns by playing a zero sum game between a generator network and a discriminator network. Let's say that a fashion designer wants to design a handbag of a specific structure and is exploring different prints. The designer might sketch the structure of the bag and then feed the sketch image into a generative adversarial network to come up with several possible final prints for the handbag. This process of style transfer can make a huge impact on the fashion industry by enabling customers to map product designs and patterns themselves, without the need to have extensive designer input. Fashion houses can also benefit by recommending products of a similar design and style to complement those that the customer already has.

In this project, we will build a smart artificial intelligence system that will generate shoes with a similar style to a given handbag and vice versa. The vanilla GAN that we discussed previously is not going to be enough to implement this project; what we need are customized versions of the GAN, such as a DiscoGAN and a CycleGAN.

In this chapter, we will cover the following topics:

- We will discuss the working principles and mathematical foundations behind DiscoGAN
- We will compare and contrast DiscoGAN with CycleGAN, which are very similar in architecture and working principles
- We will train a DiscoGAN that learns to generate images of bags from some given sketches of the bags
- Finally, we will discuss the intricacies associated with training a DiscoGAN

Technical requirements

The readers should have basic knowledge of Python 3 and artificial intelligence to go through the projects in this chapter.

The code files of this chapter can be found on GitHub:
`https://github.com/PacktPublishing/Intelligent-Projects-using-Python/tree/master/Chapter04`

Check out the following video to see the code in action:
`http://bit.ly/2CUZLQb`

DiscoGAN

A **DiscoGAN** is a generative adversarial network that generates images of products in domain B given an image in domain A. Illustrated in the following diagram is an architectural diagram of a DisoGAN network:

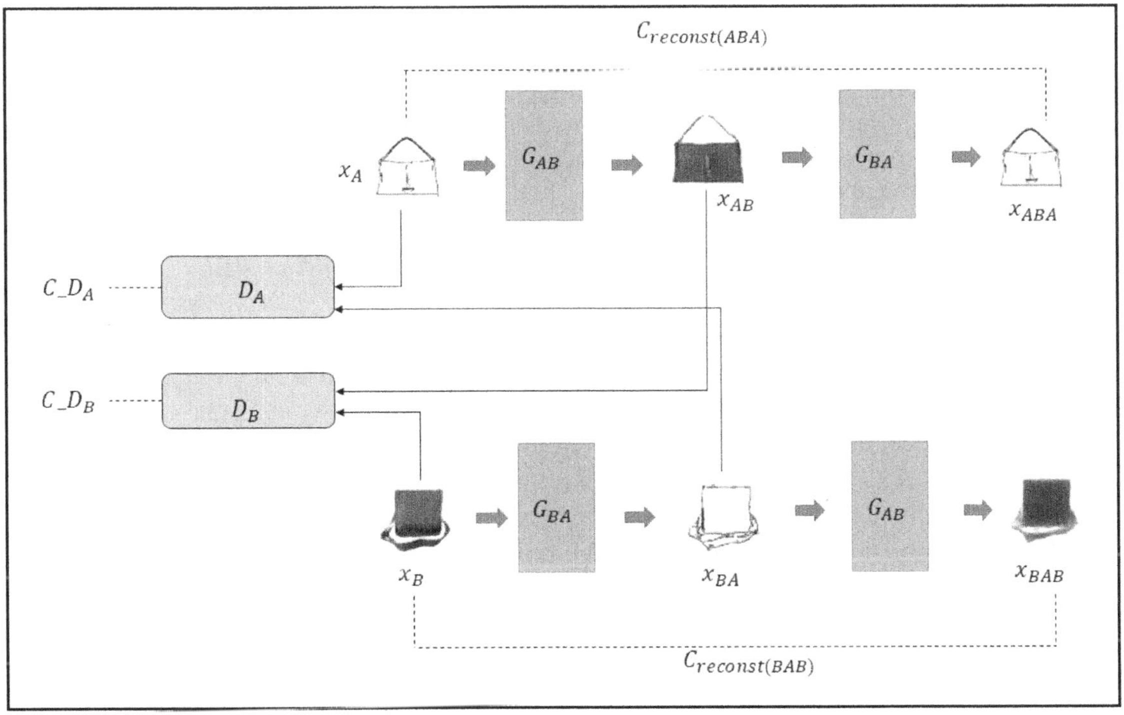

Figure 4.1: Architectural diagram of a DiscoGAN

The images generated in domain B resemble the images in domain A in both style and pattern. This relation can be learned without explicitly pairing images from the two domains during training. This is quite a powerful capability, given that the pairing of items is a time-consuming task. On a high level, it tries to learn two generator functions in the form of neural networks G_{AB} and G_{BA} so that an image x_A, when fed through the generator G_{AB}, produces an image x_{AB}, that looks realistic in domain B. Also, when this image x_{AB} is fed through the other generator network G_{BA}, it should produce an image x_{ABA} which should ideally be the same as the original image x_A. With respect to the generator function, the following relation should hold true:

$$G_{BA}G_{AB}(x_A) = x_A \qquad (1)$$

In practice, however, it is not possible for the generator functions G_{AB} and G_{BA} to be inverses of each other, so we try to minimize the loss between the reconstructed image and the original image as much as possible by choosing either a L1 or L2 normed loss. L1 normed loss is basically the sum of the absolute error for each data point while L2 normed loss represents the sum of the squared loss for each data point. We can represent the L2 normed loss for a single image as follows:

$$C = \|x_A - x_{ABA}\|_2^2 = \|x_A - G_{BA}G_{AB}(x_A)\|_2^2 \quad (2)$$

Merely minimizing the preceding loss is not going to be enough. We have to ensure that the image x_B that is created looks realistic in domain B. For instance, if we are mapping clothes in domain A to shoes in domain B, we would have to ensure that x_B resembles a shoe. A discriminator D_B on the domain B side is going to detect x_B as fake if the image is not realistic enough as a shoe and hence a loss pertaining to the same also has to be taken into account. Generally, during training, the discriminator is fed with both generated images $x_{AB} = G_{AB}(x_A)$ and original images in domain B, which we choose to represent here by y_B, so that it learns to classify real images from fake ones. As you might recall, in a GAN, the generator and the discriminator play a *zero-sum minimax game* against each other to keep getting better until an equilibrium is reached. The discriminator penalizes the fake images if they don't look realistic enough, meaning the generators have to learn to produce better images x_{AB} given an input image x_A. Taking all of this into consideration, we can formulate the loss the generator we would like to minimize as the reconstruction loss and the loss with respect to the discriminator identifying x_{AB} as fake. The second loss will attempt to make the generator produce realistic images in domain B. The generator loss of mapping an image x_A in domain A to an image in domain B can be expressed as follows:

$$C\_G_{AB} = C_{reconst(ABA)} + C_{D(AB)}$$

The reconstruction loss under the L2 norm can be expressed as follows:

$$C_{reconst(ABA)} = \|x_A - G_{BA}G_{AB}(x_A)\|_2^2 \quad (3)$$

Since we are dealing with an image, we can assume that x_A is a flattened vector of all the pixels to do justice to the L2 norm terminology. If we assume x_A is a matrix, it would be better to term $\|.\|_2^2$ as the **Frobenius norm**. However, these are just mathematical terminologies, and in essence we are just taking the sum of the square of the pixel value differences between the original image and the reconstructed image.

Let's think about the cost that the generator would try to minimize in its pursuit of making the transformed image x_{AB} look realistic to the discriminator. The discriminator would try to tag the image as a fake image, and hence the generator G_{AB} should produce x_{AB} in such a way that the log loss of it being a fake image is as small as possible. If the discriminator D_B in domain B tags real images as `1` and fake images as `0` and the probability of an image being real is given by $D_B(.)$, then the generator should make x_{AB} highly probable under the discriminator network, so that $D_B(x_B) = D_B(G_{AB}(x_A))$ is as close to `1` as possible. In terms of log loss, the generator should minimize the negative log of the preceding probability, which basically gives us $C_{D(AB)}$, as shown here:

$$C_{D(AB)} = -\log(D_B(G_{AB}(x_A))) \qquad (4)$$

Combining *(3)* and *(4)*, we can get the total generator cost C_G_{AB} of mapping an image from domain A to domain B, as shown here:

$$C\_G_{AB} = C_{reconst(ABA)} + C_{D(AB)} = \|x_A - G_{BA}G_{AB}(x_A)\|_2^2 - \log(D_B(G_{AB}(x_A))) \qquad (5)$$

The big question is, shall we stop here? Since we have images from two domains, to get a better mapping, we can take images from domain B as well and map them to domain A through a generator G_{BA}. If we take an image x_B in domain B and transform it into an image x_{BA} through the generator G_{BA} and the discriminator at domain A is given by D_A, then the cost function associated with such a transformation is given by the following:

$$C\_G_{BA} = C_{reconst(BAB)} + C_{D(BA)} = \|x_B - G_{AB}G_{BA}(x_B)\|_2^2 - \log(D_A(G_{BA}(x_B))) \qquad (6)$$

If we sum over the entire population of images in both the domains, the generator loss would be given by the sum of *(5)* and *(6)*, as shown here:

$$C_G = \mathop{\mathbb{E}}_{x_A \sim P(x_A)}[C\_G_{AB}] + \mathop{\mathbb{E}}_{x_B \sim P(x_B)}[C\_G_{BA}]$$
$$= \mathop{\mathbb{E}}_{x_A \sim P(x_A)}[\|x_A - G_{BA}G_{AB}(x_A)\|_2^2 - \log(D_B(G_{AB}(x_A)))] + \mathop{\mathbb{E}}_{y_B \sim P(x_B)}[\|x_B - G_{AB}G_{BA}(x_B)\|_2^2 - \log(D_A(G_{BA}(y_B)))] \qquad (7)$$

Now, let's build the cost functions the discriminators would try to minimize to set up the zero-sum min/max games. The discriminators in each domain would try to distinguish the real images from the fake images, and hence the discriminator G_B would try to minimize the cost C_D_B, as shown here:

$$C\_D_B = -\mathop{\mathbb{E}}_{x_B \sim P(x_B)}[\log(D_B(x_B))] - \mathop{\mathbb{E}}_{x_A \sim P(x_A)}[\log(1 - G_{AB}(x_A))] \qquad (8)$$

Similarly, the discriminator D_A would try to minimize the cost C_D_A as shown here:

$$C\_D_A = -\mathop{\mathbb{E}}_{x_A \sim P(x_A)}[\log(D_B(x_A))] - \mathop{\mathbb{E}}_{x_B \sim P(x_B)}[\log(1 - G_{BA}(x_B))] \quad (9)$$

Combining *(8)* and *(9)* the overall discriminator cost is given by C_D, as follows:

$$C_D = -\mathop{\mathbb{E}}_{y_B \sim P(y_B)}[\log(D_B(y_B))] - \mathop{\mathbb{E}}_{x_A \sim P(x_A)}[\log(1 - G_{AB}(x_A))] - \mathop{\mathbb{E}}_{x_A \sim P(x_A)}[\log(D_B(x_A))] - \mathop{\mathbb{E}}_{x_B \sim P(y_B)}[\log(1 - G_{BA}(x_B))] \quad (10)$$

If we denote the parameters of the G_{AB}, G_{BA}, D_A, and D_B as θ_{GAB},θ_{GBA},θ_{DA}, and θ_{DB}, then the optimized parameters of the networks can be represented as follows:

$$\hat{\theta}_{GAB}, \hat{\theta}_{GBA} = argmin_{\theta_{GAB}, \theta_{GBA}} \mathop{\mathbb{E}}_{x_A \sim P(x_A)}[\|x_A - G_{BA}G_{AB}(x_A)\|_2^2 - \log(D_B(G_{AB}(x_A)))] + \mathop{\mathbb{E}}_{x_B \sim P(x_B)}[\|x_B - G_{AB}G_{BA}(x_B)\|_2^2 - \log(D_A(G_{BA}(x_B)))] \quad (11)$$

$$\hat{\theta}_{DA}, \hat{\theta}_{DB} = argmin_{\theta_{DA}, \theta_{DB}} - \mathop{\mathbb{E}}_{x_B \sim P(x_B)}[\log(D_B(x_B))] - \mathop{\mathbb{E}}_{x_A \sim P(x_A)}[\log(1 - G_{AB}(x_A))] - \mathop{\mathbb{E}}_{x_A \sim P(x_A)}[\log(D_B(x_A))] - \mathop{\mathbb{E}}_{x_B \sim P(x_B)}[\log(1 - G_{BA}(x_B))] \quad (12)$$

Stochastic gradient descent, such as Adam, is performed on the cost functions to arrive at the optimal solution. Please note that, as illustrated before, the solution for a generative adversarial network is a saddle point with respect to the cost function being optimized.

CycleGAN

A **CycleGAN** is fundamentally similar to a DiscoGAN with one small modification. In a CycleGAN, we have the flexibility to determine how much weight to assign to the reconstruction loss with respect to the GAN loss or the loss attributed to the discriminator. This parameter helps in balancing the losses in correct proportions based on the problem at hand to help the network converge faster while training. The rest of the implementation of a CycleGAN is the same as that of the DiscoGAN.

Learning to generate natural handbags from sketched outlines

In this chapter, we are going to generate handbags from sketched outlines without using explicit pair matching using DiscoGAN. We denote the sketch images as belonging to domain A, while the natural handbag images to belong to domain B. There will be two generators: one that takes the images of domain A and maps them to images that would look realistic under domain B, and another that does the opposite: one that maps handbag images from domain B to images that will look realistic under domain A. The discriminators would try to identify the generator generated fake images from those of the authentic images in each domain. The generators and the discriminator would play a minimax zero- sum game against each other.

To train this network, we will require two sets of images, sketches, or outlines of handbags and natural images of handbags. The images can be downloaded from the following link: `https://people.eecs.berkeley.edu/~tinghuiz/projects/pix2pix/datasets/edges2handbags.tar.gz`.

In the next few sections, we will go through the process of defining the DiscoGAN network in TensorFlow and then training it to generate realistic handbag images using handbag sketches that act as the edges of an image. We will start by defining the architecture of the generator network.

Preprocess the Images

Each image in the `edges2handbags` dataset folder contains the picture of the `bag` and the picture of the `bag edges` in the same image. For training the network we need to separate them as images belonging to the two domains A and B that we have discussed in the architecture for DiscoGAN. The images can be split up into Domain A and Domain B images by using the following code (`image_split.py`):

```
# -*- coding: utf-8 -*-
"""
Created on Fri Apr 13 00:10:12 2018

@author: santanu
"""

import numpy as np
import os
from scipy.misc import imread
```

```
from scipy.misc import imsave
import fire
from elapsedtimer import ElapsedTimer
from pathlib import Path
import shutil
'''
Process the images in Domain A and Domain and resize appropriately
Inputs contain the Domain A and Domain B image in the same image
This program will break them up and store them in their respecective folder

'''


def process_data(path,_dir_):
    os.chdir(path)
    try:
        os.makedirs('trainA')
    except:
        print(f'Folder trainA already present, cleaning up and recreating
empty folder trainA')
        try:
            os.rmdir('trainA')
        except:
            shutil.rmtree('trainA')
        os.makedirs('trainA')

    try:
        os.makedirs('trainB')
    except:
        print(f'Folder trainA already present, cleaning up and recreating
empty folder trainB')
        try:
            os.rmdir('trainB')
        except:
            shutil.rmtree('trainB')
        os.makedirs('trainB')
    path = Path(path)
    files = os.listdir(path /_dir_)
    print('Images to process:', len(files))
    i = 0
    for f in files:
        i+=1
        img = imread(path / _dir_ / str(f))
        w,h,d = img.shape
        h_ = int(h/2)
        img_A = img[:,:h_]
        img_B = img[:,h_:]
        imsave(f'{path}/trainA/{str(f)}_A.jpg',img_A)
        imsave(f'{path}/trainB/{str(f)}_B.jpg',img_A)
```

```
        if ((i % 10000) == 0 & (i >= 10000)):
            print(f'the number of input images processed : {i}')
    files_A = os.listdir(path / 'trainA')
    files_B = os.listdir(path / 'trainB')
    print(f'No of images written to {path}/trainA is {len(files_A)}')
    print(f'No of images written to {path}/trainA is {len(files_B)}')
with ElapsedTimer('process Domain A and Domain B Images'):
    fire.Fire(process_data)
```

The `image_split.py` code can be invoked as follows:

```
python image_split.py --path /media/santanu/9eb9b6dc-b380-486e-b4fd-
c424a325b976/edges2handbags/ --_dir_ train
```

The output log is as follows:

```
Folder trainA already present, cleaning up and recreating empty folder
trainA
Folder trainA already present, cleaning up and recreating empty folder
trainB
Images to process: 138569
the number of input images processed : 10000
the number of input images processed : 20000
the number of input images processed : 30000

.....
```

The generators of the DiscoGAN

The generators of the DiscoGAN are feed-forward convolutional neural networks where the input and output are images. In the first part of the network, the images are scaled down in spatial dimensions while the number of the output feature maps increases as the layers progress. In the second part of the network, the images are scaled up along the spatial dimensions, while the number of output feature maps reduce from layer to layer. In the final output layer, an image with the same spatial dimensions as that of the input is generated. If a generator that converts an image x_A to x_{AB} from *domain A* to *domain B* is represented by G_{AB}, then we have $x_{AB} = G_{AB}(x_A)$.

Illustrated here is the `build_generator` function, which can we used to build the generators for the DiscoGAN network:

```
def build_generator(self,image,reuse=False,name='generator'):
    with tf.variable_scope(name):
        if reuse:
            tf.get_variable_scope().reuse_variables()
        else:
            assert tf.get_variable_scope().reuse is False
            """U-Net generator"""
        def lrelu(x, alpha,name='lrelu'):
            with tf.variable_scope(name):
                return tf.nn.relu(x) - alpha * tf.nn.relu(-x)
    """Layers used during downsampling"""
        def common_conv2d(layer_input,filters,f_size=4,
                          stride=2,padding='SAME',norm=True,
                          name='common_conv2d'):
            with tf.variable_scope(name):
                if reuse:
                    tf.get_variable_scope().reuse_variables()
                else:
                    assert tf.get_variable_scope().reuse is False
                d =
               tf.contrib.layers.conv2d(layer_input,filters,
                                        kernel_size=f_size,
                                        stride=stride,padding=padding)
                if norm:
                    d = tf.contrib.layers.batch_norm(d)
                d = lrelu(d,alpha=0.2)
                return d
         """Layers used during upsampling"""

       def common_deconv2d(layer_input,filters,f_size=4,
                           stride=2,padding='SAME',dropout_rate=0,
                           name='common_deconv2d'):
            with tf.variable_scope(name):
                if reuse:
                    tf.get_variable_scope().reuse_variables()
                else:
                    assert tf.get_variable_scope().reuse is False


                u =
                tf.contrib.layers.conv2d_transpose(layer_input,
                                                   filters,f_size,
                                                   stride=stride,
                                                   padding=padding)
                if dropout_rate:
```

```
                u = tf.contrib.layers.dropout(u,keep_prob=dropout_rate)
            u = tf.contrib.layers.batch_norm(u)
            u = tf.nn.relu(u)
            return u
    # Downsampling
    #  64x64 -> 32x32
    dwn1 = common_conv2d(image,self.gf,stride=2,norm=False,name='dwn1')
    #  32x32 -> 16x16
   dwn2 = common_conv2d(dwn1,self.gf*2,stride=2,name='dwn2')
    #  16x16   -> 8x8
   dwn3 = common_conv2d(dwn2,self.gf*4,stride=2,name='dwn3')
    #  8x8    -> 4x4
   dwn4 = common_conv2d(dwn3,self.gf*8,stride=2,name='dwn4')
    #  4x4    -> 1x1
   dwn5 = common_conv2d(dwn4,100,stride=1,padding='valid',name='dwn5')
    # Upsampling
    #  4x4     -> 4x4
    up1 =
   common_deconv2d(dwn5,self.gf*8,stride=1,
                   padding='valid',name='up1')
    #  4x4     -> 8x8
    up2 = common_deconv2d(up1,self.gf*4,name='up2')
    #  8x8     -> 16x16
    up3 = common_deconv2d(up2,self.gf*2,name='up3')
    #  16x16     -> 32x32
    up4 = common_deconv2d(up3,self.gf,name='up4')
   out_img = tf.contrib.layers.conv2d_transpose(up4,self.channels,
                                                  kernel_size=4,stride=2,
                                                  padding='SAME',
activation_fn=tf.nn.tanh)
   # 32x32 -> 64x64
    return out_img
```

Within the generator function, we define a leaky ReLU activation function and use a leak factor of `0.2`. We also define a convolution layer generation function, `common_conv2d`, which we use for down-sampling the image, and a `common_deconv2d`, which is used for up-sampling the down- sampled image to its original spatial dimensions.

We define the generator function with the `reuse` option by using `tf.get_variable_scope().reuse_variables()`. When the same generator function is called multiple times, the reuse option ensures that we reuse the same variables that are used by a specific generator. When we remove the reuse option, we create a new set of variables for the generator.

For instance, we might use the generator function to create two generator networks and so we would not use the `reuse` option while creating these networks for the first time. If that generator function is referred to again, we use the `reuse` option. The activation function during convolution (down sampling) and deconvolution (up sampling) is leaky ReLU preceded by batch normalization for stable and fast convergence.

The number of output feature maps in the different layers of the network is either `self.gf` or a multiple of it. For our DiscoGAN network, we have chosen `self.gf` to be `64`.

One important thing to notice in the generator is the `tanh` activation function of the output layer. This ensures that the pixel values of the images produced by the generators would be in the range of `[-1, +1]`. This makes it important for the input images to have pixel intensities in the range of `[-1, +1]`, which can be done by a simple element-wise transformation on the pixel intensities, as follows:

$$x \leftarrow (\frac{x}{127.5} - 1)$$

Similarly, to convert the image to be in a displayable 0-255 pixel intensity format, we need to apply an inverse transformation, as follows:

$$x \leftarrow (x + 1) * 127.5$$

The discriminators of the DiscoGAN

The discriminators of the DiscoGAN would learn to distinguish the real images from the fake ones in a specific domain. We will have two discriminators: one for domain A, and one for domain B. The discriminators are also convolutional networks that can perform binary classification. Unlike the traditional classification-based convolutional networks, the discriminators don't have any fully connected layers. The input images are down-sampled using convolution with a stride of two until the final layer, where the output is 1 x 1. Again, we use leaky ReLU as the activation function and batch normalization for stable and fast convergence. The following code shows the discriminator build function implementation in TensorFlow:

```
def build_discriminator(self,image,reuse=False,name='discriminator'):
    with tf.variable_scope(name):
        if reuse:
            tf.get_variable_scope().reuse_variables()
        else:
            assert tf.get_variable_scope().reuse is False
        def lrelu(x, alpha,name='lrelu'):
```

```
        with tf.variable_scope(name):
            if reuse:
                tf.get_variable_scope().reuse_variables()
            else:
                assert tf.get_variable_scope().reuse is False

        return tf.nn.relu(x) - alpha * tf.nn.relu(-x)
            """Discriminator layer"""
    def d_layer(layer_input,filters,f_size=4,stride=2,norm=True,
                name='d_layer'):
        with tf.variable_scope(name):
            if reuse:
                tf.get_variable_scope().reuse_variables()
            else:
                assert tf.get_variable_scope().reuse is False

            d =
            tf.contrib.layers.conv2d(layer_input,
                                     filters,kernel_size=f_size,
                                     stride=2, padding='SAME')
            if norm:
                d = tf.contrib.layers.batch_norm(d)
            d = lrelu(d,alpha=0.2)
            return d
    #64x64 -> 32x32
    down1 = d_layer(image,self.df, norm=False,name='down1')
    #32x32 -> 16x16
    down2 = d_layer(down1,self.df*2,name='down2')
    #16x16 -> 8x8
    down3 = d_layer(down2,self.df*4,name='down3')
    #8x8 -> 4x4
    down4 = d_layer(down3,self.df*8,name='down4')
    #4x4 -> 1x1
    down5  =
   tf.contrib.layers.conv2d(down4,1,kernel_size=4,stride=1,
                             padding='valid')
    return down5
```

The number of output feature maps in the different layers of the discriminator networks is either `self.df` or a multiple of it. For our network, we have taken `self.df` to be `64`.

Building the network and defining the cost functions

In this section, we are going to build the entire network using the generator and the discriminator functions and also define the cost function to be optimized during the training process. The TensorFlow code is as follows:

```
def build_network(self):
    def squared_loss(y_pred,labels):
        return tf.reduce_mean((y_pred - labels)**2)
   def abs_loss(y_pred,labels):
        return tf.reduce_mean(tf.abs(y_pred - labels))
   def binary_cross_entropy_loss(logits,labels):
        return tf.reduce_mean(tf.nn.sigmoid_cross_entropy_with_logits(
                                              labels=labels,logits=logits))
     self.images_real =
tf.placeholder(tf.float32,[None,self.image_size,self.image_size,self.input_
dim + self.output_dim])
    self.image_real_A = self.images_real[:,:,:,:self.input_dim]
    self.image_real_B =
    self.images_real[:,:,:,self.input_dim:self.input_dim + self.output_dim]
    self.images_fake_B =
    self.build_generator(self.image_real_A,
                         reuse=False,name='generator_AB')
    self.images_fake_A =
    self.build_generator(self.images_fake_B,
                         reuse=False,name='generator_BA')
    self.images_fake_A_ =
    self.build_generator(self.image_real_B,
                         reuse=True,name='generator_BA')
    self.images_fake_B_ =
    self.build_generator(self.images_fake_A_,
                         reuse=True,name='generator_AB')
    self.D_B_fake =
    self.build_discriminator(self.images_fake_B ,
                             reuse=False, name="discriminatorB")
    self.D_A_fake =
    self.build_discriminator(self.images_fake_A_,
                             reuse=False, name="discriminatorA")

    self.D_B_real =
    self.build_discriminator(self.image_real_B,
                             reuse=True, name="discriminatorB")
    self.D_A_real =
    self.build_discriminator(self.image_real_A,
                             reuse=True, name="discriminatorA")
```

```
    self.loss_GABA =
    self.lambda_l2*squared_loss(self.images_fake_A,self.image_real_A) +
    binary_cross_entropy_loss(labels=tf.ones_like(self.D_B_fake),
    logits=self.D_B_fake)
    self.loss_GBAB =
    self.lambda_l2*squared_loss(self.images_fake_B_,
    self.image_real_B) +
    binary_cross_entropy_loss(labels=tf.ones_like(self.D_A_fake),
    logits=self.D_A_fake)
    self.generator_loss = self.loss_GABA + self.loss_GBAB
    self.D_B_loss_real =
    binary_cross_entropy_loss(tf.ones_like(self.D_B_real),self.D_B_real)
    self.D_B_loss_fake =
    binary_cross_entropy_loss(tf.zeros_like(self.D_B_fake),self.D_B_fake)
    self.D_B_loss = (self.D_B_loss_real + self.D_B_loss_fake) / 2.0
    self.D_A_loss_real =
    binary_cross_entropy_loss(tf.ones_like(self.D_A_real),self.D_A_real)
    self.D_A_loss_fake =
    binary_cross_entropy_loss(tf.zeros_like(self.D_A_fake),self.D_A_fake)
    self.D_A_loss = (self.D_A_loss_real + self.D_A_loss_fake) / 2.0
    self.discriminator_loss = self.D_B_loss + self.D_A_loss
    self.loss_GABA_sum = tf.summary.scalar("g_loss_a2b", self.loss_GABA)
    self.loss_GBAB_sum = tf.summary.scalar("g_loss_b2a", self.loss_GBAB)
    self.g_total_loss_sum = tf.summary.scalar("g_loss",
self.generator_loss)
    self.g_sum = tf.summary.merge([self.loss_GABA_sum,
self.loss_GBAB_sum,self.g_total_loss_sum])
    self.loss_db_sum = tf.summary.scalar("db_loss", self.D_B_loss)
    self.loss_da_sum = tf.summary.scalar("da_loss", self.D_A_loss)
    self.loss_d_sum = tf.summary.scalar("d_loss",self.discriminator_loss)
    self.db_loss_real_sum = tf.summary.scalar("db_loss_real",
self.D_B_loss_real)
    self.db_loss_fake_sum = tf.summary.scalar("db_loss_fake",
self.D_B_loss_fake)
    self.da_loss_real_sum = tf.summary.scalar("da_loss_real",
self.D_A_loss_real)
    self.da_loss_fake_sum = tf.summary.scalar("da_loss_fake",
self.D_A_loss_fake)
    self.d_sum = tf.summary.merge(
          [self.loss_da_sum, self.da_loss_real_sum,
self.da_loss_fake_sum,
           self.loss_db_sum, self.db_loss_real_sum,
self.db_loss_fake_sum,
           self.loss_d_sum]
        )

    trainable_variables = tf.trainable_variables()
    self.d_variables =
```

```
[var for var in trainable_variables if 'discriminator' in var.name]
self.g_variables =
[var for var in trainable_variables if 'generator' in var.name]
print ('Variable printing start :'  )
for var in self.d_variables:
    print(var.name)
self.test_image_A =
tf.placeholder(tf.float32,[None, self.image_size,
               self.image_size,self.input_dim], name='test_A')
self.test_image_B =
tf.placeholder(tf.float32,[None, self.image_size,
               self.image_size,self.output_c_dim], name='test_B')
self.saver = tf.train.Saver()
```

In the build network, we first define the cost functions for an L2-normed error and a binary cross entropy error. The L2-normed error will be used as the reconstruction loss, while the binary cross entropy will be used as the discriminator loss. We then define the placeholder for the images in the two domains and also the TensorFlow ops for the fake images in each domain by using the generator function. We also define the ops for the discriminator output by passing the fake and real images that are specific to the domain. As well as this, we define the TensorFlow ops for the reconstructed images in each of the two domains.

Once the ops have been defined, we use them to compute the loss function considering the reconstruction loss of the images and the loss attributed to the discriminator. Note that we have used the same generator function to define the generator from domain A to B and also for the generator from B to A. The only thing that we have done differently is to provide different names to the two networks: `generator_AB` and `generator_BA`. Since the variable scope is defined as `name`, both these generators would have different sets of weights prefixed by the provided name.

The following table shows the different loss variables that we need to keep track of. All of these losses need to be minimized with respect to the parameters of the generators or the discriminators:

Variables for different Losses	**Description**
`self.D_B_loss_real`	The discriminator D_B binary cross entropy loss in classifying real images in domain B. (This loss is to be minimized with respect to the parameters of the discriminator D_B.)
`self.D_B_loss_fake`	The discriminator D_B binary cross entropy loss in classifying fake images in domain B. (This loss is to be minimized with respect to the parameters of the discriminator D_B.)

`self.D_A_loss_real`	The discriminator D_A binary cross entropy loss in classifying real images in domain A. (This loss is to be minimized with respect to the parameters of the discriminator D_A.)
`self.D_A_loss_fake`	The discriminator D_A binary cross entropy loss in classifying fake images in domain A. (This loss is to be minimized with respect to the parameters of the discriminator D_A.)
`self.loss_GABA`	The reconstruction loss of mapping an image in domain A to B and then back to A through the two generators G_{AB} and G_{BA}) plus the binary cross entropy of the fake images $G_{AB}(x_A)$ labeled as real images by discriminator in domain B. (This loss is to be minimized with respect to the parameters of the generators G_{AB} and G_{BA}.)
`self.loss_GBAB`	The reconstruction loss of mapping an image in domain B to A and then back to B through the two generators G_{BA} and G_{AB} plus binary cross entropy of fake images $G_{BA}(x_B)$ labeled as real images by discriminator in domain A. (This loss is to be minimized with respect to the parameters of the generators G_{AB} and G_{BA}.)

The first four losses make up the discriminator loss, which needs to be minimized with respect to the parameters of discriminators D_A and D_B. The last two losses make up the generator loss, which needs to be minimized with respect to the parameters of the generators G_{AB} and G_{BA}.

The loss variables are tied to TensorBoard through `tf.summary.scaler` so that these losses can be monitored during training to ensure that the losses are reducing in the desired manner. Later on, we will see how these loss traces look in TensorBoard while the training progresses.

Building the training process

In the `train_network` function, we first define the optimizers for both the generator and the discriminator loss functions. We use the Adam optimizer for both the generators and the discriminators, since this is an advanced version of the stochastic gradient descent optimizer that works really well in training GANs. Adam uses a decaying average of gradients, much like momentum for steady gradient, and a decaying average of squared gradients that provides information about the curvature of the cost function. The variables pertaining to the different losses defined by `tf.summary` are written to the log files and can therefore be monitored through TensorBoard. The following is the detailed code for the `train` function:

```
def train_network(self):
        self.learning_rate = tf.placeholder(tf.float32)
        self.d_optimizer =
tf.train.AdamOptimizer(self.learning_rate,beta1=self.beta1,beta2=self.beta2
).minimize(self.discriminator_loss,var_list=self.d_variables)
        self.g_optimizer =
tf.train.AdamOptimizer(self.learning_rate,beta1=self.beta1,beta2=self.beta2
).minimize(self.generator_loss,var_list=self.g_variables)
        self.init_op = tf.global_variables_initializer()
        self.sess = tf.Session()
        self.sess.run(self.init_op)
        #self.dataset_dir =
'/home/santanu/Downloads/DiscoGAN/edges2handbags/train/'
        self.writer = tf.summary.FileWriter("./logs", self.sess.graph)
        count = 1
        start_time = time.time()
        for epoch in range(self.epoch):
            data_A = os.listdir(self.dataset_dir + 'trainA/')
            data_B = os.listdir(self.dataset_dir + 'trainB/')
            data_A = [ (self.dataset_dir + 'trainA/' + str(file_name)) for
file_name in data_A ]

            data_B = [ (self.dataset_dir + 'trainB/' + str(file_name)) for
file_name in data_B ]
            np.random.shuffle(data_A)
            np.random.shuffle(data_B)
            batch_ids = min(min(len(data_A), len(data_B)), self.train_size)
// self.batch_size
            lr = self.l_r if epoch < self.epoch_step else
self.l_r*(self.epoch-epoch)/(self.epoch-self.epoch_step)
            for id_ in range(0, batch_ids):
                batch_files = list(zip(data_A[id_ * self.batch_size:(id_ +
1) * self.batch_size],
                                   data_B[id_ * self.batch_size:(id_ +
```

```
1) * self.batch_size]))
                batch_images = [load_train_data(batch_file, self.load_size,
self.fine_size) for batch_file in batch_files]
                batch_images = np.array(batch_images).astype(np.float32)
                    # Update G network and record fake outputs
                fake_A, fake_B, _, summary_str = self.sess.run(
[self.images_fake_A_,self.images_fake_B,self.g_optimizer,self.g_sum],
                        feed_dict={self.images_real: batch_images,
self.learning_rate:lr})
                self.writer.add_summary(summary_str, count)
                [fake_A,fake_B] = self.pool([fake_A, fake_B])
                    # Update D network
                _, summary_str = self.sess.run(
                        [self.d_optimizer,self.d_sum],
                        feed_dict={self.images_real: batch_images,
                               # self.fake_A_sample: fake_A,
                               # self.fake_B_sample: fake_B,
                                    self.learning_rate: lr})
                self.writer.add_summary(summary_str, count)
                count += 1
                print(("Epoch: [%2d] [%4d/%4d] time: %4.4f" % (
                        epoch, id_, batch_ids, time.time() - start_time)))
                if count % self.print_freq == 1:
                    self.sample_model(self.sample_dir, epoch, id_)
                if count % self.save_freq == 2:
                    self.save_model(self.checkpoint_dir, count)
```

As we can see at the end of the code, the `sample_model` function is invoked from time to time during training to check the quality of the images generated in a domain based on input images from the other domain. The model is also saved at regular intervals, based on `save_freq`.

The `sample_model` function and the `save_model` function that we referred to in the previous code are illustrated here for reference:

```
def sample_model(self, sample_dir, epoch, id_):
    if not os.path.exists(sample_dir):
        os.makedirs(sample_dir)
    data_A = os.listdir(self.dataset_dir + 'trainA/')
    data_B = os.listdir(self.dataset_dir + 'trainB/')
    data_A = [ (self.dataset_dir + 'trainA/' + str(file_name)) for
              file_name in data_A ]
    data_B = [ (self.dataset_dir + 'trainB/' + str(file_name)) for
              file_name in data_B ]
   np.random.shuffle(data_A)
    np.random.shuffle(data_B)
    batch_files =
```

```
        list(zip(data_A[:self.batch_size], data_B[:self.batch_size]))
        sample_images =
        [load_train_data(batch_file, is_testing=True) for
         batch_file in batch_files]
        sample_images = np.array(sample_images).astype(np.float32)

        fake_A, fake_B = self.sess.run(
                [self.images_fake_A_,self.images_fake_B],
                feed_dict={self.images_real: sample_images}
            )
        save_images(fake_A, [self.batch_size, 1],
                        './{}/A_{:02d}_{:04d}.jpg'.format(sample_dir, epoch,
    id_))
        save_images(fake_B, [self.batch_size, 1],
                        './{}/B_{:02d}_{:04d}.jpg'.format(sample_dir, epoch,
    id_))
```

In this `sample_model` function, randomly selected images from domain A are taken and fed to the generator G_{AB} to produce images in domain B. Similarly, randomly selected images from domain B are fed to the generator G_{BA} to produce images in domain A. These output images are generated by the two generators over different epochs, and batches are saved in a sample folder to see if the generators are improving over time in the training process to produce a better image quality.

The `save_model` function that uses the TensorFlow saver capabilities for saving models is shown as follows:

```
    def save_model(self,checkpoint_dir,step):
        model_name = "discogan.model"
        model_dir = "%s_%s" % (self.dataset_dir, self.image_size)
        checkpoint_dir = os.path.join(checkpoint_dir, model_dir)
        if not os.path.exists(checkpoint_dir):
            os.makedirs(checkpoint_dir)
        self.t(self.sess,
                        os.path.join(checkpoint_dir, model_name),
                        global_step=step)
```

Important parameter values for GAN training

In this section, we will discuss the different parameter values that are used for training the DiscoGAN. These are presented in the following table:

Parameter name	Variable name and Value set	Rationale
Learning rate for Adam optimizer	`self.l_r = 2e-4`	We should always train a GAN network with a low learning rate for better stability and a DiscoGAN is no different.
Decay rates for Adam optimizer	`self.beta1 = 0.5` `self.beta2 = 0.99`	The parameter `beta1` defines the decaying average of gradients, while the parameter `beta2` defines the decaying average of the square of the gradients.
Epochs	`self.epoch = 200`	`200` epochs is good enough for the convergence of the DiscoGAN network in this implementation.
Batch size	`self.batch_size = 64`	A batch size of `64` works well for this implementation. However, because of resource constraint, we may have to chose a smaller batch size.
Epoch beyond which learning rate falls linearly	`epoch_step = 10`	After the number of epochs specified by `epoch_step`, the learning rate falls linearly, as determined by the following scheme: `lr = self.l_r if epoch < self.epoch_step else self.l_r*(self.epoch-epoch)/(self.epoch-self.epoch_step)`

Invoking the training

All the functions we illustrated previously are created inside a `DiscoGAN()` class with the important parameter values declared in the `__init__` function, as shown in the following code block that follows. The only two parameters that needs to be passed while training the network are the `dataset_dir` and the number of `epochs` for which the training needs to be run

```
def __init__(self,dataset_dir,epochs=200):
    # Input shape
    self.dataset_dir = dataset_dir
    self.lambda_l2 = 1.0
    self.image_size = 64
    self.input_dim = 3
    self.output_dim = 3
    self.batch_size = 64
    self.df = 64
    self.gf = 64
    self.channels = 3
```

```
        self.output_c_dim = 3
        self.l_r = 2e-4
        self.beta1 = 0.5
        self.beta2 = 0.99
        self.weight_decay = 0.00001
        self.epoch = epochs
        self.train_size = 10000
        self.epoch_step = 10
        self.load_size = 64
        self.fine_size = 64
        self.checkpoint_dir = 'checkpoint'
        self.sample_dir = 'sample'
        self.print_freq = 5
        self.save_freq = 10
        self.pool = ImagePool()
        return None
```

Now that we have defined everything required to train the model, we can invoke the training through a `process_main` function as follows:

```
    def process_main(self):
        self.build_network()
        self.train_network()
```

The end to end code that we have illustrated previously for the training is in the script `cycledGAN_edges_to_bags.py`. We can train the model by running the python script `cycledGAN_edges_to_bags.py` as follows:

```
python cycledGAN_edges_to_bags.py process_main  --dataset_dir
/media/santanu/9eb9b6dc-b380-486e-b4fd-c424a325b976/edges2handbags/ epochs
100
```

The output log of the script `cycledGAN_edges_to_bags.py` execution is as follows:

```
Epoch: [ 0] [ 0/ 156] time: 3.0835
Epoch: [ 0] [ 1/ 156] time: 3.9093
Epoch: [ 0] [ 2/ 156] time: 4.3661
Epoch: [ 0] [ 3/ 156] time: 4.8208
Epoch: [ 0] [ 4/ 156] time: 5.2821
Epoch: [ 0] [ 5/ 156] time: 6.2380
Epoch: [ 0] [ 6/ 156] time: 6.6960
Epoch: [ 0] [ 7/ 156] time: 7.1528
Epoch: [ 0] [ 8/ 156] time: 7.6138
Epoch: [ 0] [ 9/ 156] time: 8.0732
Epoch: [ 0] [ 10/ 156] time: 8.8163
Epoch: [ 0] [ 11/ 156] time: 9.6669
Epoch: [ 0] [ 12/ 156] time: 10.1256
Epoch: [ 0] [ 13/ 156] time: 10.5846
Epoch: [ 0] [ 14/ 156] time: 11.0427
Epoch: [ 0] [ 15/ 156] time: 11.9135
Epoch: [ 0] [ 16/ 156] time: 12.3712
Epoch: [ 0] [ 17/ 156] time: 12.8290
Epoch: [ 0] [ 18/ 156] time: 13.2899
Epoch: [ 0] [ 19/ 156] time: 13.7525
.......
```

Monitoring the generator and the discriminator loss

The loss can be monitored in the TensorBoard dashboard. The TensorBoard dashboard can be invoked as follows:

1. From the terminal, run the following command:

   ```
   tensorboard --logdir=./logs
   ```

   `./logs` is the destination where the Tensorboard logs specific to the program are stored and should be defined in the program as follows:

```
self.writer = tf.summary.FileWriter("./logs", self.sess.graph)
```

2. Once the command in step 1 is executed, navigate to the `localhost:6006` site for TensorBoard:

   Illustrated in the following screenshot are a few traces of the generator and discriminator losses as viewed in TensorBoard during the training of the DiscoGAN implemented in the project:

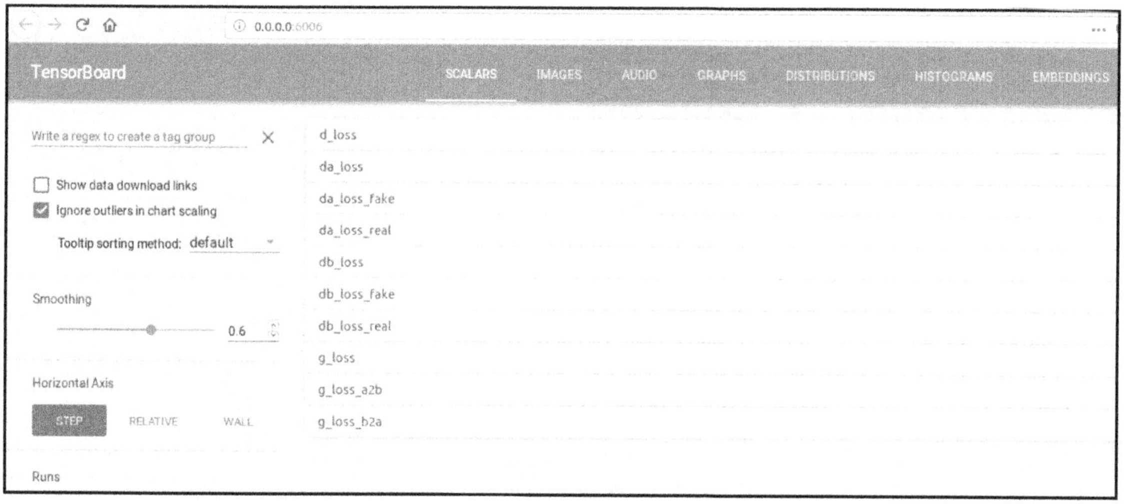

Figure 4.2: Tensorboard Scalars section containing the traces for different losses

The following screenshot shows the loss components of the discriminator in Domain A as the training progresses:

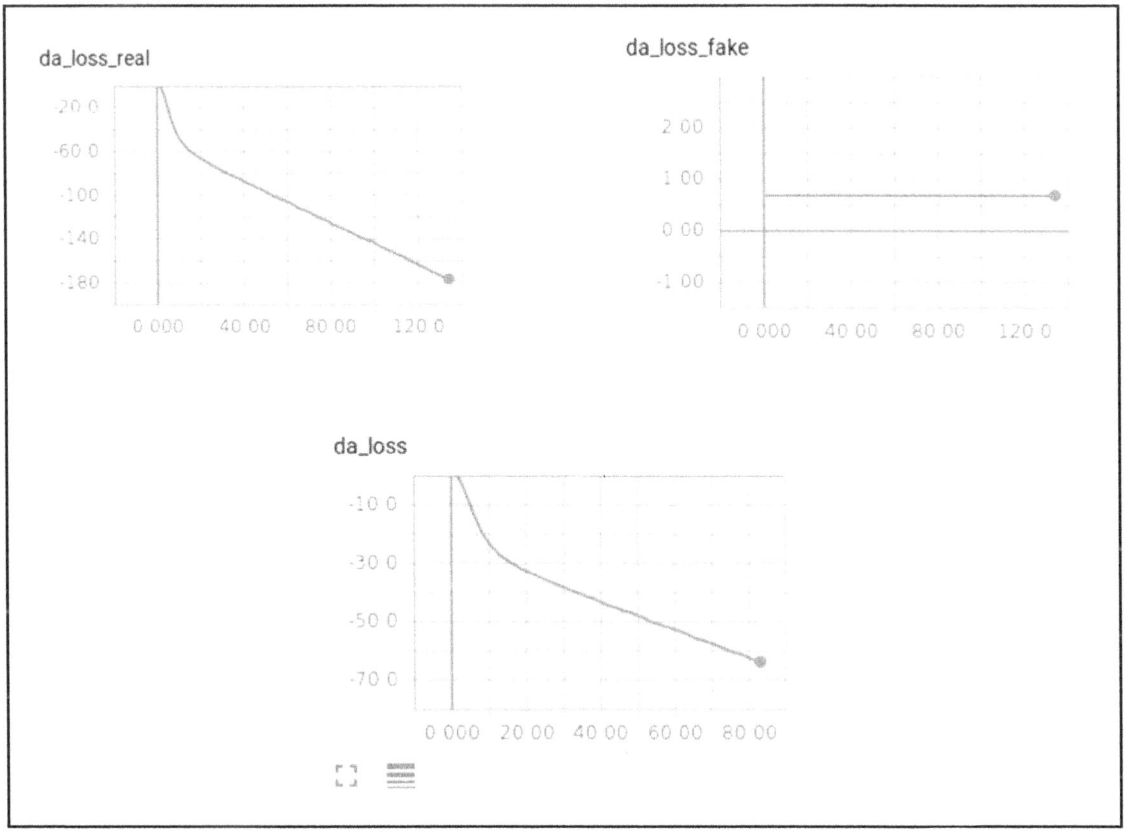

Figure 4.3: Losses of discriminator in domain A

From the preceding screenshot, we can see the losses of the discriminator in domain A over the different batches. The `da_loss` is the sum of the `da_loss_real` and `da_loss_fake` losses. The `da_loss_real` decreases steadily, since the discriminator readily learns to identify real images in domain A while the loss for the fake images is held steady at around 0.69, which is the `logloss` you can expect when a binary classifier outputs a class with 1/2 probability. This happens because the generator is also learning simultaneously to make the fake images look realistic, therefore making it tough for the discriminator to easily classify the generator images as fake. The loss profiles for the discriminator at domain B look similar to the ones illustrated in the previous screenshot for domain A.

Let's now take a look at the loss profiles for the generators, as shown here:

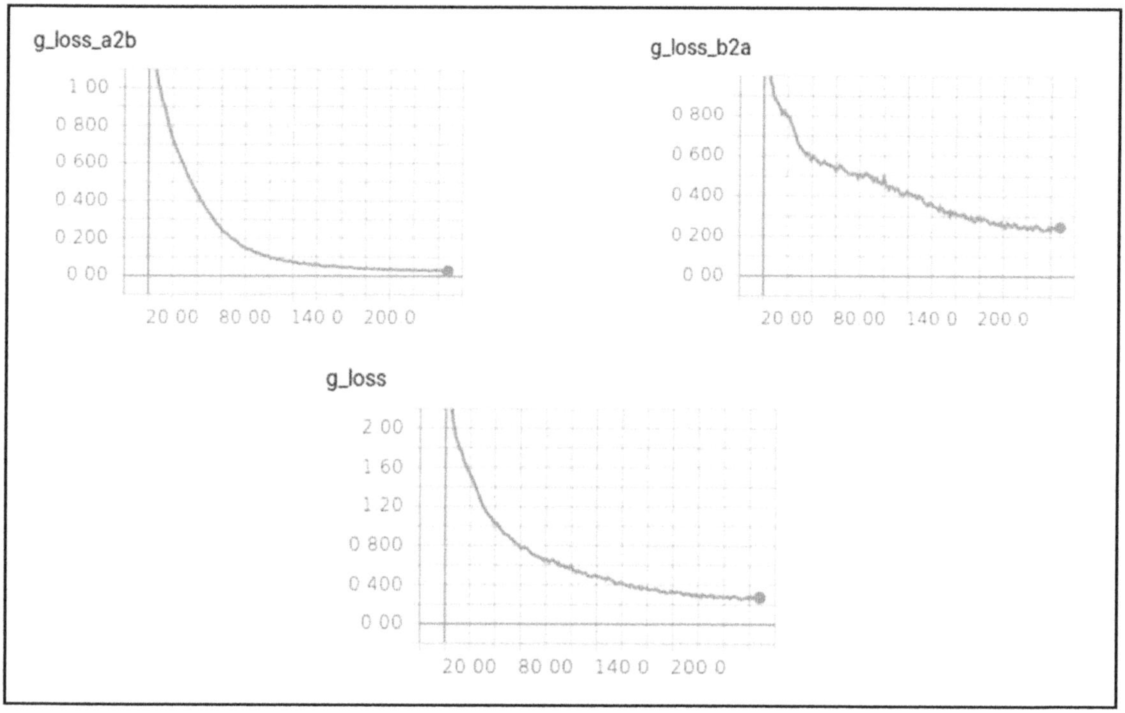

Figure 4.4: Loss profiles for the generators of the DiscoGAN

The `g_loss_a2b` is the combined generator loss of reconstructing an image from domain A to domain B and back and also the binary cross entropy loss associated with making the transformed image look realistic in the domain of B. Similarly, `g_loss_b2a` is the combined generator loss of reconstructing an image from domain B to domain A and back and also the binary cross entropy loss associated with making the transformed image look realistic in the domain of A. Both these loss profiles, along with their sum, which is `g_loss`, have a steady loss decrease as the batches progress, as we can see from the TensorBoard visuals in the previous screenshot.

Since training generative adversarial networks is generally quite tricky, it makes sense to monitor the progress of their loss profiles to understand whether the training is proceeding as desired.

Sample images generated by DiscoGAN

As we come to the end of the chapter, let's look at some of the images that were generated by the DiscoGAN in both domains:

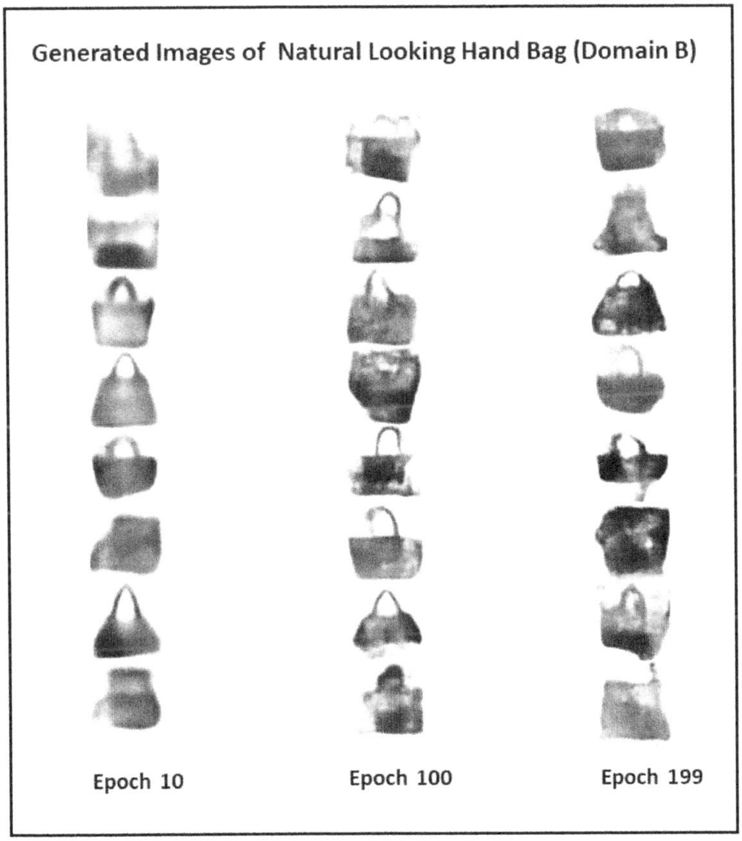

Figure 4.5: Handbag images generated given the sketches

The following screenshot contains the **Generated Images of Hand Bag Sketches (Domain A)**:

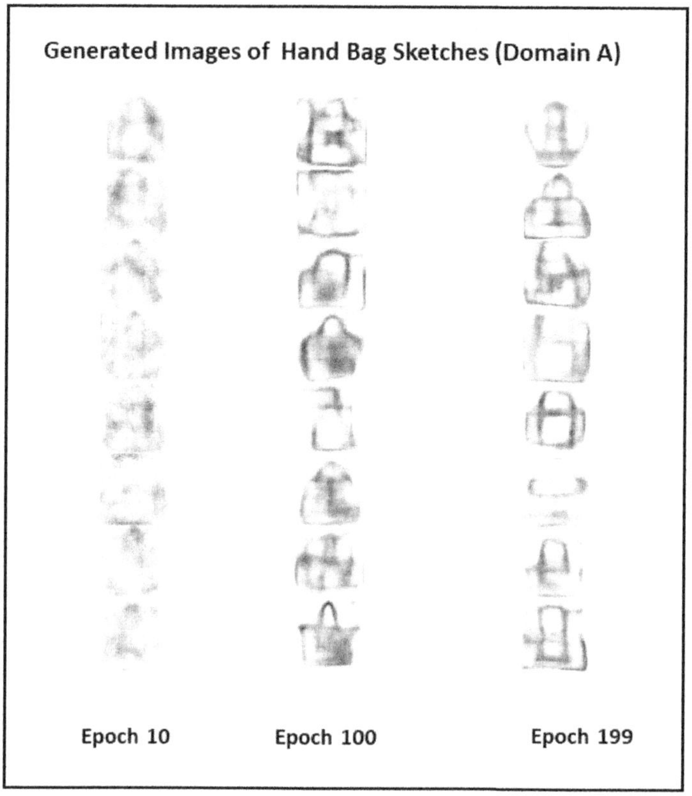

Figure 4.6: Sketches generated given the handbag images

We can see that the DiscoGAN has done a great job of converting images in either domain to high quality realistic images in the other domain.

Summary

We have now come to the end of this chapter. You should now be well-versed with the technicalities and the implementation intricacies of a DiscoGAN. The concepts we explored in this chapter can be used to implement varieties of generative adversarial networks with subtle changes that are appropriate to the problem in hand. The end-to-end implementation of this DiscoGAN network is located in the GitHub repository, at `https://github.com/PacktPublishing/Intelligent-Projects-using-Python/tree/master/Chapter04`.

In `Chapter 5`, *Video Captioning Application*, we are going to look at video-to-text translation applications, which fall under the category of expert systems in artificial intelligence.

5
Video Captioning Application

As the rate of video production increases at an exponential rate, videos have become an important medium of communication. However, videos remain inaccessible to a larger audience because of a lack of proper captioning.

Video captioning, the art of translating a video to generate a meaningful summary of the content, is a challenging task in the field of computer vision and machine learning. Traditional methods of video captioning haven't produced many success stories. However, with the recent boost in artificial intelligence aided by deep learning, video captioning has recently gained a significant amount of attention. The power of convolutional neural networks, along with recurrent neural networks, has made it possible to build end-to-end enterprise-level video-captioning systems. Convolutional neural networks process the image frames in the video to extract important features, which are processed by the recurrent neural networks sequentially to generate a meaningful summary of the video. A few important applications of video captioning systems are as follows:

- Automatic surveillance of industrial plants for safety measures
- Clustering of videos based on their content derived through video captioning
- Better security systems in banks, hospitals, and other public places
- Video searching in websites for a better user experience

Building an intelligent video-captioning system through deep learning requires primarily two types of data: videos and captions in text that act as the labels for training the end-to-end system.

As part of this chapter we are going to discuss the following:

- Discuss the roles of CNN and LSTM in video captioning
- Explore the architecture of a sequence-to-sequence video captioning system
- Build a video captioning system leveraging the *sequence-to-sequence—video to text* architecture

In the next section, we will go through how convolutional neural networks and the LSTM version of recurrent neural networks can be used to build an end-to-end video captioning system.

Technical requirements

You will require to have basic knowledge of Python 3, TensorFlow, Keras and OpenCV.

The code files of this chapter can be found on GitHub:
`https://github.com/PacktPublishing/Intelligent-Projects-using-Python/tree/master/Chapter05`

Check out the following video to see the code in action:
`http://bit.ly/2BeXK1c`

CNNs and LSTMs in video captioning

A video minus the audio can be thought of as a collection of images arranged in a sequential manner. The important features from those images can be extracted using a convolutional neural network trained on specific image classification problems, such as **ImageNet**. The activations of the last fully connected layer of a pre-trained network can be used to derive features from the sequentially sampled images from the video. The frequency rate at which to sample the images sequentially from the video depends on the type of content in the video and can be optimized through training.

Illustrated in the following diagram (*Figure 5.1*) is a pre-trained neural network used for extracting features from a video:

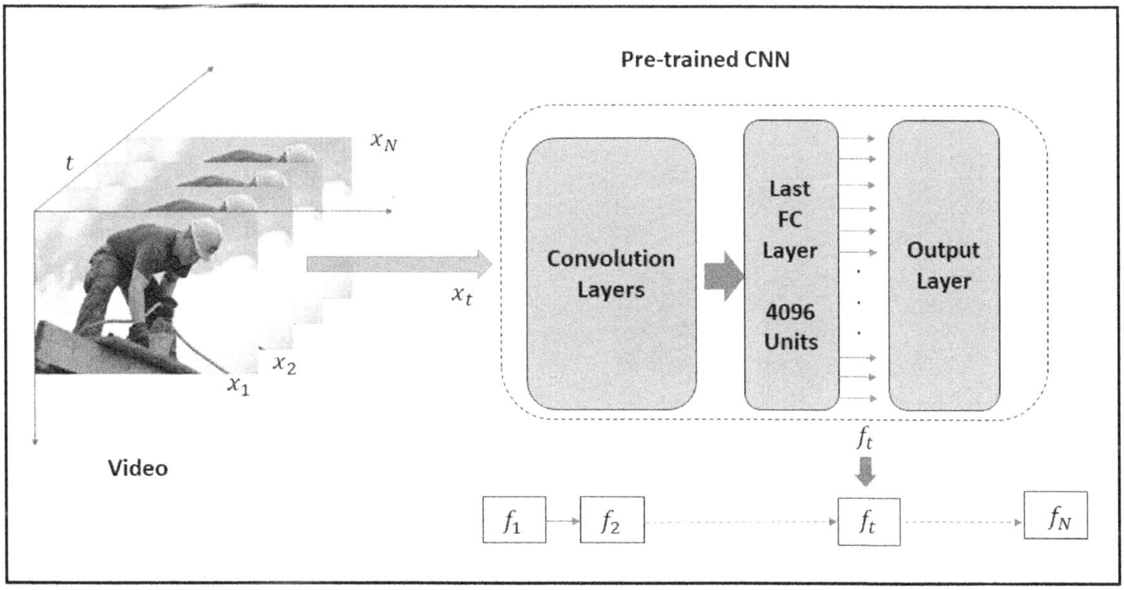

Figure 5.1: Video image feature extraction using pre-trained neural networks

As we can see from the preceding diagram, the sequentially sampled images from the video are passed through a pre-trained convolutional neural network and the activations of the `4,096` units in the last fully connected layer are taken as an output. If the video image at time t is represented as x_t and the output at the last fully connected layer is represented by $f_t \in R^{4096}$ then $f_t = f_w(x_t)$. Here, W represents the weights of the convolution neural network up to the last fully connected layer.

These series of output features $f_1, f_2, \ldots f_t \ldots f_N$ can be fed as inputs to a recurrent neural network that learns to generate text captions based on the input features, as illustrated in the following diagram (*Figure 5.2*):

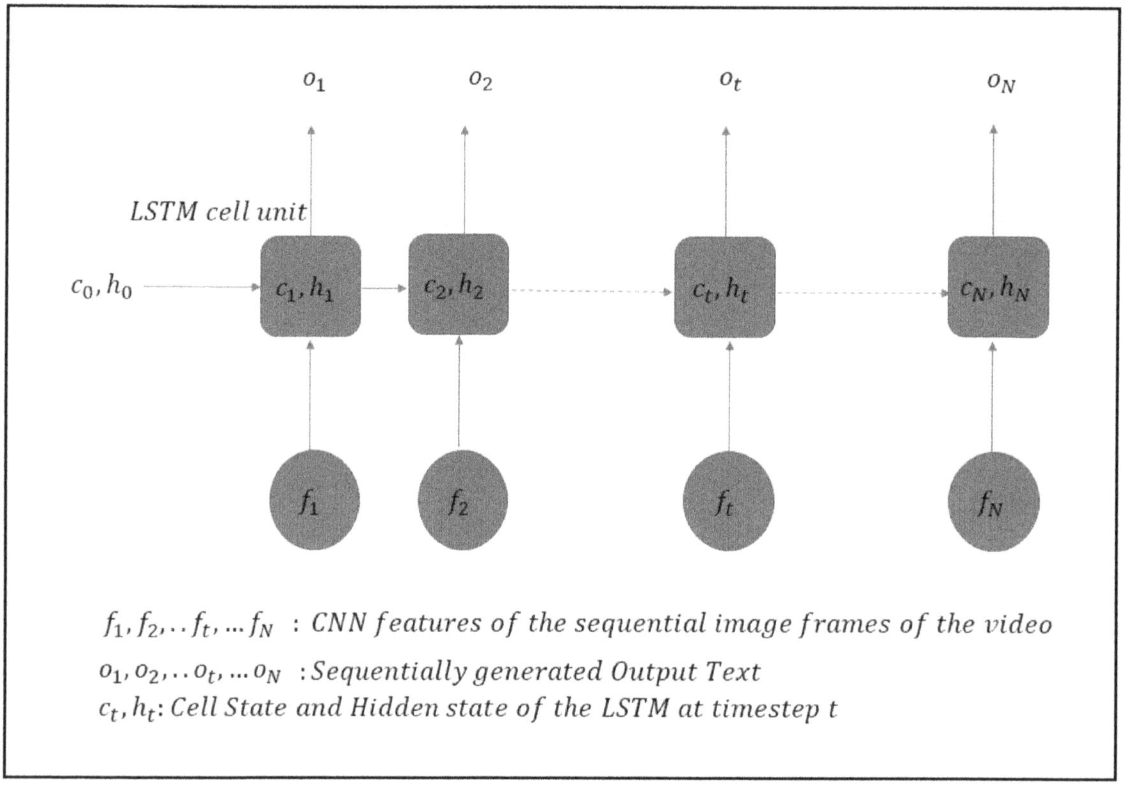

Figure 5.2: LSTM in the processing of the sequential input features from CNN

As we can see from the preceding diagram, the generated features $f_1, f_2, \ldots f_t \ldots f_N$ from the pre-trained convolutional neural is processed sequentially by the LSTM to produce the text outputs $o_1, o_2, \ldots o_t \ldots o_N$, which are the text captions for the given video. For instance, the caption for the video in the preceding diagram could be *A man in a yellow helmet is working*:

o1, o2, ... ot . . . oN = { "A ","man" "in" "a" "yellow" "helmet" "is" "working"}

Now that we have a good idea of how video captioning works in a deep-learning framework, let's discuss a more advanced video-captioning network called *sequence-to-sequence video captioning* in the next section. We will be using the same network architecture in this chapter for building a *Video-captioning system.*

A sequence-to-sequence video-captioning system

The sequence-to-sequence architecture is based on a paper called **sequence to sequence—Video to Text** authored by Subhashini Venugopalan, Marcus Rohrbach, Jeff Donahue, Raymond Mooney, Trevor Darrell, and Kate Saenko. The paper can be located at `https://arxiv.org/pdf/1505.00487.pdf`.

In the following diagram (*Figure 5.3*), a *sequence-to-sequence video-captioning* neural network architecture based on the preceding paper is illustrated:

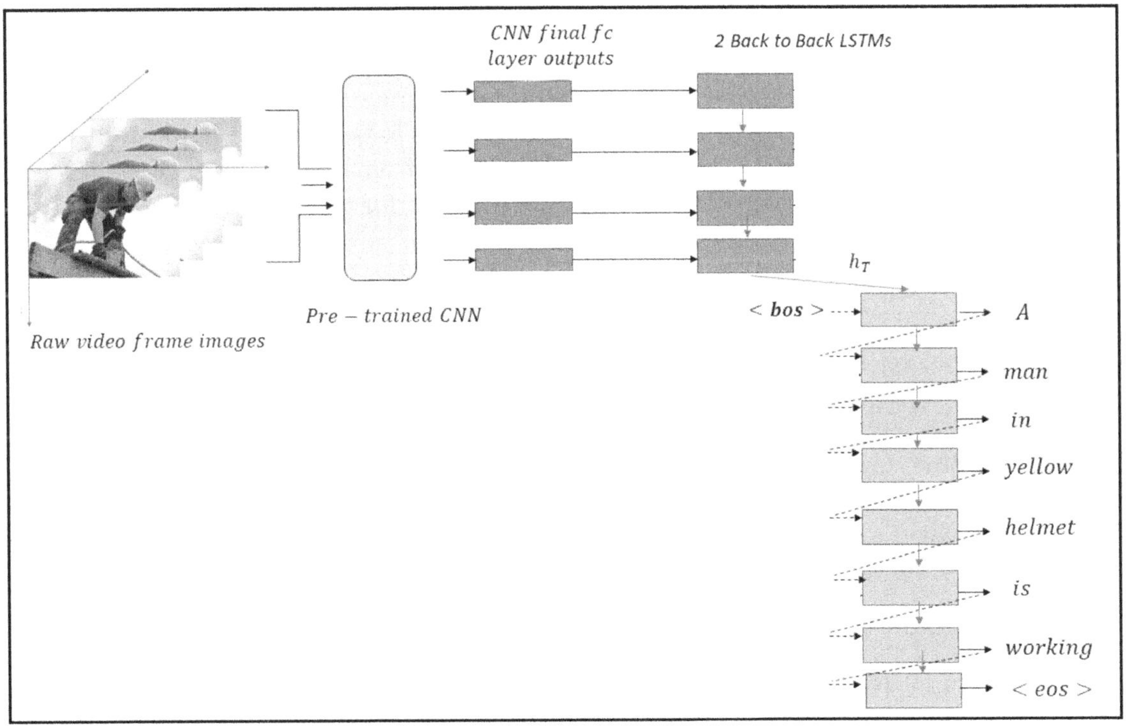

Figure 5.3: Sequence-to-sequence video-captioning network architecture

The sequence-to-sequence model processes the video image frames through a pre-trained convolutional neural network as before and the output activations of the last fully connected layer are taken as the features to be fed to the LSTMs that follow. If we denote the output activations of the last fully connected layer of the pre-trained convolutional neural network at time step *t* as $f_t \in R^{4096}$, then we would have *N* such feature vectors for the *N* image frames from the video. These *N* feature vectors $f1, f2, \ldots\ldots f_t \ldots f_N$ are fed to the LSTMs in sequence to generate the text caption.

There are two LSTMs back to back, and the number of sequences in the LSTMs is the sum of the number of image frames from the video and the maximum length of the text captions in the captions vocabulary. If the network is trained on *N* image frames of the video and the maximum text caption length in the vocabulary is *M* then the LSTMs are trained on *(N+M)* time steps. In the *N* time steps, the first LSTM processes the feature vectors $f1, f2, \ldots\ldots f_t \ldots f_N$ sequentially, and the hidden states generated by it are fed to the second LSTM. No text output target is required by the second LSTM in these *N* time steps. If we represent the hidden state of the first LSTM at time step *t* as h_t, the input to the second LSTM for the first *N* time steps is h_t. Do note that the input to the first LSTM from the N+1 time step is zero padded so that the input has no effect of the hidden state h_t for $t > N$. Do note that this doesn't guarantee that the hidden state h_t for t > N is always going to be same. In fact we can chose to feed h_t as h_T to the second LSTM for any time step $t > N$.

From the *(N+1)* time step, the second LSTM requires a text output target. The input to it at any time step $t > N$ is $[h_t, w_{t-1}]$, where h_t is the hidden state of the first LSTM at time step *t* and w_{t-1} is the text caption word at time step *(t-1)*.

At the *(N+1)* time step, the word w_N fed to the second LSTM is the start of sentence denoted by `<bos>`. The network is trained to stop generating caption words once the end of sentence symbol `<eos>` is generated. To summarize, the two LSTMs are set up in such a way that they start producing text caption words once they have processed all the video image frame features $[f_t]_{i=1}^{N}$.

One of the other ways to handle the second LSTM input for time step $t > N$ is to just feed $[w_{t-1}]$ instead of $[h_t, w_{t-1}]$ and pass on the hidden and cell state of the first LSTM at time step *T* that is $[h_T, c_T]$ to the initial hidden and the cell state of the second LSTM. The architecture of such a video captioning network can be illustrated as follows (see *Figure 5.4*):

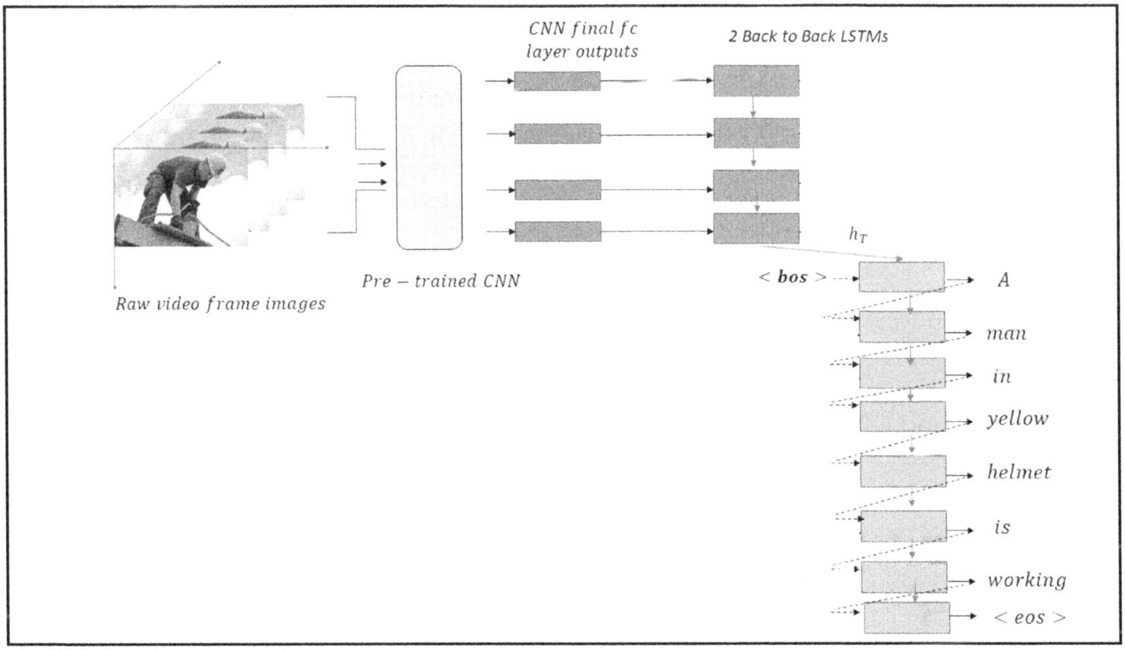

Figure 5.4: An alternate architecture for sequence to sequence model

The pre-trained convolution neural networks are generally of a common architecture such as `VGG16`, `VGG19`, `ResNet` and are pre-trained on ImageNet. However, we can retrain these architectures based on images extracted from videos in the domain for which we are building the video captioning system. We can also choose a completely new CNN architecture and train it on the video images specific to the domain.

So far, we have covered all the technical pre-requisites to develop a video-captioning system using the sequence-to-sequence architecture illustrated in this section. Do note that the alternate architectural designs suggested in this section are to encourage the readers to experiment with several designs and see which one works best for a given problem and dataset.

From the next section onward, we work towards building the intelligent video caption system.

Data for the video-captioning system

We build the video-captioning system by training the model on the `MSVD dataset`—a pre captioned YouTube video repository from Microsoft. The required data can be downloaded from the following link: `http://www.cs.utexas.edu/users/ml/clamp/videoDescription/YouTubeClips.tar`. The text captions for the videos are available at the following link: `https://github.com/jazzsaxmafia/video_to_sequence/files/387979/video_corpus.csv.zip`.

There are around `1,938` videos in the `MSVD dataset`. We will use these to train the *sequence-to- sequence video-captioning system*. Also note that we would be building the model on the sequence to sequence model illustrated in *Figure 5.3*. However readers are advised to try and train a model on the architecture presented in *Figure 5.4* and see how it fares.

Processing video images to create CNN features

Once we have downloaded the data from the specified location, the next task is to process the video image frames to extract features out of the last fully connected layers of a pre-trained convolutional neural network. We use a `VGG16` convolutional neural network that is pre-trained on ImageNet. We take the activations out of the last fully connected layer of the `VGG16`. Since the last fully connected layer of `VGG16` has `4096` units, our feature vector f_t for each time step t is a `4096`, dimensional vector that is $f_t \in R^{4096}$.

Before the images from the videos can be processed through the `VGG16`, they need to be sampled from the video. We sample images from the video in such a way that each video has `80` frames. After processing the `80` image frames from `VGG16`, each video will have `80` feature vectors $f1, f2, \ldots\ldots f_t \ldots f_{80}$. These features will be fed to the LSTMs to generate the text sequences. We use the pre-trained`VGG16` model in Keras. We create a `VideoCaptioningPreProcessing` class which first extracts `80` video frames as images from each video through the function `video_to_frames` and then those video frames are processed by a pre-trained `VGG16` convolutional neural network in the function `extract_feats_pretrained_cnn`.

The output of the `extract_feats_pretrained_cnn` are the CNN features of dimension `4096` for each video frame. Since we are dealing with `80` frames per video we would have `80` such `4096` dimensional vectors for each video.

The `video_to_frames` function can be coded as follows:

```
    def video_to_frames(self,video):
        with open(os.devnull, "w") as ffmpeg_log:
            if os.path.exists(self.temp_dest):
                print(" cleanup: " + self.temp_dest + "/")
                shutil.rmtree(self.temp_dest)
            os.makedirs(self.temp_dest)
            video_to_frames_cmd = ["ffmpeg",'-y','-i', video,
                                   '-vf', "scale=400:300",
                                   '-qscale:v', "2",
'{0}/%06d.jpg'.format(self.temp_dest)]
            subprocess.call(video_to_frames_cmd,
                            stdout=ffmpeg_log, stderr=ffmpeg_log)
```

From the preceding code, we can see that in the `video_to_frames` function, the `ffmpeg` tool is used to convert the video-to-image frames in JPEG format. The dimension specified to `ffmpeg` for the image frames is `300 x 400`. For more information on the `ffmpeg` tool, please refer to the following link: `https://www.ffmpeg.org/`.

The pre-trained CNN model to extract the features out of the last fully connected layer has been set up in the `extract_feats_pretrained_cnnfunction`. The code for the function is as follows:

```
# Extract the features from the pre-trained CNN
    def extract_feats_pretrained_cnn(self):

        model = self.model_cnn_load()
        print('Model loaded')

        if not os.path.isdir(self.feat_dir):
            os.mkdir(self.feat_dir)
        #print("save video feats to %s" % (self.dir_feat))
        video_list = glob.glob(os.path.join(self.video_dest, '*.avi'))
        #print video_list

        for video in tqdm(video_list):

            video_id = video.split("/")[-1].split(".")[0]
            print(f'Processing video {video}')

            #self.dest = 'cnn_feat' + '_' + video_id
            self.video_to_frames(video)

            image_list =
            sorted(glob.glob(os.path.join(self.temp_dest, '*.jpg')))
            samples = np.round(np.linspace(
```

```
            0, len(image_list) - 1,self.frames_step))
        image_list = [image_list[int(sample)] for sample in samples]
        images =
        np.zeros((len(image_list),self.img_dim,self.img_dim,
                 self.channels))
        for i in range(len(image_list)):
            img = self.load_image(image_list[i])
            images[i] = img
        images = np.array(images)
        fc_feats = model.predict(images,batch_size=self.batch_cnn)
        img_feats = np.array(fc_feats)
        outfile = os.path.join(self.feat_dir, video_id + '.npy')
        np.save(outfile, img_feats)
        # cleanup
        shutil.rmtree(self.temp_dest)
```

We first load the pre-trained CNN model using the `model_cnn_load` function and then for each video we extract several video frames as images using the `video_to_frames` function based on the sampling frequency specified to `ffmpeg`. We don't process all the image frames from the video created through `ffmpeg`, but instead we have taken `80` equally spaced image frames using the `np.linspace` function. The images generated by `ffmpeg` are resized to a spatial dimension of `224 x 224` using the `load_image` function. Finally these resized images are passed through the pre-trained VGG16 Convolutional Neural Network (CNN) and the output of the last fully connected layer prior to the output layer is extracted as features . These extracted feature vectors are stored in `numpy` arrays and are processed by the LSTM network in the next stage to produce video captions. The function `model_cnn_load` function defined in this section are defined as follows:

```
    def model_cnn_load(self):
            model = VGG16(weights = "imagenet", include_top=True,input_shape =
  (self.img_dim,self.img_dim,self.channels))
            out = model.layers[-2].output
            model_final = Model(input=model.input,output=out)
            return model_final
```

As can be seen from the preceding code, we are loading a `VGG16` convolutional neural network pre-trained on ImageNet and we are extracting the output of the second last layer(indexed as `-2`) as our feature vector of dimension `4096`.

The image read and resize function `load_image` that processes the raw `ffmpeg` images before feeding to the CNN is defined as follows:

```
    def load_image(self,path):
        img = cv2.imread(path)
        img = cv2.resize(img,(self.img_dim,self.img_dim))
        return img
```

The pre-processing script can be run by invoking the following command:

```
python VideoCaptioningPreProcessing.py process_main --video_dest
'/media/santanu/9eb9b6dc-b380-486e-b4fd-c424a325b976/Video
Captioning/data/' --feat_dir '/media/santanu/9eb9b6dc-b380-486e-b4fd-
c424a325b976/Video Captioning/features/' --temp_dest
'/media/santanu/9eb9b6dc-b380-486e-b4fd-c424a325b976/Video
Captioning/temp/' --img_dim 224 --channels 3 --batch_size=128 --frames_step
80
```

The output of this pre-processing step are `80` feature vectors of dimension `4096` written as a numpy array object of extension `npy`. Each video would have its own `numpy` array object stored in the `feat_dir`. The pre-processing step runs for around 28 mins as we can see from the log as follows:

```
Processing video /media/santanu/9eb9b6dc-b380-486e-b4fd-c424a325b976/Video
Captioning/data/jmoT2we_rqo_0_5.avi
100%|████████████████████████████████████████████████████████████████████| 1967/1970 [27:57<00:02, 1.09it/s]Processing video
/media/santanu/9eb9b6dc-b380-486e-b4fd-c424a325b976/Video
Captioning/data/NKtfKR4GNjU_0_20.avi
100%|████████████████████████████████████████████████████████████████████| 1968/1970 [27:58<00:02, 1.11s/it]Processing video
/media/santanu/9eb9b6dc-b380-486e-b4fd-c424a325b976/Video
Captioning/data/4cgzdXlJksU_83_90.avi
100%|████████████████████████████████████████████████████████████████████| 1969/1970 [27:59<00:01, 1.08s/it]Processing video
/media/santanu/9eb9b6dc-b380-486e-b4fd-c424a325b976/Video
Captioning/data/0IDJG0q9j_k_1_24.avi
100%|████████████████████████████████████████████████████████████████████| 1970/1970 [28:00<00:00, 1.06s/it]
28.045 min: VideoCaptioningPreProcessing
```

In the next section we deal with the pre-processing of the labelled captions of the video.

Processing the labelled captions of the video

The `corpus.csv` file contains the description of the videos in the form of text captions (see *Figure 5.5*). A snippet of the data is shown in the following screenshot. We can remove a few `[VideoID,Start,End]` combination records and treat these as test files for evaluation later on:

	A	B	C	D	E	F	G	
1	VideoID	Start	End	WorkerID	Source	AnnotationTime	Language	Description
2								
3	mv89psg6zh4	33	46	588702	unverified	55	Slovene	Papagaj se umiva pod tekočo vodo v lijaku.
4								
5	mv89psg6zh4	33	46	588702	unverified	37	Slovene	Papagaj se umiva pod tekočo vodo v lijaku.
6								
7	mv89psg6zh4	33	46	362812	unverified	11	Macedonian	папагал се бања
8								
9	mv89psg6zh4	33	46	968828	unverified	84	German	Ein Wellensittich duscht unter einem Wasserhahn.
10								
11	mv89psg6zh4	33	46	203142	unverified	14	Romanian	o pasare sta intr-o chiuveta.
12								
13	mv89psg6zh4	33	46	984231	unverified	35	Romanian	Un papagal se spala intr-o chiuveta.
14								
15	mv89psg6zh4	33	46	130914	unverified	24	Georgian	თუთიყურში რაკონაში სველდება
16								
17	mv89psg6zh4	33	46	130914	unverified	19	Georgian	თუთიყურში სველდება რაკონაში
18								
19	mv89psg6zh4	33	46	400189	unverified	23	Serbian	Papagaj se tušira u sudoperu.
20								
21	mv89psg6zh4	33	46	589431	unverified	66	Serbian	Papagaj biva kvašen u sudoperi vodom koja curi iz česme.
22								
23	mv89psg6zh4	33	46	767031	unverified	31	Serbian	Papagaj se tušira u sudoperi.
24								
25	mv89psg6zh4	33	46	649244	unverified	19	Serbian	Papagaj pije vodu u sudoperu
26								
27	mv89psg6zh4	33	46	180998	unverified	19	French	Un oiseau boit.
28								
29	mv89psg6zh4	33	46	197912	unverified	18	Gujarati	કબુતર નળ નીચે નહાય છે
30								
31	mv89psg6zh4	33	46	339861	unverified	52	Hindi	एक तोता नहा रहा है.
32								
33	mv89psg6zh4	33	46	818922	unverified	253	Hindi	बेसन वश में कुछ पढ़ा है.
34								
35	mv89psg6zh4	33	46	161492	unverified	34	Hindi	तोता नहातअ हे
36								
37	mv89psg6zh4	33	46	797651	unverified	27	Hindi	थूथ नहा रहा हे
38								
39	mv89psg6zh4	33	46	682611	clean	66	English	A bird in a sink keeps getting under the running water from a faucet.
40								
41	mv89psg6zh4	33	46	760882	clean	16	English	A bird is bathing in a sink.
42								
43	mv89psg6zh4	33	46	878566	clean	76	English	A bird is splashing around under a running faucet.

Figure 5.5: A snapshot of the format of the captions file

The `VideoID`, `Start` and `End` columns combine to form the video name in the following format: `VideoID_Start_End.avi`. Based on the video name, the features from the convolutional neural network `VGG16` has been stored as `VideoID_Start_End.npy`. Illustrated in the following code block is the function to process the text captions for the video and create the path cross reference to the video image features from `VGG16`:

```
def get_clean_caption_data(self,text_path,feat_path):
        text_data = pd.read_csv(text_path, sep=',')
        text_data = text_data[text_data['Language'] == 'English']
        text_data['video_path'] =
        text_data.apply(lambda row:
row['VideoID']+'_'+str(int(row['Start']))+'_'+str(int(row['End']))+'.npy',
         axis=1)
        text_data['video_path'] =
        text_data['video_path'].map(lambda x: os.path.join(feat_path, x))
        text_data =
        text_data[text_data['video_path'].map(lambda x: os.path.exists(x))]
        text_data =
        text_data[text_data['Description'].map(lambda x: isinstance(x,
str))]
        unique_filenames = sorted(text_data['video_path'].unique())
        data =
        text_data[text_data['video_path'].map(lambda x: x in
unique_filenames)]
        return data
```

In the defined `get_data` function we remove from the `video_corpus.csv` file all captions that are not in English . Once done, we form the link to the video features by first constructing the video name (as a concatenation of `VideoID`, `Start` and `End` features) and prefixing the features directory name to it. We then remove all video corpus file records that doesn't point to any actual video feature vector in the features directory or have invalid non text descriptions.

The data comes out as illustrated in the following diagram (*Figure 5.6*):

index	VideoID	Start	End	WorkerID	Source	AnnotationTime	Language	Description
77153	krAk8WPZRL4	207	212	281652	unverified	33	English	A car has blasted behind the people standing.
119339	lxw6wmoC_xg	116	126	280252	clean	75	English	A woman is putting a small baby in a water pip.
33060	SULWQEAErKv	13	26	919506	unverified	73	English	tortoise walking on grass
118294	1qV4wfjTYlo	151	164	948158	unverified	53	English	A cat fished a straw out of its water bowl.
35337	zHy7pM0U49w	110	116	947723	unverified	19	English	A man is chopping a tomato.
28824	bkazquPsusc	74	85	481414	clean	125	English	A cat is crawling underneath a couch.
16701	6t0BpjwYKco	71	76	829808	unverified	29	English	A lady is cutting an apple.
62353	aM-RcQj0a7I	37	55	762891	clean	30	English	The man is frying food.
40211	FCjpuJaUec0	19	26	297776	unverified	69	English	A cat plays in a toilet.
13565	ngHDYzhDBk4	5	14	762891	clean	21	English	The girls are dancing.
77485	xxHx6s_DbUo	57	61	707318	clean	11	English	A man is doing pull ups.
31845	ltFqogTmAvQ	240	246	762891	clean	14	English	The man and woman are riding a motorcycle.
62473	jfrrO5K_vKM	55	65	275759	clean	37	English	A man showing a gun packed in a box.
72911	dJCtOz32dnw	40	60	707318	unverified	16	English	A man pulls eggs out of his pants.
23996	FHwC2THZJfA	0	10	283974	unverified	106	English	Loris try to climb a rope
96143	lmCrlZeob4w	23	26	807741	unverified	42	English	Christmas in Japan
65195	ejgwQqCHN1E	7	12	688049	unverified	167	English	Love song is sing by lovers
36558	98Alrg4pFXs	148	153	135621	clean	88	English	Two black men are kick boxing.
121514	BVjvRpmHg0w	231	250	833861	unverified	207	English	The two woman's are preparing the food
82325	QTAqjSbMkXU	65	75	772960	clean	509	English	Two portions of salmon flesh are placed in a dish containing salt and whole spices and a baking sheet is spread over them.
117678	LwicaralvS0	90	104	181773	clean	37	English	A man is pouring sugar into his coffee.
58604	I_-Nb_0RxpM	1	15	772960	clean	309	English	An old man is swinging his hip with his hands placed thereon as he bends sideways standing on a pavement.
14936	L9wD3kw-8FE	65	73	553931	unverified	19	English	Someone chopped a log with a machete.
25574	J---alyznGQ	0	6	275759	clean	96	English	A cat is playing a piano.
44267	KUc1cWKXjDc	20	30	313410	unverified	57	English	Two small yellow ducks run around together in a yard.
110418	JktNQQnLblQ	4	9	418656	unverified	224	English	A woman is roasting the bread.
80187	ecm9gf2Pgkc	1	24	825347	clean	12	English	A woman is playing with a rabbit.
42987	3eqFFRSXwGE	84	96	159786	clean	1206	English	Two dogs are playing on a floor.
49600	DIToA1dDwGQ	32	42	373663	clean	28	English	A woman is riding on an elephant.
77537	ZvJvNcukZ4w	0	10	155632	clean	46	English	A badger attacks a fox.
66208	ObBss94n3gl	35	46	130040	unverified	68	English	A man slicing some vegitables
60005	9gbUM9oHBNI	557	563	303815	unverified	42	English	the person is drinking the water
15985	-7KMZQEsJW4	205	208	371782	unverified	136	English	A guy is holding the sunflower in his hand.
64925	AzMrltkXGJk	0	10	707318	unverified	20	English	A boy is looking outside a window.
34205	H1Bok7Dg7g8	21	26	373663	unverified	129	English	A puppet is talking on a phone
89675	VLBsAPZ2DDE	58	64	922727	clean	25	English	Chickens are chasing a little boy.
51448	ITA0rWPE4nY	17	23	869926	unverified	19	English	A man is washing his hands in the bathroom.
5318	vE1gvaM3iAs	39	46	467982	unverified	119	English	A man removing scratches from a dvd with some sort of chemicals.
31732	2mUMTFnQWa	1	9	696912	unverified	92	English	The girl is riding a horse around the fence.
86781	1dfR0A_BXjw	441	448	762891	clean	18	English	The man is seasoning dough.
5253	32_A0-er4Ws	16	20	534192	unverified	28	English	A woman picks a tomato outdoors.
81648	hM3jzlyNlpc	0	10	309959	clean	16	English	The hamster ran in the wheel.
54243	WPG-BIWOrG4	130	134	707318	clean	16	English	A person is baking food in the oven.

Figure 5.6: Caption data after preprocessing

Building the train and test dataset

We would like to evaluate how the model is doing once we have trained the model. We can validate the captions generated for a test dataset against the content of the videos in the test set. The train test set data sets can be created by using the following function. We can create the test dataset during training and use it for evaluation once the model has been trained:

```
def train_test_split(self,data,test_frac=0.2):
    indices = np.arange(len(data))
    np.random.shuffle(indices)
    train_indices_rec = int((1 - test_frac)*len(data))
    indices_train = indices[:train_indices_rec]
    indices_test = indices[train_indices_rec:]
    data_train, data_test =
    data.iloc[indices_train],data.iloc[indices_test]
    data_train.reset_index(inplace=True)
```

```
        data_test.reset_index(inplace=True)
        return data_train,data_test
```

Generally reserving 20% of the data for evaluation is a fair practice.

Building the model

In this section, the core model-building exercise is illustrated. We first define a embedding layer for words in the vocabulary of the text captions followed by the two LSTMs. The weights `self.encode_W` and `self.encode_b` are used to reduce the dimension of the features f_t from the convolutional neural network. For the second LSTM (LSTM 2), one of the other inputs at any time step $t > N$ is the previous word w_{t-1} along with the output h_t from the first LSTM (LSTM 1). The word embedding for w_{t-1} is fed to the LSTM 2 instead of the raw one hot encoded vector. For the first N `(self.video_lstm_step)`, the LSTM 1 processes the input features f_t from the CNN, and the output hidden state h_t*(output1)* is fed to the LSTM 2. During this encoding phase, the LSTM 2 doesn't receive any word w_{t-1} as an input.

From the *(N+1)* time step, we enter the decoding phase, where, along with the h_t*(output1)* from LSTM 1, the previous time step word embedding vector w_{t-1} is fed to the LSTM 2. In this phase, there is no input to the LSTM 1, since all the features f_t are exhausted at time step *N*. The number of time steps for the decoding phase is determined by `self.caption_lstm_step`.

Now, if we represent the activity of the LSTM 2 by a function *f2*, then $f_2(h_t, w_{t-1}) = h_{2t}$, where h_{2t} is the hidden state of the LSTM 2 at time step *t*. This hidden state h_{2t} at time *t* is translated to a probability distribution over the output words through a *softmax* function and the one that has the highest probability is chosen as the next word $\hat{o}_t$:

$$p_t = softmax(h_{2t} * W_{ho} + b)$$

$$\hat{o}_t = argmax\ p_t$$

These weights, W_{ho} and *b*, are defined in the following code block as `self.word_emb_W` and `self.word_emb_b`. Refer to the `build_model` function for more granular details. The build function has been broken down into 3 parts for easy interpretation. The build model has 3 main units

- **Definition stage**: Defining the variables, the embedding layer for the caption words and the two LSTMs for the sequence to sequence model.

- **Encoding stage**: In this stage we pass the video frame image features through the time steps of LSTM1 and the hidden state of each time step is passed onto the LSTM 2. This activity is carried out till time step *N* where *N* is the number of sampled video frame images from each video.
- **Decoding stage**: In the decoding stage the LSTM 2 starts generating the text captions. With respect to time steps Decoding Stage start from step *N +1*. The generated word from each time step of LSTM 2 is fed as input to the next state along with the hidden state of the LSTM 1.

Definition of the model variables

The variables and the other relevant definition for the video captioning model can be defined as follows:

```
Defining the weights associated with the Network
        with tf.device('/cpu:0'):
            self.word_emb =
            tf.Variable(tf.random_uniform([self.n_words, self.dim_hidden],
                        -0.1, 0.1), name='word_emb')

        self.lstm1 =
        tf.nn.rnn_cell.BasicLSTMCell(self.dim_hidden, state_is_tuple=False)
        self.lstm2 =
        tf.nn.rnn_cell.BasicLSTMCell(self.dim_hidden, state_is_tuple=False)
        self.encode_W =
        tf.Variable( tf.random_uniform([self.dim_image,self.dim_hidden],
                    -0.1, 0.1), name='encode_W')
        self.encode_b =
        tf.Variable( tf.zeros([self.dim_hidden]), name='encode_b')

        self.word_emb_W =
        tf.Variable(tf.random_uniform([self.dim_hidden,self.n_words],
        -0.1,0.1), name='word_emb_W')
        self.word_emb_b =
        tf.Variable(tf.zeros([self.n_words]), name='word_emb_b')

        # Placeholders
        video =
       tf.placeholder(tf.float32, [self.batch_size,
       self.video_lstm_step, self.dim_image])
        video_mask =
        tf.placeholder(tf.float32, [self.batch_size, self.video_lstm_step])

        caption =
```

```
        tf.placeholder(tf.int32, [self.batch_size,
self.caption_lstm_step+1])
        caption_mask =
        tf.placeholder(tf.float32, [self.batch_size,
self.caption_lstm_step+1])

        video_flat = tf.reshape(video, [-1, self.dim_image])
        image_emb = tf.nn.xw_plus_b( video_flat,
self.encode_W,self.encode_b )
        image_emb =
        tf.reshape(image_emb, [self.batch_size, self.lstm_steps,
self.dim_hidden])

        state1 = tf.zeros([self.batch_size, self.lstm1.state_size])
        state2 = tf.zeros([self.batch_size, self.lstm2.state_size])
        padding = tf.zeros([self.batch_size, self.dim_hidden])
```

All the relevant variables along with the placeholders is defined by the previous code.

Encoding stage

In the encoding stage we process each video image frame features (from CNN last layer) sequentially by passing them through the time steps of LSTM 1. The dimension of the video image frame is `4096`. Before feeding those high dimensional video frame feature vectors to the LSTM 1, they are downsized to a smaller size of `512`.

LSTM 1 processes the video frame images and passes the hidden state to the LSTM 2 at each time step and this process continues till the time step *N* (`self.video_lstm_step`). The code for the encoder is as follows:

```
probs = []
        loss = 0.0

        # Encoding Stage
        for i in range(0, self.video_lstm_step):
            if i > 0:
                tf.get_variable_scope().reuse_variables()

            with tf.variable_scope("LSTM1"):
                output1, state1 = self.lstm1(image_emb[:,i,:], state1)

            with tf.variable_scope("LSTM2"):
                output2, state2 = self.lstm2(tf.concat([padding,
output1],1), state2)
```

Decoding stage

In the decoding stage the generation of the words for the video caption takes place. There are no more inputs to the LSTM 1. However the LSTM 1 is rolled forward and the hidden state produced is fed to the LSTM 2 time steps as before. The other input to the LSTM 2 at each step is the embedding vector for the preceding word in the caption. So at each step the LSTM 2 generates a new caption word conditioned on the word predicted in the previous time step along with the hidden state from LSTM 1 at that time step. The code for the decoder is as follows is :

```
# Decoding Stage to generate Captions
        for i in range(0, self.caption_lstm_step):

            with tf.device("/cpu:0"):
                current_embed = tf.nn.embedding_lookup(self.word_emb,
caption[:, i])

            tf.get_variable_scope().reuse_variables()

            with tf.variable_scope("LSTM1"):
                output1, state1 = self.lstm1(padding, state1)

            with tf.variable_scope("LSTM2"):
                output2, state2 =
                 self.lstm2(tf.concat([current_embed, output1],1), state2)
```

Building the loss for each mini-batch

The loss optimized is the categorical cross entropy loss with respect to predicting the correct word out of the whole corpus of caption words at each time step of the LSTM 2 . The same is accumulated in each step of the Decoding phase for all the data points in the batch. The code associated with the loss accumulation during the decoding phase is as follows:

```
            labels = tf.expand_dims(caption[:, i+1], 1)
            indices = tf.expand_dims(tf.range(0, self.batch_size, 1), 1)
            concated = tf.concat([indices, labels],1)
            onehot_labels =
            tf.sparse_to_dense(concated, tf.stack
                              ([self.batch_size,self.n_words]), 1.0, 0.0)

            logit_words =
            tf.nn.xw_plus_b(output2, self.word_emb_W, self.word_emb_b)
        # Computing the loss
```

```
        cross_entropy =
        tf.nn.softmax_cross_entropy_with_logits(logits=logit_words,
        labels=onehot_labels)
        cross_entropy =
        cross_entropy * caption_mask[:,i]
        probs.append(logit_words)

        current_loss = tf.reduce_sum(cross_entropy)/self.batch_size
        loss = loss + current_loss
```

The loss can be optimised with any of the reasonable gradient descent optimizers such as Adam, RMSprop, and so on. We will chose `Adam` for out experiment since it performs well for most of the deep learning optimizations. We can define the train op using Adam optimizer as follows:

```
with tf.variable_scope(tf.get_variable_scope(),reuse=tf.AUTO_REUSE):
    train_op = tf.train.AdamOptimizer(self.learning_rate).minimize(loss)
```

Creating a word vocabulary for the captions

In this section, we create the word vocabulary for the video captions. We create some additional words that are required as follows:

```
eos => End of Sentence
bos => Beginning of Sentence
pad => When there is no word to feed,required by the LSTM 2 in the initial
N time steps
unk => A substitute for a word that is not included in the vocabulary
```

The LSTM 2, in which a word is an input, would require these four additional symbols. For the *(N+1)* time step, when we start generating the captions, we feed the word of the previous time step w_{t-1}. For the first word to be generated, there is no valid previous time step word, and so we feed the dummy word `<bos>`, which signifies the start of sentence. Similarly, when we reach the last time step, w_{t-1} is the last word of the caption. We train the model to output the final word as `<eos>`, which denotes the end of the sentence. When the end of sentence is encountered, the LSTM 2 stops emitting any further words.

To illustrate this with an example, let's take the sentence *The weather is beautiful*. The following are the input and output labels for LSTM 2 from the time step *(N+1)*:

Time step	Input	Output
N+1	`<bos>`, h_{N+1}	The
N+2	The, h_{N+2}	weather
N+3	weather, h_{N+3}	is
N+4	is,h_{N+4}	beautiful
N+5	beautiful, h_{N+5}	`<eos>`

The `create_word_dict` function to create the word vocabulary is illustrated in detail as follows:

```
    def create_word_dict(self,sentence_iterator, word_count_threshold=5):
        word_counts = {}
        sent_cnt = 0
        for sent in sentence_iterator:
            sent_cnt += 1
            for w in sent.lower().split(' '):
               word_counts[w] = word_counts.get(w, 0) + 1
        vocab = [w for w in word_counts if word_counts[w] >=
word_count_threshold]
        idx2word = {}
        idx2word[0] = '<pad>'
        idx2word[1] = '<bos>'
        idx2word[2] = '<eos>'
        idx2word[3] = '<unk>'
        word2idx = {}
        word2idx['<pad>'] = 0
        word2idx['<bos>'] = 1
        word2idx['<eos>'] = 2
        word2idx['<unk>'] = 3
        for idx, w in enumerate(vocab):
            word2idx[w] = idx+4
            idx2word[idx+4] = w
        word_counts['<pad>'] = sent_cnt
        word_counts['<bos>'] = sent_cnt
        word_counts['<eos>'] = sent_cnt
        word_counts['<unk>'] = sent_cnt
        return word2idx,idx2word
```

Training the model

In this section, we put all the pieces together to build the function for training the video-captioning model.

First, we create the word vocabulary dictionary, combining the video captions from the training and test datasets. Once this is done, we invoke the `build_model` function to create the video-captioning network, combining the two LSTMs. For each video with a specific *start* and *end,* there are multiple output video captions. Within each batch, the output video caption for a video with a specific *start* and end is randomly selected from the multiple video captions available. The input text captions to the LSTM 2 are adjusted to have the starting word at the time step *(N+1)* as `<bos>`, while the end word of the output text captions are adjusted to have the final text label as `<eos>`. The sum of the categorical cross entropy loss over each of the time steps is taken as the total cross entropy loss for a particular video. In each time step, we compute the categorical cross entropy loss over the complete word vocabulary, which can be represented as follows:

$$C^{(t)} = -\sum_{i=1}^{V} y_i^{(t)} \log(p_i^{(t)})$$

Here, $y^{(t)} = [y_1^{(t)} y_2^{(t)} y_i^{(t)} \dots . y_V^{(t)}]$ is the one hot encoded vector of the actual target word at time step *t* and $p^{(t)} = [p_1^{(t)} p_2^{(t)} p_i^{(t)} \dots . p_V^{(t)}]$ is the predicted probability vector from the model.

The loss is captured in each epoch during training to see the nature of the loss reduction. Another important thing to note here is that we are saving the trained model using TensorFlow's `tf.train.saver` function so that we can restore the model to carry out inference.

The detailed code for the `train` function is illustrated here for reference:

```
    def train(self):
        data = self.get_data(self.train_text_path,self.train_feat_path)
        self.train_data,self.test_data =
self.train_test_split(data,test_frac=0.2)
        self.train_data.to_csv(f'{self.path_prj}/train.csv',index=False)
        self.test_data.to_csv(f'{self.path_prj}/test.csv',index=False)

        print(f'Processed train file written to
{self.path_prj}/train_corpus.csv')
        print(f'Processed test file written to
{self.path_prj}/test_corpus.csv')
```

```
        train_captions = self.train_data['Description'].values
        test_captions = self.test_data['Description'].values
        captions_list = list(train_captions)
        captions = np.asarray(captions_list, dtype=np.object)
        captions = list(map(lambda x: x.replace('.', ''), captions))
        captions = list(map(lambda x: x.replace(',', ''), captions))
        captions = list(map(lambda x: x.replace('"', ''), captions))
        captions = list(map(lambda x: x.replace('\n', ''), captions))
        captions = list(map(lambda x: x.replace('?', ''), captions))
        captions = list(map(lambda x: x.replace('!', ''), captions))
        captions = list(map(lambda x: x.replace('\\', ''), captions))
        captions = list(map(lambda x: x.replace('/', ''), captions))
        self.word2idx,self.idx2word = self.create_word_dict(captions,
                                      word_count_threshold=0)
        np.save(self.path_prj/ "word2idx",self.word2idx)
        np.save(self.path_prj/ "idx2word" ,self.idx2word)
        self.n_words = len(self.word2idx)
        tf_loss, tf_video,tf_video_mask,tf_caption,tf_caption_mask,
tf_probs,train_op=
        self.build_model()
        sess = tf.InteractiveSession()
        saver = tf.train.Saver(max_to_keep=100, write_version=1)
        tf.global_variables_initializer().run()
        loss_out = open('loss.txt', 'w')
        val_loss = []
        for epoch in range(0,self.epochs):
            val_loss_epoch = []
            index = np.arange(len(self.train_data))

            self.train_data.reset_index()
            np.random.shuffle(index)
            self.train_data = self.train_data.loc[index]
            current_train_data =
            self.train_data.groupby(['video_path']).first().reset_index()

            for start, end in zip(
                    range(0, len(current_train_data),self.batch_size),
range(self.batch_size,len(current_train_data),self.batch_size)):
                start_time = time.time()
                current_batch = current_train_data[start:end]
                current_videos = current_batch['video_path'].values
                current_feats = np.zeros((self.batch_size,
                                self.video_lstm_step,self.dim_image))
                current_feats_vals = list(map(lambda vid:
np.load(vid),current_videos))
                current_feats_vals = np.array(current_feats_vals)
                current_video_masks =
np.zeros((self.batch_size,self.video_lstm_step))
```

```
                for ind,feat in enumerate(current_feats_vals):
                    current_feats[ind][:len(current_feats_vals[ind])] =
feat
                    current_video_masks[ind][:len(current_feats_vals[ind])]
= 1
                current_captions = current_batch['Description'].values
                current_captions = list(map(lambda x: '<bos> ' + x,
current_captions))
                current_captions = list(map(lambda x: x.replace('.', ''),
                                        current_captions))
                current_captions = list(map(lambda x: x.replace(',', ''),
                                       current_captions))
                current_captions = list(map(lambda x: x.replace('"', ''),
                                       current_captions))
                current_captions = list(map(lambda x: x.replace('\n', ''),
                                       current_captions))
                current_captions = list(map(lambda x: x.replace('?', ''),
                                       current_captions))
                current_captions = list(map(lambda x: x.replace('!', ''),
                                       current_captions))
                current_captions = list(map(lambda x: x.replace('\\', ''),
                                       current_captions))
                current_captions = list(map(lambda x: x.replace('/', ''),
                                       current_captions))

                for idx, each_cap in enumerate(current_captions):
                    word = each_cap.lower().split(' ')
                    if len(word) < self.caption_lstm_step:
                        current_captions[idx] = current_captions[idx] + '
<eos>'
                    else:
                        new_word = ''
                        for i in range(self.caption_lstm_step-1):
                            new_word = new_word + word[i] + ' '
                        current_captions[idx] = new_word + '<eos>'
                current_caption_ind = []
                for cap in current_captions:
                    current_word_ind = []
                    for word in cap.lower().split(' '):
                        if word in self.word2idx:
                            current_word_ind.append(self.word2idx[word])
                        else:
                            current_word_ind.append(self.word2idx['<unk>'])
                    current_caption_ind.append(current_word_ind)
                current_caption_matrix =
                sequence.pad_sequences(current_caption_ind, padding='post',
                                       maxlen=self.caption_lstm_step)
                current_caption_matrix =
```

```
                    np.hstack( [current_caption_matrix,
                            np.zeros([len(current_caption_matrix), 1] ) ]
).astype(int)
                    current_caption_masks =
                    np.zeros( (current_caption_matrix.shape[0],
                              current_caption_matrix.shape[1]) )
                    nonzeros =
                    np.array( list(map(lambda x: (x != 0).sum() + 1,
                            current_caption_matrix ) ))
                    for ind, row in enumerate(current_caption_masks):
                        row[:nonzeros[ind]] = 1
                    probs_val = sess.run(tf_probs, feed_dict={
                        tf_video:current_feats,
                        tf_caption: current_caption_matrix
                        })
                    _, loss_val = sess.run(
                            [train_op, tf_loss],
                            feed_dict={
                                tf_video: current_feats,
                                tf_video_mask : current_video_masks,
                                tf_caption: current_caption_matrix,
                                tf_caption_mask: current_caption_masks
                                })
                    val_loss_epoch.append(loss_val)
                    print('Batch starting index: ', start, " Epoch: ", epoch, "
loss: ",
                    loss_val, ' Elapsed time: ', str((time.time() -
start_time)))
                    loss_out.write('epoch ' + str(epoch) + ' loss ' +
str(loss_val) + '\n')
                # draw loss curve every epoch
                val_loss.append(np.mean(val_loss_epoch))
                plt_save_dir = self.path_prj / "loss_imgs"
                plt_save_img_name = str(epoch) + '.png'
                plt.plot(range(len(val_loss)),val_loss, color='g')
                plt.grid(True)
                plt.savefig(os.path.join(plt_save_dir, plt_save_img_name))
                if np.mod(epoch,9) == 0:
                    print ("Epoch ", epoch, " is done. Saving the model ...")
                    saver.save(sess, os.path.join(self.path_prj, 'model'),
global_step=epoch)
            loss_out.close()
```

As we can see from the preceding code we create each batch by randomly selecting a set of videos based on the `batch_size`.

For each video the labels are chosen randomly since the same video has been labelled by multiple taggers. For each of the selected caption we clean up the caption text and convert them words in them to their word indexes. The target for the captions are shifted by 1 time step since at each step we predict the word from the previous word in the caption. The model is trained for the specified number of epochs and the model is check pointed at specified intervals of epoch (9 here).

Training results

The model can be trained using the following command:

```
python Video_seq2seq.py process_main --path_prj '/media/santanu/9eb9b6dc-
b380-486e-b4fd-c424a325b976/Video Captioning/' --caption_file
video_corpus.csv --feat_dir features --cnn_feat_dim 4096 --h_dim 512 --
batch_size 32 --lstm_steps 80 --video_steps=80 --out_steps 20 --
learning_rate 1e-4--epochs=100
```

Parameter	**Value**
Optimizer	Adam
learning rate	1e-4
Batch size	32
Epochs	100
cnn_feat_dim	4096
lstm_steps	80
out_steps	20
h_dim	512

The output log of the training is as follows:

```
Batch starting index: 1728 Epoch: 99 loss: 17.723186 Elapsed time:
0.21822428703308105
Batch starting index: 1760 Epoch: 99 loss: 19.556421 Elapsed time:
0.2106935977935791
Batch starting index: 1792 Epoch: 99 loss: 21.919321 Elapsed time:
0.2206578254699707
Batch starting index: 1824 Epoch: 99 loss: 15.057275 Elapsed time:
0.21275663375854492
Batch starting index: 1856 Epoch: 99 loss: 19.633915 Elapsed time:
0.21492290496826172
Batch starting index: 1888 Epoch: 99 loss: 13.986136 Elapsed time:
0.21542596817016602
```

```
Batch starting index: 1920 Epoch: 99 loss: 14.300303 Elapsed time:
0.21855640411376953
Epoch 99 is done. Saving the model ...
24.343 min: Video Captioning
```

As we can see it takes around 24 minutes to train the model on 100 epochs using a GeForce Zotac 1070 GPU.

The training loss reduction over each epoch is as represented as follows (*Figure 5.7*):

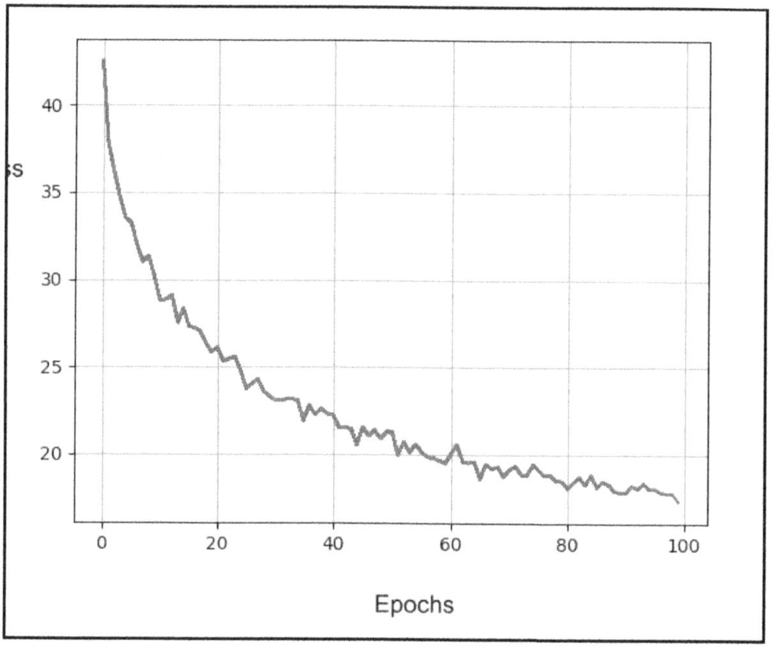

Figure 5.7 Loss profile during training

As we can see from the preceding graph (*Figure 5.7*), the loss reduction is high in the initial few epochs, and then it gradually reduces around epoch **80**. In the next section, we will illustrate how the model performs in generating captions for unseen videos.

Inference with unseen test videos

For the purpose of inference we build a generator function `build_generator` replicating the logic of the `build_model` to define all the model variables and the required TensorFlow ops to load the model and run inference on the same:

```
def build_generator(self):
    with tf.device('/cpu:0'):
        self.word_emb =
        tf.Variable(tf.random_uniform([self.n_words, self.dim_hidden],
                    -0.1, 0.1), name='word_emb')


    self.lstm1 =
    tf.nn.rnn_cell.BasicLSTMCell(self.dim_hidden, state_is_tuple=False)
    self.lstm2 =
    tf.nn.rnn_cell.BasicLSTMCell(self.dim_hidden, state_is_tuple=False)

    self.encode_W =
    tf.Variable(tf.random_uniform([self.dim_image,self.dim_hidden],
                -0.1, 0.1), name='encode_W')
    self.encode_b =
    tf.Variable(tf.zeros([self.dim_hidden]), name='encode_b')

    self.word_emb_W =
    tf.Variable(tf.random_uniform([self.dim_hidden,self.n_words],
                 -0.1,0.1), name='word_emb_W')
    self.word_emb_b =
     tf.Variable(tf.zeros([self.n_words]), name='word_emb_b')
    video =
    tf.placeholder(tf.float32, [1, self.video_lstm_step,
self.dim_image])
    video_mask =
     tf.placeholder(tf.float32, [1, self.video_lstm_step])

    video_flat = tf.reshape(video, [-1, self.dim_image])
    image_emb = tf.nn.xw_plus_b(video_flat, self.encode_W,
self.encode_b)
    image_emb = tf.reshape(image_emb, [1, self.video_lstm_step,
self.dim_hidden])

    state1 = tf.zeros([1, self.lstm1.state_size])
    state2 = tf.zeros([1, self.lstm2.state_size])
    padding = tf.zeros([1, self.dim_hidden])

    generated_words = []
```

```
        probs = []
        embeds = []

        for i in range(0, self.video_lstm_step):
            if i > 0:
                tf.get_variable_scope().reuse_variables()

            with tf.variable_scope("LSTM1"):
                output1, state1 = self.lstm1(image_emb[:, i, :], state1)

            with tf.variable_scope("LSTM2"):
                output2, state2 =
                self.lstm2(tf.concat([padding, output1],1), state2)

        for i in range(0, self.caption_lstm_step):
            tf.get_variable_scope().reuse_variables()

            if i == 0:
                with tf.device('/cpu:0'):
                    current_embed =
                    tf.nn.embedding_lookup(self.word_emb, tf.ones([1],
dtype=tf.int64))

            with tf.variable_scope("LSTM1"):
                output1, state1 = self.lstm1(padding, state1)

            with tf.variable_scope("LSTM2"):
                output2, state2 =
                self.lstm2(tf.concat([current_embed, output1],1), state2)

            logit_words =
            tf.nn.xw_plus_b( output2, self.word_emb_W, self.word_emb_b)
            max_prob_index = tf.argmax(logit_words, 1)[0]
            generated_words.append(max_prob_index)
            probs.append(logit_words)

            with tf.device("/cpu:0"):
                current_embed =
                tf.nn.embedding_lookup(self.word_emb, max_prob_index)
                current_embed = tf.expand_dims(current_embed, 0)

            embeds.append(current_embed)

        return video, video_mask, generated_words, probs, embeds
```

Inference function

During inference we call `build_generator` to define the model and other TensorFlow ops required for inference and then we load the defined model with the saved weights from the trained model using `tf.train.Saver.restoreutility`. Once the model is loaded and ready for inference for each test video we extract its corresponding video frame images pre-processed features(from CNN) and pass it to the model for inference:

```
    def inference(self):
        self.test_data =
self.get_test_data(self.test_text_path,self.test_feat_path)
        test_videos = self.test_data['video_path'].unique()
        self.idx2word =
        pd.Series(np.load(self.path_prj / "idx2word.npy").tolist())
        self.n_words = len(self.idx2word)
        video_tf, video_mask_tf, caption_tf, probs_tf, last_embed_tf =
        self.build_generator()
        sess = tf.InteractiveSession()
        saver = tf.train.Saver()
        saver.restore(sess,self.model_path)
        f = open(f'{self.path_prj}/video_captioning_results.txt', 'w')
        for idx, video_feat_path in enumerate(test_videos):
            video_feat = np.load(video_feat_path)[None,...]
            if video_feat.shape[1] == self.frame_step:
                video_mask = np.ones((video_feat.shape[0],
video_feat.shape[1]))
            else:
                continue
            gen_word_idx =
            sess.run(caption_tf, feed_dict={video_tf:video_feat,
                     video_mask_tf:video_mask})
            gen_words = self.idx2word[gen_word_idx]
            punct = np.argmax(np.array(gen_words) == '<eos>') + 1
            gen_words = gen_words[:punct]
            gen_sent = ' '.join(gen_words)
            gen_sent = gen_sent.replace('<bos> ', '')
            gen_sent = gen_sent.replace(' <eos>', '')
            print(f'Video path {video_feat_path} : Generated Caption
{gen_sent}')
            print(gen_sent,'\n')
            f.write(video_feat_path + '\n')
            f.write(gen_sent + '\n\n')
```

Inference can be run by invoking the following command:

```
python Video_seq2seq.py process_main --path_prj '/media/santanu/9eb9b6dc-
b380-486e-b4fd-c424a325b976/Video Captioning/' --caption_file
'/media/santanu/9eb9b6dc-b380-486e-b4fd-c424a325b976/Video
Captioning/test.csv' --feat_dir features --mode inference --model_path
'/media/santanu/9eb9b6dc-b380-486e-b4fd-c424a325b976/Video
Captioning/model-99'
```

Results from evaluation

The results of evaluation are very promising. The inference results on two videos from the test set `0lh_UWF9ZP4_82_87.avi` and `8MVo7fje_oE_139_144.avi` is presented as follows:

In the following screenshot, we illustrate the results of inference on video `video0lh_UWF9ZP4_82_87.avi`:

Inference on video 0lh_UWF9ZP4_82_87.avi using the trained model

In the following screenshot, we illustrate the results of inference on another `video8MVo7fje_oE_139_144.avi`:

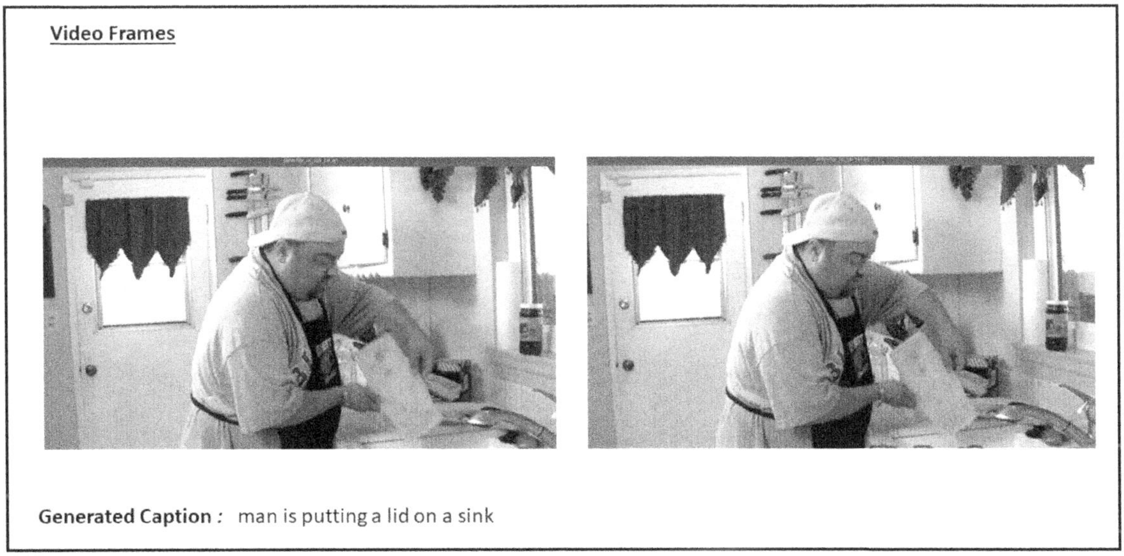

Inference on a video/8MVo7fje_oE_139_144.avi using the trained model

From the preceding screenshots, we can see that the trained model has done a good job of coming up with a good caption for the provided test videos.

The code for the project can be found in the GitHub location `https://github.com/PacktPublishing/Python-Artificial-Intelligence-Projects/tree/master/Chapter05`. The `VideoCaptioningPreProcessing.py` module can be used to pre-process the videos and create the convolutional neural network features, while the `Video_seq2seq.py` module can be used to train an end-to-end video-captioning system and run inference it.

Summary

Now we have reached the end of our exciting video-captioning project. You should be able to build your own video-captioning system using TensorFlow and Keras. You should also be able to use the technical know-hows explained in this chapter to develop other advanced models involving convolutional neural networks and recurrent neural networks. The next chapter will build an intelligent recommender system, using restricted Boltzmann machines. I look forward to your participation!

6
The Intelligent Recommender System

With the huge amount of digital information available on the internet, it becomes a challenge for users to access items efficiently. Recommender systems are information filtering systems that deal with the problem of digital data overload to pull out items or information according to the user's preferences, interests, and behavior, as inferred from previous activities.

In this chapter, we will cover the following topics:

- Introducing recommender systems
- Latent factorization-based collaborative filtering
- Using deep learning for latent factor collaborative filtering
- Using the **restricted Boltzmann machine** (**RBM**) for building recommendation systems
- Contrastive divergence for training RBMs
- Collaborative filtering using RBMs
- Implementing a collaborative filtering application using RBMs

Technical requirements

The readers should have basic knowledge of Python 3 and artificial intelligence to go through the projects in this chapter.

The code files of this chapter can be found on GitHub:
`https://github.com/PacktPublishing/Intelligent-Projects-using-Python/tree/master/Chapter06`

Check out the following video to see the code in action:
http://bit.ly/2SgcOR3

What is a recommender system?

Recommender systems are ubiquitous in today's world. Be it movie recommendations on Netflix or product recommendations on Amazon, recommender systems are making a significant impact. Recommender systems can be broadly classified into content-based filtering systems, collaborative filtering systems, and latent factor-based filtering recommender systems. **Content-based filtering** relies on hand-coding features for the items based on their content. Based on how the users have rated existing items, a user profile is created and the ranks provided by the user are given to those items:

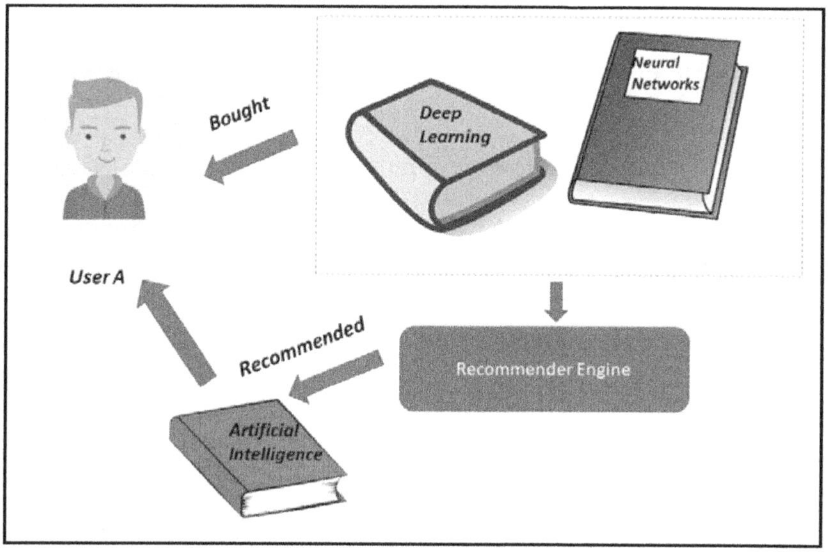

Figure 6.1: Content-based filtering illustration

As we can see in the preceding diagram (*Figure 6.1*), **User A** has bought books named **Deep Learning** and **Neural Networks**. Since the content of the book **Artificial Intelligence** is similar to the two books, the content-based recommender system has recommended the book **Artificial Intelligence** to **User A**. As we can see, in content-based filtering, the user is recommended items based on their preferences. This doesn't involve how other users have rated the book.

Collaborative filtering tries to identify similar users pertaining to a given user, and then recommends the user items that similar users have liked, bought, or rated highly. This is generally called **user-user collaborative filtering**. The opposite is to find items similar to a given item and recommend items to users who have also liked, bought, or rated other similar items highly. This goes by the name **item-item collaborative filtering**:

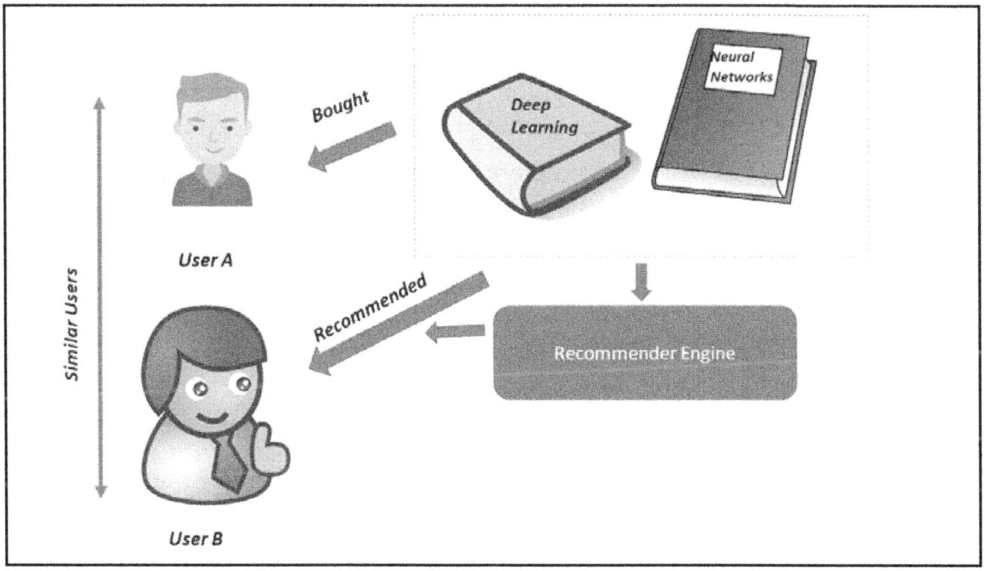

Figure 6.2: item-item collaborative filtering illustration

In the preceding diagram (*Figure 6.2*), **User A** and **User B** are very similar in terms of their taste in buying books. **User A** has recently bought the books **Deep Learning** and **Neural Networks**. Since **User B** is very similar to **User A**, the user-user collaborative recommender system recommends these books to **User B** as well.

Latent factorization-based recommendation system

Latent factorization-based filter recommendation methods attempt to discover latent features to represent user and item profiles by decomposing the ratings. Unlike the content-based filtering features, these latent features are not interpretable and can represent complicated features. For instance, in a movie recommendation system, one of the latent features might represent a linear combination of humor, suspense, and romance in a specific proportion. Generally, for already rated items, the rating r_{ij} given by an user i to an item j can be represented as $r_{ij} = u_i^T v_j$. where u_i is the user profile vector based on the latent factors and v_i is the item vector based on the same latent factors:

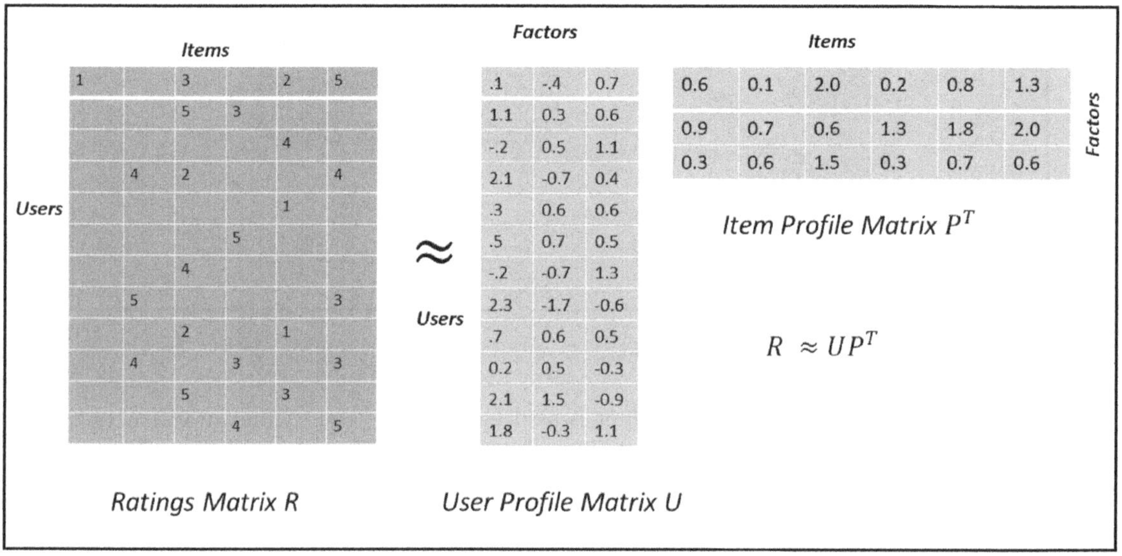

Figure 6.3: Latent factor-based filtering illustration

Illustrated in the previous diagram (*Figure 6.3*) is a latent-factor based recommendation method, where the ratings matrix $R_{m \times n}$ has been decomposed into the product of user profile matrix $U_{m \times k}$ and the transpose of the item profile matrix $P_{n \times k}$ where k is the number of the latent factors of the model. Based on these profiles, we can recommend items that have so far not been bought by the user by computing the inner product of the user profile and the item profile. The inner product gives a tentative rating that the user might have given had they bought the product.

One of the ways these user and item profiles can be created is by performing **singular value decomposition (SVD)** on the ratings matrix after filling in the missing values by some form of mean values across the users and items as appropriate. According to SVD, the rating matrix R can be decomposed as follows:

$$R = USV^T = US^{\frac{1}{2}} S^{\frac{1}{2}} V^T$$

We can take the user profile matrix as $US^{1/2}$ and then transpose of the item profile matrix as $S^{1/2} V^T$ to form the latent factor model. You might have a question as to how to perform SVD when there is missing entries in the ratings matrix corresponding to the movies that are not rated by the users. Common approaches are to impute the missing ratings by the average rating of the user, or by the global ratings average, before performing SVD.

Deep learning for latent factor collaborative filtering

Instead of using SVD, you can leverage deep learning methods to derive the user and item profile vectors of given dimensions.

For each user i, you can define a user vector $u_i \in R^k$ through an embedding layer. Similarly, for each item j, you can define a item vector $v_j \in R^k$ through another embedding layer. Then, the rating r_{ij} of a user i to an item j can be represented as the dot product of u_i and v_j as shown:

$$r_{ij} = u_i^T v_j$$

You can modify the neural network to add biases for users and items. Given that we want k latent components, the dimensions of the embedding matrix U for m users would be m x k. Similarly, the dimensions of the embedding matrix V for n items would be n x k.

In the *The deep learning-based latent factor model* section, we will use this embedding approach to create a recommender system based on the `100K Movie Lens` dataset. The dataset can be downloaded from `https://grouplens.org/datasets/movielens/`.

We will be using the `u1.base` as the training dataset and `u1.test` as the holdout test dataset.

The deep learning-based latent factor model

The deep learning-based latent factor model discussed in the *Deep learning for latent factor collaborative filtering* section can be designed as illustrated in *Figure 6.4*:

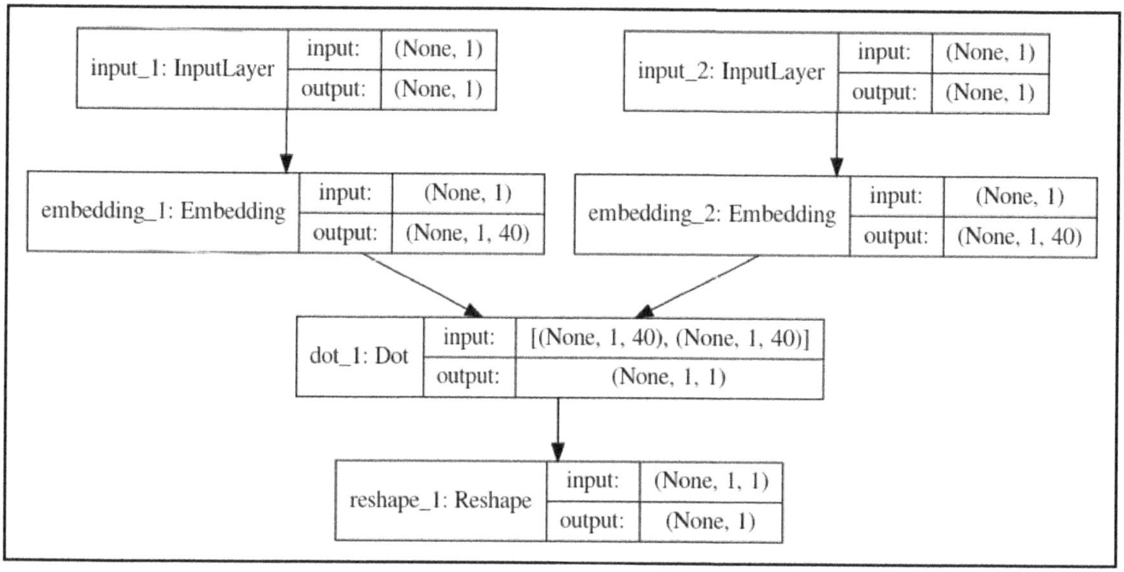

Figure 6.4: Deep learning-based latent factor model on Movie Lens 100 K dataset

The `user_ID` and the `movie_ID` picks up the user and the movie embedding vector from their corresponding embedding matrices. In the diagram, **embedding_1** represents the embedding layer for the user IDs, while **embedding_2** represents the embedding layer for movie IDs. The dot product of the user embedding vector and the movie embedding vector is performed in the **dot_1** layer to output the ratings score (one to five). The code to define the model is illustrated as follows:

```
def model(max_users,max_movies,latent_factors):
    user_ID = Input(shape=(1,))
    movie_ID = Input(shape=(1,))
    x = Embedding(max_users,latent_factors, input_length=1)(user_ID)
    y = Embedding(max_movies,latent_factors, input_length=1)(movie_ID)
    out = dot([x,y],axes=2,normalize=False)
    out= Reshape((1,))(out)
    model = Model(inputs=[user_ID,movie_ID],outputs=out)
    print(model.summary())
    return model
```

In the preceding `model` function, the `max_users` and `max_movies` determine the size of the user and the movie-embedding matrices, respectively. The parameters of the model are nothing but the components of the user and movie embedding matrices. So if we have *m* users and *n* movies, and we chose a latent dimension of *k* then we have $m \times k + n \times k = (m + n)k$ parameters to learn.

The data-processing functions can be coded as follows:

```
data_dir = Path('/home/santanu/ML_DS_Catalog-/Collaborating
Filtering/ml-100k/')
outdir = Path('/home/santanu/ML_DS_Catalog-/Collaborating
Filtering/ml-100k/')

#Function to read data
def create_data(rating,header_cols):
    data = pd.read_csv(rating,header=None,sep='\t')
    #print(data)
    data.columns = header_cols
    return data

#Movie ID to movie name dict
def create_movie_dict(movie_file):
    print(movie_file)
    df = pd.read_csv(movie_file,sep='|', encoding='latin-1',header=None)
    movie_dict = {}
    movie_ids = list(df[0].values)
    movie_name = list(df[1].values)
    for k,v in zip(movie_ids,movie_name):
        movie_dict[k] = v
    return movie_dict


# Function to create training validation and test data
def train_val(df,val_frac=None):
    X,y = df[['userID','movieID']].values,df['rating'].values
    #Offset the ids by 1 for the ids to start from zero
    X = X - 1
    if val_frac != None:
        X_train, X_test, y_train, y_val = train_test_split(X, y,
test_size=val_frac,random_state=0)
        return X_train, X_val, y_train, y_val
    else:
        return X,y
```

One thing to note is that 1 has been subtracted from both the user_ID and the movie_ID to ensure the IDs start from 0 and not from 1 so that they can properly be referenced by the embedding layers.

The code to invoke the data processing and training is as follows:

```
#Data processing and model training

train_ratings_df =
create_data(f'{data_dir}/u1.base',['userID','movieID','rating','timestamp']
)
test_ratings_df =
create_data(f'{data_dir}/u1.test',['userID','movieID','rating','timestamp']
)
X_train, X_val,y_train, y_val = train_val(train_ratings_df,val_frac=0.2)
movie_dict = create_movie_dict(f'{data_dir}/u.item')
num_users = len(train_ratings_df['userID'].unique())
num_movies = len(train_ratings_df['movieID'].unique())

print(f'Number of users {num_users}')
print(f'Number of movies {num_movies}')
model = model(num_users,num_movies,40)
plot_model(model, to_file='model_plot.png', show_shapes=True,
show_layer_names=True)
model.compile(loss='mse',optimizer='adam')
callbacks = [EarlyStopping('val_loss', patience=2),
             ModelCheckpoint(f'{outdir}/nn_factor_model.h5',
save_best_only=True)]
model.fit([X_train[:,0],X_train[:,1]], y_train, nb_epoch=30,
validation_data=([X_val[:,0],X_val[:,1]], y_val), verbose=2,
callbacks=callbacks)
```

The model has been set up to store the best model with respect to the validation error. The model converged on a validation RMSE of around 0.8872 as we can see from the training log as follows:

```
Train on 64000 samples, validate on 16000 samples
Epoch 1/30
 - 4s - loss: 8.8970 - val_loss: 2.0422
Epoch 2/30
 - 3s - loss: 1.3345 - val_loss: 1.0734
Epoch 3/30
 - 3s - loss: 0.9656 - val_loss: 0.9704
Epoch 4/30
 - 3s - loss: 0.8921 - val_loss: 0.9317
Epoch 5/30
 - 3s - loss: 0.8452 - val_loss: 0.9097
```

```
Epoch 6/30
 - 3s - loss: 0.8076 - val_loss: 0.8987
Epoch 7/30
 - 3s - loss: 0.7686 - val_loss: 0.8872
Epoch 8/30
 - 3s - loss: 0.7260 - val_loss: 0.8920
Epoch 9/30
 - 3s - loss: 0.6842 - val_loss: 0.8959
```

We now evaluate the performance of the model on the unseen test data set. The following code can be invoked to run inference on the test dataset:

```
#Evaluate on the test dataset
model = load_model(f'{outdir}/nn_factor_model.h5')
X_test,y_test = train_val(test_ratings_df,val_frac=None)
pred = model.predict([X_test[:,0],X_test[:,1]])[:,0]
print('Hold out test set RMSE:',(np.mean((pred - y_test)**2)**0.5))
pred = np.round(pred)
test_ratings_df['predictions'] = pred
test_ratings_df['movie_name'] = test_ratings_df['movieID'].apply(lambda
x:movie_dict[x])
```

The holdout test RMSE is around `0.95` as we can see from the log as follows:

```
Hold out test set RMSE: 0.9543926404313371
```

Now, we evaluate the performance of the model for the user with ID `1` in the test dataset by invoking the following line of code:

```
#Check evaluation results for the UserID = 1
test_ratings_df[test_ratings_df['userID'] ==
1].sort_values(['rating','predictions'],ascending=False)
```

We can see from the following results (*Figure 6.5*) that the model has done a good job at predicting the ratings on movies unseen during training:

userID	movieID	rating	timestamp	predictions	movie_name
1	12	5	878542960	5.0	Usual Suspects, The (1995)
1	60	5	875072370	5.0	Three Colors: Blue (1993)
1	64	5	875072404	5.0	Shawshank Redemption, The (1994)
1	100	5	878543541	5.0	Fargo (1996)
1	114	5	875072173	5.0	Wallace & Gromit: The Best of Aardman Animatio...
1	170	5	876892856	5.0	Cinema Paradiso (1988)
1	171	5	889751711	5.0	Delicatessen (1991)
1	174	5	875073198	5.0	Raiders of the Lost Ark (1981)
1	190	5	875072125	5.0	Henry V (1989)
1	6	5	887431973	4.0	Shanghai Triad (Yao a yao yao dao waipo qiao) ...

Figure 6.5: Results of evaluation for UserID 1

The code related to the deep learning method latent factor method can be found at `https://github.com/PacktPublishing/Intelligent-Projects-using-Python/tree/master/Chapter06`.

SVD++

Generally, SVD doesn't capture the user and item biases that may exist in the data. One such method that goes by the name SVD++ considers user and item biases in the latent factorization method and has been very popular in competitions such as the *Netflix challenge*.

The most common way to carry out latent factor-based recommendation is to define the user profile and biases as $u_i \in R^k$ and $b_i \in R$ and the item profiles and biases as $v_i \in R^k$ and $b_j \in R$. The rating $\hat{r}_{ij}$ provided by user i to item j is then defined to be as follows:

$$\hat{r}_{ij} = \mu + b_i + b_j + u_i^T v_j$$

μ is the global mean of all the ratings.

The user profiles and the item profiles are then determined by minimizing the sum of the square of the errors in predicting the ratings for all the items rated by the users. The squared error loss to be optimized can be represented as follows:

$$C = \sum_{i=1}^{m}\sum_{j=1}^{n} I_{ij}(r_{ij} - \hat{r}_{ij})^2$$

I_{ij} is an indicator function that is one if the user i has a rated item j; otherwise, it is zero.

The cost is minimized with respect to the parameters of the user and the item profiles. Generally, this kind of optimization leads to over-fitting, and hence the norm of the user and the item profiles are used as regularizes in the cost function, as shown here:

$$C = \sum_{i=1}^{m}\sum_{j=1}^{n} I_{ij}(r_{ij} - \hat{r}_{ij})^2 + \lambda_1 \sum_{i=1}^{m} \|u_i\|_2^2 + \lambda_2 \sum_{i=1}^{n} \|v_j\|_2^2$$

Here, λ_1 and λ_2 are the regularization constants. Generally, a popular gradient descent technique named **alternating least squares** (**ALS**) is used for optimization, which alternates updating the user profile parameters by keeping the item parameters fixed and vice versa.

The `surprise` package has a good implementation of SVD++. In the next section, we will train a model with SVD++ on the `100K movie lens` dataset and look at performance metrics.

Training model with SVD++ on the Movie Lens 100k dataset

The `surprise` package can be downloaded through `conda` using the following command:

```
conda install -c conda-forge scikit-surprise
```

The algorithm corresponding to SVD++ is named as `SVDpp` in `surprise`. We can load all the required packages as follows:

```
import numpy as np
from surprise import SVDpp # SVD++ algorithm
from surprise import Dataset
from surprise import accuracy
from surprise.model_selection import cross_validate
from surprise.model_selection import train_test_split
```

The `100K Movie lens` dataset can be downloaded and made available to the code using the `Dataset.load_builtin` utility in `surprise`. We split the data into training and holdout test set in the `80` to `20` ratio. The data-processing code lines are as follows:

```
# Load the movie lens 10k data and split the data into train test
files(80:20)
data = Dataset.load_builtin('ml-100k')
trainset, testset = train_test_split(data, test_size=.2)
```

Next, we will do `5` fold cross validations on the data and look at the cross-validation results. We chose a learning rate of `0.008` for stochastic gradient descent. Also to guard against over-fitting, we chose a regularization constant of `0.1` for both L1 and L2 regularization. Details of these code lines are as follows:

```
#Perform 5 fold cross validation with all data
algo = SVDpp(n_factors=40, n_epochs=40, lr_all=0.008, reg_all=0.1)
# Run 5-fold cross-validation and show results summary
cross_validate(algo,data, measures=['RMSE', 'MAE'], cv=5, verbose=True)
```

The results from the cross-validation are as follows:

```
Evaluating RMSE, MAE of algorithm SVDpp on 5 split(s). Fold 1 Fold 2 Fold 3
Fold 4 Fold 5 Mean Std RMSE (testset) 0.9196 0.9051 0.9037 0.9066 0.9151
0.9100 0.0062 MAE (testset) 0.7273 0.7169 0.7115 0.7143 0.7228 0.7186
0.0058 Fit time 374.57 374.58 369.74 385.44 382.36 377.34 5.72 Test time
2.53 2.63 2.74 2.79 2.84 2.71 0.11
```

We can see from the preceding results that the `5 fold cv RMSE` of the model is `0.91`. The results are impressive on the `Movie Lens 100K` dataset.

Now we will train the model on just the training dataset `trainset` and then evaluate the model on the test set. The relevant code lines are as follows:

```
model = SVDpp(n_factors=40, n_epochs=10, lr_all=0.008, reg_all=0.1)
model.fit(trainset)
```

Once the model has been trained, we evaluate the model on the holdout test dataset test set. The relevant code lines are as follows:

```
#validate the model on the testset
pred = model.test(testset)
print("SVD++ results on the Test Set")
accuracy.rmse(pred, verbose=True)
```

The output of the validation is as follows:

```
SVD++ results on the test set
RMSE: 0.9320
```

As we can see from the preceding results, the SVD++ model does really well on the test dataset with a RMSE of `0.93`. The results are comparable to the deep learning-based model latent factor model (hold out RMSE of `0.95`) that we trained prior to this.

In the *Restricted Boltzmann machines for recommendation* section, we will look at a restricted Boltzmann machine for building recommender systems. This method has gained lot of popularity in collaborative filtering since it can scale to large datasets. Most of the datasets in the collaborative filtering domain are sparse leading to difficult non-convex optimization problems. RBMs are less prone to suffer from this sparsity issue in datasets than other factorization methods such as SVD.

Restricted Boltzmann machines for recommendation

Restricted Boltzmann machines are a class of neural networks that fall under unsupervised learning techniques. **Restricted Boltzmann machines** (**RBMs**), as they are popularly known, try to learn the hidden structure of the data by projecting the input data into a hidden layer.

The hidden layer activations are expected to encode the input signal and recreate it. Restricted Boltzmann machines generally work on binary data:

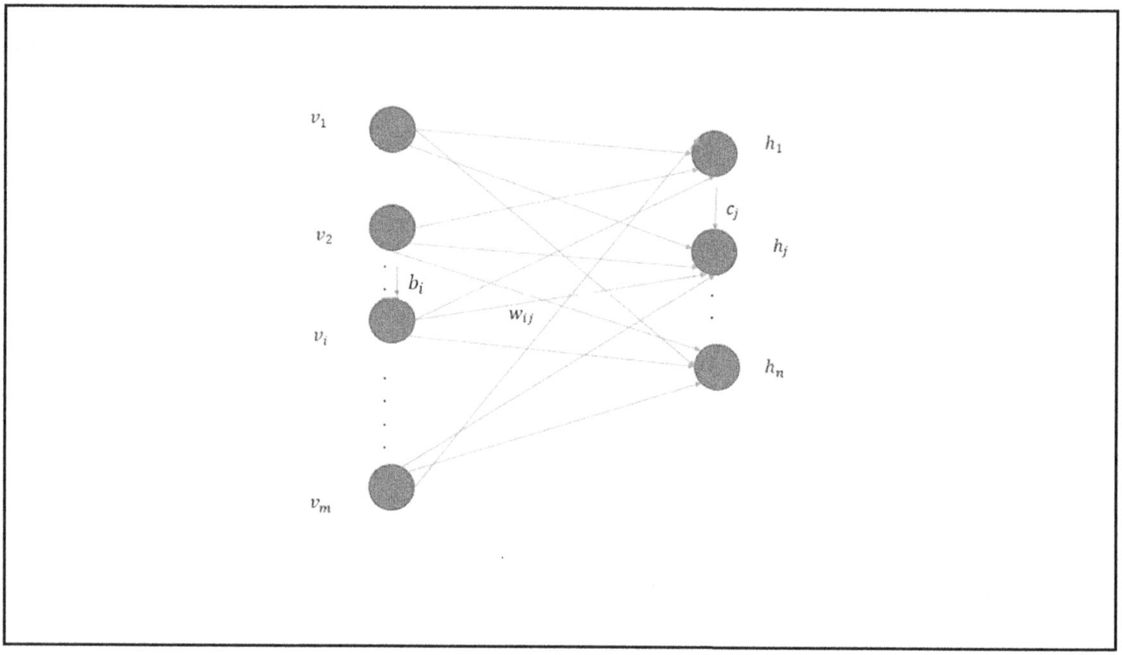

Figure 6.6: Restricted Boltzmann machines for binary data

Just to refresh our memory, the preceding diagram (*Figure 6.6*) is an RBM that has m inputs or visible units. This is projected to a hidden layer with n units. Given the visible layer inputs $v = \{v_i\}_{i=1}^{m}$, the hidden units are independent of each other and hence can be sampled as follows, where $\sigma(.)$ represents the sigmoid function:

$$P(h_j/v) = \sigma\left(\sum_{i=1}^{m} w_{ij}v_i + c_j\right)$$

Similarly, given the hidden layer activations $h = \{h_j\}_{j=1}^{n}$, the visible layer units are independent and can be sampled as follows:

$$P(v_i/h) = \sigma\left(\sum_{j=1}^{n} w_{ij}h_j + c_i\right)$$

The parameters of the RBM are the generalized weight connections $w_{ij} \in W_{m\,x\,n}$ between the visible layer unit i and the hidden layer unit j, the bias $c_i \in b$ at the visible unit i, and the bias $c_j \in c$ at the hidden layer unit j.

These parameters of the RBM are learned by maximizing the likelihood of the visible input data. If we represent the combined set of parameters by $\theta = [W; b; c]$ and we have a set of T training input data points then in the RBM, we try to maximize the likelihood function:

$$L = P(v^{(1)}v^{(2)}.....v^{(T)}/\theta) = \prod_{t=1}^{T} P(v^{(t)}/\theta)$$

Instead of working with the product form, we generally maximize the log of the likelihood, or minimize the negative of the log likelihood, to make the function mathematically more convenient. If we represent the negative of the log likelihood as our cost function C then:

$$C(\theta) = -\sum_{t=1}^{T} \log P(v^{(t)}/\theta)$$

The cost function is generally minimized by gradient descent. The gradient of the cost function with respect to the parameters consists of expectation terms and is expressed as follows:

$$\nabla_b C = \sum_{t=1}^{T} v^{(t)} - TE_{P(h,v/\theta)}[v]$$

$$\nabla_c C = \sum_{t=1}^{T} \hat{h}^{(t)} - TE_{P(h,v/\theta)}[h]$$

$$\nabla_W C = \sum_{t=1}^{T} v^{(t)}\hat{h}^{(t)^T} - TE_{P(h,v/\theta)}[vh^T]$$

The term $E_{P(h,v/\theta)}[\cdot]$ denotes the expectation of any given quantity over the joint probability distribution of the hidden and the visible units. Also, $\hat{h}$ denotes the sampled hidden layer outputs given the visible units v. Computing the expectation over the joint probability distribution within each iteration of gradient descent is computationally intractable. We resort to an intelligent method called **contrastive divergence**, discussed in the next section, to compute the expectations.

Contrastive divergence

One of the ways to compute the expectation of a joint probability distribution is to generate a lot of samples from the joint probability distribution by Gibbs sampling and then take the mean value of the samples as the expected value. In Gibbs sampling, each of the variables in the joint probability distribution can be sampled, conditioned on the rest of the variables. Since the visible units are independent, given the hidden units and vice versa, you can sample the hidden unit as $\bar{h} \leftarrow P(h/v)$ and then the visible unit activation given the hidden unit as $\bar{v} \leftarrow P(v/h = \bar{h})$. We can then take the sample $(\bar{v}, \bar{h})$ as one sampled from the joint probability distribution. In this way, we can generate a huge number of samples, say M, and take their mean to compute the desired expectation. However, doing such extensive sampling in each step of gradient descent is going to make the training process unacceptably slow, and hence, instead of computing the mean of many samples in each step of the gradient descent, we generate only one sample from the joint probability distribution that is supposed to represent the desired expectation over the entire joint probability distribution:

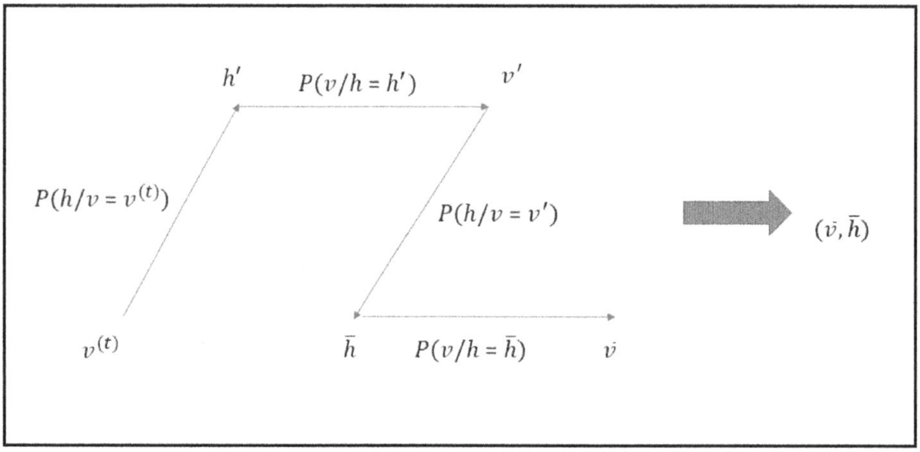

Figure 6.7: Contrastive divergence illustration

As we can see from the illustration in the preceding diagram (*Figure 6.7*), we start with the seen visible input $v^{(i)}$ and sample the hidden layer activation h' based on the conditional probability distribution $P(h/v = v^{(i)})$. Again, using the conditional probability distribution $P(v/h = h')$, we sample v'. The next sampling of the hidden unit based on the conditional probability distribution $P(h/v = v')$ gives us $\bar{h}$, and then sampling visible unit activation using $P(v/h = \bar{h})$ gives us $\bar{v}$. The sample $(\bar{v}, \bar{h})$ is taken to the representative sample for the entire joint probability distribution of v and h, that is, $P(v, h/\theta)$. The same is used for computing the expectation of any expression containing v and h. This process of sampling is known as contrastive divergence.

Starting with a visible input and then successively sampling from a conditional distribution *P(v/h)* and *P(v/h)* constitutes one step of Gibbs sampling and gives us one sample *(v/h)* from the joint distribution. Instead of picking the sample *(v/h)* at every step of Gibbs sampling, we can choose to pick the sample after several successive sampling iterations from the conditional probability distribution. If, after *k* steps of Gibbs sampling, the representative element is chosen, the contrastive divergence is termed *CD-k*. The contrastive divergence illustrated in *Figure 6.7* can be termed *CD-2*, since we choose the sample after two steps of Gibbs sampling.

Collaborative filtering using RBMs

Restricted Boltzmann machines can be used to carry out collaborative filtering when making recommendations. We will be using these RBMs to recommend movies to users. They are trained using ratings provided by the different users for different movies. A user would not have watched or rated all the movies, so this trained model can be used to recommend unseen movies to a user.

One of the first questions we should have is how to handle ranks in RBMs, since ranks are ordinal in nature, whereas RBMs work on binary data. The ranks can be treated as binary data, with the number of units to represent a rank being equal to the number of unique values for each rank. For example: in a rating system, where the ranks vary from one to five, and there would be five binary units, with the one corresponding to the rank set to one and the rest as zero. The unit visible to the RBM would be the rank provided for the user to different movies. Each rank would be represented in binary, as discussed, and there would be weight connections from all the binary visible units, corresponding to the movie rating, for each of the visible units. Since each user would have rated a different set of movies, the input for each user will be different. However, the weight connections from the movie rating units to the hidden units are common for all users.

Illustrated in the following diagrams (*Figure 6.8a* and *Figure 6.8b*) are the RBM views for **User A** and **User B**. **User A** and **User B** have rated a different set of movies. However, as we can see, the weight connections to the hidden units from each movie are the same for each user. The RBM rating with respect to **User A** is as follows:

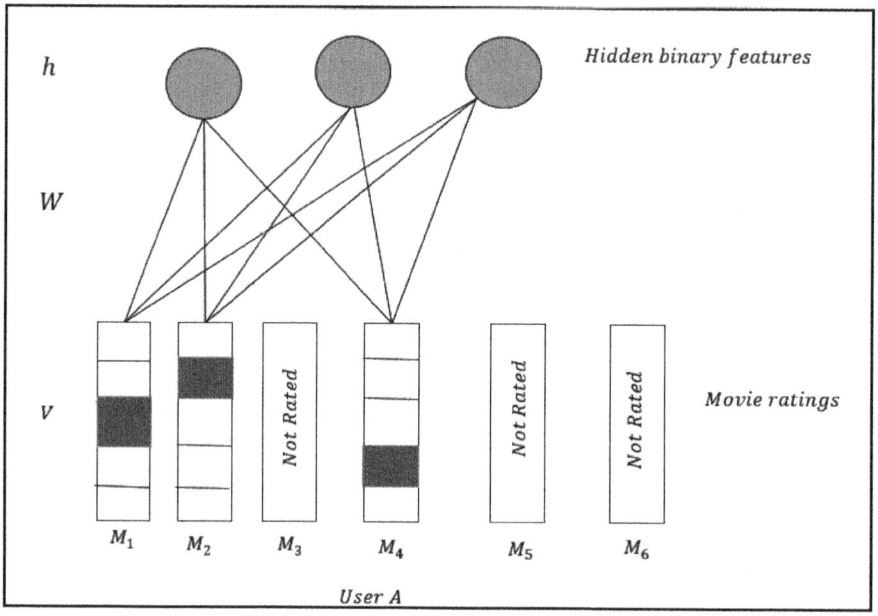

Figure 6.8a: RBM for collaborative filtering User A view

The RBM rating with respect to **User B** is as follows:

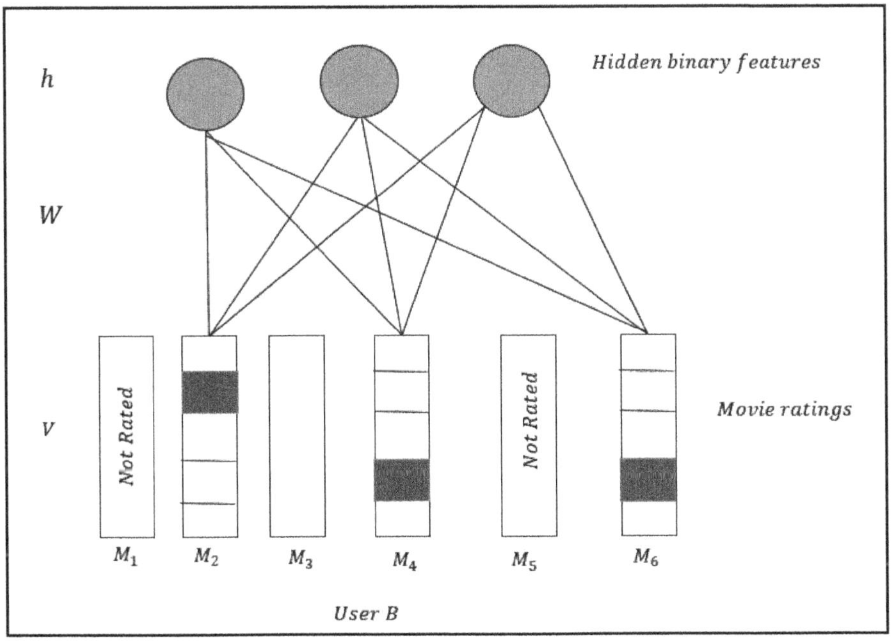

Figure 6.8b: RBM for collaborative filtering User B view

One more thing to note is that if there are M movies and if k ranks are possible for each movie, then the number of visible units to the RBM is $M * k$. Also, if the number of binary hidden units is n, then the number of weight connections in $[W]$ is equal to $M * k * n$. Each hidden unit h_j can be sampled independently of the other hidden units given the visible layer inputs as follows:

$$P(h_j/v) = \sigma(\sum_{i=1}^{m} w_{ij}v_i + c_j)$$

Here, $m = M * k$.

Unlike in a traditional RBM, the binary units in visible layers in this network cannot be independently sampled given the hidden layer activations. Each of the *k* binary units with respect to the rank of a movie are tied through a *k-way softmax* activation function. If the inputs to the visible units for a specific movie given the hidden units are $s_{i1}, s_{i2}, . s_{il} . . s_{ik}$, then the general input of the rank *l* for a movie *i* is calculated as follows:

$$s_{il} = \sum_{j=1}^{n} w_{[(i-1)k+l]j} h_j + b_{(i-1)k+l}$$

Here, *(i - 1)k + l* is the index of the visible unit of the movie *i* for rank *l*. Similarly, the visible units for any particular movie can be sampled based on their probabilities given by the soft-max function, as shown here:

$$P(v_{il}/h) = e^{s_{il}} / (\sum_{l=1}^{k} e^{s_{il}})$$

One more thing that is important in defining the outputs of both the hidden and the visible units is the need for probabilistic sampling instead of defaulting the output to be one with the maximum probability. If the probability of the hidden unit activation given the visible units is *P*, then the random number *r* in the range [0,1] is uniformly generated, and if *(P>r)* then the hidden unit activation is set to true. This scheme will ensure that over a long period of time the activations are set to true with probability *P*. Similarly, the visible units for a movie are sampled from a multinational distribution based on their probabilities given the hidden units. So, if for a specific movie, the probabilities for different ratings range from one to five, given the hidden unit activations are $(p_1, p_2, p_3, p_4, p_5)$, then the value of the rating to choose out of the five possible values can be sampled from the multinomial distribution, the probability mass function of which follows:

$$P(x_1, x_2, x_3, x_4, x_5) = p_1^{x_1} p_2^{x_2} p_3^{x_3} p_4^{x_4} p_5^{x_5}$$

Here:

$$x_1 + x_2 + x_3 + x_4 + x_5 = 1$$

$$x_i \in 0, 1 \; \forall i \in 1, 2, 3, 4, 5$$

We are now equipped with all the technical knowledge required to create a restricted Boltzmann machine for collaborative filtering.

Collaborative filtering implementation using RBM

In the next few sections, we will be implementing a collaborative filtering system using a restricted Boltzmann machine with the technical principles laid out in the earlier section. The dataset that we will be using is the MovieLens 100K dataset that contains ratings from one to five provided by users for different movies. The dataset can be downloaded from `https://grouplens.org/datasets/movielens/100k/`.

The TensorFlow implementation of this collaborative filtering system is laid out in the next few sections.

Processing the input

The input ratings file records in each row contain the fields `userId`, `movieId`, `rating`, and `timestamp`. We process each record to create a training file in the form of a `numpy` array with the three dimensions pertaining to the `userId`, the `movieId`, and the `rating`. The ratings from one to five are one-hot encoded, and hence the length along the rating dimension is five. We create the training data with 80% of the input records while the remaining 20% is reserved for test purposes. The number of movies that the users have rated is `1682`. The training file contains `943` users and hence the dimension for the training data is `(943,1682,5)`. Each user in the training file is a training record to the RBM and will contain a few movies that the user has rated and a few that the user hasn't. A few movie ratings have also been removed to be included in the test file. The RBM will be trained on the available ratings, capture the hidden structure of the input data in the hidden unit, and then try to reconstruct the input ratings for all movies for each user from the hidden structure captured. We also create a couple of dictionaries to store the cross references of the the actual movie IDs with their indices in training/test datasets. Following is the detailed code for creating the training and test files:

```
"""
@author: santanu
"""

import numpy as np
import pandas as pd
```

```
import argparse

'''
Ratings file preprocessing script to create training and hold out test
datasets
'''

def process_file(infile_path):
    infile = pd.read_csv(infile_path,sep='\t',header=None)
    infile.columns = ['userId','movieId','rating','timestamp']
    users = list(np.unique(infile.userId.values))
    movies = list(np.unique(infile.movieId.values))

    test_data = []
    ratings_matrix = np.zeros([len(users),len(movies),5])
    count = 0
    total_count = len(infile)
    for i in range(len(infile)):
        rec = infile[i:i+1]
        user_index = int(rec['userId']-1)
        movie_index = int(rec['movieId']-1)
        rating_index = int(rec['rating']-1)
        if np.random.uniform(0,1) < 0.2 :
            test_data.append([user_index,movie_index,int(rec['rating'])])

        else:
            ratings_matrix[user_index,movie_index,rating_index] = 1

        count +=1
        if (count % 100000 == 0) & (count>= 100000):
            print('Processed ' + str(count) + ' records out of ' +
str(total_count))

    np.save(path + 'train_data',ratings_matrix)
    np.save(path + 'test_data',np.array(test_data))


if __name__ == '__main__':
    parser = argparse.ArgumentParser()
    parser.add_argument('--path',help='input data path')
    parser.add_argument('--infile',help='input file name')
    args = parser.parse_args()
    path = args.path
    infile = args.infile
    process_file(path + infile)
```

The training file is a `numpy` array object of dimensions *m x n x k* where *m* is the total number of users, *n* is the total number of movies, and *k* is the number of discrete rating values (one to five). To build the test set, we randomly select 20% of the *m x n* rating entries from the training dataset. So all the *k* rating values for the test set rating samples are marked as zero in the training dataset. In the test set we don't expand the data into the three-dimensional numpy array format so it can be used for training. Rather, we just save the `userid`, `movieid` and the assigned rating in three columns. Do note that the `userid` and `movieid` stored in the train and the test files are not the actual IDs in the raw ratings data file `u.data`. They are offset by `1` to cater for Python and `numpy` indexing that starts from `0` and not from `1`

The following command can be used to invoke the data pre-processing script:

```
python preprocess_ratings.py --path '/home/santanu/ML_DS_Catalog-
/Collaborating Filtering/ml-100k/' --infile 'u.data'
```

Building the RBM network for collaborative filtering

The following function, `_network`, creates the desired RBM structure for collaborative filtering. First, we define the weights, the biases, and the placeholders for the inputs. The `sample_hidden` and `sample_visible` functions are then defined to sample the hidden and the visible activations respectively, based on the probabilities. The hidden units are sampled from Bernoulli distributions with the probabilities provided by the sigmoid function, whereas the visible units pertaining to each movie are sampled from multinomial distribution based on the probabilities provided by the softmax function. The softmax probabilities need not be created since the `tf.multinomial` function can directly sample from the logits instead of the actual probabilities.

We follow this up by defining the logic for contrastive divergence based on Gibbs sampling. The `gibbs_step` function implements one step of Gibbs sampling and then utilizes this to achieve a contrastive divergence of order *k*.

Now that we have all the necessary functions, we create the TensorFlow ops to sample the hidden state `self.h` given the visible inputs and to sample the visible units `self.x` given the sampled hidden state. We also use contrastive divergence to sample `(self.x_s,self.h_s)` as a representative sample from the joint probability distribution of v and h, that is, `P(v,h/model)`, for computing the different expectation terms in the gradients.

The final step of the `_network` function updates the weights and biases of the RBM model based on the gradients. The gradients, as we have seen earlier, are based on the hidden layer activations `self.h` given the visible layer inputs, and the representative samples from the joint probability distribution `P(v,h/model)` derived through contrastive divergence, which is `(self.x_s,self.h_s)`.

The TensorFlow ops `self.x_`, which refers to the visible layer activations given the hidden layer activations `self.h` would be useful during inference to derive the ratings for the movies that have not been rated by each user:

```
    def __network(self):
        self.x = tf.placeholder(tf.float32,
[None,self.num_movies,self.num_ranks], name="x")
        self.xr = tf.reshape(self.x, [-1,self.num_movies*self.num_ranks],
name="xr")
        self.W =
tf.Variable(tf.random_normal([self.num_movies*self.num_ranks,self.num_hidde
n], 0.01), name="W")
        self.b_h = tf.Variable(tf.zeros([1,self.num_hidden], tf.float32,
name="b_h"))
        self.b_v =
tf.Variable(tf.zeros([1,self.num_movies*self.num_ranks],tf.float32,
name="b_v"))
        self.k = 2

## Converts the probability into discrete binary states i.e. 0 and 1
        def sample_hidden(probs):
            return tf.floor(probs + tf.random_uniform(tf.shape(probs), 0,
1))

        def sample_visible(logits):
            logits = tf.reshape(logits,[-1,self.num_ranks])
            sampled_logits = tf.multinomial(logits,1)
            sampled_logits = tf.one_hot(sampled_logits,depth = 5)
            logits = tf.reshape(logits,[-1,self.num_movies*self.num_ranks])
            print(logits)
            return logits


## Gibbs sampling step
        def gibbs_step(x_k):
          # x_k = tf.reshape(x_k,[-1,self.num_movies*self.num_ranks])
            h_k = sample_hidden(tf.sigmoid(tf.matmul(x_k,self.W) +
self.b_h))
            x_k =
sample_visible(tf.add(tf.matmul(h_k,tf.transpose(self.W)),self.b_v))
            return x_k
```

```
## Run multiple gives Sampling step starting from an initital point
        def gibbs_sample(k,x_k):

            for i in range(k):
                x_k = gibbs_step(x_k)
# Returns the gibbs sample after k iterations
            return x_k

# Constrastive Divergence algorithm
# 1. Through Gibbs sampling locate a new visible state x_sample based on
the current visible state x
# 2. Based on the new x sample a new h as h_sample
        self.x_s = gibbs_sample(self.k,self.xr)
        self.h_s = sample_hidden(tf.sigmoid(tf.matmul(self.x_s,self.W) +
self.b_h))

# Sample hidden states based given visible states
        self.h = sample_hidden(tf.sigmoid(tf.matmul(self.xr,self.W) +
self.b_h))
# Sample visible states based given hidden states
        self.x_ = sample_visible(tf.matmul(self.h,tf.transpose(self.W)) +
self.b_v)

# The weight updated based on gradient descent
        #self.size_batch = tf.cast(tf.shape(x)[0], tf.float32)
        self.W_add =
tf.multiply(self.learning_rate/self.batch_size,tf.subtract(tf.matmul(tf.tra
nspose(self.xr),self.h),tf.matmul(tf.transpose(self.x_s),self.h_s)))
        self.bv_add = tf.multiply(self.learning_rate/self.batch_size,
tf.reduce_sum(tf.subtract(self.xr,self.x_s), 0, True))
        self.bh_add = tf.multiply(self.learning_rate/self.batch_size,
tf.reduce_sum(tf.subtract(self.h,self.h_s), 0, True))
        self.updt = [self.W.assign_add(self.W_add),
self.b_v.assign_add(self.bv_add), self.b_h.assign_add(self.bh_add)]
```

The data from the pre-processing step can read during training and inference using the `read_data` function illustrated as follows:

```
    def read_data(self):
        if self.mode == 'train':
           self.train_data = np.load(self.train_file)
           self.num_ranks = self.train_data.shape[2]
           self.num_movies = self.train_data.shape[1]
           self.users = self.train_data.shape[0]
        else:
           self.train_df = pd.read_csv(self.train_file)
           self.test_data = np.load(self.test_file)
           self.test_df =
```

```
pd.DataFrame(self.test_data,columns=['userid','movieid','rating'])

            if self.user_info_file != None:
                self.user_info_df =
pd.read_csv(self.user_info_file,sep='|',header=None)
self.user_info_df.columns=['userid','age','gender','occupation','zipcode']

            if self.movie_info_file != None:
                self.movie_info_df =
pd.read_csv(self.movie_info_file,sep='|',encoding='latin-1',header=None)
                self.movie_info_df = self.movie_info_df[[0,1]]
                self.movie_info_df.columns = ['movieid','movie Title']
```

Also, during the inference process, along with the test file we read in a prediction file CSV (`self.train_file` here in the inference part of the previous code) for all movies and ratings irrespective of whether they have been rated. The prediction is performed once the model has been trained. Since we already have the ratings predicted after training, all we need to do during inference time is combine the rating prediction information with the test file's actual rating information (more details in the `train` and `inference` sections to follow). Also, we read information from the user and movie meta data file for later use.

Training the RBM

The `_train` function illustrated here can be used to train the RBM. In this function, we first invoke the `_network` function to build the RBM network structure and then we train the model for a specified number of epochs within an activated TensorFlow session. The model is saved at specified intervals using TensorFlow's `saver` function:

```
    def _train(self):

        self.__network()
       # TensorFlow graph execution

        with tf.Session() as sess:
            self.saver = tf.train.Saver()
            #saver = tf.train.Saver(write_version=tf.train.SaverDef.V2)
            # Initialize the variables of the Model
            init = tf.global_variables_initializer()
            sess.run(init)

            total_batches = self.train_data.shape[0]//self.batch_size
            batch_gen = self.next_batch()
            # Start the training
            for epoch in range(self.epochs):
                if epoch < 150:
```

```
                    self.k = 2

                if (epoch > 150) & (epoch < 250):
                    self.k = 3

                if (epoch > 250) & (epoch < 350):
                    self.k = 5

                if (epoch > 350) & (epoch < 500):
                    self.k = 9

                    # Loop over all batches
                for i in range(total_batches):
                    self.X_train = next(batch_gen)
                    # Run the weight update
                    #batch_xs = (batch_xs > 0)*1
                    _ =
sess.run([self.updt],feed_dict={self.x:self.X_train})

                # Display the running step
                if epoch % self.display_step == 0:
                    print("Epoch:", '%04d' % (epoch+1))
                    print(self.outdir)
                    self.saver.save(sess,os.path.join(self.outdir,'model'),
                                    global_step=epoch)
            # Do the prediction for all users all items irrespective of
whether they
              have been rated
             self.logits_pred = tf.reshape(self.x_,
            [self.users,self.num_movies,self.num_ranks])
             self.probs = tf.nn.softmax(self.logits_pred,axis=2)
             out = sess.run(self.probs,feed_dict={self.x:self.train_data})
             recs = []
             for i in range(self.users):
                 for j in range(self.num_movies):
                     rec = [i,j,np.argmax(out[i,j,:]) +1]
                     recs.append(rec)
             recs = np.array(recs)
             df_pred = pd.DataFrame(recs,columns=
             ['userid','movieid','predicted_rating'])
             df_pred.to_csv(self.outdir + 'pred_all_recs.csv',index=False)

             print("RBM training Completed !")
```

An important thing to highlight in the preceding function is the creation of random batches using a custom `next_batch` function. The function is as defined in the following code snippet and it is used to define an iterator `batch_gen` that can be invoked by the `next` method to retrieve the next mini-batch:

```
def next_batch(self):
    while True:
        ix =
np.random.choice(np.arange(self.data.shape[0]),self.batch_size)
        train_X = self.data[ix,:,:]
        yield train_X
```

One thing to note is that at the end of the training, we predict the ratings for all movies from all users, irrespective of whether they are rated. The ratings with the maximum probability, which will be given out of the five possible ratings (that is from one to five) as the final rating. Since in Python the indexing starts from zero we add one to get the actual rating after using `argmax` to get the location of the rating with the highest probability. So, at the end of the training, we have a `pred_all_recs.csv` file containing the predicted rating for all the training and test records. Do note that the test records are embedded in the training records with all the indices of the rating for from one to five being set to zero.

However, once we have trained the model sufficiently from the hidden representation of the movies that the user has watched it learns to generate ratings from the movies that the user hasn't seen.

The model can be trained by invoking the following commands:

```
python rbm.py main_process --mode train --train_file
'/home/santanu/ML_DS_Catalog-/Collaborating
Filtering/ml-100k/train_data.npy' --outdir '/home/santanu/ML_DS_Catalog-
/Collaborating Filtering/' --num_hidden 5 --epochs 1000
```

Training the model for `1000` epochs with just `5` hidden layers takes around `52` seconds, as we can see from the log:

```
RBM training Completed !
52.012 s: process RBM
```

Note that the Restricted Boltzmann Machine Network has been trained on an Ubuntu machine with a GeForce Zotac 1070 GPU and 64 GB of RAM. Training time may vary based on the system used to train the network.

Inference using the trained RBM

Inference for the RBM is pretty straightforward given that we have already generated the file `pred_all_recs.csv` with all the predictions during training. All we need to do is just extract the test records from the `pred_all_recs.csv` based on the provided test file. Also, we resort to the original `userid` and `movieid` by adding `1` to their current values. The purpose of going back to the original ID is to be able to add the user and movie information from the `u.user` and `u.item` files.

The inference block is as follows:

```
    def inference(self):

        self.df_result =
self.test_df.merge(self.train_df,on=['userid','movieid'])
        # in order to get the original ids we just need to add 1
        self.df_result['userid'] = self.df_result['userid'] + 1
        self.df_result['movieid'] = self.df_result['movieid'] + 1
        if self.user_info_file != None:
            self.df_result.merge(self.user_info_df,on=['userid'])
        if self.movie_info_file != None:
            self.df_result.merge(self.movie_info_df,on=['movieid'])
        self.df_result.to_csv(self.outdir + 'test_results.csv',index=False)


        print(f'output written to {self.outdir}test_results.csv')
        test_rmse = (np.mean((self.df_result['rating'].values -
        self.df_result['predicted_rating'].values)**2))**0.5
        print(f'test RMSE : {test_rmse}')
```

Inference can be invoked as follows:

```
python rbm.py main_process --mode test --train_file
'/home/santanu/ML_DS_Catalog-/Collaborating Filtering/pred_all_recs.csv' --
test_file '/home/santanu/ML_DS_Catalog-/Collaborating
Filtering/ml-100k/test_data.npy' --outdir '/home/santanu/ML_DS_Catalog-
/Collaborating Filtering/' --user_info_file '/home/santanu/ML_DS_Catalog-
/Collaborating Filtering/ml-100k/u.user' --movie_info_file
'/home/santanu/ML_DS_Catalog-/Collaborating Filtering/ml-100k/u.item'
```

By using only `5` hidden units in the RBM we achieve a test RMSE of around `1.19` which is commendable given that we have chosen such a simple network. The output log of inference is provided in the following code block for reference:

```
output written to /home/santanu/ML_DS_Catalog-/Collaborating
Filtering/test_results.csv
test RMSE : 1.1999306704742303
458.058 ms: process RBM
```

We look at the inference results for `userid 1` from the `test_results.csv` as follows (see *Figure 6.9*):

userid	movieid	rating	predicted_rating	age	gender	occupation	zipcode	movie Title
1	181	5	5	24	M	technician	85711	Return of the Jedi (1983)
1	265	4	4	24	M	technician	85711	Hunt for Red October, The (1990)
1	7	4	4	24	M	technician	85711	Twelve Monkeys (1995)
1	89	5	4	24	M	technician	85711	Blade Runner (1982)
1	232	3	3	24	M	technician	85711	Young Guns (1988)
1	210	4	4	24	M	technician	85711	Indiana Jones and the Last Crusade (1989)
1	212	4	4	24	M	technician	85711	Unbearable Lightness of Being, The (1988)
1	87	5	4	24	M	technician	85711	Searching for Bobby Fischer (1993)
1	190	5	4	24	M	technician	85711	Henry V (1989)
1	61	4	4	24	M	technician	85711	Three Colors: White (1994)
1	240	3	3	24	M	technician	85711	Beavis and Butt-head Do America (1996)
1	121	4	4	24	M	technician	85711	Independence Day (ID4) (1996)
1	218	3	3	24	M	technician	85711	Cape Fear (1991)
1	160	4	4	24	M	technician	85711	Glengarry Glen Ross (1992)
1	97	3	4	24	M	technician	85711	Dances with Wolves (1990)
1	107	4	3	24	M	technician	85711	Moll Flanders (1996)
1	201	3	4	24	M	technician	85711	Evil Dead II (1987)
1	177	5	4	24	M	technician	85711	Good, The Bad and The Ugly, The (1966)
1	68	4	4	24	M	technician	85711	Crow, The (1994)
1	27	2	3	24	M	technician	85711	Bad Boys (1995)
1	66	4	3	24	M	technician	85711	While You Were Sleeping (1995)
1	228	5	3	24	M	technician	85711	Star Trek: The Wrath of Khan (1982)
1	176	5	4	24	M	technician	85711	Aliens (1986)
1	138	1	3	24	M	technician	85711	D3: The Mighty Ducks (1996)
1	268	5	4	24	M	technician	85711	Chasing Amy (1997)
1	155	2	2	24	M	technician	85711	Dirty Dancing (1987)
1	195	5	4	24	M	technician	85711	Terminator, The (1984)
1	64	5	5	24	M	technician	85711	Shawshank Redemption, The (1994)
1	44	5	4	24	M	technician	85711	Dolores Claiborne (1994)
1	223	5	4	24	M	technician	85711	Sling Blade (1996)

Figure 6.9: Holdout data validation results on userid 1

We can see from the predictions in the preceding screenshot (*Figure 6.9*) that the RBM has done a good job of predicting the holdout set of movies for `userid 1`.

You are advised to take the final rating prediction as the expectation of the ratings over the multinomial probability distribution for each movie-rating prediction and see how it fares in comparison to the approach, where we are taking the final rating as the one with the highest probability over the multinomial distribution. The RBM paper for collaborative filtering can be located at `https://www.cs.toronto.edu/~rsalakhu/papers/rbmcf.pd`. The code related to the restricted Boltzmann machine can be located at `https://github.com/PacktPublishing/Intelligent-Projects-using-Python/blob/master/Chapter06/rbm.py`.

Summary

After going through this chapter, you should now be able to build an intelligent recommender system using restricted Boltzmann machines and extend it in interesting ways based on your domain and requirements. For a detailed implementation of the project illustrated in this chapter, refer to the GiHub link for this project at `https://github.com/PacktPublishing/Intelligent-Projects-using-Python/blob/master/Chapter06`.

In the next chapter, we will deal with the creation of a mobile app to perform sentiment analysis of movie reviews. I look forward to your participation.

7
Mobile App for Movie Review Sentiment Analysis

In this modern age, sending data to AI-based applications in the cloud for inference is commonplace. For instance, a user can send an image taken on a mobile phone to the Amazon Rekognition API, and the service can tag the various objects, people, text, scenes, and so on, present in the image. The advantage of employing the service of an AI-based application that's hosted in the cloud is its ease of use. The mobile app just needs to make an HTTPS request to the AI-based service, along with the image, and, within a few seconds, the service will provide the inference results. A few of these **machine learning as a service** providers are as follows:

- Amazon Rekognition
- Amazon Polly
- Amazon Lex
- Microsoft Azure Cognitive Services
- IBM Watson
- Google Cloud Vision

The following diagram, *Figure 7.1,* illustrates the architecture of this kind of application as it's hosted on the cloud, and how it interacts with a mobile device:

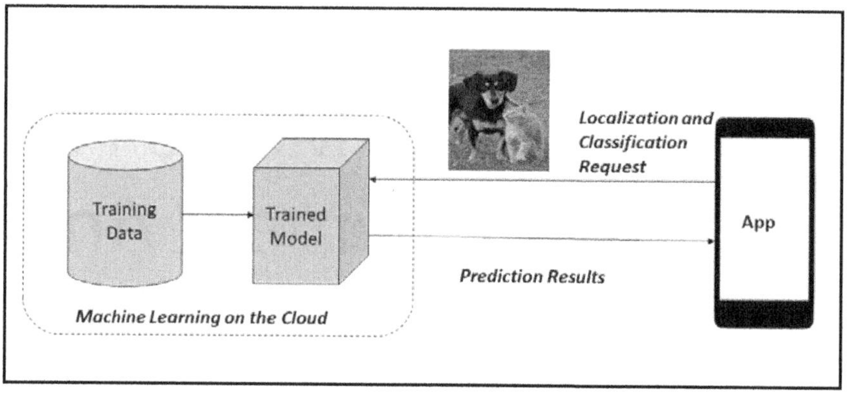

Figure 7.1: Mobile app communicating with an AI model hosted on the cloud

As you can see in the preceding diagram, the mobile app sends an image localization and classification request to the model hosted on the cloud, along with an image, and the model sends back the results, after running inference on the provided image. The advantages of using such a service on the cloud are as follows:

- There is no need to gather data for training this kind of model
- There is no pain associated with hosting the AI model as a service
- There is no need to worry about re-training the model

All of the preceding will be taken care of by the service provider. However, using this kind of AI application on the cloud does have several disadvantages, as well, which include the following:

- The user cannot run inference on the mobile device locally. All inference needs to be done by sending a network request to the server where the AI application is hosted. The mobile app won't work in the absence of network connectivity. Also, there may be some delays in getting the predictions from the model through the network.
- If it is not a freely hosted cloud application, the user typically pays for the number of inferences they run.
- The models hosted on the cloud are very generic, and the user has no control over training those models with their own data. If the data is unique, this kind of application, which is trained on generic data, might not provide great results.

The preceding shortcomings of AI applications deployed on the cloud can be overcome by running inference on the mobile device itself, instead of sending the data to the AI application over the internet.

The model can be trained on any system with the appropriate CPU and GPU, using training data specific to the problem that the mobile app is designed for. The trained model can then be converted to an optimized file format, with only the weights and ops required to run the inference. The optimized model can then be integrated with the mobile app, and the whole project can be loaded as an app on the mobile device. The optimized file for the trained model should be as light in size as possible, since the model is going to be stored on the mobile itself, along with the rest of the mobile app code. In this chapter, we are going to develop an Android mobile app, using TensorFlow mobile.

Technical requirements

You will require to have basic knowledge of Python 3, TensorFlow, and Java

The code files of this chapter can be found on GitHub:
`https://github.com/PacktPublishing/Intelligent-Projects-using-Python/tree/master/Chapter07`

Check out the following video to see the code in action:
`http://bit.ly/2S1sddw`

Building an Android mobile app using TensorFlow mobile

In this project, we will be using TensorFlow's mobile capabilities to optimize a trained model as a protocol buffer object. We will then integrate the model with an Android app, the logic of which will be written in Java. We need to carry out the following steps:

1. Build a model in TensorFlow and train it with the relevant data.
2. Once the model performs satisfactorily on the validation dataset, convert the TensorFlow model to the optimized protobuf object (for example, `optimized_model.pb`).

3. Download Android Studio and its prerequisites. Develop the core application logic in Java and the interfacing pages using XML.
4. Integrate the TensorFlow trained model protobuf object and its associated dependencies in the assets folder within the project.
5. Build the project and run it.

The implementation of this Android app is illustrated in the following diagram (*Figure 7.2*):

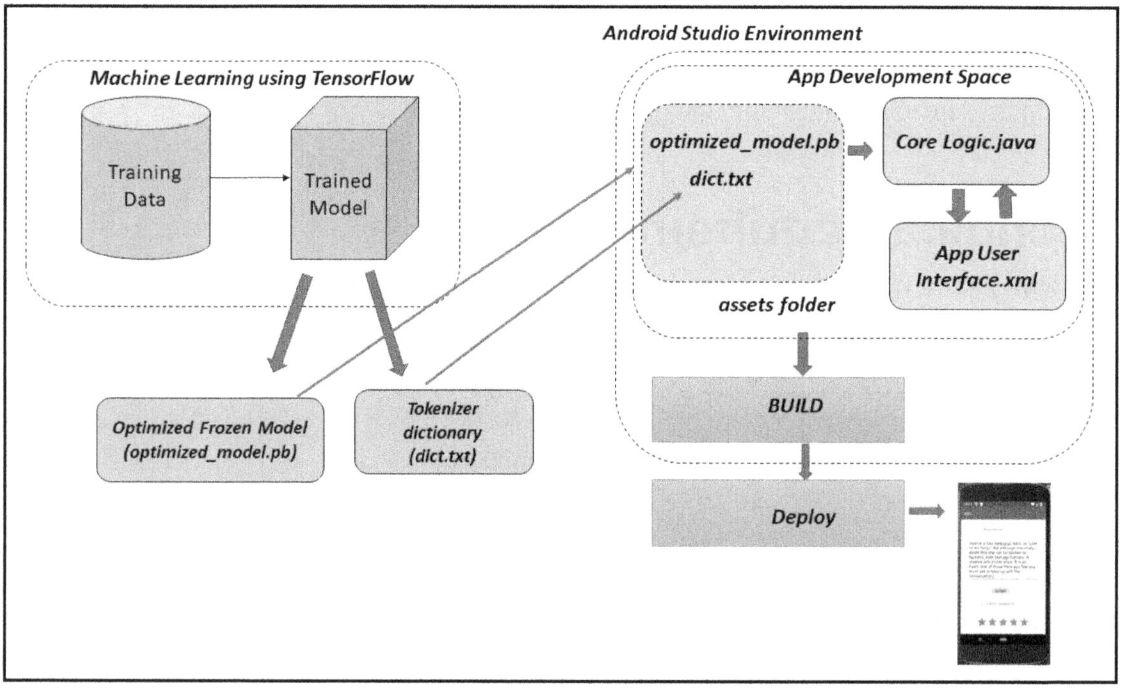

Figure 7.2: Mobile app deployment architectural diagram

Movie review rating in an Android app

We will be building an Android app that will take movie reviews as input and provide a rating from `0` to `5` as an output, based on a sentiment analysis of the movie review. An LSTM version of the recurrent neural network would first be trained to carry out a binary classification on the sentiment of the movie. The training data would consist of text-based movie reviews, along with a binary label of `0` or `1`. A label of `1` stands for a review that has a positive sentiment, while `0` denotes that the movie has a negative sentiment. From the model, we will predict the probability of the sentiment being positive, and then scale up the probability by a factor of five, to convert it into a reasonable rating. The model will be built using TensorFlow, and then the trained model will be converted to an optimized frozen protobuf object, to be integrated with the Android app logic. The frozen object will be of a much smaller size than the original trained model, and will only be used for inference purposes.

We will use the dataset available at `http://ai.stanford.edu/~amaas/data/sentiment/`, used in the following paper, titled *Learning Word Vectors for Sentiment Analysis*:

```
@InProceedings{maas-EtAl:2011:ACL-HLT2011,
  author    = {Maas, Andrew L.  and  Daly, Raymond E.  and  Pham, Peter T.
and  Huang, Dan  and  Ng, Andrew Y.  and  Potts, Christopher},
  title     = {Learning Word Vectors for Sentiment Analysis},
  booktitle = {Proceedings of the 49th Annual Meeting of the Association
for Computational Linguistics: Human Language Technologies},
  month     = {June},
  year      = {2011},
  address   = {Portland, Oregon, USA},
  publisher = {Association for Computational Linguistics},
  pages     = {142--150},
  url       = {http://www.aclweb.org/anthology/P11-1015}
}
```

Preprocessing the movie review text

The movie review text needs to be preprocessed and converted to numerical tokens, corresponding to different words in the corpus. The Keras tokenizer will be used to convert the words into numerical indices, or tokens, by taking the first `50000` frequent words. We have restricted the movie reviews to have a maximum of `1000` word tokens. If a movie review has less than `1000` word tokens, the review is padded with zeros at the beginning. After the preprocessing, the data is split into train, validation, and test sets. The Keras `Tokenizer` object is saved for use during inference.

The detailed code(preprocess.py) for preprocessing the movie reviews is as follows:

```
# -*- coding: utf-8 -*-
"""
Created on Sun Jun 17 22:36:00 2018
@author: santanu
"""
import numpy as np
import pandas as pd
import os
import re
from keras.preprocessing.text import Tokenizer
from keras.preprocessing.sequence import pad_sequences
import pickle
import fire
from elapsedtimer import ElapsedTimer


# Function to clean the text and convert it into lower case
def text_clean(text):
    letters = re.sub("[^a-zA-z0-9\s]", " ",text)
    words = letters.lower().split()
    text = " ".join(words)
    return text


def process_train(path):
    review_dest = []
    reviews = []
    train_review_files_pos = os.listdir(path + 'train/pos/')
    review_dest.append(path + 'train/pos/')
    train_review_files_neg = os.listdir(path + 'train/neg/')
    review_dest.append(path + 'train/neg/')
    test_review_files_pos = os.listdir(path + 'test/pos/')
    review_dest.append(path + 'test/pos/')
    test_review_files_neg = os.listdir(path + 'test/neg/')
    review_dest.append(path + 'test/neg/')
    sentiment_label = [1]*len(train_review_files_pos) + \
                      [0]*len(train_review_files_neg) + \
                      [1]*len(test_review_files_pos) + \
                      [0]*len(test_review_files_neg)
    review_train_test = ['train']*len(train_review_files_pos) + \
                        ['train']*len(train_review_files_neg) + \
                        ['test']*len(test_review_files_pos) + \
                        ['test']*len(test_review_files_neg)
    reviews_count = 0
    for dest in review_dest:
        files = os.listdir(dest)
```

```
        for f in files:
            fl = open(dest + f,'r')
            review = fl.readlines()
            review_clean = text_clean(review[0])
            reviews.append(review_clean)
            reviews_count +=1
    df = pd.DataFrame()
    df['Train_test_ind'] = review_train_test
    df['review'] = reviews
    df['sentiment_label'] = sentiment_label
    df.to_csv(path + 'processed_file.csv',index=False)
    print ('records_processed',reviews_count)
    return df
def process_main(path):
    df = process_train(path)
    # We will tokenize the text for the most common 50000 words.
    max_fatures = 50000
    tokenizer = Tokenizer(num_words=max_fatures, split=' ')
    tokenizer.fit_on_texts(df['review'].values)
    X = tokenizer.texts_to_sequences(df['review'].values)
    X_ = []
    for x in X:
        x = x[:1000]
        X_.append(x)
    X_ = pad_sequences(X_)
    y = df['sentiment_label'].values
    index = list(range(X_.shape[0]))
    np.random.shuffle(index)
    train_record_count = int(len(index)*0.7)
    validation_record_count = int(len(index)*0.15)

    train_indices = index[:train_record_count]
    validation_indices = index[train_record_count:train_record_count +
                               validation_record_count]
    test_indices = index[train_record_count + validation_record_count:]
    X_train,y_train = X_[train_indices],y[train_indices]
    X_val,y_val = X_[validation_indices],y[validation_indices]
    X_test,y_test = X_[test_indices],y[test_indices]
    np.save(path + 'X_train',X_train)
    np.save(path + 'y_train',y_train)
    np.save(path + 'X_val',X_val)
    np.save(path + 'y_val',y_val)
    np.save(path + 'X_test',X_test)
    np.save(path + 'y_test',y_test)

    # saving the tokenizer oject for inference
    with open(path + 'tokenizer.pickle', 'wb') as handle:
        pickle.dump(tokenizer, handle, protocol=pickle.HIGHEST_PROTOCOL)
```

```
if __name__ == '__main__':
    with ElapsedTimer('Process'):
        fire.Fire(process_main)
```

The code `preprocess.py` can be invoked as follows:

```
python preprocess.py --path /home/santanu/Downloads/Mobile_App/aclImdb/
```

The output log for the same would be as follows:

```
Using TensorFlow backend.
records_processed 50000
24.949 s: Process
```

Building the model

We will build a simple LSTM version of the recurrent neural network, with an embedding layer following the input layer. The embedding layer word vectors are initialized with the pretrained Glove vectors with a dimension of 100, and the layer is defined as `trainable`, so that the word vector embedding can update itself based on the training data. The dimension of the hidden states and the cell states is also kept as `100`. The model is trained using binary cross-entropy loss. To avoid overfitting, ridge regularization is added to the loss function. The **Adam optimizer** is used for training the model.

The following code snippet shows the function used to build the model in TensorFlow:

```
def _build_model(self):
        with tf.variable_scope('inputs'):
            self.X = tf.placeholder(shape=[None,
self.sentence_length],dtype=tf.int32,name="X")
            print (self.X)
            self.y = tf.placeholder(shape=[None,1],
dtype=tf.float32,name="y")
            self.emd_placeholder =
tf.placeholder(tf.float32,shape=[self.n_words,self.embedding_dim])

        with tf.variable_scope('embedding'):
            # create embedding variable
            self.emb_W =tf.get_variable('word_embeddings',[self.n_words,
self.embedding_dim],initializer=tf.random_uniform_initializer(-1, 1,
0),trainable=True,dtype=tf.float32)
            self.assign_ops = tf.assign(self.emb_W,self.emd_placeholder)
            # do embedding lookup
```

```
            self.embedding_input =
tf.nn.embedding_lookup(self.emb_W,self.X,"embedding_input")
            print( self.embedding_input )
            self.embedding_input =
tf.unstack(self.embedding_input,self.sentence_length,1)
            #rint( self.embedding_input)

        # define the LSTM cell
        with tf.variable_scope('LSTM_cell'):
            self.cell = tf.nn.rnn_cell.BasicLSTMCell(self.hidden_states)

        # define the LSTM operation
        with tf.variable_scope('ops'):
            self.output, self.state =
tf.nn.static_rnn(self.cell,self.embedding_input,dtype=tf.float32)
        with tf.variable_scope('classifier'):
            self.w = tf.get_variable(name="W",
shape=[self.hidden_states,1],dtype=tf.float32)
            self.b = tf.get_variable(name="b", shape=[1], dtype=tf.float32)
        self.l2_loss = tf.nn.l2_loss(self.w,name="l2_loss")
        self.scores =
tf.nn.xw_plus_b(self.output[-1],self.w,self.b,name="logits")
        self.prediction_probability =
tf.nn.sigmoid(self.scores,name='positive_sentiment_probability')
        print (self.prediction_probability)
        self.predictions =
tf.round(self.prediction_probability,name='final_prediction')

        self.losses =
tf.nn.sigmoid_cross_entropy_with_logits(logits=self.scores,labels=self.y)
        self.loss = tf.reduce_mean(self.losses) + self.lambda1*self.l2_loss
        tf.summary.scalar('loss', self.loss)
        self.optimizer =
tf.train.AdamOptimizer(self.learning_rate).minimize(self.losses)

        self.correct_predictions =
tf.equal(self.predictions,tf.round(self.y))
        print (self.correct_predictions)

        self.accuracy = tf.reduce_mean(tf.cast(self.correct_predictions,
"float"),          name="accuracy")
        tf.summary.scalar('accuracy', self.accuracy)
```

Training the model

In this section, we will illustrate the TensorFlow code for training the model. The model is trained for a modest `10 epochs`, to avoid overfitting. The learning rate used for the optimizer is `0.001`, while the training batch size and the validation batch size are set at `250` and `50`, respectively. One thing to note is that we are saving the model graph definition in the `model.pbtxt` file, using the `tf.train.write_graph` function. Also, once the model is trained, we will save the model weights in the checkpoint file, `model_ckpt`, using the `tf.train.Saver` function. The `model.pbtxt` and `model_ckpt` files will be used to create an optimized version of the TensorFlow model in the protobuf format, which can be integrated with the Android app:

```
    def _train(self):
          self.num_batches = int(self.X_train.shape[0]//self.batch_size)
          self._build_model()
          self.saver = tf.train.Saver()
          with tf.Session() as sess:
               init = tf.global_variables_initializer()
               sess.run(init)
sess.run(self.assign_ops,feed_dict={self.emd_placeholder:self.embedding_mat
rix})
               tf.train.write_graph(sess.graph_def, self.path, 'model.pbtxt')
               print (self.batch_size,self.batch_size_val)
               for epoch in range(self.epochs):
                   gen_batch =
self.batch_gen(self.X_train,self.y_train,self.batch_size)
                   gen_batch_val =
self.batch_gen(self.X_val,self.y_val,self.batch_size_val)
                   for batch in range(self.num_batches):
                       X_batch,y_batch = next(gen_batch)
                       X_batch_val,y_batch_val = next(gen_batch_val)
sess.run(self.optimizer,feed_dict={self.X:X_batch,self.y:y_batch})
                       c,a =
sess.run([self.loss,self.accuracy],feed_dict={self.X:X_batch,self.y:y_batch
})
                       print(" Epoch=",epoch," Batch=",batch," Training Loss:
","{:.9f}".format(c), " Training Accuracy=", "{:.9f}".format(a))
                       c1,a1 =
sess.run([self.loss,self.accuracy],feed_dict={self.X:X_batch_val,self.y:y_b
atch_val})
                       print(" Epoch=",epoch," Validation Loss:
","{:.9f}".format(c1), " Validation Accuracy=", "{:.9f}".format(a1))
                   results =
sess.run(self.prediction_probability,feed_dict={self.X:X_batch_val})
                   print(results)
```

```
                if epoch % self.checkpoint_step == 0:
                    self.saver.save(sess, os.path.join(self.path,'model'),
global_step=epoch)
            self.saver.save(sess,self.path + 'model_ckpt')
            results =
sess.run(self.prediction_probability,feed_dict={self.X:X_batch_val})
            print(results)
```

The batch generator

In the `train` function, we will use a batch generator to produce random batches, based on the batch sizes passed. The generator functions can be defined as follows. Note that the functions use `yield` in place of `return`. By calling the functions with the required parameters, an iterator object of batches will be created. The batches can be retrieved by applying the `next` method to the iterator object. We will call the generator functions at the start of each epoch, so that the batches will be random in each epoch.

The following code snippet illustrates the function used to generate the batch iterator object:

```
def batch_gen(self,X,y,batch_size):
        index = list(range(X.shape[0]))
        np.random.shuffle(index)
        batches = int(X.shape[0]//batch_size)
        for b in range(batches):
            X_train,y_train = X[index[b*batch_size: (b+1)*batch_size],:],
                                     y[index[b*batch_size:
(b+1)*batch_size]]
            yield X_train,y_train
```

The detailed code for the model training activity is present in the script **`movie_review_model_train.py`** . The training for the same can be invoked as follows:

```
python movie_review_model_train.py process_main --path
/home/santanu/Downloads/Mobile_App/ --epochs 10
```

The output from training is as follows:

```
Using TensorFlow backend.
(35000, 1000) (35000, 1)
(7500, 1000) (7500, 1)
```

```
(7500, 1000) (7500, 1)
no of positive class in train: 17497
no of positive class in test: 3735
Tensor("inputs/X:0", shape=(?, 1000), dtype=int32)
Tensor("embedding/embedding_lookup:0", shape=(?, 1000, 100), dtype=float32)
Tensor("positive_sentiment_probability:0", shape=(?, 1), dtype=float32)
.....
25.043 min: Model train
```

Freezing the model to a protobuf format

The saved, trained model, in the form of the `model.pbtxt` and `model_ckpt` files, cannot be used by the Android app directly. We need to convert it to an optimized protobuf format (a `.pb` extension file), which can be integrated with the Android app. The file size of the optimized protobuf format will be much smaller than the combined size of the `model.pbtxt` and `model_ckpt` files.

The following code(`freeze_code.py`) will create the optimized protobuf model from the `model.pbtxt` and the `model_ckpt` files:

```
# -*- coding: utf-8 -*-

import sys
import tensorflow as tf
from tensorflow.python.tools import freeze_graph
from tensorflow.python.tools import optimize_for_inference_lib
import fire
from elapsedtimer import ElapsedTimer

#path = '/home/santanu/Downloads/Mobile_App/'
#MODEL_NAME = 'model'

def model_freeze(path,MODEL_NAME='model'):

    # Freeze the graph

    input_graph_path = path + MODEL_NAME+'.pbtxt'
    checkpoint_path = path + 'model_ckpt'
    input_saver_def_path = ""
    input_binary = False
    output_node_names = 'positive_sentiment_probability'
    restore_op_name = "save/restore_all"
    filename_tensor_name = "save/Const:0"
    output_frozen_graph_name = path + 'frozen_'+MODEL_NAME+'.pb'
```

```
    output_optimized_graph_name = path + 'optimized_'+MODEL_NAME+'.pb'
    clear_devices = True


    freeze_graph.freeze_graph(input_graph_path, input_saver_def_path,
                              input_binary, checkpoint_path,
output_node_names,
                              restore_op_name, filename_tensor_name,
    output_frozen_graph_name, clear_devices, "")

    input_graph_def = tf.GraphDef()

    with tf.gfile.Open(output_frozen_graph_name, "rb") as f:
        data = f.read()
        input_graph_def.ParseFromString(data)

    output_graph_def = optimize_for_inference_lib.optimize_for_inference(
            input_graph_def,
            ["inputs/X" ],#an array of the input node(s)
            ["positive_sentiment_probability"],
            tf.int32.as_datatype_enum # an array of output nodes
            )

    # Save the optimized graph

    f = tf.gfile.FastGFile(output_optimized_graph_name, "w")
    f.write(output_graph_def.SerializeToString())

if __name__ == '__main__':
    with ElapsedTimer('Model Freeze'):
        fire.Fire(model_freeze)
```

As you can see in the preceding code, we first declare the input tensor and the output tensor, by referring to their names as defined while declaring the model. Using the input and the output tensors, as well as the `model.pbtxt` and `model_ckpt` files, the model is frozen by utilizing the `freeze_graph` function from `tensorflow.python.tools`. In the next step, the frozen model is further optimized, using the `optimize_for_inference_lib` function from `tensorflow.python.tools` to create the protobuf model, named `optimized_model.pb`. This optimized protobuf model, `optimized_model.pb`, will be integrated with the Android app, for inference.

The `freeze_code.py` model can be invoked to create the protobuf format file as follows:

```
python freeze_code.py --path /home/santanu/Downloads/Mobile_App/ --
MODEL_NAME model
```

The output of the execution of the preceding command is as follows:

```
39.623 s: Model Freeze
```

Creating a word-to-token dictionary for inference

During preprocessing, we trained a Keras tokenizer to replace the words with their numerical word indices, so that the processed movie reviews could be fed to the LSTM model for training. We have also kept the first `50000` words with the highest word frequency, and have set the review sequences to be of a maximum length of `1000`. Although the trained Keras tokenizer was saved for inference, it cannot be used by the Android app directly. We can restore the Keras tokenizer and save the first `50000` words and their corresponding word indices in a text file. This text file can be used in the Android app, in order to build a **word-to-indices dictionary** to convert the words of the review text to their word indices. It is important to note that the word to indices mapping can be retrieved from the loaded Keras tokenizer object, by referring to `tokenizer.word_index`. The detailed code to do this activity `tokenizer_2_txt.py` is as follows:

```
import keras
import pickle
import fire
from elapsedtimer import ElapsedTimer

#path = '/home/santanu/Downloads/Mobile_App/aclImdb/tokenizer.pickle'
#path_out = '/home/santanu/Downloads/Mobile_App/word_ind.txt'
def tokenize(path,path_out):
    with open(path, 'rb') as handle:
        tokenizer = pickle.load(handle)



    dict_ = tokenizer.word_index

    keys = list(dict_.keys())[:50000]
    values = list(dict_.values())[:50000]
    total_words = len(keys)
```

```
    f = open(path_out,'w')
    for i in range(total_words):
        line = str(keys[i]) + ',' + str(values[i]) + '\n'
        f.write(line)

    f.close()

if __name__ == '__main__':
    with ElapsedTimer('Tokeize'):
        fire.Fire(tokenize)
```

The `tokenizer_2_txt.py` can be run as follows:

```
python tokenizer_2_txt.py --path
'/home/santanu/Downloads/Mobile_App/aclImdb/tokenizer.pickle' --path_out
'/home/santanu/Downloads/Mobile_App/word_ind.txt'
```

The output log of the preceding command is as follows:

```
Using TensorFlow backend.
165.235 ms: Tokenize
```

App interface page design

A simple mobile app interface can be designed using Android Studio, and the relevant code will be generated as an XML file. As you can see in the following screenshot (*Figure 7.3*), the app consists of a simple movie review textbox, where the users can input their movie reviews, and, once done, press the **SUBMIT** button. Once the **SUBMIT** button is pressed, the review will be passed to the core app logic, which will process the movie review text and pass it to the TensorFlow optimized model for inference.

As a part of the inference, a sentiment score will be computed, which will be displayed on the mobile app and also showcased as a star rating:

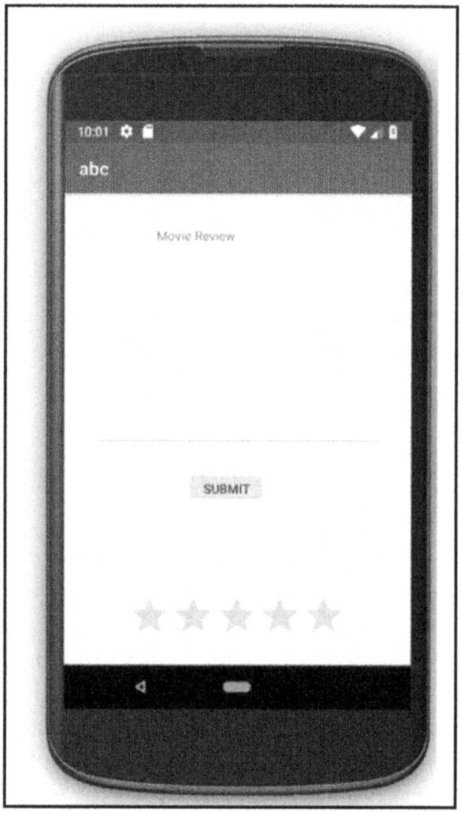

Figure 7.3: Mobile app user interface page format

The XML file required to generate the previously mentioned view of the mobile app is illustrated as follows:

```
<?xml version="1.0" encoding="utf-8"?>
<android.support.constraint.ConstraintLayout
xmlns:android="http://schemas.android.com/apk/res/android"
    xmlns:app="http://schemas.android.com/apk/res-auto"
    xmlns:tools="http://schemas.android.com/tools"
    android:layout_width="match_parent"
    android:layout_height="match_parent"
    tools:context=".MainActivity"
    tools:layout_editor_absoluteY="81dp">
```

```
<TextView
    android:id="@+id/desc"
    android:layout_width="100dp"
    android:layout_height="26dp"
    android:layout_marginEnd="8dp"
    android:layout_marginLeft="44dp"
    android:layout_marginRight="8dp"
    android:layout_marginStart="44dp"
    android:layout_marginTop="36dp"
    android:text="Movie Review"
    app:layout_constraintEnd_toEndOf="parent"
    app:layout_constraintHorizontal_bias="0.254"
    app:layout_constraintStart_toStartOf="parent"
    app:layout_constraintTop_toTopOf="parent"
    tools:ignore="HardcodedText" />

<EditText
    android:id="@+id/Review"
    android:layout_width="319dp"
    android:layout_height="191dp"
    android:layout_marginEnd="8dp"
    android:layout_marginLeft="8dp"
    android:layout_marginRight="8dp"
    android:layout_marginStart="8dp"
    android:layout_marginTop="24dp"
    app:layout_constraintEnd_toEndOf="parent"
    app:layout_constraintStart_toStartOf="parent"
    app:layout_constraintTop_toBottomOf="@+id/desc" />

<RatingBar
    android:id="@+id/ratingBar"
    android:layout_width="240dp"
    android:layout_height="49dp"
    android:layout_marginEnd="8dp"
    android:layout_marginLeft="52dp"
    android:layout_marginRight="8dp"
    android:layout_marginStart="52dp"
    android:layout_marginTop="28dp"
    app:layout_constraintEnd_toEndOf="parent"
    app:layout_constraintHorizontal_bias="0.238"
    app:layout_constraintStart_toStartOf="parent"
    app:layout_constraintTop_toBottomOf="@+id/score"
    tools:ignore="MissingConstraints" />

<TextView
    android:id="@+id/score"
    android:layout_width="125dp"
    android:layout_height="39dp"
```

```
        android:layout_marginEnd="8dp"
        android:layout_marginLeft="96dp"
        android:layout_marginRight="8dp"
        android:layout_marginStart="96dp"
        android:layout_marginTop="32dp"
        android:ems="10"
        android:inputType="numberDecimal"
        app:layout_constraintEnd_toEndOf="parent"
        app:layout_constraintHorizontal_bias="0.135"
        app:layout_constraintStart_toStartOf="parent"
        app:layout_constraintTop_toBottomOf="@+id/submit" />

    <Button
        android:id="@+id/submit"
        android:layout_width="wrap_content"
        android:layout_height="35dp"
        android:layout_marginEnd="8dp"
        android:layout_marginLeft="136dp"
        android:layout_marginRight="8dp"
        android:layout_marginStart="136dp"
        android:layout_marginTop="24dp"
        android:text="SUBMIT"
        app:layout_constraintEnd_toEndOf="parent"
        app:layout_constraintHorizontal_bias="0.0"
        app:layout_constraintStart_toStartOf="parent"
        app:layout_constraintTop_toBottomOf="@+id/Review" />

</android.support.constraint.ConstraintLayout>
```

One thing to note is that the variables through which the user and the mobile app core logic interact with each other are declared in the XML file, in the `android:id` option. For instance, the movie review that the user provides will be handled by the `Review` variable, as is defined in the XML file shown here:

```
android:id="@+id/Review"
```

The core logic of the Android app

The core logic of the Android app is to process the user requests, along with the data passed, and then send the results back to the user. As a part of this mobile app, the core logic will accept the movie review provided by the user, process the raw data, and convert it to a format that the trained LSTM model can run an inference on. The `OnClickListener` functionality in Java is utilized to monitor whether the user has submitted a processing request. Each of the words in the provided movie review needs to be changed to their indices, before the input can be fed directly to the optimized trained LSTM model for inference. Aside from the optimized protobuf model, a dictionary of the words and their corresponding indices is also stored for this purpose. The `TensorFlowInferenceInterface` methods are used to run inferences with the trained model. The optimized protobuf model and the dictionary of the words and their corresponding indices are stored in the `assets` folder. To summarize, the tasks performed by the app's core logic are as follows:

1. Load the words in the index dictionary into a `WordToInd` `HashMap`. The word-to-index dictionary is derived from the tokenizer during the preprocessing of the texts, before training the model.
2. Monitor whether a user has submitted a movie review for inference by using the `OnClickListener` method.
3. If a movie review has been submitted, the review will be read from the `Review` variable tied to the XML. The review is cleaned by removing punctuation, and so on, and is then split into words. Each of these words is converted to its corresponding indices, using the `HashMap` function `WordToInd`. These indices form the `InputVec` input to our TensorFlow model, for inference. The input vector length is `1000`; so, if the review has fewer than `1000` words, the vector is padded with zeros at the beginning.

4. In the next step, the optimized protobuf model (with a `.pb` extension) is loaded into the memory from the `assets` folder, using the `TensorFlowInferenceInterface` capabilities to create an `mInferenceInterface` object. The input node and the output node of the TensorFlow model, which are to be referred to for inference, need to be defined, as in the original model. For our model, they are defined as `INPUT_NODE` and `OUTPUT_NODE`, and they contain the name of the TensorFlow input placeholder and the output sentiment probability ops, respectively. The `feed` method of the `mInferenceInterface` object is used to assign the `InputVec` values to the `INPUT_NODE` of the model, while the `run` method of `mInferenceInterface` executes the `OUTPUT_NODE`. Finally, the `fetch` method of `mInferenceInterface` is used to populate the results of inference to a float variable, `value_`.
5. The sentiment score (the probability of the sentiment being positive) is converted to a rating by multiplying by five. This is then fed to the Android app user interface through the `ratingBar` variable.

The core logic of the mobile app in Java is as follows:

```
package com.example.santanu.abc;
import android.content.res.AssetManager;
import android.support.v7.app.AppCompatActivity;
import android.os.Bundle;
import android.view.View;
import android.widget.RatingBar;
import android.widget.TextView;
import android.widget.Button;
import android.widget.EditText;
import java.io.BufferedReader;
import java.io.FileReader;
import java.io.IOException;
import java.io.InputStreamReader;
import java.util.HashMap;
import java.util.Map;
import org.tensorflow.contrib.android.TensorFlowInferenceInterface;


public class MainActivity extends AppCompatActivity {

    private TensorFlowInferenceInterface mInferenceInterface;
    private static final String MODEL_FILE =
"file:///android_asset/optimized_model.pb";
    private static final String INPUT_NODE = "inputs/X";
    private static final String OUTPUT_NODE =
```

```
"positive_sentiment_probability";


    @Override
    protected void onCreate(Bundle savedInstanceState) {
        super.onCreate(savedInstanceState);
        setContentView(R.layout.activity_main);
        // Create references to the widget variables

        final TextView desc = (TextView) findViewById(R.id.desc);
        final Button submit = (Button) findViewById(R.id.submit);
        final EditText Review = (EditText) findViewById(R.id.Review);
        final TextView score = (TextView) findViewById(R.id.score);
        final RatingBar ratingBar = (RatingBar)
findViewById(R.id.ratingBar);

        //String filePath =
"/home/santanu/Downloads/Mobile_App/word2ind.txt";
        final Map<String,Integer> WordToInd = new
HashMap<String,Integer>();
        //String line;

        //reader = new BufferedReader(new
InputStreamReader(getAssets().open("word2ind.txt")));

        BufferedReader reader = null;
        try {
            reader = new BufferedReader(
                    new
InputStreamReader(getAssets().open("word_ind.txt")));

            // do reading, usually loop until end of file reading
            String line;
            while ((line = reader.readLine()) != null)
            {
                String[] parts = line.split("\n")[0].split(",",2);
                if (parts.length >= 2)
                {

                    String key = parts[0];
                    //System.out.println(key);
                    int value = Integer.parseInt(parts[1]);
                    //System.out.println(value);
                    WordToInd.put(key,value);
                } else

                {
                    //System.out.println("ignoring line: " + line);
```

```
                }
            }
        } catch (IOException e) {
            //log the exception
        } finally {
            if (reader != null) {
                try {
                    reader.close();
                } catch (IOException e) {
                    //log the exception
                }
            }
        }

        //line = reader.readLine();



        // Create Button Submit Listener

        submit.setOnClickListener(new View.OnClickListener() {

            @Override
            public void onClick(View v) {
                // Read Values
                String reviewInput = Review.getText().toString().trim();
                System.out.println(reviewInput);

                String[] WordVec = reviewInput.replaceAll("[^a-zA-z0-9 ]",
"").toLowerCase().split("\\s+");
                System.out.println(WordVec.length);

                int[] InputVec = new int[1000];
                // Initialize the input
                for (int i = 0; i < 1000; i++) {
                    InputVec[i] = 0;
                }
                // Convert the words by their indices

                int i = 1000 - 1 ;
                for (int k = WordVec.length -1 ; k > -1 ; k--) {
                    try {
                        InputVec[i] = WordToInd.get(WordVec[k]);
                        System.out.println(WordVec[k]);
                        System.out.println(InputVec[i]);

                    }
```

```
                    catch (Exception e) {
                        InputVec[i] = 0;

                    }
                    i = i-1;
                }

                if (mInferenceInterface == null) {
                    AssetManager assetManager = getAssets();
                    mInferenceInterface = new
TensorFlowInferenceInterface(assetManager,MODEL_FILE);
                }


                float[] value_ = new float[1];


                mInferenceInterface.feed(INPUT_NODE,InputVec,1,1000);
                mInferenceInterface.run(new String[] {OUTPUT_NODE}, false);
                System.out.println(Float.toString(value_[0]));
                mInferenceInterface.fetch(OUTPUT_NODE, value_);
                double scoreIn;
                scoreIn = value_[0]*5;
                double ratingIn = scoreIn;
                String stringDouble = Double.toString(scoreIn);
                score.setText(stringDouble);
                ratingBar.setRating((float) ratingIn);


            }

        });

    }
}
```

One of the points to note is that we might need to edit the `build.gradle` file for the app, in order to add the package to the dependencies:

```
org.tensorflow:tensorflow-android:1.7.0
```

Testing the mobile app

We will test the mobile app with the reviews of two movies: *Avatar* and *Interstellar*. The *Avatar* movie review has been taken from `https://www.rogerebert.com/reviews/avatar-2009`, and is as follows:

"Watching Avatar, I felt sort of the same as when I saw Star Wars in 1977. That was another movie I walked into with uncertain expectations. James Cameron's film has been the subject of relentlessly dubious advance buzz, just as his Titanic was. Once again, he has silenced the doubters by simply delivering an extraordinary film. There is still at least one man in Hollywood who knows how to spend $250 million, or was it $300 million, wisely.

"Avatar is not simply a sensational entertainment, although it is that. It's a technical breakthrough. It has a flat-out Green and anti-war message. It is predestined to launch a cult. It contains such visual detailing that it would reward repeating viewings. It invents a new language, Na'vi, as Lord of the Rings did, although mercifully I doubt this one can be spoken by humans, even teenage humans. It creates new movie stars. It is an Event, one of those films you feel you must see to keep up with the conversation."

The reviewer has given the movie a rating of 4/5, while the the mobile app gives a rating of around 4.8/5, as illustrated in the following screenshot (*Figure 7.4*):

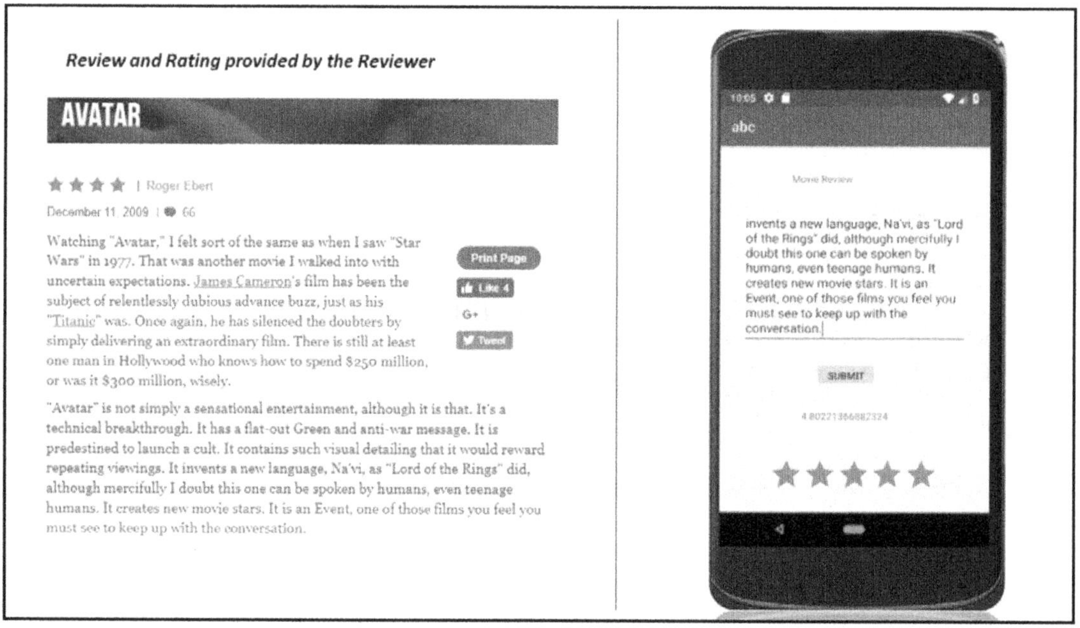

Figure 7.4. Mobile app review rating of the movie Avatar

Similarly, we will evaluate the rating provided by the app for the movie *Interstellar*, with a review taken from `https://www.rottentomatoes.com/m/interstellar_2014/`. The review is as follows:

"Interstellar represents more of the thrilling, thought-provoking, and visually resplendent film making moviegoers have come to expect from writer-director Christopher Nolan, even if its intellectual reach somewhat exceeds its grasp."

The average rating of the movie on *Rotten Tomatoes* is 7/10, which, when scaled to 5, gives a score of 3.5/5, while the mobile app predicts a rating of 3.37, as illustrated in the following screenshot (*Figure 7.5*):

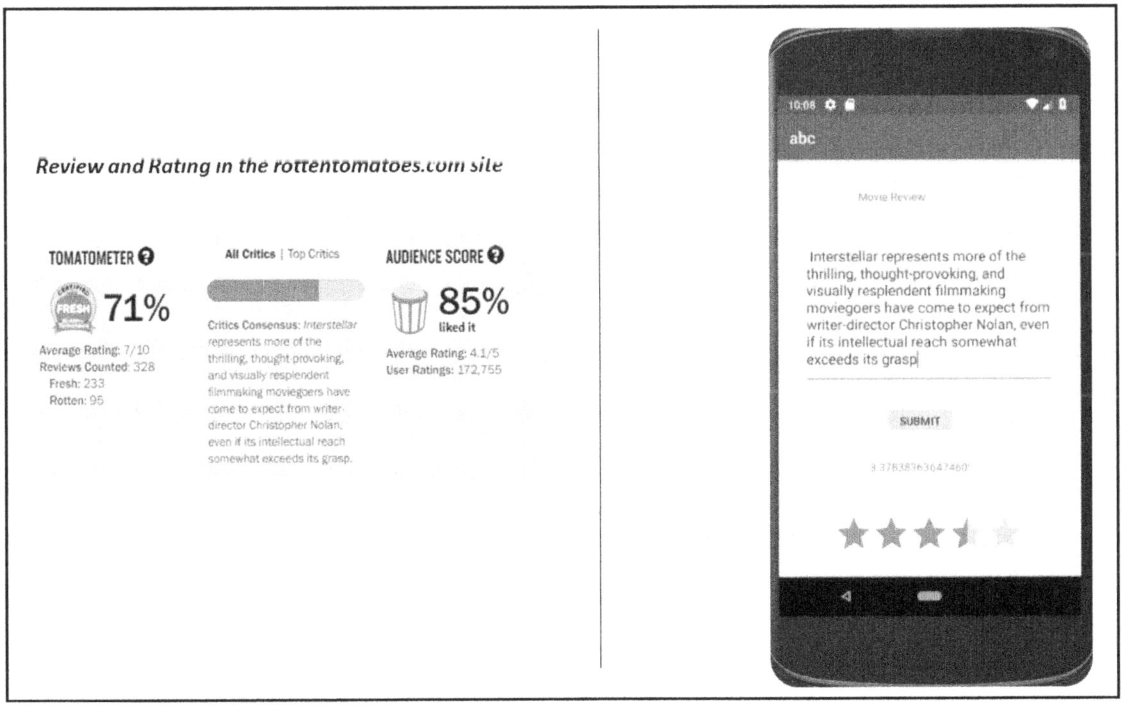

Figure 7.5. Mobile app review rating of the movie Interstellar

As you can see in the two preceding illustrations, the mobile movie review rating app does a great job of providing a reasonable rating for movie reviews.

Summary

Having finished this chapter, the reader should have a fair idea of how to deploy deep learning models in an Android app, using TensorFlow's mobile capabilities. The technicalities and the implementation details that were touched upon in this chapter should be beneficial for the reader, helping them to build smart Android mobile applications and extend them in interesting ways. The detailed code for this project is located at `https://github.com/PacktPublishing/Python-Artificial-Intelligence-Projects/Chapter07`.

In the next chapter, we will build a conversational AI chatbot for customer service. We look forward to your participation.

8
Conversational AI Chatbots for Customer Service

Conversational chatbots have produced a lot of hype recently because of their role in enhancing customer experience. Modern businesses have started using the capabilities of chatbots in several different processes. Because of the wide acceptance of conversational AIs, the tedious task of filling out forms or sending information over the internet has become much more streamlined. One of the desired qualities of a conversational chatbot is that it should be able to respond to a user request in the current context. The players in a conversational chatbot system are the user and the bot respectively. There are many advantages of using conversational chatbots, as shown in the following list:

- **Personalized assistance**: Creating a personalized experience for all customers might be a tedious task, but not doing so can make a business suffer. Conversational chatbots are a convenient alternative to providing a personalized experience to each and every customer.
- **Around-the-clock support**: Using customer service representatives 24/7 is expensive. Using chatbots for customer service out of office hours removes the need to hire extra customer representatives.
- **Consistency of responses**: Responses provided by the chatbot are likely to be consistent, whereas responses given to the same questions by different customer service representatives are likely to vary. This removes the need for a customer to call multiple times if they are not satisfied with the answer provided by a customer service representative.
- **Patience**: While customer service representatives might lose their patience when attending to a customer, this is not a possibility for a chatbot.
- **Querying records**: Chatbots are much more efficient in querying records than human customer service representatives.

Chatbots are not a recent thing, and their origin can be traced back to the 1950s. Just following World War II, Alan Turing developed the **Turing test** to see whether a person can distinguish a human from a machine. Years later, in 1966, Joseph Weizenbaum developed some software named *Eliza*, which imitated the language of a psychotherapist. The tool can be still located at `http://psych.fullerton.edu/mbirnbaum/psych101/Eliza.htm`.

Chatbots can perform a varied set of tasks, a few of which are shown in the following list to emphasize their versatility:

- Answering to queries regarding products
- Providing recommendations to customers
- Performing sentence-completion activities
- Conversational chatbots
- Negotiating prices with customers and taking part in bidding

Many times, businesses have a hard time figuring out whether they need a chatbot or not. Whether a business needs a chatbot can be determined by the flowchart in *Figure 8.1*:

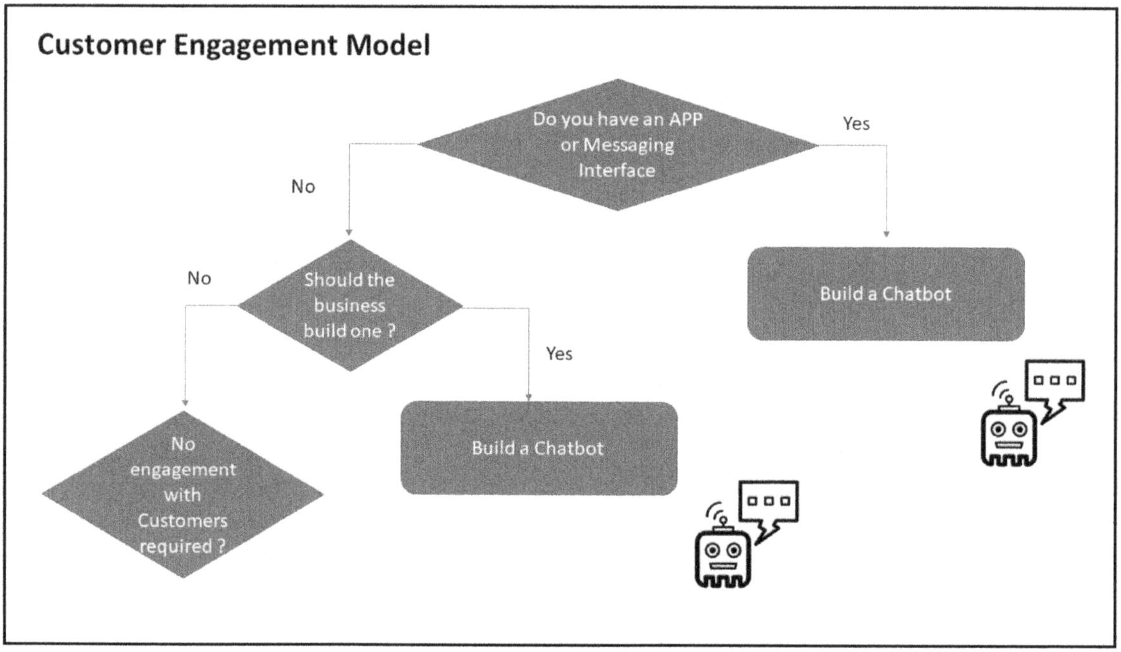

Figure 8.1: Customer engagement model

As part of this chapter, we will be covering the following topics:

- Chatbot architecture
- LSTM sequence-to-sequence model for chatbots
- Building a sequence-to-sequence model for a Twitter support chatbot

Technical requirements

You will require to have basic knowledge of Python 3, TensorFlow and Keras

The code files of this chapter can be found on GitHub:
`https://github.com/PacktPublishing/Intelligent-Projects-using-Python/tree/master/Chapter08`

Check out the following video to see the code in action:
`http://bit.ly/2G9AyoB`

Chatbot architecture

The core component of a chatbot is its natural-language processing framework. Chatbots process data presented to them using natural-language processing through a process commonly known as **parsing**. The parsed user input is then interpreted and an appropriate response is sent back to the user based on what the user wants, as deciphered from the input. The chatbot might need to seek help from a knowledge base and historical transaction data store to deal with the user's request appropriately.

Chatbots can be broadly grouped into the following two categories:

- **Retrieval-based models**: These models generally rely on lookup tables or a knowledge base to select an answer from a predefined set of answers. Although this method might seem naive, most chatbots in production are of this kind. Of course, there can be various degrees of sophistication with regard to selecting the best answer from the lookup tables or knowledge base.
- **Generative models**: Generative models generate responses on the fly instead of adopting a lookup-based approach. They are mostly probabilistic models or models based on machine learning. Up until recently, Markov chains were mostly used as generative models; however, with the recent success of deep learning, recurrent neural network-based approaches have gained popularity. Generally, the LSTM version of RNNs is used as a generative model for chatbots, since it is better at handling long sequences.

Both retrieval-based models and generative models come with their own set of pros and cons. Since retrieval-based models answer from a fixed set of answers, they are not able to handle unseen questions or requests for which there are no appropriate predefined responses. Generative models are much more sophisticated; they can understand the entities in the user input and generate human-like responses. However, they are harder to train and generally require much more data to train. They are also prone to making grammatical mistakes, which retrieval-based models cannot make.

A sequence-to-sequence model using an LSTM

The sequence-to-sequence model architecture is well suited for capturing the context of the customer input and then generating appropriate responses based on that. *Figure 8.2* shows a sequence-to-sequence model framework that can respond to questions just as a chatbot would:

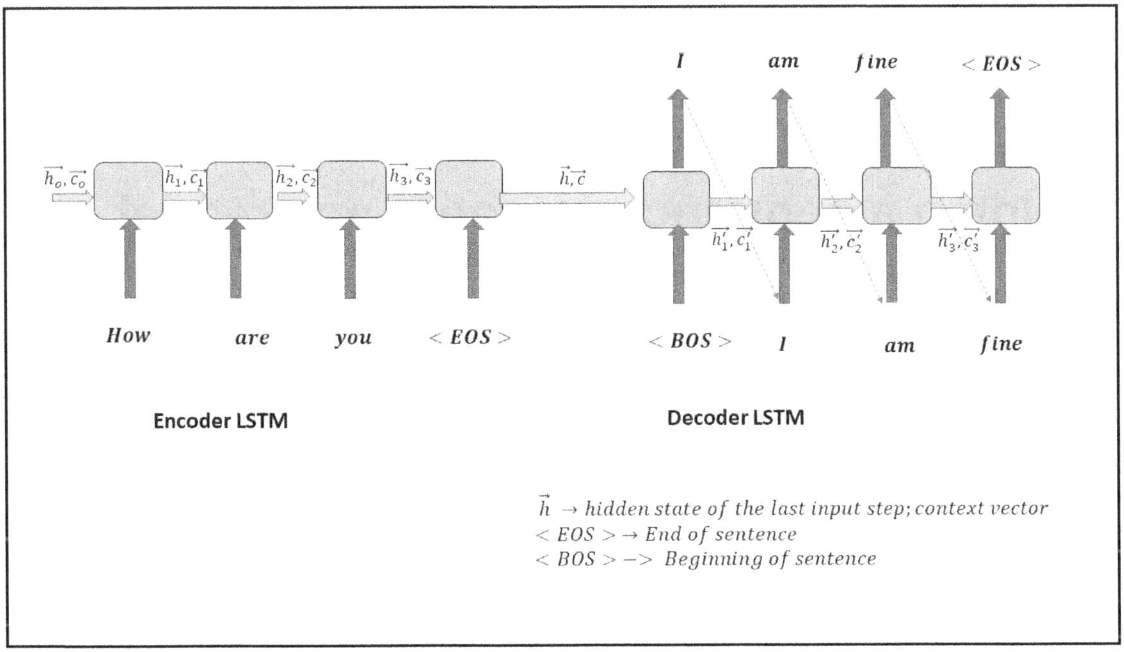

Figure 8.2: Sequence-to-sequence model using an LSTM

We can see from the preceding diagram (*Figure 8.2*) that the **Encoder LSTM** takes the input sequence of words and encodes it into a hidden state vector, $\vec{h}$, and a cell state vector, $\vec{c}$. The vectors, $\vec{h}$, and $\vec{c}$ are the hidden and cell states of the last step of the LSTM encoder. They would essentially capture the context of the whole input sentence.

The encoded information in the form of $\vec{h}$ and $\vec{c}$ is then fed to the **Decoder LSTM** as its initial hidden and cell states. The **Decoder LSTM** in each step tries to predict the next word conditioned on the current word. This means that, the input to each step of the **Decoder LSTM** is the current word.

To predict the first word, the LSTM would be provided with a dummy start keyword **<BOS>** that represents the beginning of the sentence. Similarly, the **<EOS>** dummy keyword represents the end of the sentence, and once this is predicted, the output generation should stop.

During the training of a sequence-to-sequence model for each target word, we know *apriori* the previous word that is an input to the **Decoder LSTM**. However, during inference, we won't have these target words, and so we would have to feed the previous step as an input.

Building a sequence-to-sequence model

The architecture of the sequence-to-sequence model that we will be using for building the chatbot will have slight modifications to the basic sequence-to-sequence architecture illustrated previously in *Figure 8.2*. The modified architecture can be seen in the following diagram (*Figure 8.3*):

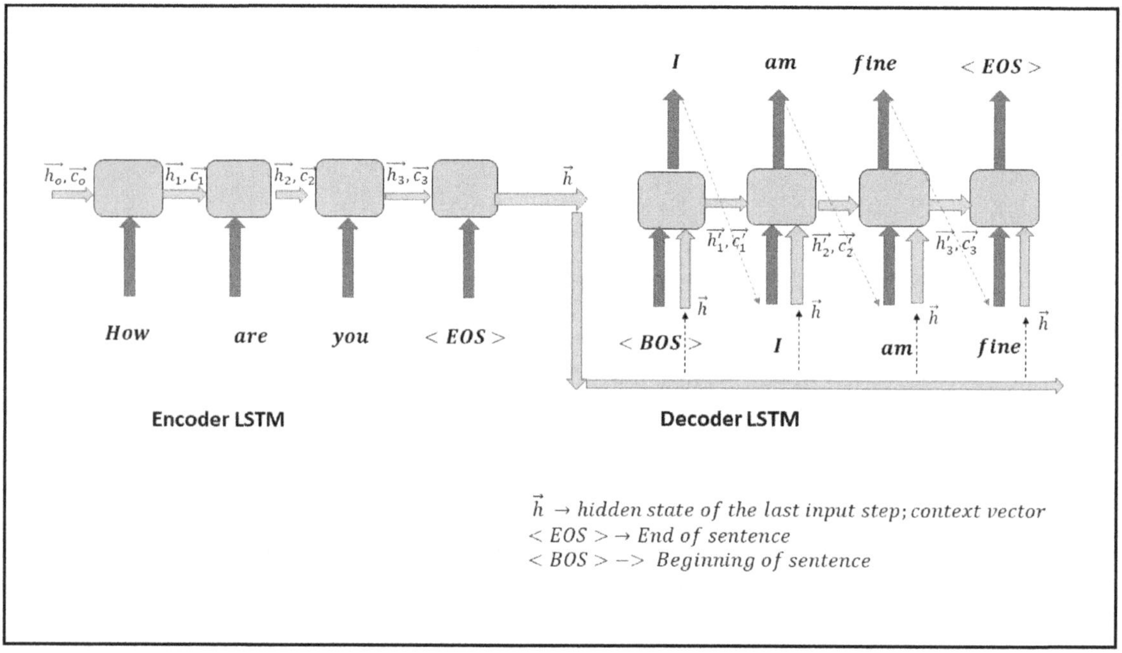

Figure 8.3: Sequence-to-sequence model

Instead of feeding the hidden state $\vec{h}$ and the cell state $\vec{c}$ of the last step of the encoder to the initial hidden and cell states of the **Decoder LSTM**, we feed the hidden state $\vec{h}$ at each input step of the decoder. To predict the target word w_t at any step t, the inputs are the previous target word, w_{t-1}, at any step, $t-1$, and the hidden state $\vec{h}$.

Customer support on Twitter

Now that we have some idea of how to build a chatbot using a recurrent neural network, we will build a chatbot using the customer service responses of 20 big brands to tweets posted by customers. The dataset `twcs.zip` can be located at `https://www.kaggle.com/thoughtvector/customer-support-on-twitter`. Each tweet is identified by the `tweet_id` and the tweet content is in the `text` field. The tweets posted by the customers can be identified by the `in_response_to_tweet_id` field. This should contain null values for customer tweets. For customer service tweets, this `in_response_to_tweet_id` field should point to the customer `tweet_id` to which this tweet is directed.

Creating data for training the chatbot

To extract all the inbound tweets that are posted by customers, we need to fetch all the tweets that have the `in_response_to_tweet_id` field as `null`. The outbound file that contains the customer service representative responses can be extracted by filtering by tweets where the `in_response_to_tweet_id` field is not null. Once we have the inbound and the outbound files, we need to merge them on the `tweet_id` of the inbound file and the `in_response_to_tweet_id` of the outbound file. This will give us our file with the *tweets in* by the customers and the *tweets out* by the customer service representatives in response. The data creation function can be coded as follows:

```
def process_data(self,path):
    data = pd.read_csv(path)

   if self.mode == 'train':
        data = pd.read_csv(path)
        data['in_response_to_tweet_id'].fillna(-12345,inplace=True)
        tweets_in =  data[data['in_response_to_tweet_id'] == -12345]
        tweets_in_out =
        tweets_in.merge(data,left_on=['tweet_id'],right_on=
        ['in_response_to_tweet_id'])
        return tweets_in_out[:self.num_train_records]
    elif self.mode == 'inference':
        return data
```

Tokenizing the text into word indices

The tweets need to be tokenized and converted into numbers before they can be fed to the neural network. The **count vectorizer** is used to determine a fixed number of frequent words that form the vocabulary space for the chatbot. We also introduce three new tokens that signify the start of a sentence (`START`), the end of a sentence (`PAD`), and also any unknown words (`UNK`). The function to tokenize tweets is shown here for reference:

```
    def tokenize_text(self,in_text,out_text):
        count_vectorizer = CountVectorizer(tokenizer=casual_tokenize,
max_features=self.max_vocab_size - 3)
        count_vectorizer.fit(in_text + out_text)
        self.analyzer = count_vectorizer.build_analyzer()
        self.vocabulary =
        {key_: value_ + 3 for key_,value_ in
count_vectorizer.vocabulary_.items()}
        self.vocabulary['UNK'] = self.UNK
        self.vocabulary['PAD'] = self.PAD
        self.vocabulary['START'] = self.START
        self.reverse_vocabulary =
        {value_: key_ for key_, value_ in self.vocabulary.items()}
        joblib.dump(self.vocabulary,self.outpath + 'vocabulary.pkl')
        joblib.dump(self.reverse_vocabulary,self.outpath +
'reverse_vocabulary.pkl')
        joblib.dump(count_vectorizer,self.outpath + 'count_vectorizer.pkl')
        #pickle.dump(self.count_vectorizer,open(self.outpath +
        'count_vectorizer.pkl',"wb"))
```

Now, the tokenized words need to be converted to word indices so that they can be fed to the recurrent neural network, as shown in the following code:

```
def words_to_indices(self,sent):
        word_indices =
       [self.vocabulary.get(token,self.UNK) for token in
self.analyzer(sent)] +
        [self.PAD]*self.max_seq_len
        word_indices = word_indices[:self.max_seq_len]
        return word_indices
```

We would also like to convert the word indices predicted by the recurrent neural network into words to form a sentence. The function for this can be coded as follows:

```
 def indices_to_words(self,indices):
        return ' '.join(self.reverse_vocabulary[id] for id in indices if id
!= self.PAD).strip()
```

Replacing anonymized screen names

Before we tokenize the tweet, it might be worthwhile replacing the anonymized screen names in the tweets to a common name so that the responses generalize better. The function for this can be coded as follows:

```
    def replace_anonymized_names(self,data):

        def replace_name(match):
            cname = match.group(2).lower()
            if not cname.isnumeric():
                return match.group(1) + match.group(2)
            return '@__cname__'
        re_pattern = re.compile('(\W@|^@)([a-zA-Z0-9_]+)')
        if self.mode == 'train':

            in_text = data['text_x'].apply(lambda
txt:re_pattern.sub(replace_name,txt))
            out_text = data['text_y'].apply(lambda
            txt:re_pattern.sub(replace_name,txt))
            return list(in_text.values),list(out_text.values)
        else:
            return map(lambda x:re_pattern.sub(replace_name,x),data)
```

Defining the model

The LSTM version of the RNN is used to build the sequence-to-sequence model. This is because LSTMs are much more efficient in remembering long-term dependencies in long sequences of text. The three gates in the LSTM architecture enable it to remember long-term sequences efficiently. A basic RNN is unable to remember long-term dependencies because of the vanishing gradient problems that are associated with its architecture.

In this model, we are using two LSTMs. The first LSTM would encode the input tweet into a context vector. This context vector is nothing but the last hidden state $\vec{h} \in R^n$ of the encoder LSTM, *n* being the dimension of the hidden state vector. The input tweet $\vec{x} \in R^k$ is fed into the encoder LSTM as a sequence of word indices, *k* being the sequence length of the input tweet. These word indices are mapped to word embedding $w \in R^m$ before being fed to the LSTM. The word embeddings are housed in an embedding matrix, $[W \in R^{m \times N}]$, where *N* denotes the number of the words in the vocabulary.

The second LSTM works as the decoder. It tries to decode the context vector $\vec{h}$ created by the encoder LSTM into a meaningful response. As part of this approach, we feed the context vector at each time step along with the previous word to generate the current word. At the first time step, we don't have any previous word to condition the LSTM on, and so we use the proxy `START` word to start the process of generating the sequence of words from the decoder LSTM. How we input the previous word at a current time step during inference differs from the method we use during training. In training, since we know the previous words *apriori*, at each time step, we don't have any problems feeding them accordingly. However, during inference, since we don't have the actual previous word at the current time step, the predicted word at the previous time step is fed. The hidden state $\vec{h}_t'$ of each time step *t* is fed through a few fully connected layers before the final big softmax *N*. The word that gets the maximum probability in this softmax layer is the predicted word for the time step. This word is then fed to the input of the next step, which is step *t + 1* of the decoder LSTM.

The `TimeDistributed` function in Keras allows for an efficient implementation of getting a prediction at each time step of the decoder LSTM, as shown in the following code:

```
    def define_model(self):
        # Embedding Layer
        embedding = Embedding(
            output_dim=self.embedding_dim,
            input_dim=self.max_vocab_size,
            input_length=self.max_seq_len,
            name='embedding',
        )
        # Encoder input
        encoder_input = Input(
            shape=(self.max_seq_len,),
            dtype='int32',
            name='encoder_input',
        )
        embedded_input = embedding(encoder_input)

        encoder_rnn = LSTM(
            self.hidden_state_dim,
            name='encoder',
            dropout=self.dropout
        )
        # Context is repeated to the max sequence length so that the same
context
        # can be feed at each step of decoder
        context =
RepeatVector(self.max_seq_len)(encoder_rnn(embedded_input))
        # Decoder
```

```
        last_word_input = Input(
            shape=(self.max_seq_len,),
            dtype='int32',
            name='last_word_input',
        )
        embedded_last_word = embedding(last_word_input)
        # Combines the context produced by the encoder and the last word
uttered as
        inputs
        # to the decoder.
        decoder_input = concatenate([embedded_last_word, context],axis=2)

        # return_sequences causes LSTM to produce one output per timestep
instead of
        one at the
        # end of the intput, which is important for sequence producing
models.
        decoder_rnn = LSTM(
            self.hidden_state_dim,
            name='decoder',
            return_sequences=True,
            dropout=self.dropout
        )
        decoder_output = decoder_rnn(decoder_input)
        # TimeDistributed allows the dense layer to be applied to each
decoder output
       per timestep
        next_word_dense = TimeDistributed(
            Dense(int(self.max_vocab_size/20),activation='relu'),
            name='next_word_dense',
        )(decoder_output)
        next_word = TimeDistributed(
            Dense(self.max_vocab_size,activation='softmax'),
            name='next_word_softmax'
        )(next_word_dense)
        return Model(inputs=[encoder_input,last_word_input],
outputs=[next_word])
```

Loss function for training the model

The model is trained on categorical cross-entropy loss to predict the target words in each time step of the decoder LSTM. The categorical cross-entropy loss in any step would be over all the words of the vocabulary, and can be represented as follows:

$$C_t = -\sum_{i=1}^{N} y_i \, log \, p_i$$

The label $[y_i]_{i=1}^{N}$ represents the one hot-encoded version of the target word. Only the label corresponding to the actual word would be *one*; the rest would be *zero*. The term *Pi* represents the probability that the actual target word is the word indexed by *i*. To get the total loss, *C*, for each input/output tweet pair, we need to sum up the losses over all the time steps of the decoder LSTM. Since the vocabulary size might get very large, creating a one hot-encoded vector $\overrightarrow{y_t} = [y_i]_{i=1}^{N}$ for the target label in each time step would be costly. The `sparse_categorical_crossentropy` loss becomes very beneficial here, since we don't need to convert the target word into a one hot-encoded vector, but instead we can just feed the index of the target word as the target label.

Training the model

The model can be trained with the Adam optimizer, since it reliably provides stable convergence. Since RNNs are prone to exploding gradient problems (although this is not so problematic for LSTMs), it is better to clip the gradients if they become too large. The given model can be defined and compiled with the Adam optimizer and `sparse_categorical_crossentropy`, as shown in the following code block:

```
    def create_model(self):
        _model_ = self.define_model()
        adam = Adam(lr=self.learning_rate,clipvalue=5.0)
_model_.compile(optimizer=adam,loss='sparse_categorical_crossentropy')
        return _model_
```

Now that we have looked at all the basic functions, the training function can be coded as follows:

```
def train_model(self,model,X_train,X_test,y_train,y_test):
        input_y_train = self.include_start_token(y_train)
        print(input_y_train.shape)
        input_y_test = self.include_start_token(y_test)
```

```
        print(input_y_test.shape)
        early = EarlyStopping(monitor='val_loss',patience=10,mode='auto')

        checkpoint =
        ModelCheckpoint(self.outpath + 's2s_model_' + str(self.version) +
'_.h5',monitor='val_loss',verbose=1,save_best_only=True,mode='auto')
        lr_reduce =
        ReduceLROnPlateau(monitor='val_loss',factor=0.5, patience=2,
verbose=0,
         mode='auto')
        model.fit([X_train,input_y_train],y_train,
              epochs=self.epochs,
              batch_size=self.batch_size,
              validation_data=[[X_test,input_y_test],y_test],
              callbacks=[early,checkpoint,lr_reduce],
              shuffle=True)
        return model
```

At the beginning of the `train_model` function, we create `input_y_train` and `input_y_test`, which are copies of `y_train` and `y_test` respectively and are shifted from them by one time step so that they can act as the input for the previous word at each time step of the decoder. The first word of these shifted sequences is the `START` keyword that is fed at the first time step of the decoder LSTM. The `include_start_token` custom utility function is as follows:

```
def include_start_token(self,Y):
    print(Y.shape)
    Y = Y.reshape((Y.shape[0],Y.shape[1]))
    Y = np.hstack((self.START*np.ones((Y.shape[0],1)),Y[:, :-1]))
    return Y
```

Coming back to the training function, `train_model`, we see that early stopping is enabled using the `EarlyStopping` callback facility if the loss doesn't decrease in `10` epochs. Similarly, the `ReduceLROnPlateau` callback would reduce the existing learning rate by half (`0.5`) if the error doesn't reduce in two epochs. The model is saved through the `ModelCheckpoint` callback whenever the error reduces in an epoch.

Generating output responses from the model

Once the model is trained, we want to use it to generate responses given an input tweet. The same can be done in the following steps:

1. Replace the anonymized screen names in the input tweet with the common name.
2. Convert the modified input tweet into word indices.
3. Feed the word indices to the encoder LSTM and the `START` keyword to the decoder LSTM to generate the first predicted word. From the next step onward, feed the predicted word from the previous time step instead of the `START` keyword.
4. Continue doing this until the end-of-sentence keyword is predicted. We have represented this with `PAD`.
5. Look at the inverse vocabulary dictionary to get the words from the predicted word indexes.

The `respond_to_input` function that can do the work of generating output sequences given the input tweet is illustrated in the following code for reference:

```
def respond_to_input(self,model,input_sent):
        input_y = self.include_start_token(self.PAD *
np.ones((1,self.max_seq_len)))
        ids =
np.array(self.words_to_indices(input_sent)).reshape((1,self.max_seq_len))
        for pos in range(self.max_seq_len -1):
            pred = model.predict([ids, input_y]).argmax(axis=2)[0]
            #pred = model.predict([ids, input_y])[0]
            input_y[:,pos + 1] = pred[pos]
        return
self.indices_to_words(model.predict([ids,input_y]).argmax(axis=2)[0])
```

Putting it all together

Putting it all together, the `main` function can be defined as having two flows: one for training and the other for inference. Even in the training function, we generate a few responses to the input tweet sequences to check how well we trained the model. The following code shows the `main` function for reference:

```
def main(self):
    if self.mode == 'train':
```

```
            X_train, X_test, y_train, y_test,test_sentences =
self.data_creation()
            print(X_train.shape,y_train.shape,X_test.shape,y_test.shape)
            print('Data Creation completed')
            model = self.create_model()
            print("Model creation completed")
            model = self.train_model(model,X_train,X_test,y_train,y_test)
            test_responses = self.generate_response(model,test_sentences)
            print(test_sentences)
            print(test_responses)
            pd.DataFrame(test_responses).to_csv(self.outpath +
            'output_response.csv',index=False)

        elif self.mode == 'inference':

            model = load_model(self.load_model_from)
            self.vocabulary = joblib.load(self.vocabulary_path)
            self.reverse_vocabulary =
joblib.load(self.reverse_vocabulary_path)
            #nalyzer_file = open(self.analyzer_path,"rb")
            count_vectorizer = joblib.load(self.count_vectorizer_path)
            self.analyzer = count_vectorizer.build_analyzer()
            data = self.process_data(self.data_path)
            col = data.columns.tolist()[0]
            test_sentences = list(data[col].values)
            test_sentences = self.replace_anonymized_names(test_sentences)
            responses = self.generate_response(model,test_sentences)
            print(responses)
            responses.to_csv(self.outpath + 'responses_' +
str(self.version) +
            '_.csv',index=False)
```

Invoking the training

The training can be invoked by running the `chatbot.py` (see the code in the GitHub for this project) module with several arguments, as shown in the following command:

```
python chatbot.py --max_vocab_size 50000 --max_seq_len 30 --embedding_dim
100 --hidden_state_dim 100 --epochs 80 --batch_size 128 --learning_rate
1e-4 --data_path /home/santanu/chatbot/data/twcs.csv --outpath
/home/santanu/chatbot/ --dropout 0.3 --mode train --num_train_records 50000
--version v1
```

The following are some of the important arguments, along with their description and used values for invoking the training of the chatbot sequence-to-sequence model:

Parameters	Description	Values used for training
`max_vocab_size`	Number of words to take in the vocabulary	`50,000`
`max_seq_len`	The maximum length the tweets are to be restricted to for feeding to the LSTM	`30`
`hidden_state_dim`	Hidden state $\vec{h}$ dimension of the LSTM	`100`
`embedding_dim`	Dimension of the word embedding	`100`
`learning rate`	Starting learning rate to be used for the optimizer	`0.0001`
`dropout`	Dropout to be used for regularization purposes	`0.3`
`Mode`	Train/inference	For training use `train` for inference use `inference`

Results of inference on some input tweets

The trained sequence-to-sequence model generated some relevant tweets in response to some input tweets. The sample inference command is shown in the following command. The `data_path` argument contains the location of the test input tweets:

```
python chatbot.py --max_vocab_size 50000 --max_seq_len 30 --embedding_dim
100 --hidden_state_dim 100  --data_path /home/santanu/chatbot/data/test.csv
--outpath /home/santanu/chatbot/ --dropout 0.3 --mode inference --version
v1 --load_model_from /home/santanu/chatbot/s2s_model_v1_.h5  --
vocabulary_path /home/santanu/chatbot/vocabulary.pkl --
reverse_vocabulary_path /home/santanu/chatbot/reverse_vocabulary.pkl --
count_vectorizer_path /home/santanu/chatbot/count_vectorizer.pkl
```

The results of the inference are shown in the following table:

Tweet in	Tweet out
`@sprintcare` is the worst customer service.	`@__cname__` Hey there! Can you dm us your account's email address? We'll take a look backstage / dn `https://t.co/ldfdzrinat`.
`@__cname__` Y'all lie about your *great* connection. 5 bars LTE, still won't load something. Smh.	`@__cname__` We apologize for the trouble. Please send us a dm with your email address so we can connect.
`@__cname__` Whenever I contact customer support, they tell me I have shortcode enabled on my account, but I have never in the 4 years I've tried `https://t.co/0G98RtNxPK`.	`@__cname__` Hi there, we are sorry to hear this. Please send us a dm with your email address and phone number so we can look into this for.

Actually that's a broken link you sent me and incorrect information `https://t.co/V4yfrHR8VI`.	`@__cname__` Hi, we are sorry to hear this. Please dm us your contact info and we'll be happy to help. ^kk
Yo `@Ask_Spectrum`, your customer service reps are super nice— but imma start trippin if y'all don't get my service going!	`@__cname__` We apologize for the trouble. Please send us a dm with your email address so we can connect.
My picture on `@Ask_Spectrum` pretty much every day. Why should I pay $171 per month? `https://t.co/U6ptkQa5Ik`.	`@__cname__` Hi, we are sorry to hear this. Please dm us your contact info and we'll be happy to help. ^kk
Somebody from `@VerizonSupport` please help me �������� I'm having the worst luck with your customer service.	`@__cname__` We apologize for the trouble. Please dm us your contact info and phone number so we can assist.
`@VerizonSupport` My friend is without internet we need to play video games together please our skills diminish every moment without internetz.	`@__cname__` Hey there! Can you dm us your account's email address? we'll take a look backstage / dn `https://t.co/ldfdzrinat`
`@__cname__` tried to pay a bill for 60 days. No service, rude CS, and several transfers. Look up my equipment # and give me an acct #!	`@__cname__` Hi, we are sorry to hear this. Please dm us your contact info and we'll be happy to help. ^kk
`@__cname__` is the worst ISP I've ever had.	`@__cname__` Hey there! Can you dm us your account's email address? We'll take a look backstage / dn `https://t.co/ldfdzrinat`
`@__cname__` fix your app it won't even open.	`@__cname__` Hi there! We don't have any info on this issue. Please send us a dm with your name and phone number and the full service address.

Summary

And now, we come to the end of the chapter. Having looked through the various concepts related to chatbots and sequence-to-sequence models illustrated in this chapter, the reader should now be able to build a chatbot implementation of their own and extend it in interesting ways. Sequence-to-sequence models, as we know, not only apply to chatbots, but to a whole range of natural-language processing domains, such as machine translation. The code for this chapter can be located at the GitHub location `https://github.com/PacktPublishing/Python-Artificial-Intelligence-Projects/tree/master/Chapter08`.

In the next chapter, we are going to use reinforcement learning to get a racing car to learn to drive by itself. We look forward to your participation.

9
Autonomous Self-Driving Car Through Reinforcement Learning

Reinforcement learning, in which an agent learns to make decisions by interacting with the environment, has really taken off in the last few years. It is one of the hottest topics in artificial intelligence and machine learning these days, and research in this domain is progressing at a fast pace. In **reinforcement learning** (**RL**), an agent converts their actions and experiences into learning to make better decisions in the future.

Reinforcement learning doesn't fall under the supervised or unsupervised machine learning paradigm, as it is a field in its own right. In supervised learning, we try to learn a mapping $F: X \rightarrow Y$ that maps input X to output Y, whereas in reinforcement learning, the agent learns to take the best action through trial and error. When an agent performs a task well, a reward is assigned, whereas when the agent performs poorly, it pays a penalty. The agent tries to assimilate this information and learns not to repeat these mistakes under similar conditions. These conditions that the agent is exposed to are referred to as states. *Figure 9.1* shows the interaction of an agent in an environment in a reinforcement learning framework:

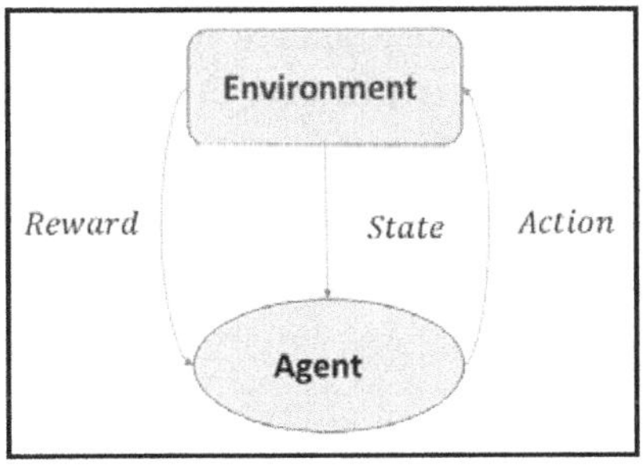

Figure 9.1: Illustration of agent and environment interaction

Technical requirements

You will require to have basic knowledge of Python 3, TensorFlow, Keras and OpenCV.

The code files of this chapter can be found on GitHub:
`https://github.com/PacktPublishing/Intelligent-Projects-using-Python/tree/master/Chapter09`

Check out the following video to see the code in action:
`http://bit.ly/2WxfwpF`

Markov decision process

Any reinforcement learning problem can be viewed as a **Markov decision process**, which we briefly looked at in `Chapter 1`, *Foundations of Artificial Intelligence Based Systems*. We will look at this again in more detail for your benefit. In the Markov decision process, we have an agent interacting with an environment. At any given instance, the t agent is exposed to one of many states: $(s^{(t)} = s) \in S$. Based on the agent's action $(a^{(t)} = a) \in A$ in the state $s^{(t)}$ the agent is presented with a new state $(s^{(t+1)} = s') \in S$. Here, S denotes the set of all states the agent may be exposed to, while A denotes the possible actions the agent can partake in.

You may now wonder how an agent takes action. Should it be random or based on heuristics? Well, it depends how much the agent has interacted with the environment in question. In the initial phase, the agent might take random actions, since they have no knowledge of the environment. However, once the agent has interacted with the environment enough, based on the rewards and the penalties, the agent learns what might be a suitable action to take in a given state. Similar to how people tend to take actions that benefit the long term rewards, an RL agent also takes his action, which maximizes the long-term reward.

Mathematically, the agent tries to learn a Q value $Q(s, a)$ for every state action pair $(s \in S, a \in A)$. For a given state $s^{(t)}$ an RL agent selects the action a, which gives the maximum Q value. The action $a^{(t)}$ taken by the agent can be expressed as follows:

$$a^{(t)} = \arg\max_a Q(s^{(t)}, a)$$

Once the agent takes an action $a^{(t)}$ in the state $s^{(t)}$, a new state $s^{(t+1)}$ is presented to the agent to be dealt with. This new state $s^{(t+1)}$ is generally not deterministic and is generally expressed as a probability distribution condition on the current state $s^{(t)}$ and action $a^{(t)}$.These probabilities are referred to as **state transition probabilities** and can be expressed as follows:

$$P(s^{(t+1)} = s' / s^{(t)} = s, a^{(t)} = a)$$

Whenever an agent takes an action $a^{(t)}$ at state $s^{(t)}$ and reaches a new state $s^{(t+1)}$ an immediate reward is awarded to the agent that can be expressed as follows:

$$R_{a^{(t)}}\left(s^{(t)}, s^{(t+1)}\right)$$

Now we have everything we need to define a Markov decision process. A Markov decision process is a system that is characterized by the four elements as follows:

- A set of states S
- A set of actions A
- A set of rewards R
- State transition probability $P(s^{(t+1)} = s'/s^{(t)} = s, a^{(t)} = a)$:

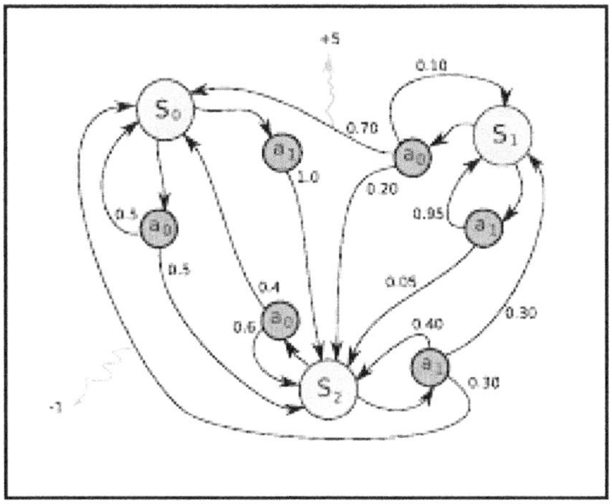

Figure 9.2: Illustration of a Markov decision process with three states

Learning the Q value function

For an RL agent to make a decision, it is important for the agent to learn the Q value function. The Q value function can be learned iteratively via **Bellman's equation**. When the agent starts to interact with the environment, it starts with a random state $s^{(0)}$ and random state of Q values for every state action pair. The agent's action would also be somewhat random, since it has no state Q values to make informed decisions. For each action taken, the environment would return a reward based on which agent starts to build the Q value tables, and improves over time.

At any exposed state $s^{(t)}$ at iteration t the agent would take an action $a^{(t)}$ that maximizes its long-term reward. The Q table holds the long-term reward values, and hence the chosen $a^{(t)}$ would be based on the following heuristics:

$$a^{(t)} = \arg\max_{a} Q^{(t)}(s^{(t)}, a)$$

The Q value table is also indexed by iteration t, since the agent can only look at the Q table build so far which is going to improve as the agent interacts with the environment more.

Based on the action $a^{(t)}$ taken the environment will present the agent with a reward $r^{(t)}$ and a new state $s^{(t+1)}$. The agent will update the Q table in such a way that its total long-term expected reward is maximized. The long term reward $r'^{(t)}$ can be written as follows:

$$r'^{(t)} = r^{(t)} + \gamma \max_{a'} Q^{(t)}(s^{(t+1)}, a')$$

Here, γ is a discount factor. As we can see, the long term reward combines the immediate reward $r^{(t)}$ and the cumulative future reward based on the next state $s^{(t+1)}$ presented.

Based on the computed long-term reward, the existing Q value of the state action pair ($s^{(t)}$, $a^{(t)}$) is updated as follows:

$$Q^{(t+1)}(s^{(t)}, a^{(t)}) = (1 - \alpha) * Q^{(t)}(s^{(t)}, a^{(t)}) + \alpha * r'^{(t)}$$

$$= (1 - \alpha) * Q^{(t)}(s^{(t)}, a^{(t)}) + \alpha * (r^{(t)} + \gamma \max_{a'} Q^{(t)}(s^{(t+1)}, a))$$

Deep Q learning

Deep Q learning leverages deep learning networks in learning the Q value function. Illustrated in the following diagram, *Figure 9.3*, is the architecture of a deep Q learning network:

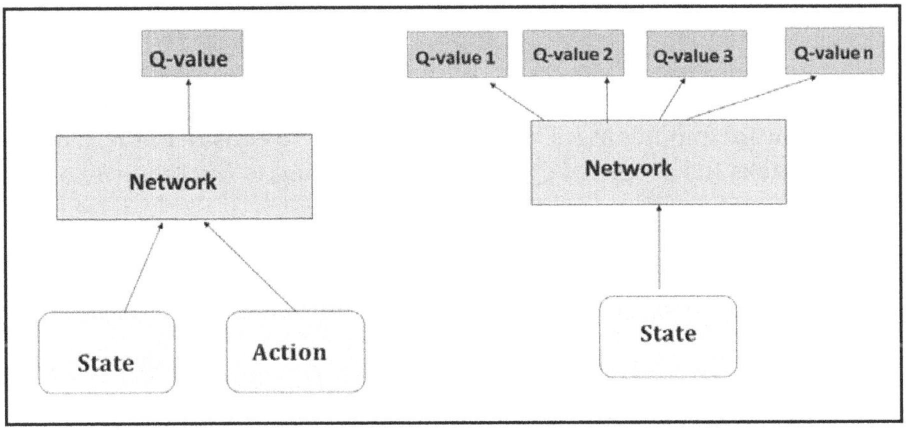

Figure 9.3: Illustration of a deep Q network

The diagram learns to map every pair of states *(s, a)* and actions into an output Q value output *Q(s, a)*, while in the diagram on the right, for every state *s*, we learn Q values pertaining to every action *a*. If there are *n* possible actions for every state, the output of the network produces *n* outputs $Q(s, a_1)$, $Q(s, a_2)$, ... $Q(s, a_n)$.

The deep Q learning networks are trained with a very simple idea called experience replay. Let the RL agent interact with the environment and store experience in the tuple form of (s, a, r, s') in a replay buffer. Mini-batches can be sampled from this replay buffer to train the network. In the beginning, the replay buffer is stored with random experiences.

Formulating the cost function

It is easier to work with the architecture where we get the Q values for all the actions for a given state the network is fed with. The same is illustrated in the right-hand side of *Figure 9.3*. We would let the agent interact with the environment and collect states and rewards based on which we will learn the Q functions. In fact, the network would learn the Q function by minimizing the predicted Q values for all actions $[a_i]_{i=1}^{n}$ for a given state *s* with those of the target Q values. Each training record is a tuple $(s^{(t)}, a^{(t)}, r^{(t)}, s^{(t+1)})$.

Bear in mind that the target Q values are to be computed based on the network itself. Let's consider the fact that the network is parametrized by the $W \in R^d$ weights and we learn mapping from the states to the Q values for each action given the state. For n set of actions $[a_i]_{i=1}^{n}$ the network would predict i Q values pertaining to each of the actions. The mapping function can be denoted as follows:

$$f_W(s) = [Q(s, a_1)\ Q(s, a_2)\ Q(s, a_3) \ldots.\ Q(s, a_n)]^T$$

This mapping is used to predict the Q values given a state $s^{(t)}$ and this prediction $\hat{p}^{(t)}$ goes to the cost function we are minimizing. The only technicality to consider here is that we would just need to take the predicted Q value corresponding to the action $a^{(t)}$ observed at the instance t.

We can use the same mapping to build the target Q values based on the next state $s^{(t+1)}$. As illustrated in the prior section, the candidate update to the Q value is as follows:

$$r^{(t)} + \gamma \max_{a'} Q^{(t)}(s^{(t+1)}, a')$$

Consequently, the target Q values can be calculated like so:

$$y_{t+1} = r^{(t)} + \max_{a'} f_W(s^{(t+1)})$$

$$= r^{(t)} + \max_{a'}[Q(s, a_1)\ Q(s, a_2)\ Q(s, a_3) \ldots.\ Q(s, a_n)]^T$$

To learn the functional mapping from the states to the Q values, we minimize the squared loss or other relevant loss with respect to the weights of the neural network:

$$\hat{W} = \sum_{i=1}^{m}(y_i^{(t)} - \hat{p}_i^{(t)})^2$$

Double deep Q learning

One of the issues with deep Q learning is that we use the same network weights W to estimate the target and the Q value. As a result, there is a large correlation between the Q values we are predicting and the target Q values, since they both use the same changing weights. This makes both the predicted and the target Q values shift at every step of training, leading to oscillations.

To stabilize this, we use a copy of the original network to estimate the target Q values and the weights of the target network is copied from the original network at specific intervals during the steps. This variant of the deep Q learning network is called **double deep Q learning** and generally leads to stable training. The working mechanics of the double deep Q learning is illustrated in the following diagrams *Figure 9.4A* and *Figure 9.4B*:

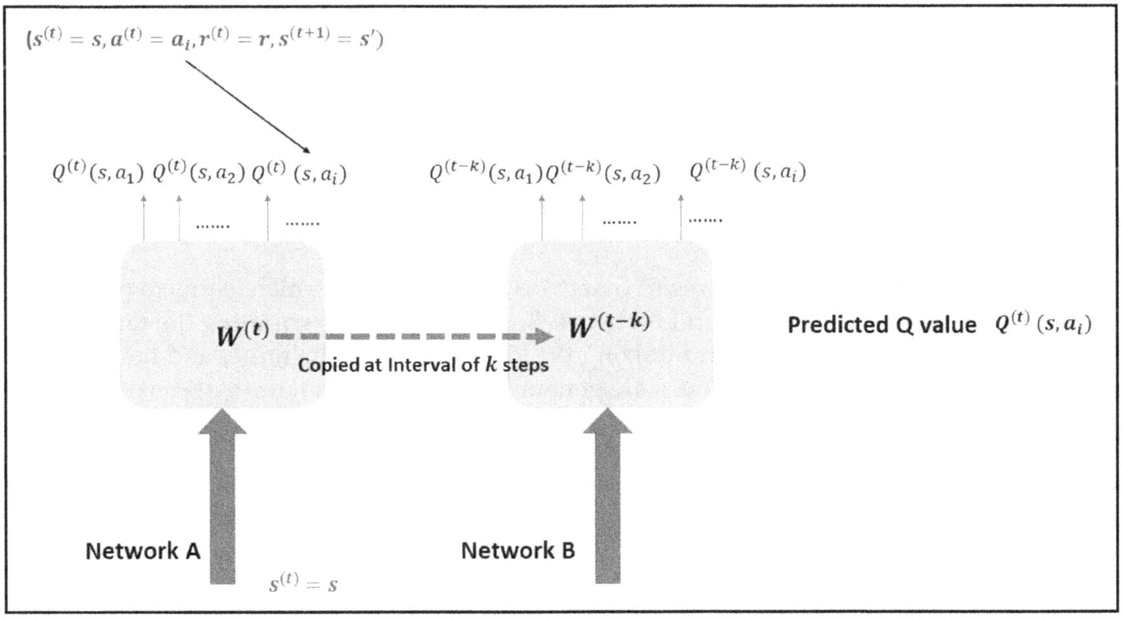

Figure 9.4A: Illustration of double deep Q learning

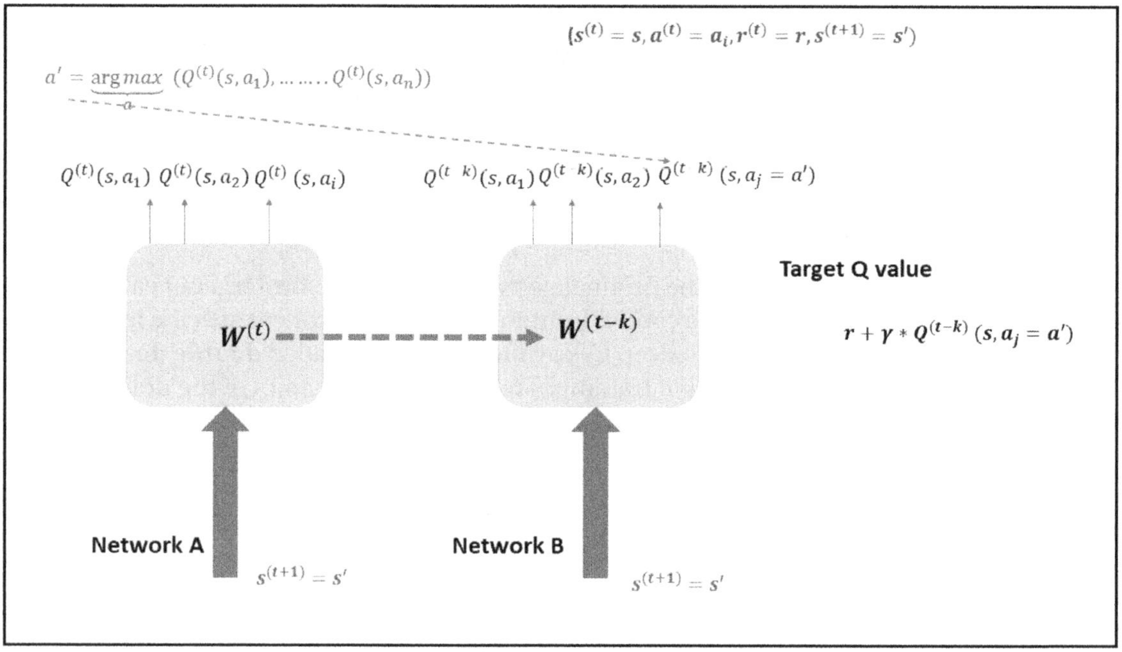

Figure 9.4B: Illustration of double deep Q learning

In the preceding diagram, we can see two networks: **Network A**, which learns to predict the actual Q values given a state, and **Network B** which helps in computing the target Q values. **Network A** improves by minimizing the loss function of the target and the predicted Q values. Since the Q values are generally continuous in nature, some of the valid loss functions are `mean squared error`, `mean absolute error`, `Huber Loss`, `log-cosh loss`, and so on.

Network B is basically a copy of **Network A**, and hence they share the same architecture. The weights from **Network A** are generally copied to **Network B** at specified intervals. This is to ensure that the same set of network weights are not used to predict the Q values and also formulate the target Q values, as it leads to unstable training. Given the single training tuple $(s^{(t)} = s, a^{(t)} = a, r^{(t)} = r, s^{(t+1)} = s')$, the **Network A** gives the prediction for the Q values given the state $s^{(t)} = s$ for all the possible actions. Since we know the actual action $a^{(t)} = a$, we choose the Q value $Q^{(t)}\ (s^{(t)} = s, a^{(t)} = a)$. This will act as our predicted Q value $\hat{y}$.

Computing the target is now a little more difficult, since it involves both networks. We know the candidate Q value at any state $s^{(t)}$ at step t is the immediate reward $r^{(t)}$ at time t plus the maximum Q value at the next step $(t + 1)$ given the new state $s^{(t+1)}$. The candidate Q value can be expressed as follows:

$$r^{(t)} + \gamma \max_{a'} Q^{(t)}(s^{(t+1)}, a) = r + \gamma \max_{a'} Q^{(t)}(s', a)$$

This is the case when γ is a constant discount factor. The reward r is already a part of the training tuple. Consequently, the only thing that we need to compute the target is the action a' that gives the maximum Q and takes the corresponding Q value to that corresponding action a'. This problem of computing $\max_{a'} Q^{(t)}(s', a)$ is broken down into two parts:

- **Network A** determines the action a' that gives the maximum Q value given the state s'. However, we won't take the Q value corresponding to the action a' and state s' from **Network A.**
- **Network B** is used to extract the Q value $Q^{(t-k)}(s', a')$ corresponding to the state s' and action a'.

This leads to much stable training in comparison to that of a basic `DQN`.

Implementing an autonomous self-driving car

We will now look at implementing an autonomous self-driving racing car that learns to drive by itself on a racing track using deep Q networks. The driver and the car will act as the agent, while the racing track and its surroundings act as the environment. We will be using an OpenAI Gym `CarRacing-v0` framework as the environment. The states and the rewards are going to be presented to the agent by the environment, while the agent will act upon those by taking appropriate actions. The states are in the form of images taken from a camera in front of the car. The actions that the environment accepts are in the form of the three-dimensional vector $a \in R^3$ where the first component is used for turning left, the second component is used for moving forward and the third component is used for moving right. The agent will interact with the environment and will convert the interaction into tuples of the form $(s, a, r, s')_{i=1}^{m}$. These interaction tuples will act as our training data.

The architecture would be similar to what we have illustrated on the right side of the diagrams (*Figure 9.4A* and *Figure 9.4B*).

Discretizing actions for deep Q learning

Discretizing actions for deep Q learning is very important, since a three-dimensional continuous action space can have infinite Q values, and it would not be possible to have separate units for each of them in the output layer of the Deep Q network. The three dimensions of the actions space are as follows:

Steering: $\in [-1, 1]$

Gas: $\in [0, 1]$

Break: $\in [0, 1]$

We convert this three dimensional action space into four actions of interest to us as follows:

```
Brake :       [0.0, 0.0, 0.0]
Sharp Left:   [-0.6, 0.05, 0.0]
Sharp Right:  [0.6, 0.05, 0.0]
Straight:     [0.0, 0.3, 0.0]
```

Implementing the Double Deep Q network

The network architecture of the **Double Deep Q network** is illustrated as follows. The networks have CNN architecture to process the states as images and output Q values for all possible actions. The detailed code(`DQN.py`) is as follows:

```
import keras
from keras import optimizers
from keras.layers import Convolution2D
from keras.layers import Dense, Flatten, Input, concatenate, Dropout
from keras.models import Model
from keras.utils import plot_model
from keras import backend as K
import numpy as np

'''
Double Deep Q Network Implementation
'''

learning_rate = 0.0001
```

```
BATCH_SIZE = 128

class DQN:

    def __init__(self,num_states,num_actions,model_path):
        self.num_states = num_states
        print(num_states)
        self.num_actions = num_actions
        self.model = self.build_model() # Base Model
        self.model_ = self.build_model()
       # target Model (copy of Base Model)
        self.model_chkpoint_1 = model_path +"CarRacing_DDQN_model_1.h5"
        self.model_chkpoint_2 = model_path +"CarRacing_DDQN_model_2.h5"
        save_best = keras.callbacks.ModelCheckpoint(self.model_chkpoint_1,
                                                monitor='loss',
                                                verbose=1,
                                                save_best_only=True,
                                                mode='min',
                                                period=20)
        save_per = keras.callbacks.ModelCheckpoint(self.model_chkpoint_2,
                                                monitor='loss',
                                                verbose=1,
                                                save_best_only=False,
                                                mode='min',
                                                period=400)
        self.callbacks_list = [save_best,save_per]
    # Convolutional Neural Network that takes in the state and outputs the
Q values for all the possible actions.
    def build_model(self):

        states_in = Input(shape=self.num_states,name='states_in')
        x =
Convolution2D(32,(8,8),strides=(4,4),activation='relu')(states_in)
        x = Convolution2D(64,(4,4), strides=(2,2), activation='relu')(x)
        x = Convolution2D(64,(3,3), strides=(1,1), activation='relu')(x)
        x = Flatten(name='flattened')(x)
        x = Dense(512,activation='relu')(x)
        x = Dense(self.num_actions,activation="linear")(x)

        model = Model(inputs=states_in, outputs=x)
        self.opt = optimizers.Adam(lr=learning_rate, beta_1=0.9,
beta_2=0.999, epsilon=None,decay=0.0, amsgrad=False)
        model.compile(loss=keras.losses.mse,optimizer=self.opt)
        plot_model(model,to_file='model_architecture.png',show_shapes=True)

        return model

    # Train function
```

```
    def train(self,x,y,epochs=10,verbose=0):
        self.model.fit(x,y,batch_size=(BATCH_SIZE), epochs=epochs,
verbose=verbose, callbacks=self.callbacks_list)
   #Predict function
    def predict(self,state,target=False):
        if target:
            # Return the Q value for an action given a state from thr
target Network
            return self.model_.predict(state)
        else:
            # Return the Q value from the original Network
            return self.model.predict(state)
    # Predict for single state function
    def predict_single_state(self,state,target=False):
        x = state[np.newaxis,:,:,:]
        return self.predict(x,target)
    #Update the target Model with the Base Model weights
    def target_model_update(self):
        self.model_.set_weights(self.model.get_weights())
```

As we can see in the preceding code we are having two models where one is a copy of the other. The base and the target models are saved as`CarRacing_DDQN_model_1.h5` and `CarRacing_DDQN_model_2.h5`.

By invoking the `target_model_update` the target model is updated to have the same weights as the base model.

Designing the agent

The agent will interact with the environment and, given a state, will try to execute the best action. The agent will initially execute random actions and, as the training progresses, the actions will be based more on the Q values given a state. The value of the **epsilon** parameter determines the probability of the action being random. Initially **epsilon** is set to `1` to make the actions random. When the agent has collected a specified number of training samples, the epsilon is reduced in each step so that the probability of the action being random is reduced. This scheme of basing the action on the value of the epsilon is called the Epsilon greedy algorithm. We define two agent classes as follows:

- `Agent`: Executes actions based on the Q values given a state
- `RandomAgent`: Executes random action

The agent class has three functions with the following functionalities:

- `act`: The agent decides the action to take based on the state
- `observe`: The agent captures the state and the target Q values
- `replay`: The agent trains the model based on the observations

The detailed code for the agent(`Agents.py`) is illustrated as follows:

```
import math
from Memory import Memory
from DQN import DQN
import numpy as np
import random
from helper_functions import sel_action,sel_action_index

# Agent and Random Agent implementations

max_reward = 10
grass_penalty = 0.4
action_repeat_num = 8
max_num_episodes = 1000
memory_size = 10000
max_num_steps = action_repeat_num * 100
gamma = 0.99
max_eps = 0.1
min_eps = 0.02
EXPLORATION_STOP = int(max_num_steps*10)
_lambda_ = - np.log(0.001) / EXPLORATION_STOP
UPDATE_TARGET_FREQUENCY = int(50)
batch_size = 128



class Agent:
    steps = 0
    epsilon = max_eps
    memory = Memory(memory_size)
    def __init__(self, num_states,num_actions,img_dim,model_path):
        self.num_states = num_states
        self.num_actions = num_actions
        self.DQN = DQN(num_states,num_actions,model_path)
        self.no_state = np.zeros(num_states)
        self.x = np.zeros((batch_size,)+img_dim)
        self.y = np.zeros([batch_size,num_actions])
        self.errors = np.zeros(batch_size)
        self.rand = False
        self.agent_type = 'Learning'
```

```
            self.maxEpsilone = max_eps
        def act(self,s):
            print(self.epsilon)
            if random.random() < self.epsilon:
                best_act = np.random.randint(self.num_actions)
                self.rand=True
                return sel_action(best_act), sel_action(best_act)
            else:
                act_soft = self.DQN.predict_single_state(s)
                best_act = np.argmax(act_soft)
                self.rand=False
                return sel_action(best_act),act_soft

        def compute_targets(self,batch):
            # 0 -> Index for current state
            # 1 -> Index for action
            # 2 -> Index for reward
            # 3 -> Index for next state
            states = np.array([rec[1][0] for rec in batch])
            states_ = np.array([(self.no_state if rec[1][3] is None else
    rec[1][3]) for rec in batch])
            p = self.DQN.predict(states)
            p_ = self.DQN.predict(states_,target=False)
            p_t = self.DQN.predict(states_,target=True)
            act_ctr = np.zeros(self.num_actions)
            for i in range(len(batch)):
                rec = batch[i][1]
                s = rec[0]; a = rec[1]; r = rec[2]; s_ = rec[3]
                a = sel_action_index(a)
                t = p[i]
                act_ctr[a] += 1
                oldVal = t[a]
                if s_ is None:
                    t[a] = r
                else:
                    t[a] = r + gamma * p_t[i][ np.argmax(p_[i])] # DDQN
                self.x[i] = s
                self.y[i] = t
                if self.steps % 20 == 0 and i == len(batch)-1:
                    print('t',t[a], 'r: %.4f' % r,'mean t',np.mean(t))
                    print ('act ctr: ', act_ctr)
                self.errors[i] = abs(oldVal - t[a])

            return (self.x, self.y,self.errors)


        def observe(self,sample): # in (s, a, r, s_) format
            _,_,errors = self.compute_targets([(0,sample)])
```

```
        self.memory.add(errors[0], sample)

        if self.steps % UPDATE_TARGET_FREQUENCY == 0:
            self.DQN.target_model_update()
        self.steps += 1
        self.epsilon = min_eps + (self.maxEpsilone - min_eps) *
np.exp(-1*_lambda_ * self.steps)


    def replay(self):
        batch = self.memory.sample(batch_size)
        x, y,errors = self.compute_targets(batch)
        for i in range(len(batch)):
            idx = batch[i][0]
            self.memory.update(idx, errors[i])

        self.DQN.train(x,y)
class RandomAgent:
    memory = Memory(memory_size)
    exp = 0
    steps = 0

    def __init__(self, num_actions):
        self.num_actions = num_actions
        self.agent_type = 'Learning'
        self.rand = True

    def act(self, s):
        best_act = np.random.randint(self.num_actions)
        return sel_action(best_act), sel_action(best_act)

    def observe(self, sample): # in (s, a, r, s_) format
        error = abs(sample[2]) # reward
        self.memory.add(error, sample)
        self.exp += 1
        self.steps += 1
    def replay(self):
        pass
```

The environment for the self-driving car

The environment for the self-driving car is `CarRacing-v0` from the **OpenAI Gym.** The states presented to the agent from this OpenAI environment are images from the front of the simulated car in `CarRacing-v0`. The environment also returns a reward based on the action taken by the agent at a given state. We penalize the reward if the car treads on grass and also normalize the reward to be in the range of `(-1,1)` for stable training. The detailed code for the environment is as below

```
import gym
from gym import envs
import numpy as np
from helper_functions import
rgb2gray,action_list,sel_action,sel_action_index
from keras import backend as K

seed_gym = 3
action_repeat_num = 8
patience_count = 200
epsilon_greedy = True
max_reward = 10
grass_penalty = 0.8
max_num_steps = 200
max_num_episodes = action_repeat_num*100

'''
Enviroment to interact with the Agent
'''

class environment:
    def __init__(self,
environment_name,img_dim,num_stack,num_actions,render,lr):
        self.environment_name = environment_name
        print(self.environment_name)
        self.env = gym.make(self.environment_name)
        envs.box2d.car_racing.WINDOW_H = 500
        envs.box2d.car_racing.WINDOW_W = 600
        self.episode = 0
        self.reward = []
        self.step = 0
        self.stuck_at_local_minima = 0
        self.img_dim = img_dim
        self.num_stack = num_stack
        self.num_actions = num_actions
        self.render = render
        self.lr = lr
        if self.render == True:
```

```
            print("Rendering proeprly set")
        else:
            print("issue in Rendering")
    # Agent performing its task
    def run(self,agent):
        self.env.seed(seed_gym)
        img = self.env.reset()
        img = rgb2gray(img, True)
        s = np.zeros(self.img_dim)
        #Collecting the state
        for i in range(self.num_stack):
            s[:,:,i] = img

        s_ = s
        R = 0
        self.step = 0
        a_soft = a_old = np.zeros(self.num_actions)
        a = action_list[0]
        #print(agent.agent_type)
        while True:
            if agent.agent_type == 'Learning' :
                if self.render == True :
                    self.env.render("human")


            if self.step % action_repeat_num == 0:
                if agent.rand == False:
                    a_old = a_soft
                #Agent outputs the action
                a,a_soft = agent.act(s)
                # Rescue Agent stuck at local minima
                if epsilon_greedy:
                    if agent.rand == False:
                        if a_soft.argmax() == a_old.argmax():
                            self.stuck_at_local_minima += 1
                            if self.stuck_at_local_minima >=
patience_count:
                                print('Stuck in local minimum, reset
learning rate')
                                agent.steps = 0
                                K.set_value(agent.DQN.opt.lr,self.lr*10)
                                self.stuck_at_local_minima = 0
                        else:
                            self.stuck_at_local_minima =
                            max(self.stuck_at_local_minima -2, 0)
                            K.set_value(agent.DQN.opt.lr,self.lr)
                #Perform the action on the environment
                img_rgb, r,done,info = self.env.step(a)
```

```
                if not done:
                    # Create the next state
                    img = rgb2gray(img_rgb, True)
                    for i in range(self.num_stack-1):
                        s_[:,:,i] = s_[:,:,i+1]
                    s_[:,:,self.num_stack-1] = img
                else:
                   s_ = None
                # Cumulative reward tracking
                R += r
                # Normalize reward given by the gym environment
                r = (r/max_reward)
                if np.mean(img_rgb[:,:,1]) > 185.0:
                # Penalize if the car is on the grass
                    r -= grass_penalty
                # Keeping the value of reward within -1 and 1
                r = np.clip(r, -1 ,1)
            #Agent has a whole state,action,reward,and next state to learn
from
                agent.observe( (s, a, r, s_) )
                agent.replay()
                s = s_
            else:
                img_rgb, r, done, info = self.env.step(a)
                if not done:
                    img = rgb2gray(img_rgb, True)
                    for i in range(self.num_stack-1):
                        s_[:,:,i] = s_[:,:,i+1]
                    s_[:,:,self.num_stack-1] = img
                else:
                   s_ = None

                R += r
                s = s_
            if (self.step % (action_repeat_num * 5) == 0) and
               (agent.agent_type=='Learning'):
                print('step:', self.step, 'R: %.1f' % R, a, 'rand:',
agent.rand)
            self.step += 1
            if done or (R <-5) or (self.step > max_num_steps) or
             np.mean(img_rgb[:,:,1]) > 185.1:
                self.episode += 1
                self.reward.append(R)
                print('Done:', done, 'R<-5:', (R<-5), 'Green
                      >185.1:',np.mean(img_rgb[:,:,1]))
                break

        print("Episode ",self.episode,"/",
```

```
max_num_episodes,agent.agent_type)
        print("Average Episode Reward:", R/self.step, "Total Reward:",
              sum(self.reward))
    def test(self,agent):
        self.env.seed(seed_gym)
        img= self.env.reset()
        img = rgb2gray(img, True)
        s = np.zeros(self.img_dim)
        for i in range(self.num_stack):
            s[:,:,i] = img

        R = 0
        self.step = 0
        done = False
        while True :
            self.env.render('human')
            if self.step % action_repeat_num == 0:
                if(agent.agent_type == 'Learning'):
                    act1 = agent.DQN.predict_single_state(s)
                    act = sel_action(np.argmax(act1))
                else:
                    act = agent.act(s)
                if self.step <= 8:
                    act = sel_action(3)
                img_rgb, r, done,info = self.env.step(act)
                img = rgb2gray(img_rgb, True)
                R += r
                for i in range(self.num_stack-1):
                    s[:,:,i] = s[:,:,i+1]
                s[:,:,self.num_stack-1] = img
            if(self.step % 10) == 0:
                print('Step:', self.step, 'action:',act, 'R: %.1f' % R)
                print(np.mean(img_rgb[:,:,0]), np.mean(img_rgb[:,:,1]),
                      np.mean(img_rgb[:,:,2]))
            self.step += 1
            if done or (R< -5) or (agent.steps > max_num_steps) or
              np.mean(img_rgb[:,:,1]) > 185.1:
                R = 0
                self.step = 0
                print('Done:', done, 'R<-5:', (R<-5), 'Green>
                 185.1:',np.mean(img_rgb[:,:,1]))
                break
```

The `run` function in the above code denotes the activity of the agent in the context of the environment.

Putting it all together

The `main.py` script puts together the logic of the environment, `DQN`, and `agent` appropriately, enabling the car to learn driving through reinforcement learning. Detailed code is as follows:

```
import sys
#sys.path.append('/home/santanu/ML_DS_Catalog-/Python-Artificial-
Intelligence-Projects_backup/Python-Artificial-Intelligence-
Projects/Chapter09/Scripts/')
from gym import envs
from Agents import Agent,RandomAgent
from helper_functions import action_list,model_save
from environment import environment
import argparse
import numpy as np
import random
from sum_tree import sum_tree
from sklearn.externals import joblib

'''
This is the main module for training and testing the CarRacing Application
from gym
'''

if __name__ == "__main__":
    #Define the Parameters for training the Model

    parser = argparse.ArgumentParser(description='arguments')
    parser.add_argument('--environment_name',default='CarRacing-v0')
    parser.add_argument('--model_path',help='model_path')
    parser.add_argument('--train_mode',type=bool,default=True)
    parser.add_argument('--test_mode',type=bool,default=False)
    parser.add_argument('--epsilon_greedy',default=True)
    parser.add_argument('--render',type=bool,default=True)
    parser.add_argument('--width',type=int,default=96)
    parser.add_argument('--height',type=int,default=96)
    parser.add_argument('--num_stack',type=int,default=4)
    parser.add_argument('--lr',type=float,default=1e-3)
    parser.add_argument('--huber_loss_thresh',type=float,default=1.)
    parser.add_argument('--dropout',type=float,default=1.)
    parser.add_argument('--memory_size',type=int,default=10000)
    parser.add_argument('--batch_size',type=int,default=128)
    parser.add_argument('--max_num_episodes',type=int,default=500)
    args = parser.parse_args()
    environment_name = args.environment_name
    model_path = args.model_path
```

```
    test_mode = args.test_mode
    train_mode = args.train_mode
    epsilon_greedy = args.epsilon_greedy
    render = args.render
    width = args.width
    height = args.height
    num_stack = args.num_stack
    lr = args.lr
    huber_loss_thresh = args.huber_loss_thresh
    dropout = args.dropout
    memory_size = args.memory_size
    dropout = args.dropout
    batch_size = args.batch_size
    max_num_episodes = args.max_num_episodes
    max_eps = 1
    min_eps = 0.02
    seed_gym = 2 # Random state
    img_dim = (width,height,num_stack)
    num_actions = len(action_list)

if __name__ == '__main__':

    environment_name = 'CarRacing-v0'
    env =
environment(environment_name,img_dim,num_stack,num_actions,render,lr)
    num_states = img_dim
    print(env.env.action_space.shape)
    action_dim = env.env.action_space.shape[0]
    assert action_list.shape[1] ==
    action_dim,"length of Env action space does not match action buffer"
    num_actions = action_list.shape[0]
    # Setting random seeds with respect to python inbuilt random and numpy
random
    random.seed(901)
    np.random.seed(1)
    agent = Agent(num_states, num_actions,img_dim,model_path)
    randomAgent = RandomAgent(num_actions)

    print(test_mode,train_mode)
    try:
        #Train agent
        if test_mode:
            if train_mode:
                print("Initialization with random agent. Fill memory")
                while randomAgent.exp < memory_size:
                    env.run(randomAgent)
                    print(randomAgent.exp, "/", memory_size)
                agent.memory = randomAgent.memory
```

```
                randomAgent = None
                print("Starts learning")
                while env.episode < max_num_episodes:
                    env.run(agent)
                model_save(model_path, "DDQN_model.h5", agent, env.reward)
            else:
                # Load train Model
                print('Load pre-trained agent and learn')
                agent.DQN.model.load_weights(model_path+"DDQN_model.h5")
                agent.DQN.target_model_update()
                try :
                    agent.memory =
joblib.load(model_path+"DDQN_model.h5"+"Memory")
                    Params =
joblib.load(model_path+"DDQN_model.h5"+"agent_param")
                    agent.epsilon = Params[0]
                    agent.steps = Params[1]
                    opt = Params[2]
                    agent.DQN.opt.decay.set_value(opt['decay'])
                    agent.DQN.opt.epsilon = opt['epsilon']
                    agent.DQN.opt.lr.set_value(opt['lr'])
                    agent.DQN.opt.rho.set_value(opt['rho'])
                    env.reward =
joblib.load(model_path+"DDQN_model.h5"+"Rewards")
                    del Params, opt
                except:
                    print("Invalid DDQL_Memory_.csv to load")
                    print("Initialization with random agent. Fill memory")
                    while randomAgent.exp < memory_size:
                        env.run(randomAgent)
                        print(randomAgent.exp, "/", memory_size)
                    agent.memory = randomAgent.memory
                    randomAgent = None
                    agent.maxEpsilone = max_eps/5
                print("Starts learning")
                while env.episode < max_num_episodes:
                    env.run(agent)
                model_save(model_path, "DDQN_model.h5", agent, env.reward)
        else:
            print('Load agent and play')
            agent.DQN.model.load_weights(model_path+"DDQN_model.h5")
            done_ctr = 0
            while done_ctr < 5 :
                env.test(agent)
                done_ctr += 1
            env.env.close()
    #Graceful exit
    except KeyboardInterrupt:
```

```
        print('User interrupt..gracefule exit')
        env.env.close()
        if test_mode == False:
            # Prompt for Model save
             print('Save model: Y or N?')
             save = input()
             if save.lower() == 'y':
                 model_save(model_path, "DDQN_model.h5", agent, env.reward)
             else:
                print('Model is not saved!')
```

Helper functions

The following are a few of the helper functions that are used in this reinforcement learning framework for the purpose of action selection, storing observations used for training, state image processing and saving the weights of the trained model:

```
"""
Created on Thu Nov  2 16:03:46 2017

@author: Santanu Pattanayak
"""
from keras import backend as K
import numpy as np
import shutil, os
import numpy as np
import pandas as pd
from scipy import misc
import pickle
import matplotlib.pyplot as plt
from sklearn.externals import joblib


huber_loss_thresh = 1
action_list = np.array([
                    [0.0, 0.0, 0.0],      #Brake
                    [-0.6, 0.05, 0.0],    #Sharp left
                    [0.6, 0.05, 0.0],     #Sharp right
                    [0.0, 0.3, 0.0]] )    #Staight

rgb_mode = True

num_actions = len(action_list)
def sel_action(action_index):
    return action_list[action_index]
```

```
def sel_action_index(action):
    for i in range(num_actions):
        if np.all(action == action_list[i]):
            return i
    raise ValueError('Selected action not in list')

def huber_loss(y_true,y_pred):
    error = (y_true - y_pred)

    cond = K.abs(error) <= huber_loss_thresh
    if cond == True:
        loss = 0.5 * K.square(error)
    else:
        loss = 0.5 *huber_loss_thresh**2 + huber_loss_thresh*(K.abs(error)
- huber_loss_thresh)
    return K.mean(loss)


def rgb2gray(rgb,norm=True):
    gray = np.dot(rgb[...,:3], [0.299, 0.587, 0.114])
    if norm:
        # normalize
        gray = gray.astype('float32') / 128 - 1

    return gray

def data_store(path,action,reward,state):

    if not os.path.exists(path):
        os.makedirs(path)
    else:
        shutil.rmtree(path)
        os.makedirs(path)
    df = pd.DataFrame(action, columns=["Steering", "Throttle", "Brake"])
    df["Reward"] = reward
    df.to_csv(path +'car_racing_actions_rewards.csv', index=False)
    for i in range(len(state)):
        if rgb_mode == False:
            image = rgb2gray(state[i])
        else:
            image = state[i]

    misc.imsave( path + "img" + str(i) +".png", image)


def model_save(path,name,agent,R):
    ''' Saves actions, rewards and states (images) in DataPath'''
    if not os.path.exists(path):
```

```
            os.makedirs(path)
        agent.DQN.model.save(path + name)
        print(name, "saved")
        print('...')
        joblib.dump(agent.memory,path+name+'Memory')
        joblib.dump([agent.epsilon,agent.steps,agent.DQN.opt.get_config()],
    path+name+'AgentParam')
        joblib.dump(R,path+name+'Rewards')
        print('Memory pickle dumped')
```

Training of the Reinforcement Learning Process for the Self Driving Car can be invoked as below

```
 python main.py --environment_name 'CarRacing-v0' --model_path
'/home/santanu/Autonomous Car/train/' --train_mode True --test_mode False -
-epsilon_greedy True --render True --width 96 --height 96 --num_stack 4 --
huber_loss_thresh 1 --dropout 0.2 --memory_size 10000 --batch_size 128 --
max_num_episodes 500
```

Results from the training

Initially, the self-driving car makes mistakes, but after a period of time, the car learns from its mistakes through training, and therefore gets better. This screenshot shows images of the car's activity during the initial part of the training and then from the later part of the training when it has learned from its previous mistakes. This has been illustrated in the following screenshots (*Figure 9.5(A)* and *Figure 9.5(B)*):

Figure 9.5(A): The car making mistakes in the initial part of the training

The following result shows the car driving successfully after enough training:

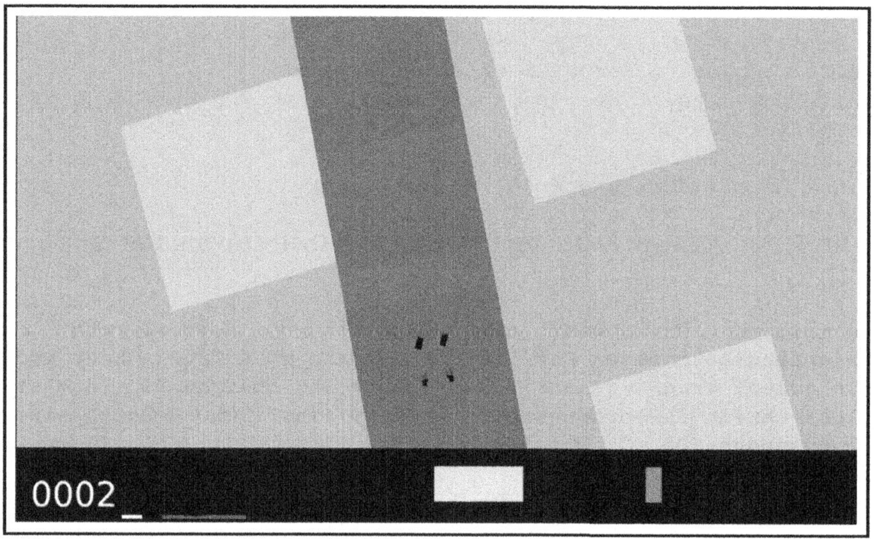

Figure 9.5(B): The car driving successfully after sufficient training

Summary

With this, we come to the end of this chapter. The topics discussed in this chapter will help you to get up to speed with the reinforcement learning paradigm as well as enable you to build intelligent RL systems. Also, the reader is expected to apply the technicalities learned in this project to other RL-based problems.

In the next chapter we are going to look at CAPTCHAs from a deep learning perspective and build some interesting projects around it. Look forward to your participation.

10 CAPTCHA from a Deep-Learning Perspective

The term **CAPTCHA** is an acronym for **completely automated public Turing test to tell computers and humans apart**. This is a computer program designed to distinguish between a human user and a machine or a bot, typically as a security measure to prevent spam and data misuse. The concept of CAPTCHA was introduced as early as 1997, when the internet search company AltaVista was trying to block automatic URL submissions to the platform that were skewing their search engine algorithms. To tackle this problem, AltaVista's chief scientist, Andrei Broder, came up with an algorithm to randomly generate images of text that could easily be identified by humans, but not by bots. Later, in 2003, Luis von Ahn, Manuel Blum, Nicholas J Hopper, and John Langford perfected this technology and called it CAPTCHA. The most common form of CAPTCHA requires a user to recognize the letters and numbers in a distorted image. This test is done in the hope that humans would easily be able to distinguish the characters in the distorted image, while an automated program or bot will not be able to distinguish them. The CAPTCHA test is sometimes called a reverse Turing test since it is performed by a computer as opposed to a human.

As of recently, CAPTCHA has started to serve a much bigger role than just preventing bot frauds. For instance, Google used CAPTCHA and one of its variants, reCAPTCHA, when they digitized the archives of New York Times and some books in Google Books. This is typically done by asking the user to correctly enter the characters of more than one CAPTCHA. Only one of the CAPTCHAs is actually labelled and used to validate whether the user is human.

The rest of the CAPTCHAs are labelled by the user. Currently, Google uses image-based CAPTCHA to help label its autonomous car-driving dataset as shown in the following screenshot:

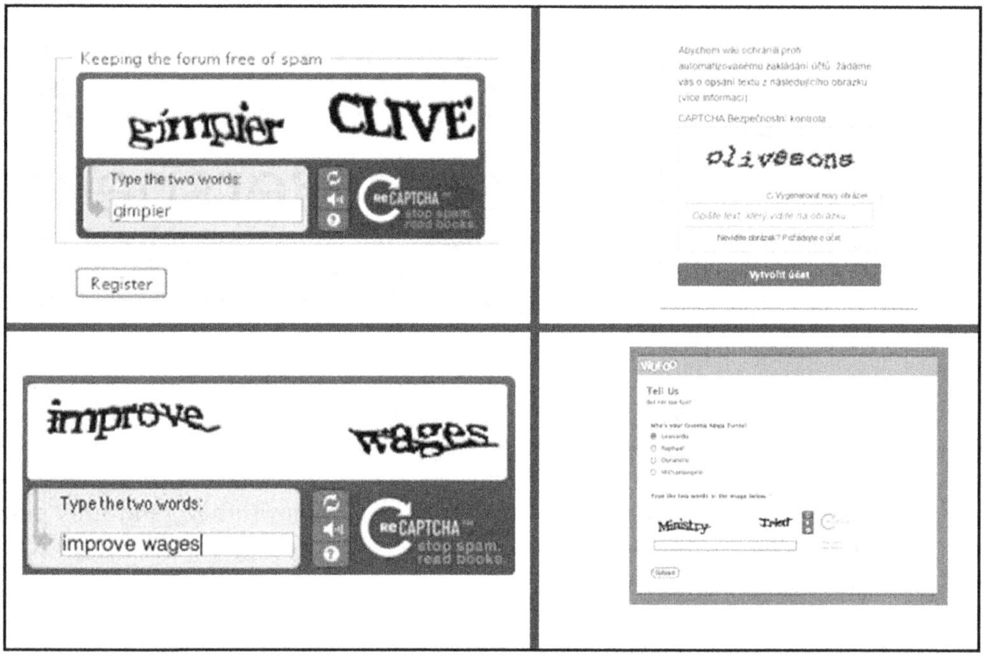

Figure 10.1: Some common CAPTCHAs on various websites

In this chapter, we will cover the following topics:

- What are CAPTCHAs
- Breaking CAPTCHAs using deep learning to expose their vulnerability
- Generating CAPTCHAs using adversarial learning

Technical requirements

You will require to have basic knowledge of Python 3, TensorFlow, Keras and OpenCV.

The code files of this chapter can be found on GitHub:
`https://github.com/PacktPublishing/Intelligent-Projects-using-Python/tree/master/Chapter10`

Check out the following video to see the code in action:
http://bit.ly/2SgwR6P

Breaking CAPTCHAs with deep learning

With the recent success of **convolutional neural networks** (**CNNs**) in computer vision tasks, breaking basic CAPTCHAs in a few minutes is a relatively easy task. Consequently, CAPTCHAs need to be much more evolved than they have in the past. In the first part of this chapter, we are going to expose the vulnerability of basic CAPTCHAs being automatically detected using bots with a deep-learning framework. We are going to follow this up by exploiting GAN to create CAPTCHAs that are harder for bots to detect.

Generating basic CAPTCHAs

CAPTCHAs can be generated using the `Claptcha` package in Python. We use this to generate CAPTCHA images of four characters consisting of numbers and text. Consequently, each character can be any one of `26` letters and `10` digits. The following code can be used for generating CAPTCHAs with a random selection of letters and digits:

```
alphabets = 'abcdefghijklmnopqrstuvwxyz'
alphabets = alphabets.upper()
font =
"/home/santanu/Android/Sdk/platforms/android-28/data/fonts/DancingScript-
Regular.ttf"
# For each of the 4 characters determine randomly whether its a digit or
alphabet
char_num_ind = list(np.random.randint(0,2,4))
text = ''
for ind in char_num_ind:
    if ind == 1:
    # for indicator 1 select character else number
        loc = np.random.randint(0,26,1)
        text = text + alphabets[np.random.randint(0,26,1)[0]]
    else:
        text = text + str(np.random.randint(0,10,1)[0])

c = Claptcha(text,font)
text,image = c.image
plt.imshow(image)
```

The following screenshot (*Figure 10.2*) is the random CAPTCHA generated by the preceding code:

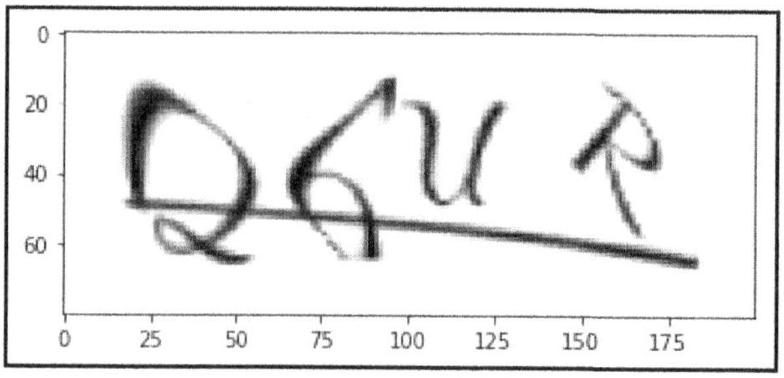

Figure 10.2: Random CAPTCHA with the characters 26UR

Along with the text, the `Claptcha` tool requires the font in which to print the text as input. As we can see, it has added noise to the image in the form of a somewhat distorted line across the horizontal axis.

Generating data for training a CAPTCHA breaker

In this section, we are going to generate several CAPTCHAs using the `Claptcha` tool for training a CNN model. The CNN model will learn to identify the characters in the CAPTCHA through supervised training. We are going to generate a training and validation set for training the CNN model. In addition to this, we are going to generate a separate test set to evaluate its ability to generalize unseen data. The `CaptchaGenerator.py` script can be coded as follows to generate CAPTCHA data:

```
from claptcha import Claptcha
import os
import numpy as np
import cv2
import fire
from elapsedtimer import ElasedTimer

def generate_captcha(outdir,font,num_captchas=20000):
    alphabets = 'abcdefghijklmnopqrstuvwxyz'
    alphabets = alphabets.upper()
    try:
        os.mkdir(outdir)
    except:
        'Directory already present,writing captchas to the same'
    #rint(char_num_ind)
    # select one alphabet if indicator 1 else number
```

```
    for i in range(num_captchas):
        char_num_ind = list(np.random.randint(0,2,4))
        text = ''
        for ind in char_num_ind:
            if ind == 1:
                loc = np.random.randint(0,26,1)
                text = text + alphabets[np.random.randint(0,26,1)[0]]
            else:
                text = text + str(np.random.randint(0,10,1)[0])
        c = Claptcha(text,font)
        text,image = c.image
        image.save(outdir + text + '.png')

def main_process(outdir_train,num_captchas_train,
                  outdir_val,num_captchas_val,
                  outdir_test,num_captchas_test,
                 font):

    generate_captcha(outdir_train,font,num_captchas_train)
    generate_captcha(outdir_val,font,num_captchas_val)
    generate_captcha(outdir_test,font,num_captchas_test)


if __name__ == '__main__':
    with ElasedTimer('main_process'):
        fire.Fire(main_process)
```

One thing to note is that most of the CAPTCHA generators use a `ttf` file to get a font pattern for the CAPTCHA.

We can generate training set, validation, and the test set of size `16000`, `4000`, and `4000`, by using the `CaptchaGenerator.py` script as follows:

```
python CaptchaGenerator.py --outdir_train '/home/santanu/Downloads/Captcha
Generation/captcha_train/' --num_captchas_train 16000 --outdir_val
'/home/santanu/Downloads/Captcha Generation/captcha_val/' --
num_captchas_val 4000
--outdir_test '/home/santanu/Downloads/Captcha Generation/captcha_test/' --
num_captchas_test 4000 --font
"/home/santanu/Android/Sdk/platforms/android-28/data/fonts/DancingScript-
Regular.ttf"
```

The script took `3.328 mins` to generate `16000` training CAPTCHAs, `4000` validation CAPTCHAs, and `4000` test CAPTCHAs, as we can see from the following log of the script:

```
3.328 min: main_process
```

In the next section, we are going to discuss the CAPTCHA breaker's convolutional neural network architecture.

Captcha breaker CNN architecture

We are going to use a CNN architecture to identify the characters in the CAPTCHA. The CNN would have two pairs of convolution and pooling before the dense layers. Instead of feeding the whole CAPTCHA to the network, we are going to break the CAPTCHA into four characters and feed them individually to the model. This requires the final output layer of the CNN to predict one of the `36` classes pertaining to the `26` letters and `10` digits.

The model can be defined as shown in the following code by the function `_model_`:

```
def _model_(n_classes):
    # Build the neural network
    input_ = Input(shape=(40,25,1))
    # First convolutional layer with max pooling
    x = Conv2D(20, (5, 5), padding="same",activation="relu")(input_)
    x = MaxPooling2D(pool_size=(2, 2), strides=(2, 2))(x)
    x = Dropout(0.2)(x)
    # Second convolutional layer with max pooling
    x = Conv2D(50, (5, 5), padding="same", activation="relu")(x)
    x = MaxPooling2D(pool_size=(2, 2), strides=(2, 2))(x)
    x = Dropout(0.2)(x)
    # Hidden layer with 1024 nodes
    x = Flatten()(x)
    x = Dense(1024, activation="relu")(x)
    # Output layer with 36 nodes (one for each possible alphabet/digit we
predict)
    out = Dense(n_classes,activation='softmax')(x)
    model = Model(inputs=[input_],outputs=out)

    model.compile(loss="sparse_categorical_crossentropy", optimizer="adam",
metrics=
    ["accuracy"])
    return model
```

The CAPTCHA breaker CNN model can be pictorially depicted as shown in the following diagram (*Figure 10.3*):

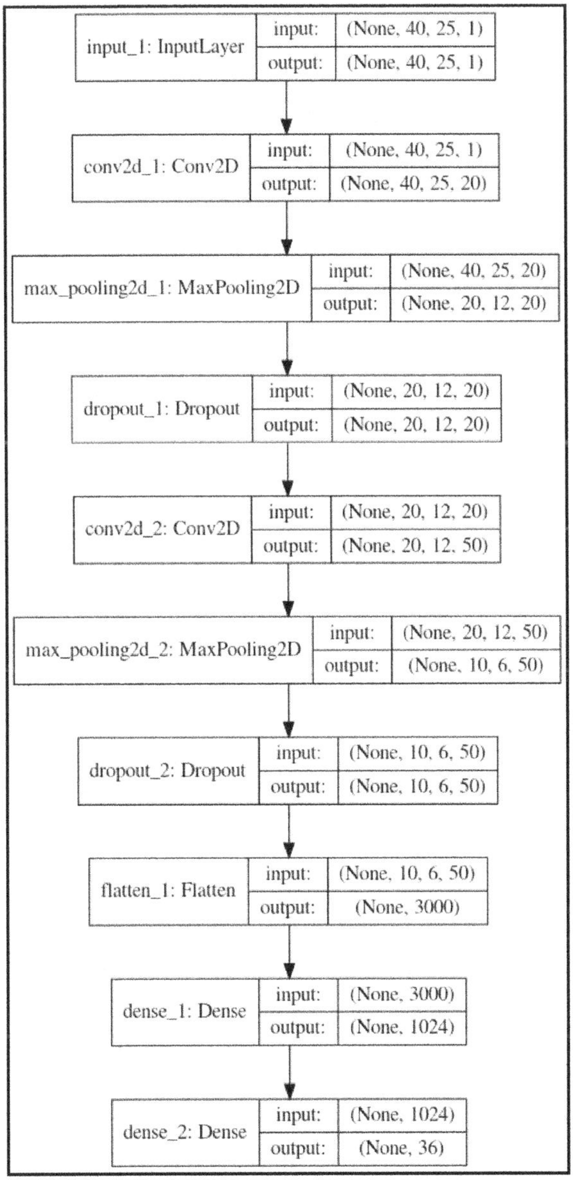

Figure 10.3: The CAPTCHA breaker CNN architecture

Pre-processing the CAPTCHA images

The raw pixels of the images don't work well with the CNN architecture. It's always a good idea to normalize the images for the CNN to converge faster. Two methods that are generally used as normalizing schemes is the mean pixel subtraction method or scaling the pixels to lie in the range of `[0,1]` by dividing the pixel values by `255`. For our CNN network, we are going to normalize the images to lie in the range of `[0,1]`. We are also going to process the grayscale images of the CAPTCHA, which means that we would be dealing with only one color channel. The `load_img` function can be used to load and pre-process the CAPTCHA image, as shown in the following code:

```
def load_img(path,dim=(100,40)):
    img = cv2.imread(path,cv2.IMREAD_GRAYSCALE)
    img = cv2.resize(img,dim)
    img = img.reshape((dim[1],dim[0],1))
    #print(img.shape)
    return img/255.
```

Converting the CAPTCHA characters to classes

The raw characters of the CAPTCHA need to be converted to numerical classes for training purposes. The `create_dict_char_to_index` function can be used to convert the raw characters into class labels:

```
def create_dict_char_to_index():
    chars = 'abcdefghijklmnopqrstuvwxyz0123456789'.upper()
    chars = list(chars)
    index = np.arange(len(chars))
    char_to_index_dict,index_to_char_dict = {},{}
    for v,k in zip(index,chars):
        char_to_index_dict[k] = v
        index_to_char_dict[v] = k

    return char_to_index_dict,index_to_char_dict
```

Data generator

Dynamically generating batches of training and validation data is important for training the CNN in an efficient manner. Loading all the data in memory before the start of training can lead to data storage issues, and it therefore makes sense to read the CAPTCHAs and build batches dynamically during training time. This leads to the optimal use of resources.

We are going to use a data generator that can be leveraged for building both training and validation batches. The generator will store the CAPTCHA file location during initialization and dynamically build batches in each epoch. The order of the files is randomly shuffled after each so that the CAPTCHA images are not traversed in the same order in each epoch. This generally ensures that the model doesn't get stuck at a bad local minima during training. The data generator class can be coded as follows:

```
class DataGenerator(keras.utils.Sequence):
    'Generates data for Keras'
    def
__init__(self,dest,char_to_index_dict,batch_size=32,n_classes=36,dim=(40,10
0,1),shuffle=True):
        'Initialization'
        self.dest = dest
        self.files = os.listdir(self.dest)
        self.char_to_index_dict = char_to_index_dict
        self.batch_size = batch_size
        self.n_classes = n_classes
        self.dim = (40,100)
        self.shuffle = shuffle
        self.on_epoch_end()

    def __len__(self):
        'Denotes the number of batches per epoch'
        return int(np.floor(len(self.files) / self.batch_size))

    def __getitem__(self, index):
        'Generate one batch of data'
        # Generate indexes of the batch
        indexes =
self.indexes[index*self.batch_size:(index+1)*self.batch_size]

        # Find list of files to be processed in the batch
        list_files = [self.files[k] for k in indexes]

        # Generate data
        X, y = self.__data_generation(list_files)

        return X, y

    def on_epoch_end(self):
        'Updates indexes after each epoch'
        self.indexes = np.arange(len(self.files))
        if self.shuffle == True:
            np.random.shuffle(self.indexes)

    def __data_generation(self,list_files):
```

```
        'Generates data containing batch_size samples' # X :
         (n_samples, *dim, n_channels)
        # Initialization
        dim_h = dim[0]
        dim_w = dim[1]//4
        channels = dim[2]
        X = np.empty((4*len(list_files),dim_h,dim_w,channels))
        y = np.empty((4*len(list_files)),dtype=int)
       # print(X.shape,y.shape)

        # Generate data
        k = -1
        for f in list_files:
            target = list(f.split('.')[0])
            target = [self.char_to_index_dict[c] for c in target]
            img = load_img(self.dest + f)
            img_h,img_w = img.shape[0],img.shape[1]
            crop_w = img.shape[1]//4
            for i in range(4):
                img_crop = img[:,i*crop_w:(i+1)*crop_w]
                k+=1
                X[k,] = img_crop
                y[k] = int(target[i])

        return X,y
```

Training the CAPTCHA breaker

The CAPTCHA breaker model can be trained by invoking the `train` function as follows:

```
def
train(dest_train,dest_val,outdir,batch_size,n_classes,dim,shuffle,epochs,lr
):
    char_to_index_dict,index_to_char_dict = create_dict_char_to_index()
    model = _model_(n_classes)
    train_generator =
DataGenerator(dest_train,char_to_index_dict,batch_size,n_classes,dim,shuffl
e)
    val_generator =
DataGenerator(dest_val,char_to_index_dict,batch_size,n_classes,dim,shuffle)
model.fit_generator(train_generator,epochs=epochs,validation_data=val_gener
ator)
    model.save(outdir + 'captcha_breaker.h5')
```

For the CAPTCHAs in the batch, all four characters are considered for training. We define the `train_generator` and `val_generator` object using the `DataGenerator` class. These data generators dynamically provide batches for training and validation.

The training can be invoked by running the `captcha_solver.py` script with the `train` argument as follows:

```
python captcha_solver.py train --dest_train
'/home/santanu/Downloads/Captcha Generation/captcha_train/' --dest_val
'/home/santanu/Downloads/Captcha Generation/captcha_val/' --outdir
'/home/santanu/ML_DS_Catalog-/captcha/model/' --batch_size 16 --lr 1e-3 --
epochs 20 --n_classes 36 --shuffle True --dim '(40,100,1)'
```

In just `20` epochs of training, the model achieves a validation accuracy of around 98.3% per character level of the CAPTCHA, as seen from the following output log as follows:

```
Epoch 17/20
1954/1954 [==============================] - 14s 7ms/step - loss: 0.0340 -
acc: 0.9896 - val_loss: 0.0781 - val_acc: 0.9835
Epoch 18/20
1954/1954 [==============================] - 13s 7ms/step - loss: 0.0310 -
acc: 0.9904 - val_loss: 0.0679 - val_acc: 0.9851
Epoch 19/20
1954/1954 [==============================] - 13s 7ms/step - loss: 0.0315 -
acc: 0.9904 - val_loss: 0.0813 - val_acc: 0.9822
Epoch 20/20
1954/1954 [==============================] - 13s 7ms/step - loss: 0.0297 -
acc: 0.9910 - val_loss: 0.0824 - val_acc: 0.9832
4.412 min: captcha_solver
```

The training time for `20` epochs with roughly `16000` 98.3s (that is, `64000` CAPTCHA characters) is around `4.412 min` using a GeForce GTX 1070 GPU. Readers are advised to use a GPU based machine for faster training.

Accuracy on the test data set

The inference of the test data can be run by invoking the `evaluate` function. The `evaluate` function is illustrated as follows for reference. Do note that the evaluate should be designed to look at the accuracy from the overall CAPTCHA perspective and not on the character level of the CAPTCHA. So, only when all four characters of the CAPTCHA target matches the prediction can we flag the CAPTCHA as being correctly identified by the CNN.

The `evaluate` function for running inference on test CAPTCHAs can be coded as follows:

```
def evaluate(model_path,eval_dest,outdir,fetch_target=True):
    char_to_index_dict,index_to_char_dict = create_dict_char_to_index()
    files = os.listdir(eval_dest)
    model = keras.models.load_model(model_path)
    predictions,targets = [],[]
    for f in files:
        if fetch_target == True:
            target = list(f.split('.')[0])
            targets.append(target)

        pred = []
        img = load_img(eval_dest + f)
        img_h,img_w = img.shape[0],img.shape[1]
        crop_w = img.shape[1]//4
        for i in range(4):
            img_crop = img[:,i*crop_w:(i+1)*crop_w]
            img_crop = img_crop[np.newaxis,:]
            pred_index  = np.argmax(model.predict(img_crop),axis=1)
            #print(pred_index)
            pred_char   = index_to_char_dict[pred_index[0]]
            pred.append(pred_char)
        predictions.append(pred)

    df = pd.DataFrame()
    df['files'] = files
    df['predictions'] = predictions

    if fetch_target == True:
        match = []
        df['targets'] = targets

        accuracy_count = 0
        for i in range(len(files)):
            if targets[i] == predictions[i]:
                accuracy_count+= 1
                match.append(1)
            else:
                match.append(0)
        print(f'Accuracy: {accuracy_count/float(len(files))} ')
        eval_file = outdir + 'evaluation.csv'
        df['match'] = match
        df.to_csv(eval_file,index=False)
        print(f'Evaluation file written at: {eval_file} ')
```

The following command can be run to invoke the `evaluate` function of the `captcha_solver.py` script for inference:

```
python captcha_solver.py evaluate  --model_path
/home/santanu/ML_DS_Catalog-/captcha/model/captcha_breaker.h5 --eval_dest
'/home/santanu/Downloads/Captcha Generation/captcha_test/' --outdir
/home/santanu/ML_DS_Catalog-/captcha/ --fetch_target True
```

The accuracy achieved on the test dataset of `4000` CAPTCHAs is around 93%. The output of running the `evaluate` function is as follows:

```
Accuracy: 0.9320972187421699
Evaluation file written at: /home/santanu/ML_DS_Catalog-
/captcha/evaluation.csv
13.564 s: captcha_solver
```

We can also see that the inference on those `4000` CAPTCHAs took around 14 seconds and the output of the evaluations is written in the `/home/santanu/ML_DS_Catalog-/captcha/evaluation.csv` file.

We will look at some of the targets and predictions where the model has not done well in the following screenshot (*Figure 10.4*):

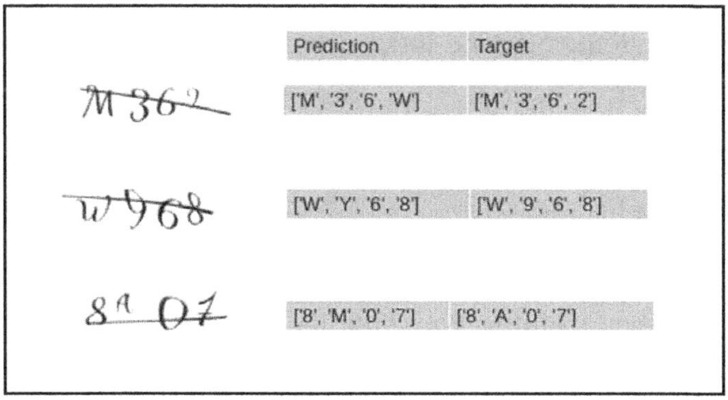

Figure 10.4: CAPTCHAs where the CAPTCHA solver model failed

CAPTCHA generation through adversarial learning

In this section, we are going to work through creating CAPTCHAs through a generative adversarial network. We are going to generate images similar to those in the **Street View House Numbers** dataset (**SVHN** dataset). The idea is to use these GAN generated images as CAPTCHAs. Only when we have trained the GAN would they be easy to sample from a noise distribution. This would alleviate the need to create CAPTCHAs through a more complicated method. It would also provide some variety to the SVHN street numbers used in CAPTCHAs.

The SVHN is a real world dataset that is very much popular in the machine learning and deep-learning field for its use in the object recognition algorithm. As its name suggests, the dataset contains real images of house numbers obtained from Google Street View Images. The dataset can be downloaded from the following link: `http://ufldl.stanford.edu/housenumbers/`.

We are going to work with the resized house numbers dataset where the images have been resized to dimension `(32,32)`. The dataset of interest to us is `train_32x32.mat`.

Through this **generative adversarial network** (**GAN**) we are going to generate house number images from random noise and the generated images would be much like those in the SVHN dataset.

Just to recap, in a GAN we have a generator (*G*) and a discriminator(*D*), which play a zero sum minimax game with each other with respect to a loss function. Over time, both the generator and the discriminator get better at their jobs until we reach a stationary point where both cannot improve any further. This stationary point is the saddle point with respect to the loss function. For our application, the Generator G is going to convert a noise z from a given distribution $P(z)$ into a house number image x such that $x = G(z)$.

This generated image is passed through the discriminator D which tries to detect this generated image x as fake and the real house number images from the SVHN dataset as real. At the same time the generator would try to create the image $x = G(z)$ in such a way that the discriminator finds the images to be real. If we tag the real images as `1` and the fake images generated by the generator as `0` then the discriminator would try to minimize the binary cross entropy loss as a classifier network given two classes. The loss minimized by the discriminator D can be written as follows:

$$-E_{z \sim p_Z(z)}[\log D(G(z)) - E_{x \sim p_X(x)}[log(1 - D(G(x))] \qquad (1)$$

In the preceding expression *D(.)* is the discriminator function, and its output denotes the probability of tagging an image as real. $P_z(z)$ denotes the distribution of the random variable noise *z*, while $P_X(x)$ denotes the distribution of the real house number images. *G(.)* and *D(.)* denotes the generator network function and the discriminator network function respectively. These would be parameterized by the weights of the network that we have conveniently skipped for the clutter of notation. If we denote the parameters of the generator network weights by θ and those of the discriminator network by ϕ then the discriminator would learn to minimize the loss in *(1)* with respect to ϕ while the generator would aim to maximize the same loss in *(1)* with respect to θ. We can refer to the loss optimized in *(1)* as a utility function that both the generator and the discriminator are optimizing with respect to their parameters. The utility function *U* can be written as a function of the parameters of the generator and discriminator as follows:

$$U(\theta, \phi) = -E_{z \sim p_Z(z)}[\log D(G(z)) - E_{x \sim p_X(x)}[log(1 - D(G(x))]$$

From the game theory perspective, the generator *G* and the discriminator *D* plays a zero sum minmax game with each other with the utility function $U(\theta, \phi)$ and the optimization problem of the minimax game can then be expressed as follows:

$$\hat{\theta}, \hat{\phi} = \max_{\theta} \min_{\phi} U(\theta, \phi)$$

$$= \max_{\phi_G} \min_{\phi_D} -E_{z \sim p_Z(z)} \log D(G(z)) - E_{x \sim p_X(x)} \log(1 - D(G(x))) \qquad (2)$$

At a point in the parameter space, if a function is a local maxima, with respect to some parameters and a local minima, with respect to the rest of the parameters, then the point is called a **saddle point**. Consequently, the point given by $(\hat{\theta}, \hat{\phi})$ would be a saddle point for the utility function $U(\theta, \phi)$. This saddle point is the nash equilibrium of the minimax zero sum game and the parameters $\hat{\theta}, \hat{\phi}$ are the most optimal with respect to utility the generator and discriminator is optimizing. In terms of the problem at hand, the generator *G* would produce the most difficult CAPTCHAs for the discriminator to detect with $\hat{\theta}$ as its parameters. Similarly, the discriminator is most adapted to detect fake CAPTCHAs with ϕ as its parameters.

The simplest of functions that has a saddle point is $x^2 - y^2$ and the saddle point is the origin: `(0,0)`.

Optimizing the GAN loss

In the previous section, we have seen that the optimal state of the generator and the discriminator with respect to the parameters of their respective networks is given by this:

$$\hat{\theta}, \hat{\phi} = \max_{\theta} \min_{\phi} U(\theta, \phi) = \max_{\phi_G} \min_{\phi_D} -E_{z \sim p_Z(z)} \log D(G(z)) - E_{x \sim p_X(x)} \log(1 - D(G(x)))$$

For maximizing an objective function, we generally use gradient ascent, whereas for minimizing a cost function, we use gradient descent. The preceding optimization problem can be broken down into two parts: the generator and the discriminator optimizing the utility function in turns by gradient ascent and gradient descent respectively. At any step t during the optimization, the discriminator would try to move to a new state by minimizing the utility as follows:

$$\min_{\phi} -E_{z \sim p_Z(z)} \log D(G(z)) - E_{x \sim p_X(x)} \log(1 - D(G(x)))$$

Alternatively, the generator would try to maximize the same utility. Since the discriminator D doesn't have any parameters of the generator, the second term of the utility doesn't influence the generator's optimization. The same can be expressed as follows:

$$\max_{\theta} -E_{z \sim p_Z(z)} \log D(G(z)) - E_{x \sim p_X(x)} \log(1 - D(G(x)))$$

$$= \max_{\theta} -E_{z \sim p_Z(z)} \log D(G(z))$$

$$= \min_{\theta} E_{z \sim p_Z(z)} \log D(G(z))$$

We have converted both the generator and the discriminator optimization objective as a minimization problem. The optimization by both the discriminator and generator is performed using gradient descent until we reach the saddle point of the objective function.

Generator network

The generator network would take in random noise and try to output images similar to the SVHN images as output. The random noise is a `100` dimensional input vector. Each of the dimensions is a random variable following the standard normal distribution with a mean of `0` and a standard deviation of `1`.

The initial dense layer has `8192` units, which is reshaped to a three-dimensional tensor of a shape 4 x 4 x 512 . The tensor can be thought of as a 4 x 4 image with `512` filters. To increase the spatial dimensions of the tensor, we do a series of transpose 2D convolutions with a stride of `2` and a kernel filter size of the dimensions 5 x 5. The stride size determines the scaling of the transpose convolution. For instance, a stride of 2 doubles each of the spatial dimensions of the input image followed by the transpose convolutions are generally accompanied by batch normalization for better convergence. The network uses `LeakyReLU` as the activation function except for the activation layer. The final output of the network is an image of dimension 32 x 32 x 3.

The `tanh` activation is used in the final layer in order to normalize the image pixel values in the range of `[-1,1]`.

The generator can be coded as illustrated as follows:

```
def generator(input_dim,alpha=0.2):
    model = Sequential()
    model.add(Dense(input_dim=input_dim, output_dim=4*4*512))
    model.add(Reshape(target_shape=(4,4,512)))
    model.add(BatchNormalization())
    model.add(LeakyReLU(alpha))
    model.add(Conv2DTranspose(256, kernel_size=5, strides=2,
                              padding='same'))
    model.add(BatchNormalization())
    model.add(LeakyReLU(alpha))
    model.add(Conv2DTranspose(128, kernel_size=5, strides=2,
                              padding='same'))
    model.add(BatchNormalization())
    model.add(LeakyReLU(alpha))
    model.add(Conv2DTranspose(3, kernel_size=5, strides=2,
                              padding='same'))
    model.add(Activation('tanh'))
    return model
```

The network architecture of the generator is depicted in the following diagram (*Figure 10.5*) for reference:

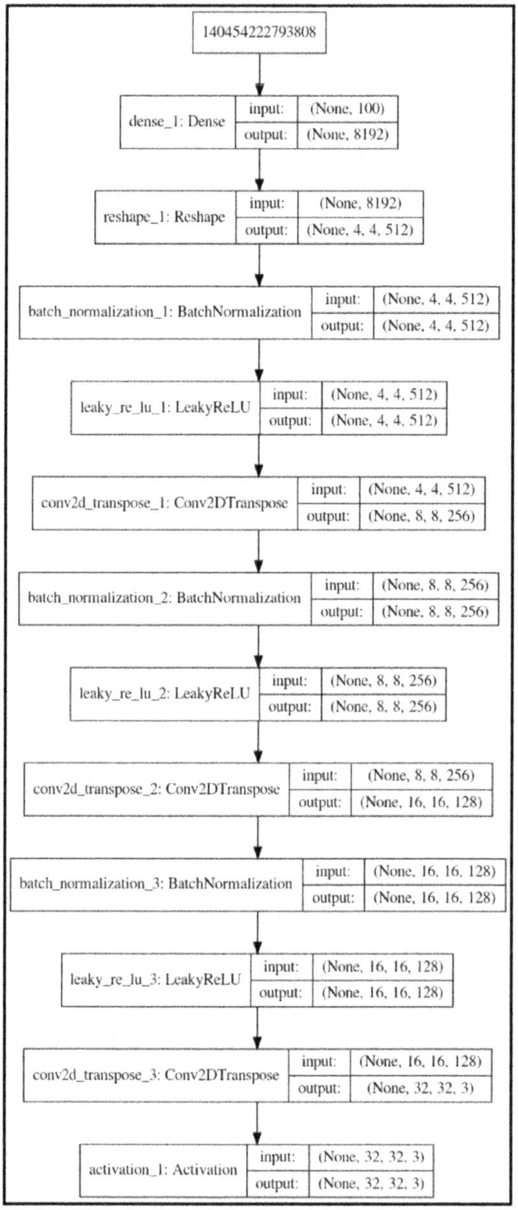

Figure 10.5: Generator network graph

Discriminator network

The discriminator will be a classic binary classification convolutional neural network that can classify the generator images as fake and the actual SVHN dataset images as real.

The discriminator network can be coded as follows:

```
def discriminator(img_dim,alpha=0.2):
    model = Sequential()
    model.add(
            Conv2D(64, kernel_size=5,strides=2,
            padding='same',
            input_shape=img_dim)
            )
    model.add(LeakyReLU(alpha))
    model.add(Conv2D(128,kernel_size=5,strides=2,padding='same'))
    model.add(BatchNormalization())
    model.add(LeakyReLU(alpha))
    model.add(Conv2D(256,kernel_size=5,strides=2,padding='same'))
    model.add(BatchNormalization())
    model.add(LeakyReLU(alpha))
    model.add(Flatten())
    model.add(Dense(1))
    model.add(Activation('sigmoid'))
    return model
```

The defined discriminator network in the previous code block takes the fake generator images, and the real SVHN images as input and passes them through `3` sets of 2D convolutions before the final output layer. The convolutions in this network are not followed by pooling but by batch normalization and `LeakyReLU` activations.

The network architecture of the discriminator is represented in the following diagram (*Figure 10.6*):

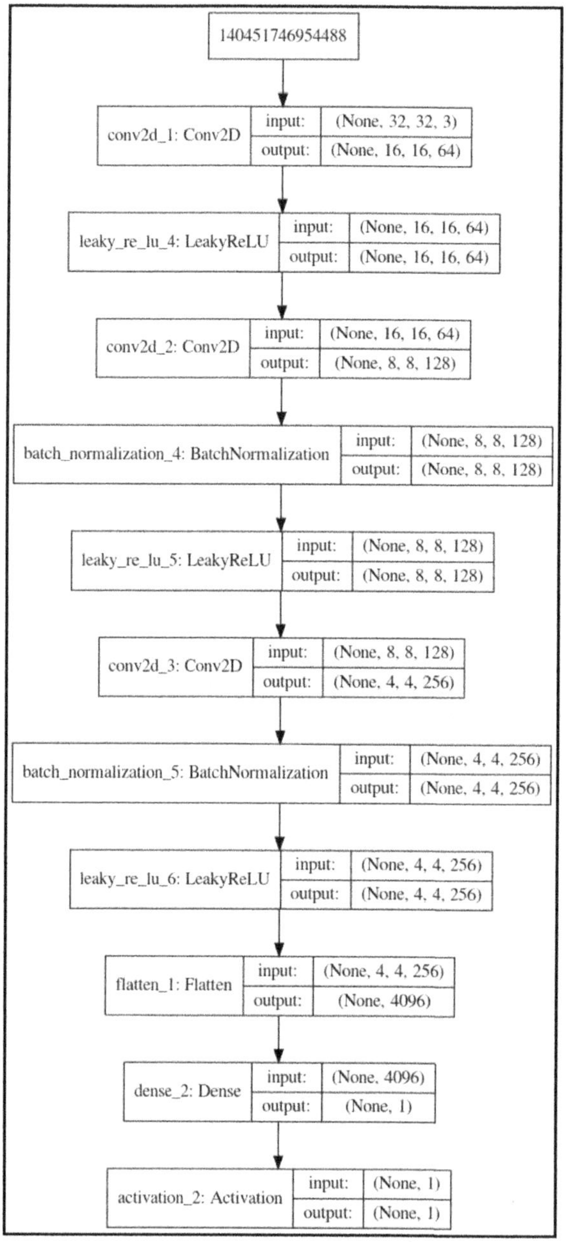

Figure 10.6: Discriminator network graph

The output activation function of the discriminator is a sigmoid. This aids the binary classification of the fake generated images from the real SVHN images.

Training the GAN

Setting up a training flow for a generative adversarial network is not straight forward, as it demands a lot of technical considerations. We define three networks for training as follows:

- The generator network g with parameters θ
- The discriminator network d with parameters ϕ
- The combined generator discriminator network denoted by g_d with weights θ and ϕ

The generator g creates fake images that the d discriminator would evaluate and try to label as fake.

In the g_d network, the g generator creates fake images and then tries to fool the d discriminator into believing them as real. The discriminator network is compiled with the binary cross-entropy loss, and the loss is optimized with respect to the discriminator parameters ϕ, whereas the g_d network is compiled with respect to the parameters θ of the g generator in order to fool the discriminator. Consequently, the g_d network loss is the binary cross entropy loss related to the discriminator tagging all fake images as real. In each mini-batch the generator and the discriminator weights are updated based on the optimization of the loss associated with the g_d and d networks:

```
def train(dest_train,outdir,
        gen_input_dim,gen_lr,gen_beta1,
        dis_input_dim,dis_lr,dis_beta1,
        epochs,batch_size,alpha=0.2,smooth_coef=0.1):

    #X_train,X_test = read_data(dest_train),read_data(dest_test)
    train_data = loadmat(dest_train + 'train_32x32.mat')
    X_train, y_train = train_data['X'], train_data['y']
    X_train = np.rollaxis(X_train, 3)
    print(X_train.shape)
    #Image pixels are normalized between -1 to +1 so that one can use the
tanh activation function
    #_train = (X_train.astype(np.float32) - 127.5)/127.5
    X_train = (X_train/255)*2-1
    g = generator(gen_input_dim,alpha)
    plot_model(g,show_shapes=True, to_file='generator_model.png')
    d = discriminator(dis_input_dim,alpha)
    d_optim = Adam(lr=dis_lr,beta_1=dis_beta1)
```

```
    d.compile(loss='binary_crossentropy',optimizer=d_optim)
    plot_model(d,show_shapes=True, to_file='discriminator_model.png')
    g_d = generator_discriminator(g, d)
    g_optim = Adam(lr=gen_lr,beta_1=gen_beta1)
    g_d.compile(loss='binary_crossentropy', optimizer=g_optim)
    plot_model(g_d,show_shapes=True, to_file=
    'generator_discriminator_model.png')
    for epoch in range(epochs):
        print("Epoch is", epoch)
        print("Number of batches", int(X_train.shape[0]/batch_size))
        for index in range(int(X_train.shape[0]/batch_size)):
            noise =
            np.random.normal(loc=0, scale=1,
size=(batch_size,gen_input_dim))
            image_batch = X_train[index*batch_size:(index+1)*batch_size,:]
            generated_images = g.predict(noise, verbose=0)
            if index % 20 == 0:
                combine_images(generated_images,outdir,epoch,index)
                # Images converted back to be within 0 to 255
            print(image_batch.shape,generated_images.shape)
            X = np.concatenate((image_batch, generated_images))
            d1 = d.train_on_batch(image_batch,[1 - smooth_coef]*batch_size)
            d2 = d.train_on_batch(generated_images,[0]*batch_size)

            y = [1] * batch_size + [0] * batch_size
            # Train the Discriminator on both real and fake images
            make_trainable(d,True)
            #_loss = d.train_on_batch(X, y)
            d_loss = d1 + d2

            print("batch %d d_loss : %f" % (index, d_loss))
            noise =
            np.random.normal(loc=0, scale=1,
size=(batch_size,gen_input_dim))
            make_trainable(d,False)
            #d.trainable = False
            # Train the generator on fake images from Noise
            g_loss = g_d.train_on_batch(noise, [1] * batch_size)
            print("batch %d g_loss : %f" % (index, g_loss))
            if index % 10 == 9:
                g.save_weights('generator', True)
                d.save_weights('discriminator', True)
```

The `Adam` optimizer is used for the optimisation of both networks. One thing to note is that the network `g_d` needs to be compiled to optimize the loss with respect to parameters of generator *G* only. Consequently, we need to disable the training of the parameters of the discriminator *D* in network `g_d`.

We can use the following function to disable or enable learning of the parameters of the network:

```
def make_trainable(model, trainable):
    for layer in model.layers:
        layer.trainable = trainable
```

We can disable learning of the parameters by setting the trainable to `False`, whereas if we want to enable the training of these parameters, we need to set it to `True`.

Noise distribution

The noise that is input to the GAN needs to follow a specific probability distribution. generally uniform distribution `U[-1,1]` or standard normal distribution that is, normal distribution with mean `0` and standard deviation `1` is used to sample each dimension of the noise vector. Empirically it has been seen that sampling noise from standard normal distribution seems to work better than sampling from uniform distribution. We would be using standard normal distribution to sample random noise in this implementation.

Data preprocessing

As discussed previously, we would be working with the SVHN dataset images of dimensions `32 x 32 x 3`.

The dataset images are readily available in matrix data form. The raw pixel of the images are normalized within the range of `[-1,1]` for faster and stable convergence. Because of this transformation, the final activation of the generator is kept `tanh` to ensure the generated image has pixel values within `[-1,1]`.

The `read_data` can be used to process the input data. The `dir_flag` is used to determine whether we have the raw processed data matrix file or the image directory. For instance, when we work with the SVHN dataset, the `dir_flag` should be set to `False`, since we already have a pre-processed data matrix file named `train_32x32.mat`.

However, it is better to keep the `read_data` function generic, since this allows us to reuse the script for other datasets. The `loadmat` function from `scipy.io` can be used for reading the `train_32x32.mat`.

If the inputs are raw images placed in a directory, then we can read the image files available in the directory and read them through `opencv`. The `load_img` function can be used to read the raw images using `opencv`.

Finally, the pixel intensity is normalized to be in the range of `[-1,1]` for better convergence of the network:

```
def load_img(path,dim=(32,32)):

    img = cv2.imread(path)
    img = cv2.resize(img,dim)
    img = img.reshape((dim[1],dim[0],3))
    return img


def read_data(dest,dir_flag=False):

  if dir_flag == True:
  files = os.listdir(dest)
  X = []
  for f in files:
  img = load_img(dest + f)
  X.append(img)
  return X
  else:
  train_data = loadmat(path)
  X,y = train_data['X'], train_data['y']
  X = np.rollaxis(X,3)
  X = (X/255)*2-1
  return X
```

Invoking the training

The training of the GAN can be invoked by running the `train` function of the `captcha_gan.py` script with the parameters as follows:

```
python captcha_gan.py train --dest_train
'/home/santanu/Downloads/train_32x32.mat' --outdir
'/home/santanu/ML_DS_Catalog-/captcha/SVHN/' --dir_flag False --batch_size
100 --gen_input_dim 100 --gen_beta1 0.5 --gen_lr 0.0001 --dis_input_dim
'(32,32,3)' --dis_lr 0.001 --dis_beta1 0.5 --alpha 0.2 --epochs 100 --
smooth_coef 0.1
```

The preceding script uses the `fire` Python package to invoke a user specified function, which is `train` in our case. The good thing about `fire` is that all the inputs to the function can be supplied by the user as arguments as we can see from the previous command.

GANs are notoriously hard to train and therefore these parameters need to be tuned in order for the model to function properly. Following are a few of the important parameters:

Parameters	**Values**	**Comment**
`batch_size`	`100`	The batch size for mini batch stochastic gradient descent.
`gen_input_dim`	`100`	The input random noise vector dimension.
`gen_lr`	`0.0001`	Generator learning rate.
`gen_beta1`	`0.5`	`beta_1` is the parameter for the Adam optimizer for the generator.
`dis_input_dim`	`(32,32,3)`	Shape of the real and fake housing number images to the discriminator.
`dis_lr`	`0.001`	Learning rate of the discriminator network.
`dis_beta1`	`0.5`	`beta_1` is the parameter for the Adam optimizer for discriminator.
`alpha`	`0.2`	This is the leak factor of the `LeakyReLU` activation. This helps to provide a gradient (`0.2` here) when the input to the `activation` function is negative. It helps solve the dying `ReLU` problem. The gradient of the output of the ReLU function with respect to its input is `0` if the input is less than or equal to `0`. The back-propagated error from later layers gets multiplied by this `0` and no error passes to the earlier layers though the neuron associated with this `ReLU`. The ReLU is said to have died and many such dead `ReLUs` can affect the training. `LeakyReLU` overcomes this problem by providing small gradient even for negative input values, thus ensuring that the training never stops due to lack of gradient.
`epochs`	`100`	This is the number of epochs to run.
`smooth_coef`	`0.1`	This smooth coefficient is designed to reduce the weight of the loss of real samples to the discriminator. For instance, the `smooth_coef` of `0.1` would reduce the loss attributed to the real images to 90% of the original loss. This helps the GANs to converge better.

Training the GAN with these parameters takes around 3.12 hours, using a GeForce GTX 1070 GPU. Readers are advised to use a GPU for faster training.

The quality of CAPTCHAs during training

Let's now investigate the quality of the CAPTCHAs generated at various epochs during training. The following are the images of CAPTCHAs after epoch `5` (see *Figure 10.7a*), epoch `51` (see *Figure 10.7b*), and epoch `100` (see *Figure 10.7c*). We can see that the quality of the CAPTCHA images has improved as thc training progresses. The following screenshot shows the result for sample CAPTCHAs generated at epoch 5:

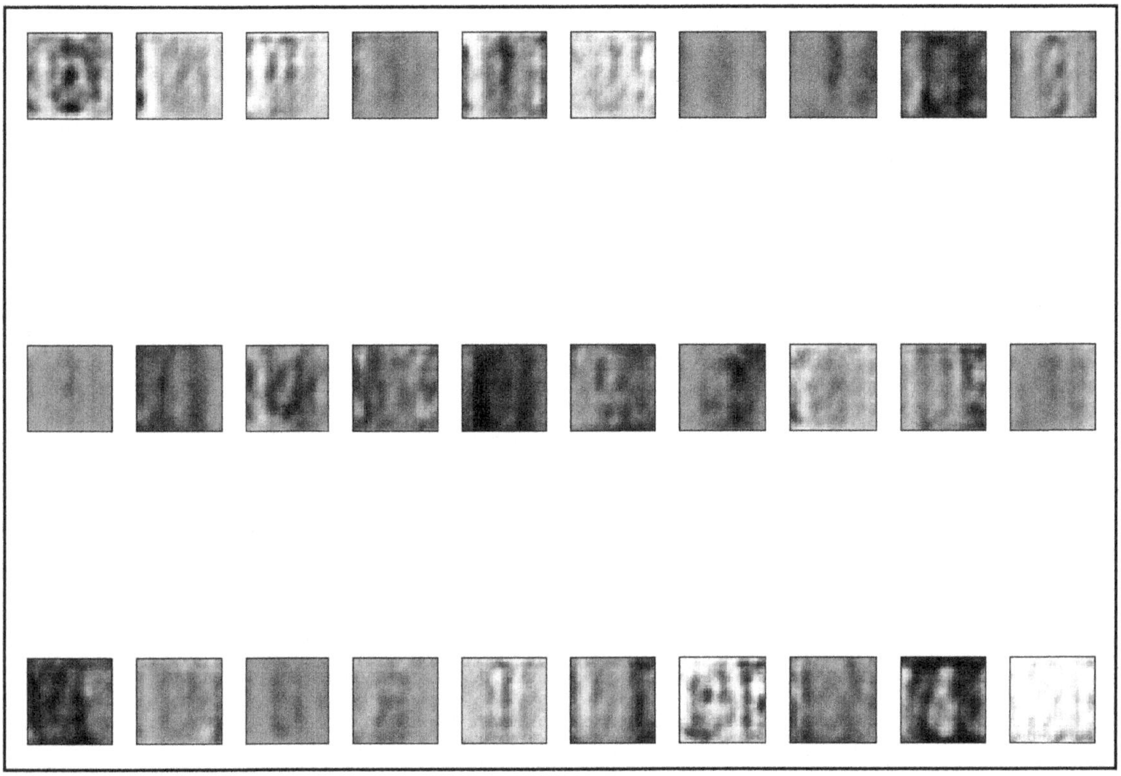

Figure 10.7a: Sample CAPTCHAs generated at epoch 5

The following screenshot shows the result for sample CAPTCHAs generated at epoch 51:

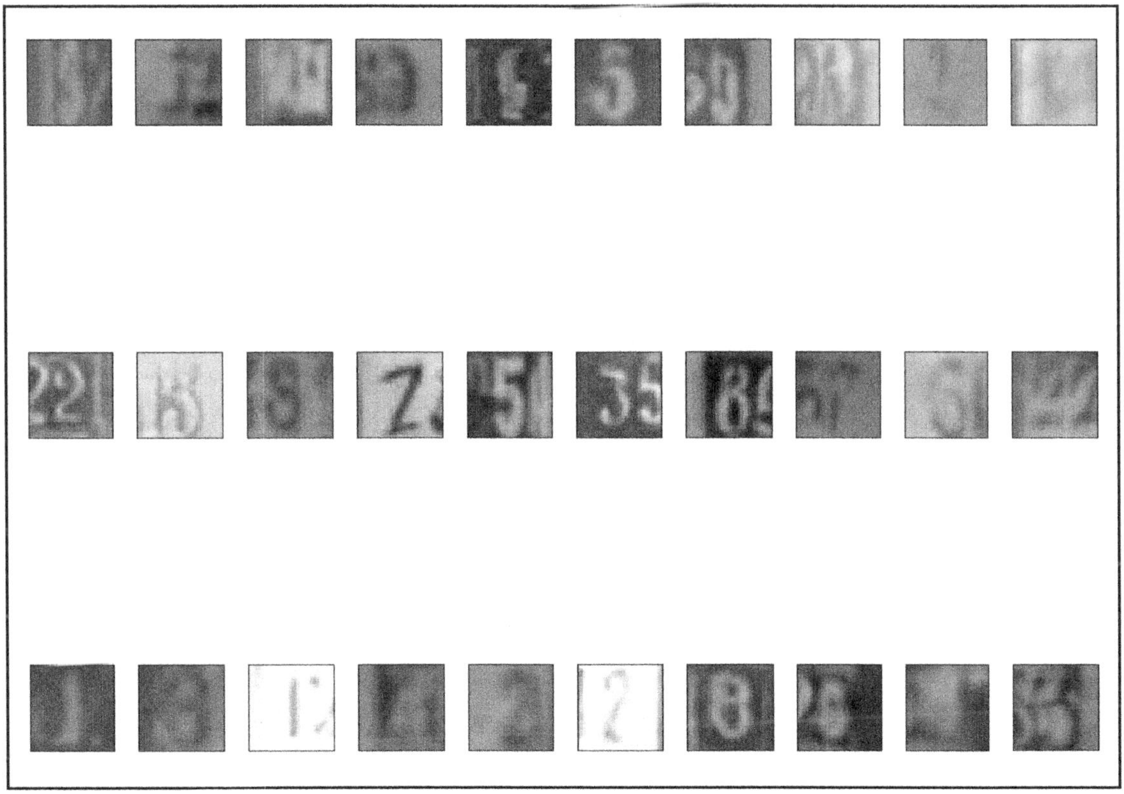

Figure 10.7b: Sample CAPTCHAs generated at epoch 51

The following screenshot shows the result for sample CAPTCHAs generated at epoch 100:

Figure 10.7c: Sample CAPTCHAs generated at epoch 100

Using the trained generator to create CAPTCHAs for use

The trained GAN network can be loaded at run time to generate street view housing numbers like CAPTCHA for use. The `generate_captcha` function can be used to generate CAPTCHAs for use, illustrated as follows:

```
def generate_captcha(gen_input_dim,alpha,
             num_images,model_dir,outdir):

    g = generator(gen_input_dim,alpha)
    g.load_weights(model_dir + 'generator')
    noise =
    np.random.normal(loc=0, scale=1, size=(num_images,gen_input_dim))
    generated_images = g.predict(noise, verbose=1)
    for i in range(num_images):
        img = generated_images[i,:]
        img = np.uint8(((img+1)/2)*255)
        img = Image.fromarray(img)
        img.save(outdir + 'captcha_' + str(i) + '.png')
```

You may be wondering how it is possible to have the label for these generated CAPTCHAs, since they are required to verify whether the user is a human or a bot. The idea is very simple: send the unlabelled CAPTCHAs along with some labelled CAPTCHAs so that the user doesn't know which CAPTCHA is going to be evaluated. Once you have enough labels for the generated CAPTCHA take the majority label as the actual label and use it for evaluation henceforth.

The `generate_captcha` function can be invoked from the `captcha_gan.py` script by invoking the following command:

```
python captcha_gan.py generate-captcha --gen_input_dim 100 --num_images 200
--model_dir '/home/santanu/ML_DS_Catalog-/captcha/' --outdir
'/home/santanu/ML_DS_Catalog-/captcha/captcha_for_use/' --alpha 0.2
```

The following screenshot (*Figure 10.8*) depicts a few of the CAPTCHAs generated by invoking the `generate_captcha` function. We can see that the images are decent enough to be used as CAPTCHAs:

Figure 10.8: Generated CAPTCHAs using the generator of the trained GAN network

Summary

With this, we come to the end of the chapter. All the code related to this chapter can be located in the GitHub link found at: `https://github.com/PacktPublishing/Intelligent-Projects-using-Python/tree/master/Chapter10`. You will now have a fair idea about how deep learning can influence CAPTCHAs. At one end of the spectrum, we can see how easily CAPTCHAs can be solved by bots with deep-learning AI applications in them. However, at the other end, we see how deep learning can be used to leverage a given dataset and create new CAPTCHAs from random noise. You can extend the technicalities learned about generative adversarial networks in this chapter to build a smart CAPTCHA generation system, using deep learning. And now, we come to the end of this book. I hope that this journey through the nine practical artificial intelligence-based applications has been an enriching one. All the best!

Other Books You May Enjoy

If you enjoyed this book, you may be interested in these other books by Packt:

Artificial Intelligence By Example
Denis Rothman

ISBN: 978-1-78899-054-7

- Use adaptive thinking to solve real-life AI case studies
- Rise beyond being a modern-day factory code worker
- Acquire advanced AI, machine learning, and deep learning designing skills
- Learn about cognitive NLP chatbots, quantum computing, and IoT and blockchain technology
- Understand future AI solutions and adapt quickly to them
- Develop out-of-the-box thinking to face any challenge the market presents

Artificial Intelligence for Big Data
Anand Deshpande, Manish Kumar

ISBN: 978-1-78847-217-3

- Manage Artificial Intelligence techniques for big data with Java
- Build smart systems to analyze data for enhanced customer experience
- Learn to use Artificial Intelligence frameworks for big data
- Understand complex problems with algorithms and Neuro-Fuzzy systems
- Design stratagems to leverage data using Machine Learning process
- Apply Deep Learning techniques to prepare data for modeling
- Construct models that learn from data using open source tools
- Analyze big data problems using scalable Machine Learning algorithms

Leave a review - let other readers know what you think

Please share your thoughts on this book with others by leaving a review on the site that you bought it from. If you purchased the book from Amazon, please leave us an honest review on this book's Amazon page. This is vital so that other potential readers can see and use your unbiased opinion to make purchasing decisions, we can understand what our customers think about our products, and our authors can see your feedback on the title that they have worked with Packt to create. It will only take a few minutes of your time, but is valuable to other potential customers, our authors, and Packt. Thank you!

Index

D

E

F

G

H

Q

R

S

T

V

W

Made in the USA
Monee, IL
19 April 2020

26029066R00188